POLISH AMERICANS IN CALIFORNIA

1827-1977

AND WHO'S WHO

Edited by
Jacek Przygoda

Foreword
Doyce B. Nunis, Jr.

Polish American Historical Association
California Chapter
LOYOLA MARYMOUNT UNIVERSITY
Los Angeles

I

COVER
The cover depicts the historic fusion of American and Polish national colors.
The United States Bicentennial underscored the blessings of Liberty with
Responsibility. Poles in their one-hundred-fifty year long presence in
California are priding themselves in being a distinct part of the Golden State
and American history in Freedom. — *Gloria M. Jeschke*
Cover design — Leonard Konopelski

II

This Project
of the Polish American
Bicentennial Committee in Los Angeles
is dedicated to
the Memory of All Those
Whose Ancestors
came from Poland
and have established Their Home
in California
to make the Golden State grow.

CONTENTS

	Page
Acknowledgments	VIII
Preface — *Charles S. Casassa*	X
Foreword — *Doyce B. Nunis, Jr.*	XI
Prologue — *Francis J. Weber*	XIII
Introduction — *Jacek Przygoda/Anthony F. Turhollow*	XV

Illustrations Follow Throughout Narrative Parts of the Text

PART ONE

AMERICA AND POLAND IN RETROSPECT	1
Poland's Conversion to Christianity	2
America — Poland: The Way It Was — *Henryk Moscicki*	4
American Revolution and The Poland of Stanislaw August Poniatowski: A Bicentennial Tribute — *Alfred J. Wrobel*	14

PART TWO

VIGNETTES OF POLES IN NINETEENTH CENTURY CALIFORNIA	21
Poles in California, 1827-1977: An Overview — *Jacek Przygoda*	22
California Localities Connected with Poland and Poles *Richard C. Lewanski*	28
Poles in Northern California in the 1840s and 1850s — *Witold S. Sworakowski*	34
Felix P. Wierzbicki — *Ladislas J. Siekaniec*	39
Helena Modjeska: The California Years — *Ellen K. Lee*	42
Post-Script on Modjeska — *Ellen K. Lee*	54
Ralph Modjeski: Famous Builder of Bridges — *Tom Szatkowski*	56
Sienkiewicz in California — *Gillian Olechno-Huszcza*	60
Paderewski in Paso Robles — *Margaret Prasniewski*	66
Helena Paderewska: Passing Through Paso Robles — *Helena Liibke/Anne Strakacz Appleton*	70
Polish Prince Brings Power to San Francisco — *Don J. Baxter*	72

PART THREE

VIGNETTES OF POLES IN TWENTIETH CENTURY CALIFORNIA	75
The Works of Jan de Rosen in Southern California — *Gene H. Zygmont*	74
Wiktor Podoski — *J. George Szeptycki*	78
Jan Styka and "The Crucifixion" — *Gene H. Zygmont*	82
Introduction to Mrozewski — *Boleslaw Mastai*	85

Stefan Mrozewski's Creativity — *Stanley L. Cuba* 87
Stanislaw Szukalski — *Gene H. Zygmont* 90
Wladyslaw Gawlinski — *Doris Bernhagen* 93
Wladyslaw (Walter) Zawojski — *Jacek Przygoda* 95
The Art of Kali-Weynerowska — *James I. Rambo* 99
Edward H. Hicks — *Jacek Przygoda* 102
Anton Grot — *Donald Deschner* 104
Polish Art and Film (Reproduction) 107
Life of Ryszard Boleslawski — *Boguslaw Rostworowski* 108
Polish Art and Film (Reproduction) 111
Zygmunt Sulistrowski — *Kathy S. Hayes* 112
Jaroslaw Zielinski 115
Roman Maciejewski — *Slawa Krance* 116
Ryszard Rodzinski — *Slawa Krance* 117
Stephan Pasternacki — *Kathy S. Hayes* 118
Wladziu Liberace — *Mindy Kaye* 120
Bronislaw Kaper — *Mindy Kaye* 122
Harry Lojewski — *Mindy Kaye* 123
Henry Vars — *Mindy Kaye* 125
Bobby Vinton — *Mindy Kaye* 128
Jerry Kasper — *Jacek Przygoda* 130
The Semonski Family — *Mindy Kaye* 132
Ganna Walska — *Jacek Przygoda* 134
Pola Negri — *K.Cz./Cz. Olechno-Huszcza* 136
Ted Knight — *Mindy Kaye* 138
Karl Lukas — *Kathy S. Hayes* 140
Loretta Swit — *Mindy Kaye* 142
The "Krakusy" — *Andrzej Nizynski* 144
Jan Prasniewski — *Margaret Kirk* 146
John D.F. Black — *Mindy Kaye* 149
Frank Stanley — *Mindy Kaye* 152
Connie Gale — *Jacek Przygoda* 153
Szczepan K. Zimmer — *Jacek Przygoda* 156
Stanislaw Karpinski — *Szczepan K. Zimmer* 159
Alicja Pomian-Pozerska — *Jacek Przygoda* 161
Victor Londzin — *Jacek Przygoda* 164
Ewa Emill — *Halina Zimmer* 165
Edward J. Tolosko — *Jacek Przygoda* 168

PART FOUR

POLISH AMERICAN SOCIETAL LIFE IN CALIFORNIA 171
Immigrant ... Musical Chairs — *E.G. Dabrowska Wissema* 172
America Needs Ethnicity — *Geno Baroni* 173
Profile of the Polish American Community in
Northern California — *Jan Kowalik* 175

P.A.C. — Northern California — W.J. 180
Polish Clubs in the San Francisco Bay Area —
  Zdzislaw Zakrzewski 181
Polish Cultural Hour Radio Program — W.J. 182
POLAM — Bruno Shatyn 184
Polish Veterans WW II, Oakland — Kazimierz Porebski 185
Polish Social Club, Sacramento — B. Witkowski/J. Prasniewski .. 186
Ongoing Wonder — Jacek Przygoda 187
Polish Parish Elementary School — Alice Parka 193
St. Stanislaus Club — Bernice Ault 194
Polish Retirement Foundation — Alice Parka 195
Guardian Angel P.N.C. Church — Robert J. Vrablik 196
P.A.C. — California-Arizona Division — Anthony Saran 198
"Samopomoc" — Izabella Z. Macander 200
Polish Center in Los Angeles — Helena Stelmach 202
P.A.C. Federal Credit Union — Henryk Westwalewicz 203
Polish Scouting in California — Gena Kliszewska 204
Polish Women's Alliance in Southern California 206
P.A.V.A. in Los Angeles 207
Polish Veterans WW II, Southern California Chapter 208
P.A.F.A. — Pacific Coast Wing — Marek J. Mazynski 209
Polish Home Army Association, Los Angeles — Kathy S. Hayes 210
Polish University Club — Michele M. Sawa 213
Polish Library in Los Angeles — Danuta Zawadzka 214
Polish American Business & Professional Club — Jean M. Breese 216
P.N.A. White Eagle Lodge, San Fernando — Wanda Korba 217
Polish American Citizens Club — Jean M. Breese 218
Polish Philatelic & Numismatic Society — Wally Pawlowski 219
Polish Community in San Diego — Jozef Patyk 220
P.A.A.A. of Santa Barbara — Jolanta Skrzynska 224
Polish Parish Council in Santa Barbara — Catherine Deresiewicz . 225
Restoration — E.G. Dabrowska Wissema 226

PART FIVE

DOCUMENTARY:
  BICENTENNIAL-PEOPLE-IDEAS-DEEDS 227
Introductory Remarks 228
First U.S. Bicentennial Heritage Meeting, L.A., Minutes 229
Polish Heritage Weekend, LMU., April 26-27, 1975 —
  Jacek Przygoda 231
Polish American Participation in the U.S. Bicentennial in L.A. —
  Halina Gawlinska 235
International Heritage Festival, Los Angeles, May 22-23, 1976 —
  Mark Bielski 239
Polish American Bicentennial Grand Ball — Tom Szatkowski 243

Leon S. Kawecki: Echo of The Bicentennial — *Kathy S. Hayes* .. 245
1973 P.A.H.A. — California Chapter Meeting, Minutes —
Helena H. Grams 246
Bulletin & Newsletter, P.A.H.A. — California Chapter, Spring 1977
— *Jerome S. Laskowski* 250
P.A.H.A., Student Chapter, Loyola Marymount University —
Donald Malin/Anthony Turhollow, Jr. 254
Bishop Thaddeus A. Shubsda — *Jacek Przygoda* 256
Rev. Anthony Saran — *Kathy S. Hayes* 260
Contemporary Church Architecture in Southern California —
J. George Szeptycki 262
Mieczyslaw G. Bekker 268
Lech Niemo-Niemojewski — *Stephan Pasternacki* 271
Jozefa Kudlicka — *Stephan Pasternacki* 272
Thomas M. Potasz — *Michele M. Sawa* 274
Sylwin G. Strakacz — *Anne Strakacz Appleton* 276
Helen E. Bayer — *Michele M. Sawa* 278
Helena Liibke — *Jacek Przygoda* 280
Tadeusz Zielinski — *Jacek Przygoda* 282
The Michal Cieslak Family — *Jacek Przygoda* 284
Marie Zingel — *Halina Gawlinska* 287
Felicia Kwasieborska — *Jacek Przygoda* 289
Edward P. Drake — *Jacek Przygoda* 290
Edmund T. Dombrowski, Sr. — *Kathy S. Hayes* 291
Eastern Dental Mfg. Company — *Jacek Przygoda* 293
Bruno Mudy: EMCO Engineering — *Jacek Przygoa* 295
WARNO Development Company — *Jacek Przygoda* 296
Walter J. Archer — *Jacek Przygoda* 297
T.T. Stanley — *Jacek Przygoda* 298
Wally Pawlowski: Odyssey of An Immigrant — *Kathy S. Hayes* 299
Andrew Cichy: One of Many — *Kathy S. Hayes* 300
Seweryn Kulesza: Olympic Medalist — *Kathy S. Hayes* 301
Conclusion — *Jacek Przygoda/Anthony F. Turhollow* 303
Index of Names 311

PART SIX

POLISH AMERICAN *WHO'S WHO* IN CALIFORNIA 319
Introduction 321
Form of the Biographical Questionnaire 322
WHO'S WHO Information Sequence 324
Key of Abbreviations & Biographical Code 324
WHO'S WHO 331
List of Subscribers 365

ACKNOWLEDGMENTS

The editor's deep gratitude for all kinds of help while working on this book can hardly be expressed.

First of all, the Polish American Bicentennial Committee in Los Angeles deserves very special recognition. Two of its enthusiastic members, Joan Dorothy Sovinski and Wanda B. Szatkowski, instilled the needed initial confidence in the undertaking by organizing the Bicentennial Grand Ball Committee with its proceeds going for this book.

Mary W. Wegner and Krystyna Zielkiewicz spearheaded the preparatory work. With the assistance of Jean Breese, Mindy Kay, Hedy Pawlowski, Catherine M. Deresiewicz and Maria T. Halstead of Santa Barbara, they all excelled in promoting the book. As a matter of fact, Mrs. Mary W. Wegner has been a truly dedicated and selfless co-worker.

Special thanks go to the following: associate editor Margaret Prasniewski for her knowledgeable advice and toil with some manuscripts; to the local P.A.H.A. chapter president, Dr. Anthony F. Turhollow, for his standby assistance throughout the work; to Jerome A. Simons, managing editor, and to his daughter Denise, for clerical work.

Further thanks are extended to Mr. and Mrs. Ludwik Klimes, Professor and Mrs. Czeslaw Olechno-Huszcza; Mrs. Frank Tabasz and Mrs. Gene H. Zygmont, who helped as translators; to Kathy Hayes, Rosemary Dunlap, Halina Gawlinska and Ingeborg M. Klimes for typing; to Doris Bernhagen, Clarence Morrissey and Stephan Pasternacki for research; to Edward M. Kaminski, Arthur L. Zygmont and again to Gene H. Zygmont for working on the "Who's Who" part of the book; to James Jeschke, art director, and Martin Dabrowski, photographer.

Thanks also go to all generous contributors and publishers for their permission to reprint articles. Sincere thanks are likewise extended to Rev. Donald Bilinski, O.F.M., Curator, The Polish Museum of America in Chicago; the U.S. Geological Survey in Menlo Park, and the State Department of Transportation, Division of Highways, in Sacramento.

Without the pre-publication subscribers, especially respondents to the "Who's Who" questionnaire, as well as societies' sponsorship and donors, this book could never have been published. My heartfelt thanks go to all of them. I am especially indebted to Mr. and Mrs. Eugeniusz Szczepanski for their encouragements and substantial contribution, and also to Mr. and Mrs. Jerzy Wdowiak.

I appreciate the interest of Rev. Msgr. John J. Reilly in the progress of the work on the book, as I have lived and worked since June 1, 1976 at Queen of Angels Seminary in San Fernando, California, where he is the rector. I am obliged to Fr. Patrick Ziemann for the use of his library, rich in "Californiana." And also to Rev. Msgr. Francis J. Weber for his valuable help at the Los Angeles Archdiocesan Archives as well as to Dr. Karl W. Kleinz and Sr. Patrice for their literary assistance.

I am no less indebted to Dr. Ray A. Billington from The Huntington Library, Dr. Andrew F. Rolle from Occidental College and Msgr. John J. Reilly for reading the manuscript of the book and kindly appraising it, as well as to Msgr. Francis J. Weber for writing the Prologue.

I greatly appreciate the kindness of the Very Rev. Charles S. Casassa, S.J., Chancellor of Loyola Marymount University, in writing the Preface in his official capacity as Chairman of the Los Angeles City American Revolution Bicentennial Committee.

I am most grateful to Dr. Doyce B. Nunis, Jr., Professor of History at the University of Southern California, for the Foreword, and for his gracious help in many other ways.

Jacek Przygoda

PREFACE

The Los Angeles City American Revolution Bicentennial Committee completed its work at the end of 1976 as did most city, state and federal bicentennial committees. Whatever carry-over has survived has been largely in the minds and hearts of individual citizens — fond memories, some joy, some sadness, a mixture of gladness and disappointment over what happened or failed to happen. In some cases further action has taken place. A case in point is this book, *The Polish Americans in California, 1827-1977*. The Los Angeles Polish American Committee for the Bicentennial cooperated whole-heartedly with the City Committee by putting on several programs of its own and by joining with other civic groups for still other programs. For the co-chairmen of the Los Angeles Polish American Committee, Rev. Jacek Przygoda and Dr. Anthony F. Turhollow, and the other members of the Committee, this was not enough. They looked for a more permanent expression of their ideas and ideals. This book is that expression. As the Chairman of the Los Angeles City American Revolution Bicentennial Committee, I am deeply gratified by the publication of this book. The City of Los Angeles and the State of California are indebted to the book's editor, Rev. Jacek Przygoda, and its contributors. They have developed a resource that tells much about one ethnic group in California over a period of one hundred and fifty years.

Charles S. Casassa, S.J.
Chairman, Los Angeles City
American Revolution Bicentennial Committee

FOREWORD

From the beginning of European colonization, California's population has been cosmopolitan. The initial settlers were of Spanish, Indian and Negro descent. In the early decades of the nineteenth century, prior to Mexican independence from Spain, foreign visitors, though actually forbidden by Spanish policy, included French, Russian, British and American sojourners. With an exception or two, these early visitors did not settle.

As a Mexican province, California was opened to all nationalities for settlement, thanks to a generous and inviting land policy and liberal naturalization laws adopted by the Mexican Congress. The end results are reflected in two censuses taken in the Los Angeles district, the most populous area in Mexican California, in 1836 and 1844.

The 1836 census recorded a district-wide population of 2228 people. Of that number, 553 were Indians living in *rancherias;* the rest were whites —603 men, 421 women and 651 children under twelve years of age. Among the men were fifty registered foreigners. The largest contingent were Americans, twenty-nine in number. The remaining twenty-one came from various parts of the world: five from France, four from England, three from Portugal, two from Africa, and one each from such widely dispersed countries as Canada, Curacao, Germany, Ireland, Italy, Norway and Scotland.

By 1844, the area's population, excluding Indians, totaled 1847 — 627 men, 500 women, 720 children. The birthplace of most of the names listed in the 1844 *padron* indicates a large number of native-born *Californios.* Mexico appears as the country sending the greatest number of settlers. But new arrivals from South American countries — Chile, Columbia and Peru — are listed, along with one man from the Philippine Islands. Foreign residents included twenty-six Americans, seven Frenchmen, four Englishmen, two Germans and two Portuguese, as well as three Spaniards. Los Angeles, indeed, was cosmopolitan.

The first federal census of California, after its acquisition and admission to statehood, continued to reflect the cosmopolitan pattern. Varied nationalities were attracted by the magnet of gold and flocked to the mines. The gold rush era enriched the human fabric in

California by attracting people from around the world — the state became a promising cultural mosaic. Although the 1850 census was imperfect due to the loss of several county returns, it recorded 69,610 native-born Americans and 22,358 foreign born. The latter group represented twenty-nine distinct countries or continents, as well as some 400 placed under the category of "other foreign countries," a tidy but misleading catch all. Thus, even in the first year of statehood, California's cosmopolitan population continued to grow rapidly in number.

The 1860 federal census registered 146,528 foreign-born, a dramatic increase in a single decade. And, significantly, for the first time, 730 were listed as being born in Poland. By 1870, that number rose to 804. Growth in the Polish-born population continued to increase gradually over the ensuing decades.

Although a native-born Pole visited Mexican California as captain of a Russian American Fur Company vessel with a call at Bodega Bay, Poles did come to California in the early days of the gold rush, even though they sparsely registered in the 1850 census. Proof of that fact is easy to come by. One Pole heralded the way as early as 1847.

Felix P. Wierzbicki, M.D., was born in Czerniowce, Poland, and as a youth studied medicine in Warsaw. An ardent Polish revolutionary, he fled his native land for the United States in 1834. After a brief residence in Illinois, he moved east to Connecticut to complete his medical studies. By 1846, he was practicing in Providence, Rhode Island. On America's entry into war with Mexico, Dr. Wierzbicki, failing to receive a commission, joined Stevenson's New York Volunteers as a hospital steward, and came round-the-Horn with that expeditionary force in 1847. He spent the remainder of his life in California, dying in San Francisco, December 26, 1860, at the age of forty-five.

In 1849, he published in San Francisco the first book to be printed in English west of the Mississippi River and north of Mexico, entitled *California As It Is, and As It May Be, or, A Guide to the Gold Region,* a great Californiana rarity. Later that year, he revised his initial text by adding two chapters, one of which was "Medical Observations Upon the People & Country." This chapter is the second known published medical treatise on California, the first being an essay written by Dr. M. Rollin, a French visitor in 1787 with the Laperouse expedition, which was printed in 1797. Equally important, Dr. Wierzbicki was one of the first trained physicians to practice medicine in San Francisco.

His life and story are representative of the many sterling contributions made to California's growth and development by Polish-born citizens. Now, for the first time, the story of that contribution is told in abundant detail in this book. The role played by Polish-born and Polish Americans in California's history is clearly etched in the narrative which follows. These proud people have given their full measure to the evolution of the commonwealth in many varied and fascinating ways.

Pride in one's national origins is not new to Californians. In 1878, Hugh Quigley published his history of *The Irish Race in California and on the Pacific Coast*. The second nationality to be singled out for similar consideration was the French. Daniel Lévy undertook that task in his *Les Francais en Californie*, published in San Francisco in 1884, but never translated into English. Since these pioneer efforts, a succession of books have dealt with such diverse racial and national origins as the Chinese, Japanese, Filipinos, Italians, Portuguese and Blacks, while broader studies on a national or regional basis have dealt with Basques, Cornish and Scandinavians, to mention three.

This history of the Polish in California fills a void that has long existed. Now, one more segment in the human composition of California's cosmopolitan history is placed in the broader mosaic of the state's greatest heritage — its diverse peoples and the attendant contributions made by that diversity in the enrichment of the state — yesterday, today and tomorrow.

University of Southern California   *Doyce B. Nunis, Jr.*

PROLOGUE

The initial Polish imprint on Alta California can be traced to May 1, 1805, when Captain William Shaler's 175 ton *Lelia Byrd* put into a bay on Santa Catalina Island for repairs.

Because the bay which served the weary seamen as an hospitable haven had not yet been designated with a name, Shaler, the proto navigator to visit and survey the area, "took the liberty of naming it after my much respected friend, M. de Rouissillon." The conferral of his Polish companion's name was the first such appellation applied in California by an American.

John, the Count of Rouissillon (1772-1803), was a Polish nobleman of considerable prominence in his native land. An accomplished scholar in the fields of astronomy, mathematics and music, the count was conversant with almost every European language and dialect.

Rouissillon had fought for the liberty of his country as an aide-de-camp to Tadeusz Kosciuszko when that famed Polish general led a force of 4,000 peasants, armed only with crude scythes and other farming implements, against the Russians at Raclawice.

Subsequently exiled in Hamburg to avoid reprisals from his nation's enemies, Rouissillon met William Shaler and Richard Cleveland when the two New England merchant-adventurers arrived to purchase a vessel on which to visit the western shores of America. Reared on the continent, Rouissillon had never been to sea. Yet such a challenge fascinated him and he readily accepted the offer to join Shaler and Cleveland on their epochal journey.

The *Lelia Byrd* sailed from Cuxhaven on November 8, 1801. After a brief stop at the Canary Islands, the ship reached Rio de Janeiro early the next year. Rounding Cape Horn, Shaler, Cleveland, Rouissillon and their eight crewmen sailed into the harbor of Valparaiso on February 24th. There the entire crew was briefly imprisoned for infringing on the Spanish trade monopoly.

The *Lelia Byrd* encountered further difficulties at San Blas, Mexico, where officials raised new objections to their docking. After personally appealing to the local governor and then to the viceroy himself, Rouissillon finally secured permission to dispose of their wares and reprovision the ship. Then it was on to Alta California.

Though he remained behind in Mexico to acquaint himself with the seat of an ancient and vibrant culture, Rouissillon fully intended to rejoin his friends in the United States, where he hoped to live out his years in an atmosphere of liberty. Those expectations were unfortunately thwarted by a premature death in 1803.

Richard Cleveland described the count as a strong "advocate of liberty" who "could not brook the subjugation of his country." He was likewise an outstanding Catholic, whose knowledge of theology and practice of virtue further endowed his valiant personality.

Though Port Rouissillon does not survive in the Golden State's geographic nomenclature, present-day Avalon remains the scene of the first link in what has become a formidable Polish presence in California.

This enlightening and penetrating publication of Father Jacek Przygoda continues the narrative of Polish presence along the Pacific Slope since 1805. Though their numbers have never been large, the Poles have left a noble record in western American annals. One writer says that "here in the sunny land they found freedom and new homes, they found friends and a measure of prosperity. They repaid the young commonwealth with the best that was in them." This they surely did and today their numbers even include a member of the California hierarchy, the Most Reverend Thaddeus Shubsda, Auxiliary Bishop of Los Angeles and Episcopal Vicar for Santa Barbara.

It is indeed a pleasure to recommend this work.

Msgr. Francis J. Weber
Archivist
Archdiocese of Los Angeles

INTRODUCTION

No one anticipated this book when, on April 17, 1974, the Very Reverend Charles S. Casassa, S.J., Chancellor, Loyola Marymount University, and Chairman of the Los Angeles Bicentennial Committee, invited the Polish American Historical Association, California Chapter, to participate in the city-wide bicentennial celebrations.

From the initial deliberations of the International Heritage Bicentennial Subcommittee, in which Father Przygoda participated, came the stimulus to produce a publication on Poles in Los Angeles. For it was during the second meeting, June 18, 1974, that Barbara Perry, then Executive Director of the Los Angeles Bicentennial Committee, suggested that the ethnic groups in the metropolitan region of the city prepare their respective "Who's Who." This was meant to serve as a lasting memento of the United States bicentennial commemorations in this area.

However, on second thought, such a "Who's Who" of Polish American achievers in their various professional, cultural, social and business fields seemed insufficient to honor appropriately this historical event. It appeared advisable to present, first, some available historical materials pertaining to the Polish past in California.

Thus, a handful of enthusiasts, functioning within the Polish American Bicentennial Committee of Los Angeles, held several exploratory meetings. There developed a two-pronged plan of action. First, the need for the effective participation by the local Polish American community in the over-all bicentennial celebrations was unequivocally ascertained, and the representatives to the International Heritage Bicentennial Committee were chosen. Second, the organization of a Polish American Bicentennial Grand Ball Committee became a reality; the proceeds of their work would defray the cost of the main project, a book on Polish Americans in California, including an emphasis on "Who's Who" among them. A striking paucity of books on this subject reinforced the resolution to undertake the publication project on a larger scale.

The plan became a necessity after realizing that 44,198 people of Polish foreign stock lived in Los Angeles according to U.S. Census

XVII

Bureau of 1960; 73,959 in the Los Angeles Standard Metropolitan Statistical Area in 1970 and this same census registered 115,833 Poles and Polish descendants in California. These demographic figures should speak for themselves, and indicate a wealth of publications about Polish people in the state. But do they?

Yes, books such as those by Lynn Bowman, Robert Glass Cleland, Rockwell D. Hunt, Anne Loftis, William M'Collum, Carey McWilliams, Harris Newmark, Harry T. Peters, Andrew F. Rolle, and Hubert H. Bancroft, did recognize the names of Helena Modjeska, Felix P. Wierzbicki, C. Bielawski, James C. Zabriskie, A. Zakrzewski, John Strentzel, Ralph Modjeski, Henryk Sienkiewicz, and I.J. Paderewski, but that is almost all "things Polish" in California. The persistent lack of adequate, up-dated information on Californians of Polish heritage is probably responsible for the lack of treatment of Poles in popular books and textbooks on and about California today.

A booklet, *Polish Pioneers of California,* written by Miecislaus Haiman and published in Chicago in 1940 is not available in high schools, nor in college libraries throughout the state. Also unknown in the Los Angeles area is a commemorative publication, *Slavs in California,* published in Oakland in 1937, with a three-page text penned by Jozefa Kudlicka, "Poles in Los Angeles." Only an unpublished M.A. thesis (University of Southern California, 1952) by Milton L. Kosberg and a Ph.D. dissertation by Neil C. Sandberg (at the same university), published in New York in 1974, deal with Polish topics in California.

Since 1972, a Polish and English bilingual biannual, *Migrant Echo,* has been published and edited by Andrew Woznicki in San Francisco. One of its contributors is a well-known Polish historiographer, Jan Kowalik; he has lately devoted his time and energy to researching and writing on Poles in California. He is also the founder of the American-Polish Documentation Studio, presently in San Jose.

Thus, the primary purpose of this book is to start the process of filling "the Polish gap" in the demographic as well as historical picture of California. Collecting and compiling unpublished and published materials in this pilot book may provide the impetus for further scholarly research along these lines and thus recapture the heritage of all Californians.

There are two secondary goals of this venture. First, the realization, in part, of the plan cherished by the Los Angeles International Heritage Bicentennial Subcommittee in 1974. Second, since a truly integrated American society is vital to all of us, it is hoped that some knowledge about Polish Americans, in this most populous state of the

XVIII

Union, will contribute to a social cohesiveness, along with a cultural appreciation.

Part One of the book presents a brief historical background. To refresh the reader's memory, the relationship between Poland, America during its Revolutionary War, and the United States is outlined. Parts Two and Three, respectively, feature a mosaic of Polish American personalities who made noteworthy contributions to the American society in California. Part Four focuses on Polish American societal life in California. Part Five contains some documentary materials. Part Six gives a sample of Polish American *Who's Who* in California.

Maps and illustrations are interspersed throughout the text. Neither the editor nor contributors intend to present in this fragmentary picture a claim to any glorification of Polish Americans. However, as any claim to superiority is repulsive, so ignorance is also unfair.

Thus, mindful of a thought expressed by Antoine Lavoisier that, "Like three impressions of the same seal, the word ought to produce the idea, and the idea ought to be a picture of the fact," we hope that this fruition of a three-year effort will serve as a reference source in libraries for general and individual readers across the state.

Los Angeles   Jacek Przygoda/Anthony F. Turhollow
Fourth of July 1977

ROUNCE & COFFIN CLUB, LOS ANGELES

AWARD OF MERIT

WESTERN BOOKS EXHIBITION, 1977

THIS IS TO CERTIFY THAT

Sarmatia

SUBMITTED BY

Bogdan Deresiewicz

HAS BEEN CHOSEN AS ONE OF THE

WESTERN BOOKS OF 1977

Richard Doctor

CHAIRMAN OF THE EXHIBITION

PART
ONE

AMERICA AND POLAND
IN RETROSPECT

When a society
or civilization
perishes, one condition
can always be found.
They forgot where
they came from.

Carl Sandburg

Wood engraving by Stefan Mrozewski

Conversion to Christianity

In the year 966, Mieszko, the first historic ruler of Poland's Piast dynasty, accepted Christianity for himself and for his nation. Helped by his Christian wife, Princess Dobrawa, he brought Poland into the European community of Christian nations by adopting the pattern of Western culture and civilization.

To counter German threats to his lands, Mieszko placed the Church of Poland under the direct authority of Rome. This action put Poland under the special protection of the Holy See.

In the thousand years which followed, Poland has been a part of Western culture and its furthermost outpost in Europe.

Text by Helena Sworakowska

AMERICA — POLAND: The Way It Was

Henryk Moscicki

Towards the end of the 17th century, Stefan Klonowicz alluded to America in a poem entitled "Flis" by saying:
Happy isles — heroic land of bliss,
Known to our country long ere this . . .
It seems as though Klonowicz was under the influence of a prophetic inspiration when he predicted the heroic future of those "happy isles," that were neither strange nor indifferent to Poland.

It was early indeed that Poland learned of America. Knowledge of the discovery of the New World soon reached Krakow, where, in the Jagiellonian Academy, active interest was manifested in the acquisitions of bold voyagers and learned geographers. The first, though inaccurate, reference to a land called the "New World" (*Novum Mundum*) is found in a book printed in Krakow in 1506, the work of John of Hollywood (Sacrabosco) with comments by John of Glogowo, a professor of the Krakow University. The next, much more detailed, mention of America is made by John Stobnica, who succeeded John of Glogowo to the Krakow chair. In his *Introductio in Ptholomei Cosmographiam*, printed in 1512, this Polish geographer endeavors to fix the geographical location of the new part of the world, and to this end, provides his book with a reproduction of a map drawn by Waldseemuller in 1507. The third "Americana" to originate in Poland is a volume published in 1522, which is similar to the first in that it also contains comments on the work of Sacrabosco. Finally, mention is also made of America in the work of the immortal astronomer, Nicholas Copernicus (Mikolaj Kopernik), which was published under the title *De revolutionibus orbium coelestium*, in 1543.

Copernicus uses the discovery of America as one of the important arguments upon which he bases his famous theory that the earth is spheroid with a single center.

The first to publish knowledge on America in the Polish language was Martin Bielski. In his *Kroniki wszystkiego swiata* (Chronicles of the

Excerpts from a paper read in the Warsaw Town Hall on July 4, 1926. Henryk Moscicki (1881-1952), among several books, wrote *General Jasinski i Powstanie Kosciuszkowskie* (General Jasinski and the Kosciuszko Insurrection), in 1917.

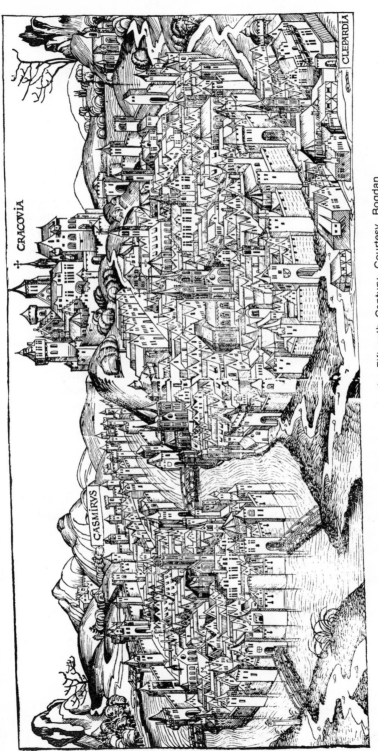

Cracovia — (Cracow, Krakow) — in the Fifteenth Century. Courtesy, Bogdan Deresiewicz, translator of *Sarmatia the Early Polish Kingdom*; published in Los Angeles, The Plantin Press, 1976.

Entire World), published in Krakow in 1551, this geographer writes: "America, an isle in the west, is located on a great ocean and is so large that it is considered as a fourth grand division of the earth."

* * *

In the 17th century, there are instances of the settlement of Poles in America. Foremost among them were the Zabrieskies or, more correctly, the Zborowskis, descendants of Wojciech Zborowski, son of Martin, Castellain of Krakow, whose brother Samuel was beheaded in the castle at Krakow during the reign of Stefan Batory. The Zborowskis-Zabrieskies settled near the town of Hackensack, New Jersey, during the second half of the 17th century.

During that period there also settled in America the Laskis, Zubrzyckis and the Sadowskis. Furthermore, a certain Pole, a "professor," was said to have come to Manhattan Island in 1659 to teach the Dutch colonists.

The first Polish immigrants were, of course, too few to bring about close amicable relations between Poland and the New World. It was not until the second half of the 18th century, upon the outbreak of the War of Independence, that Poland showed a great interest in the American Colonies and sympathized profoundly with them.

* * *

The words which open and close the memorable Declaration of Independence, reverberated throughout Poland in the minds of patriotic citizens, as they witnessed the dismemberment of their country. King Stanislas August heartily sympathized with the aspirations of the American people for freedom, while the democratic slogans of that young republic were eagerly incorporated into political literature, and were, moreover, reflected in the reform ideas of Staszic and Kollataj.

At a time when despotism was approaching its pinnacle in Europe, and when by partitioning Poland Catherine II and Frederick the Great endeavored to prove to the world that their system was excellent, and after having imposed the "spirit of servility" upon the dismembered country, received humble homages in return from debased magnates — at such a seemingly triumphal moment for tyranny, there burst forth a rebellion against the British Monarch, with Americans, as Kosciuszko was to say later, "daring to conquer over their tyrants. . ."

Each word of the sublime Act of Independence sounded in the hearts of the Polish people as if it were spoken in their own tongue. For the

Polish-Lithuanian Republic was composed of a few nations, united together by Jagiellonian vows, in order that they might benefit from "the freedom and liberties of the Kingdom of Poland, the same as all the other citizens of the Polish Crown. . . and that happiness may be derived therefrom for all time by them and their posterity." The evolving American Union was realizing this ideal of Polish liberty. Hence, "wherever on the globe they are fighting for liberty, it is as if it was our own affair."

A Polish noble, Mr. Kosciuszko, landed in America in 1776, to become the first Pole and one of the first Europeans to take up arms in America's defense; he preceded Lafayette by one year. He quickly appraised the strength and purity of the American cause, which was then held in Europe to be reckless and lost. He astonished Americans by his military knowledge and by the breadth of his ideas on democracy. It was with great pleasure that Thomas Jefferson informed General Gates that Kosciuszko "is the purest Son of Liberty that I have ever seen, and of that Liberty that embraces all, not alone a handful of the chosen and wealthy." Jefferson was not mistaken.

Kosciuszko's enlistment brought other Polish volunteers to America, cavalry officers of the first French Foreign Legion: Captain John Mieszkowski, Lieutenant Grabowski, Kossowski and Uzdowski, and a number of other officers and common soldiers. Above all, there was Pulaski, "A big-hearted, chivalrous man," who met with a heroic death on October 9, 1779, while leading a furious charge near Savannah. The Legion formed by Pulaski counted several Poles in its ranks, among them, Captain John Zielinski, a relative of Pulaski, killed August 25, 1779; Maciej Rogowski, a Bar Confederate; Colonel Michael Kowacz, a Slav or Pole, killed near Charleston on May 11, 1779; Lieutenant Carl Litomski; Colonel Baron de Botzen (or De Boze), also said to be a Pole, killed during the treacherous assault at Egg Harbor, and a number of others, whose names time has effaced.

Totally different from his many countrymen and towering above them was Kosciuszko. What marked him out was initiative to serve and, more particularly, a loftier, more rugged spirit, which seemed to be better suited to the new times and to the New World. His type of virtue agreed well with the primitive colonial puritanism. "Kosciuszko," wrote Washington, "is better adapted to the genius and spirit of our people." In reality, he became very much attached to the Americans, and not only showed a keen interest in military matters, but took their internal affairs warmly to heart. He showed great tact in the face of local quarrels. "Your principles and aspirations," wrote Jefferson to Kosciuszko, "are such that they must be praised, respected and loved. Faithful to one aim — liberty and human happiness, they did not traffic with renegades and apostates."

Shortly after peace was signed in 1783, Kosciuszko left America with the rank of Brigadier General, bestowed "for long, faithful and useful services," and with the medal of the Order of Cincinnatus, whose motto, "Omnia reliquit servare Republicam" (He relinquished all things to serve the Republic) he had truly fulfilled. In the person of Kosciuszko, Poland took from Free America a priceless, everlasting treasure — a treasure of great ideas.

*   *   *

The downfall of Poland was sincerely regretted in America. Jefferson called this happening a "pernicious precedent," a "crime," a "horror." Henry Wheaton, a noted American jurist and statesman, was of the opinion that the dismemberment of Poland was "the most glaring insult to natural justice and international law, an insult that was not seen since Europe rose from a state of barbarism." The countryless Polish wanderers found willing aid and relief on the American soil, and shared in the warm sympathy for the lost Polish cause which Kosciuszko and Niemcewicz had aroused by their service in America. Among those Poles was a certain Stadnicki who, in conjunction with a company of Dutch colonists, founded the city of Buffalo in 1796, on a site occupied by an Indian village called Tu-shava.

During a visit paid to the United States in 1783-1784 Kajetan Wegierski, a poet, acquired a sincere admiration for — as he described — the "youth and health-abounding American Nation." "I travelled a few thousand miles," he wrote to Washington from Princeton on October 18, 1784, "to see and to become acquainted with the founders of American liberty; not only to be able to say that I have seen them, but to learn how to preserve for the people their most precious rights."

In 1803 and 1804, many of the Polish Legionnaires, who took part in the unfortunate San Domingo Expedition, settled permanently in the United States, and, in time, became completely assimilated. In 1795, Bishop John Carroll of Baltimore ordained into the priesthood Prince Golicyn, a Russian noble who came to the United States in 1792, and placed in his charge a church and parish established for Poles and other Slavs in Bohemia Manor, Cecil County, Maryland. Golicyn wrote to the Jesuits in the Province of Bialorus and induced several to come to America, a few Poles among them. (Rev. Norbert Korsak, Rev. Bonifacy Krukowski and Rev. Franciszek Dzierozynski).

*   *   *

prominently in the American army. About this time there were founded the first Polish associations: "The Society of Poles in America" in 1842 and "The Democratic Society of Polish Exiles" in 1852, both in New York. Apart from propagating the idea of an armed return to Poland, the "Democratic Society," in keeping with Kosciuszko's ideals, heartily supported the Republican Party, which aimed to abolish slavery in America.

When war broke out in 1861, a large number of Poles joined the ranks of the Union army. Among the officers whose bravery and faithfulness to the cause rendered them conspicuous were: Rosenkranz, Szeinic, Ludwik Zychlinski and, particularly, General Wlodzimierz Krzyzanowski. As a youth barely out of his teens, Krzyzanowski took part in Mieroslawski's Insurrection of Poznan. He luckily escaped arrest and sailed for America, where, through hard work, he in time became quite independent. The hard knocks he received in life did not kill the ideals of his youth however, and, conscious of the inner command that induces every sensitive Pole to stand faithfully in the defense of mankind's highest gift, liberty, he voluntarily joined Lincoln's army. The son of "a land that is above everything the dearest to me, mindful of its misfortune, I fought for an idea, for freedom and liberty," such were the words Krzyzanowski used to describe his decision.

It is as if there existed a spiritual bond which spanned a century to unite Kosciuszko with Krzyzanowski — two Poles who, in the defeats experienced while fighting for their country, did not lose their faith in the triumph of truth and goodness. Krzyzanowski went through the entire campaign of 1861-1864 and won successively the rank of captain, colonel and general.

*   *   *

Worry and deep concern overcame the Poles in the American army when news of the outbreak of the January Insurrection arrived from Poland. Their hearts went out to their bleeding country. A few, among them Zychlinski, succeeded in obtaining their release, to reach their country and join the ranks of their brethren. Contributions poured into the National Fund, numerous meetings were convened, and a newspaper was founded in New York on June 1, 1861, under the name of *Echo from Poland;* it had for its motto: "Know first the affairs of our country—and its adversities and its glories." Henry Kalinowski, a Commissioner of the National Committee and Comptroller of the National Fund, conducted an extensive publicity campaign on Poland's behalf. He also organized a Polish Central Committee, which was composed of Dr. Mackiewicz, Gacek, Jaworowski, the editor of *Echo,* and W. Piotrowski. It is worthy of note that American Poles of "Mosaic faith" and Czechs held meetings and gatherings which revealed their friendly attitude towards Poland.

The insurrection failed and with it the hope of restoring an independent Poland. Again, new hosts of Polish wanderers arrived in hospitable America in search of bread. There they met and benefited from her youthful strength, her unrestrained freedom, and her power of recognizing the rights of every active and creative individual to live.

Finally there came the time when the prophecies of Jefferson, Howe and the many other noble Americans were fulfilled. The Declaration of Independence, the product of Washington's and Kosciuszko's sword, was applied by word and act to Poland by Woodrow Wilson. In a speech made before the Senate on January 22, 1917, he presented to the world the idea of resuscitating Poland. He again mentioned Poland when addressing Congress on December 4, 1917, in connection with the declaration of war against Austria. Among the "fourteen points" contained in his Congressional message of January 8, 1918, he clearly stated the unexpired right of re-establishing a free Polish state, and in a similar speech delivered on February 11, 1918, he emphasized the European significance of Poland's restoration. Two years after his speech to the Senate, in a telegram sent to Paderewski on January 22, 1919, he recognized the Government of Poland in free Warsaw.

*   *   *

A century and a half separates us from the moment when the world was moved by the resounding words of the Declaration of Independence. During the first few years in which the United States was strengthening its acquired freedom, the foundations of the Polish homeland were crumbling to pieces, the conquered nation was being driven to an unknown destiny, and the Polish soul was being destroyed by persecution and Prusso-Muscovite expropriations. Fanatic hatred built a veritable wall of prejudice against us. Our deeds, our faith, and our speech were slandered. Our virtue was exhibited in the light of falsity and hypocrisy. We were looked upon as renegades. Our very right to live a cultural and independent life was questioned. We were not known in Europe. But the American nation did not even then deny its sympathy for Poland. It comforted her by word and substantial aid; the star-spangled banner of the United States shielded the bleeding breast of the White Eagle.

Because, Americans, you remembered Washington's memorable words "be true to yourselves" with regard to Poland; because you have always been faithful to far away Poland; because, through the tears of our misery there shone the bright beams of your optimism and consolation; because your hands saved the Polish child; because amid the hardships of molding an independent existence you awakened faith in us; because your sword tilted the scales of justice; and because the words of your distinguished men reflected an understanding of our historical mission — for these gifts of your noble soul, tribute and thanks are paid to you by the Poland of Kosciuszko, of Pulaski, of Niemcewicz, of Krzyzanowski; paid in the whispers of the Polish child in the words of our poet:

Happy Isles — heroic land of bliss,
Known to our country long ere this . . .

THE AMERICAN REVOLUTION AND THE POLAND OF STANISLAW AUGUST PONIATOWSKI:
A Bicentennial Tribute

Alfred J. Wrobel

In 1790 a Polish patriot, Hugo Kollataj, wondered what the new United States would mean to the ancient kingdom of Poland. "If nothing more," he thought, "we are a strange, old man full of bad habits in contrast with a well-educated young man whose heart has not yet been stained by evil examples." It would seem fitting in America's Bicentennial Year to see what impact this "well-educated young man" had upon the Poland of Stanislaw August Poniatowski, the last eighteenth century King of Poland.

Poland in the eighteenth century was not a great power, but its strategic geographical position and size made it a victim of diplomatic intrigue, which often involved the powerful nations of Russia, Prussia, Austria, France and Great Britain. Stanislaw August was a confirmed Anglophile, but he chose to keep Poland neutral during the American Revolution in the hope that such a position would bring some western "golden liberties" such as the "liberum veto" in which a single defiant deputy could break up a Diet meeting. Poland, as John Adams observed, had "no balance," only "a king and an assembly of nobles and nothing more."

It was within this framework that serious efforts would be made to reform an almost anarchistic system. And one important source of inspiration for reform was the developing American Revolution.

II

Early in his reign Stanislaw August realized the importance of the press in reform. He sent agents abroad to promote a favorable picture of Poland in the Dutch, French and English press. At home he saw newspapers mushroom from one, in 1774, to more than a dozen by 1795. And he encouraged the publication of a magazine, the *Monitor*, as the "leading organ of the early Polish Enlightenment." The general

Alfred J. Wrobel teaches history at El Camino College, El Camino, California.

features of the Polish Enlightenment are somewhat similar to those found in most western European countries: a vogue for all things French; a widespread acquaintance with such figures as Rousseau, Raynal, Mably, Voltaire, Montesquieu, and others; the immense popularity of science; and the acceptance of free masonry by Stanislaw August and influential members of the nobility.

The international character of Polish masonry at this time was revealed in a proposal to George Washington for Congressional nomination of a number of "American Characters as Members" of the Polish Order of Knights of Divine Providence. Congress, however, could not "consistently with the principles of the Confederation, accept their obliging proposal."

The American Bald Eagle. Sculpture by Antoni Pedzich. Photo, Martin Dabrowski.

One important Polish journalist was unhappy with this direction of thought and activity. Father Stefan Luskina, nobleman, traveler, scholar, educator, and eventually editor of the influential *Gazeta Warszawska* (Warsaw Gazette), saw the Enlightenment as a threat to the Monarchy and to the Church. He chose the American colonial conflict to inform his readers of the consequences of such revolutionary ideas. While his newspaper selected and edited the colonial events from essentially foreign newspaper sources, the astonishing amount of such news in this bi-weekly newspaper provided the Polish reader with a greater sophistication than could be expected of a remotely situated Eastern European capital such as Warsaw.

If the intent of Luskina was to create some fear for the consequences of a liberal impulse of the European Enlightenment, he may have been disappointed. The total impression of the overwhelming mass of information about the American conflict was favorable to the American cause. By condemning the British, he in effect gave moral approval to the American struggle.

Yet Luskina's conservative instinct was repelled by the social experimentation implied in the American Revolution. He chose to ignore the concept of equality; on the other hand, he had no quarrel with the political struggle. Since the Poles were in a similar position of being politically oppressed, his gentry readers could identify sympathetically with the Americans. In this way the *Gazeta Warszawska* did much to create a popular image of the Americans in the Polish quest for political independence.

Many of the *szlachta* kept abreast of American news by having their secretaries summarize foreign newspaper accounts, while some of the gentry encountered in their travels such prominent Americans as Benjamin Franklin and Thomas Jefferson. Prince Adam Czartoryski and his wife, Izabela, were very impressed with Franklin's hospitality, which even included twelve lessons on the harmonica. The Polish reformer, Stanislaw Staszic, considered Franklin a great scientist, politician and statesman. Later in Paris, Jefferson entertained political writer and activist Julian Niemcewicz, and statesman Ignacy Potocki.

Above all, the increase in Polish books and articles about America brought a widespread awareness of a new political and social experiment taking place in the New World. The earliest of these foreign translated works came with official court approval in 1778. Father Pawel Kollacz translated from an anonymous German source, the *Rewolucya teraznieysza Ameryki Polnocney w dwunastu zkonfederowanych osadach* (The Present Revolution in the Twelve Confederated Colonies of North America). Although adding little in the way of analysis of the Revolution, the translator did hail "a new epoch of happiness for America."

One of the most influential monthly magazines was the *Pamietnik historyczno-polityczny* (Historical-Political Memoir). An ex-Jesuit, Piotr Switkowski, was the editor, and with tireless effort he sought to make Poland a strong nation. He remained steadfastly an Anglophile; nonetheless, he presented to his readers generous selections from the French author and soldier, the Marquis de Chastellux, who gave a vivid and fairly accurate picture of life in the United States. For a more romantic view, he included American author and agriculturist, J. Hector St. John Crevecoeur and his *Letters From an American Farmer*. Special attention was usually given to Benjamin Franklin, already an international figure of considerable admiration. His *Poor Richard's Almanac* soon helped to establish a Polish literary vogue in aphorism. Switkowski hoped to push for constitutional reform in Poland and American independence was an inspired example. But he had no desire to imitate the American system. The reformer wanted to strengthen the ineffective Monarchy rather than give further justification to republicanism in Poland.

III

In this era of reform, the Poles sought a better understanding of the United States for which two of them had fought; Kazimierz Pulaski, who perished at the siege of Savannah in 1779, and Tadeusz Kosciuszko, who survived to come home for another historical role.

Stanislaw August's private secretary, Piotr Maurycy Glayre, expressed an undisguised enthusiasm for the Americans, while one of the King's advisors, Abbe Piotolli, read John Adams and Thomas Paine. The statesman, reformer and philosopher, Hugo Kollataj, translated Paine and was impressed with his agrarian schemes of reform. The Polish poet, Kajetan Wegierski, wrote personally to John Dickerson for a copy of his writings, while Poland's diplomatic agent in Paris, Filipio Mazzei, passed on Jefferson's *Notes on Virginia* for the King's perusal. It was, incidentally, Mazzei, with Jefferson's approval, who wrote a four volume treatise correcting French misconceptions about the United States. Within a short time, the United States Constitution was familiar to the various factions engaged in the reform of the Polish constitution.

The King also had by this time developed an admiration for the Americans — in part to make the best of a revolutionary situation, and in part the result of the enthusiasm of his own advisors. He desired a bust of George Washington, and on at least one occasion he actually wrote Washington, noting how the General's "conduct in war and peace has inspired me for a long time with a desire of expressing to you the highest esteem in which I bear you." Furthermore, "it would be pleasing to me that an American shall bear the marks of my esteem and affection in the midst of his compatriots, in the midst of that nation which has known how to win for itself already such an opinion from the inhabitants of the Old Hemisphere, that is able in many ways to serve them as a lesson and model."

The American chosen to be honored by the King was Lewis Littlepage, a recently created Knight of the Order of Saint Stanislaw, and since 1787 a chamberlain at the Polish Court. This wandering Virginian, whose diplomatic and military career in America and Europe was steeped in controversy, provided information and advice to the Polish court on American affairs. One such area of concern was the future economic relationship of the new nation with Poland. As early as 1781 the Department of Foreign Affairs requested the Polish Minister in London, Franciszek Bukaty, to prepare an economic analysis on the impact of future American trade upon Poland.

Bukaty foresaw a "new epoch of trade," but he was confident that the Baltic advantages over some American products, such as timber and potash, would remain secure, "as long as they did not permit the Americans to exceed the quality of their products." But such an interpretation was conditional because of the "cruel obstacles to our own free port facilities." He had in mind the Prussian dominance of the Polish Baltic trade. When, in 1794, Stanislaw August considered the establishment of trade with the United States, it was on the basis that the Anglo-American trade would be normalized. Polish diplomatic efforts never lost sight of winning British support for Poland.

Minister Bukaty was involved in a plan to attract American workers to Poland to improve the quality of Polish-Ukrainian tobacco. With the approval of the Treasury Commission, Bukaty in 1791 engaged the services of an adventurous Virginian speculator, Richard Claiborne. Soon afterwards, however, the Polish Minister had to withdraw the contract "because of the unfortunate occurrence of Revolution in Poland." Claiborne was paid "with a Hundred Pounds Sterling for the disappointment," and Bukaty "at least received from him a Manuscript on the Cultivation of Tobaccos in his country." Bukaty then expressed the hope "that even England, having at present no particular connections or impulse towards preference for America, would import our tobacco." But such hopefulness was based upon some assurance of internal reform to attract substantial British support.

IV

Poland's internal reform movement already had reached a crucial stage with the meeting of the Great Diet in 1788. At the beginning of this famous Four Years' Diet, two groups developed: the Republicans and the Patriots. The former were represented by reactionary magnates (men like the Grand hetman of the Army, Seweryn Rzewuski) who, in their obstinacy and selfishness, sought a return to the "misguided democratic anarchy" which existed before 1764. On the other hand, the Patriots, desiring a thorough reform of the Polish constitution, represented the best minds of the country. Led by such men as the popular Prince Adam Kazimierz Czartoryski, the Patriots joined the Republicans in the long-awaited opportunity to challenge the Russian domination of Poland.

In the ensuing polemic warfare, Republicans and Patriots were sharply divided over such issues as executive power. To Seweryn Rzewuski, Poland was a "Democracy of Nobles" in which it was "better to have less tranquility with a limitation on freedom." To the Patriots such a position was nothing less than anarchy. And Rzewuski, accordingly, set out to defend his position on elective monarchy.

In his defense, Rzewuski cited England as an example of the loss of freedom under a hereditary monarchy. Americans had no choice but to fight this system, and once free, rejected the idea of a king in their government, since "a hereditary monarchy cannot be in accord with freedom." "Is England," he asked, "the kind of government the Poles need, in which the King is everything, the Nation nothing?"

Rzewuski, in effect, viewed the American Revolution as a failure of the British system in not preserving American freedom. The ultimate proof of this was in the rejection of the monarchy for a federal system of government. By implication, he reasoned, federalism could then be applied to strengthen the Polish republic. The magnate also felt that the Poles should follow the example of Franklin and Washington "who have shown to the world that in Republics, a free Nation, itself the creator of good and bad faith, necessarily does not need Kings for its happiness."

It was the Patriot, Hugo Kollataj, who took up the challenge of Rzewuski. This skillful politician-scholar also knew "Franklin's language." He had no quarrel with Rzewuski's use of Franklin and Washington, so long as the object would be the freedom of all persons in Polish society. What particularly disturbed Kollataj was the deliberate misuse of these Americans to defend the existing political order. To Kollataj, freedom, as exemplified by Franklin and Washington, was for the entire nation and not for any particular class. Furthermore, Kollataj saw the American Revolution not as a battle over the merits of the British system but rather over the preservation of rights under that system.

Could such a system be applied to Poland? Kollataj warned his audience against using foreign models. He felt that the Poles should imitate the American experience but only in the sense that "the system of Franklin is concerned with the freedom of man and not with the means by which everywhere he will try to recover his rights." Kollataj therefore favored the strengthening of the Monarchy to preserve this "freedom of man."

At this time such arguments gave the Poles a unique distinction among European nations in considering the merits of the American political system in their own constitutional reform. In the end the Patriots would see the elective monarchy abandoned and a hereditary monarchy settled on the House of Saxony. John Adams shrewdly observed that the new Constitution "opened a futurity to the popular will," and, "a step in advance toward liberal institutions." Gouverneur Morris in Paris felt that the "Kingdom of Poland has formed a new Constitution which I think will change the political face of Europe by drawing that Kingdom of Anarchy into Power." John Paul Jones sent his congratulations to the King, and Thomas Paine considered applying for Polish citizenship.

But power was not what the surrounding European countries had in mind. In a short time another partition was in the making. Under these trying circumstances, Tadeusz Kosciuszko of American Revolutionary fame, was to become the hero. Americans toasted him in the hope that he would become "the Washington of Poland." Kosciuszko was soon leading an armed insurrection. Unfortunately for the Polish cause, Russia, Prussia and Austria combined their military power to end this "threat" to Eastern Europe.

The "Enlightened" monarchs were to undo the work of the Polish Patriots, but the legend of Kosciuszko was complete. He helped the Poles justify their political existence — and the inspiration of the American Revolution would always remain in the background — a befitting Bicentennial tribute.

This article is based upon the author's Ph.D. (1967) dissertation, *The American Revolution and the Poland of Stanislaus Augustus Poniatowski (1763-1795)*. See *Dissertation Abstracts* (1968). For more information, contact University Microfilms, Ann Arbor, Michigan 48106.

PART TWO

VIGNETTES OF POLES IN NINETEENTH CENTURY CALIFORNIA

America is a combination
of a common sharing
of many cultural ideas
with distinctive facets.

Zbigniew Brzezinski

POLES IN CALIFORNIA, 1827-1977: AN OVERVIEW

Jacek Przygoda

"The West was not exclusively Anglo-Saxon in character, nor was it composed of native stock. Italians, Poles, Germans, and French settlers also favored life beyond the Rocky Mountains." (I. Harold Sharfman)[1]

The historic 1976, the year of the United States Bicentennial Observance, might have been commemorated as the Sesquicentennial of the Polish Story in California. One hundred and fifty years ago a Pole, Dionisius Zaremba (Zarembo), a sea captain in the service of Russia, set on colonizing Western America, brought his brig within reach of Fort Ross into Bodega Bay. Later, about 1845, he was in charge of closing the cumbersome sales transaction of Fort Ross to John A. Sutter for the Russian American Company.

Other Polish seamen followed: Stephen Vallivode (Waliwoda) came to Northern California shores in 1830-40. Henry Lyons Brolaski (Brolaskey), Stanislaus Pongowski, Francis Surok (Syrec), and Albert Pulaski (Pollaskey) followed shortly thereafter by overland roads.[2]

Two hundred years ago, in 1775-76, a Spaniard, Juan Bautista de Anza, led a second expedition to California from Sonora, Mexico. The first one had ended in Monterey; this time he reached San Francisco. Like the first, this caravan passed through the San Jacinto Mountains, named after a 13th Century missionary, a Polish Dominican Father. His name in Spanish is Jacinto; in English, Hyacinth; in Polish — Jacek.

In the year 1876 the acclaim of the American theatre for forty years —Helena Modjeska — with her husband, Karol Bozenta Chlapowski and their entourage, arrived in Anaheim. They had been preceded by the future Nobel Prize winner (for the novel *Quo Vadis*), Henryk Sienkiewicz.

In the year 1976, near the same San Jacinto Pass used by de Anza expeditions, bicycling "San Jacinto Street for two miles out of Hemet to the town of San Jacinto, about three miles from Anza's camp on the San Jacinto River" was Frank Riley. His grandfather came to this country from Poland.[3]

One might say all these events were purely coincidental, but Poles have been connected with California history and life from the beginning.

For example, Modest Maryanski was a trapper and gold prospector in the Mono Lake region; he also owned the Shasta gold mine. Count Ladislaus Poniatowski, at one time president of the San Francisco Jockey Club, owned a big gold and silver mine. So did Prince John Sapieha, who also lived in San Francisco about 1876-1880. Sapieha married into the Astor family and founded a bank in New York.

And then there was the Solinski (Solinskey, Solinsky) family. Hugo Charles Solinski came to California in the 1830s and became an agent for Pacific Express and one of Wells Fargo Bank. C.W.H. Solinski was postmaster of Chinese Camp in Tuolomne County, and Francis Solinski was one of the first graduates of the University of California (1877) and a noted mining expert. Irene D. Paden and Margaret E. Schlichtmann in their book *The Big Oak Flat Road* credited one of the Solinskis with building the access road to Yosemite.

"But maybe," wrote Jan Kowalik, "the most fascinating of them all was Gabriel Sovulewski, master of Yosemite and Yosemite National Park superintendent. He built many hundred miles of trails in the Sierras, rejected (however) all attempts to christen any natural monument after him." (*Migrant Echo*, Vol. V, No. 3). And how the name of Jacob Rogenade (!) be omitted here? H.H. Bancroft wrote of him, "native of Poland who came with the U.S. dragoons; murdered at Los Angeles '54." (*History of California*, Vol. V, p. 702). (Other personalities of that and the following era are presented in a more detailed way further in the text.)

Nor can be overlooked, in this century, the "United Polish Societies of Los Angeles." Although it only operated from 1939 to 1944, the U.P.S. of Los Angeles, in conjunction with the Polish American Council headquartered in Chicago, held the President's War Relief Control Board Permit No. 26.

Officers of U.P.S. of Los Angeles included: Frank Danielski, president; Helena E. Bayer, Wanda Bell and Mrs. P. Stefanowski, vice presidents; Zygmunt Baranowski, treasurer; Adam Stefanowski, financial secretary; Marie Toporkiewicz, R.N., American Red Cross Representative, and B.A. Zaremba, recording secretary. (Zaremba later published *Jednodniowka*, a Polish monthly). Advisory Board members included: A. Rybicki, chairman, Walter Danielski, Mrs. M. Olewicz, Mrs. Regina Wasick and Henrietta Danuta (Bobby) Koshade, an actress and a great swimmer who won eight gold medals, and one with a diamond.

Another echo from those years brings back the name of a Polish patriot, Karol Demant, from Los Angeles, and a Polish general, Stanislaw Kwasniewski, poet and writer (post-World War II emigre) who lived and died in Santa Monica.

Francis Bolek, editor of *Who's Who in Polish America*, listed 56 California personalities in the 1943 edition. By 1977 their number had reached 257, and future editions of *Polish Americans WHO'S WHO in California* will list several times that number.

Like almost everyone moving to California, particularly its southern part, the Poles too were attracted either by the climate, by economic considerations (aircraft, electronics and naval industries), or they were prompted by an artistic creativity (with the magic name of Hollywood leading in its field of the film industry). Some were simply moved by the feeling of freedom. A different category of newcomers consisted of clergy, teachers, artists of all sorts, government employees and ex-military personnel.

The majority of Poles arriving after World War II chose Los Angeles and its environs, the San Francisco-Oakland-San Jose area, Santa Barbara, San Diego, as well as many other places in the state, to settle for still another reason. Their native country, Poland, for whose political and economic freedom many of them had fought between 1939 and 1945, was again not a "free, sovereign and independent state."

In retrospect, five periods of Polish immigration history in California are chronologically discernible:

The first lasted approximately 25 years, and comprised the pre-Forty-Niners (1825-1849).

The second period saw the arrival of Polish Forty-Niners and their families, as well as the post-Forty-Niners — the settlers from other states and immigrants from Poland. This period spanned some 45 years (1849-1895).

The third phase can be placed between the middle of the last decade of the 19th Century to the end of World War II, again roughly 50 years in duration (1895-1945). The bulk of the new arrivals then were Polish Americans, mainly people discharged from the armed services, professionals (actors, musicians, government employees, etc.), and retired people.

It is noteworthy to single out at this point that already in 1910 there were in the state 3,595 inhabitants whose mother tongue was Polish.

The fourth period lasted a decade (1946-1956) and witnessed the coming of displaced persons (after 1952): Polish combatants from Great Britain, West Germany, and other countries of the free world. Naturally, some internal migration also took place then.

The fifth, and current, period, after 1957, resumes immigration directly from Poland, along with Poles arriving from the rest of Europe, Canada, and South America, as well as Polish Americans coming to the state to retire or to find work.

The prevailing psychological type of Polish immigrant to California in the last thirty years is a very special one. In most cases, Poles reached this country after having been forcefully displaced from their own, after suffering temporary transitional living conditions in Argentina, Austria, Baltic and Scandinavian states, Belgium, Canada, France, Germany, Great Britain, Hungary, Italy, the Middle East, Rumania and Russia. The atrocities of the 1939-45 war, deportations and forced labor camps, prisons, P.O.W. and concentration camps, separation of families, a seemingly hopeless waiting, worry and a growing anxiety for opportunity to escape from slavery of one sort or another — all such experiences have added extra dimensions to the spiritual makeup of this latest Polish immigration.

At the time when Patrick Henry's challenge, "Give me liberty or give me death," is about to succumb to a threatening wave of patriotic indifference, the freedom fighters' legacy of martyrdom becomes much more significant. Besides the fact that while their individual and national life is permeated with a fierce love of freedom, Poles have been recognized for another basic characteristic: a strong, strong religious faith. Those two principal traits of the Polish personality in general are conspicuous in Poland's history since the year 966.

This notion is underlined by Poles of Mosaic religious beliefs. The Jews, after being expelled in the 14th Century from German states, were accepted with customary hospitality in Poland and grew in numbers as well as attachment to the Polish soil and way of life. The same outstanding qualities of love for freedom and religion, plus the added support of close family ties, were subsequently brought from Poland to all countries of immigration. As will be seen elsewhere in this book, religious services in Polish, along with the concomitant pastoral care by their own priests, became one of the primary concerns of Poles in Los Angeles. In fact as early as 1908 there was a Polish priest ministering to the faithful here. Others are encountered in San Francisco, in San Bernardino County (Fontana) and more recently, in the city of San Diego and Orange Diocese.

Another aspect of the cultivation of the Polish heritage in California can be found in instruction in the Polish language, which has been done from the elementary to the college level for years; the Polish parish on West Adams Boulevard in Los Angeles has given courses and, in 1976-77, for the first time ever, Polish courses were initiated at Loyola Marymount University. Prior to this the University of California (Berkeley and Los Angeles campuses) has been providing sporadic extension courses in Polish language and literature. More evidence of Polish culture may be discovered in published periodicals, Polish radio programs, and, above all, in the array of societies, fraternal organizations, associations and clubs.

For Polish people in the United States in general, and California in particular, they have been the means to recover from endless shocks, to restore confidence in people and human institutions, to make some sense of the world and to find a real freedom that works, day after day. Finally, they could live decently, with the unquestionable dignity of free human beings.

After the initial bewilderment, Poles began life in earnest in the country of their dreams. Understandably, there were growing pains. For many the language barrier had to be overcome. And for all, the age-old problem of employment had to be solved. Despite illusions and at times disillusions, the new Poles somehow managed to move slowly into the mainstream of American life, as had their predecessors a century or so ago in Chicago, Detroit, Buffalo, Cleveland, Philadelphia, New York, Boston, and countless other localities. This time, in California, the transition period was shorter, easier. Although there were and are cultural, social, and economic victims of the new socio-cultural and industrial systems, Polish Americans fare rather well.

What has helped the Polish immigrants and Polish American migrants in California is the high population mobility in this dynamic state. This mobility, coupled with the flexibility of the labor force, helped qualified arrivals not only to adjust, but to prosper.

One example of Poles' professional preparation and their abilities to handle work assignments emerges from the fact that out of one immigrant group of some eighty members in Los Angeles, there were in 1976 eight Ph.D's, fourteen graduates of schools of engineering, 31 industrial technicians and seven mechanics, seven office workers, four businessmen and eleven professionals.

Another example is provided by the Ampex Corporation, in Marina Del Rey, where several Poles worked, including Klimuszko, drafting supervisor, Nizynski, production manager, and Victor Sell, assistant to the president. The 1976 Hughes Corporation telephone directory reveals employees named Chojnacki, Cybulski, Dombrowski, Gurski, Haponski, Kaminski, Kuzma, Makowski, Nowakowski, Nowicki, and so on. This indicates the employment integration of Polish Americans at one particular electronics industry.

Another list of achievers is headed by Most Reverend Thaddeus Shubsda, the first auxiliary Bishop of Polish descent in Los Angeles. Al Antczak is the managing editor of the Los Angeles diocesan weekly, *The Tidings*. Walter Pudinski was recently at the helm of the California Highway Patrol. Joseph S. Myslicki is the 1977 Knights of Columbus State high official.

Deployment of a scholarly acumen is attested by 28 Polish Americans in California on the Polish Institute of Arts and Sciences in America membership roster (New York, 1975). The Polish American Historical Association, California Chapter, organized at Loyola Marymount University in 1972, has 110 members, one fifth of the national list. The Polish American Arts Association of Santa Barbara recruited in 1976 some 60 members in that city alone.

All in all, this overview is dedicated to all those who weathered the storms, both emotional and financial, by means of their indomitable courage and hard work, and who have created a beautiful place for themselves and their families in California.

Their contributions, both cultural and economic, have enriched us all.

References

1) Dr. I. Harold Sharfman, *Nothing Left to Commemorate,* the story of the Pioneer Jews of Jackson, Amador County, California. Preface.

2) H.H. Bancroft, *History of California,* Vol. II, p. 731, M. Haiman, *Polish Pioneers of California,* pp. 36-39.

3) Frank Riley, *De Anza's Trail Today,* p. 57.

CALIFORNIA LOCALITIES CONNECTED WITH POLAND AND POLES

Richard C. Lewanski

AVALON City, port on Santa Catalina Island.

The present port of Avalon, capital of Santa Catalina Island near Long Beach, was discovered by William Shaler, captain of "Lelia Byrd," and named Port Rousillon in May, 1805. Count John de Rousillon was a 28year-old officer, a mathematician and linguist serving as Kosciuszko's aide-de-camp. In 1802 he traveled with Shaler from Hamburg to Rio, Cape Horn, Valparaiso, Galapagos and San Blas, Mexico, where he died in 1803. "Rousillon" was quite likely an assumed name of a Polish political emigre who left following the partition of Poland.

BIELAWSKI Mountain, in Santa Clara County.

This 3,269-feet-high mountain near Highway 101 in Santa Clara County was named by J.D. Whitney in 1861, after the chief draughtsman of the Surveyor General's Office, Captain Casimir Bielawski. He was born in 1815, came to California in 1853, and died in San Francisco in 1905.

BUCHON Point, in San Luis Obispo County.

The soldiers of the Portola Expedition, seeking Monterey, named the locality "Buchon" when they camped here on September 4, 1769 and met a local chief with "a large goiter which hangs from his neck." Father Juan Crespi, however, gave the point a more dignified name of San Ladislao after the Franciscan Friar, Ladislaus of Gielniow in Poland, who died in 1505. But the priest's name has vanished, and the soldier's remains.

COPERNICUS PEAK. This 4,372 feet mountain in eastern part of Santa Clara County was named after the famous Polish astronomer by Casimir Bielawski.

Adapted from an article published in *Polish American Studies*. Vol. XIV, No. 1 — 2.Jan. — June, 1957.

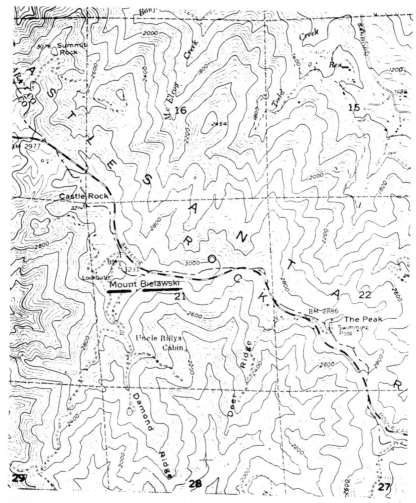

Courtesy: United States, Department of the Interior, Geological Survey; Menlo Park, California. Mount Bielawski, underlined.

FRIANT City, dam in Fresno County.

Friant was originally named Pollasky after Marcus Pollasky, a financial genius who came to Fresno and persuaded people to invest in the land for the railroad which was to tap timberland in the Sierras. In 1891 town lots were sold in the San Joaquin Valley, and Pollasky City was founded. It became the terminus of the Southern Pacific Railroad, and only in 1920 was it renamed Friant. The northeastern branch of the Southern Pacific is still called Pollasky Road.

GLENDALE, Los Angeles County.

At Forest Lawn Memorial Park in Glendale the largest and probably most impressive religious painting in the world, "The Crucifixion," is permanently exhibited. This panoramic canvas was conceived by Ignace Jan Paderewski and painted by Jan Styka of Lwow.

MARIPOSA, Town in Mariposa County.

In 1877 Henryk Sienkiewicz, special correspondent for Warsaw newspapers, visited this town and stayed at Billing Hotel, owned by a German who came to California from Baden. Mr. Billing was an enthusiast of the Polish revolutionary leader, Gen. Ludwik Mieroslawski, under whom he had fought some thirty years earlier. Billing introduced Sienkiewicz to a local Polish squatter named Putrament; that acquaintance formed the basis for one of Sienkiewicz's most famous short stories, *Wspomnienia z Maripozy*.

MODJESKA Peak and Canyon, Orange County.

The name Modjeska is an abbreviation of the Polish family name, Modrzejewska. It refers to Helena Opid, born in Krakow on October 12, 1840, who married first Gustaw Modrzejewski and later Karol Chlapowski. She is listed in the *California Hall of Fame* by Rockwell D. Hunt. She died in Newport Beach, California, on April 8, 1909.

LA POLKA Rancho, southern Santa Clara County.

La Polka Rancho was a one-square league parcel of the original San Ysidro land grant. In 1833 it was granted by the county to Isabel Ortega. In 1849 it was purchased by Daniel Murphy and named La Polka, a name suggested by the new dance which was at the peak of its popularity at that time. Another locality, Polka Bar, is a mining site of 1851 on the Trinity River.

POLONIO Pass, State Highway 41.

This Pass through Diablo Ridge, connecting Paso Robles and Fresno, has an elevation of 2,000 feet.

ROSS Fort, State Historical Monument.

There were several Poles in the Russian expeditionary forces in California. One of them, Korsakowski, became governor of all Russian possessions in America ten years after the Russians landed in Bodega Bay in 1811. About 1840 John Sutter purchased Fort Ross, and Captain Dionizy Zaremba, a skipper, became the Russian agent in charge of all matters connected with the sale.

SAN FRANCISCO.

One of the largest churches in the United States, the Grace Episcopalian Cathedral atop Nob Hill, is embellished with exciting murals painted by Jan de Rosen. These famous murals, adapted to the Gothic style of church, were painted in colors made from an emulsion of wax and water rather than oils applied to plaster. The murals

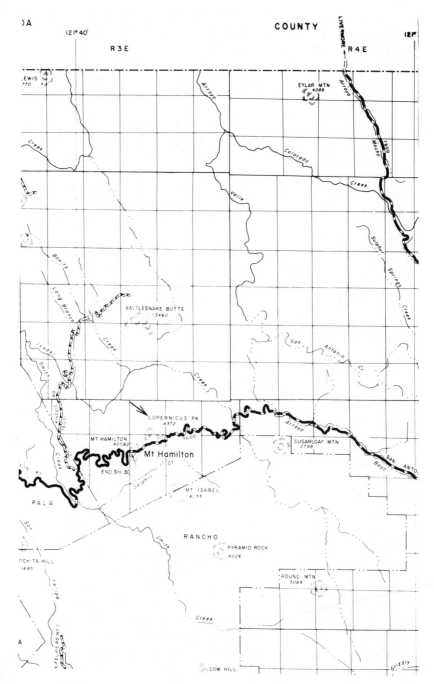

Arrow indicates the location of Copernicus Peak.

represent the Nativity, the first Anglican service in California, Bishop Kip, Samuel Seabury, St. Augustine and King Ethelbert, Father Junipero Serra and Don Gaspar De Portola, and St. Clare.

SAN JACINTO Mountains, San Bernardino County.

San Jacinto, the mountains, the river and the town, honor a thirteenth century Polish Dominican Saint, Jacek (Jacinto in Spanish).

SEBASTOPOL, Sonoma County.

The city was named by its founder, Captain Rudolf Korwin-Piotrowski, after he learned of the Allied victory over Russia during the Crimean War. Piotrowski was born in Kamien near Lublin, Poland, in 1814, and took part in the November Uprising of 1830-31. He was a friend of two California governors, Booth and Pacheco. He died in Paris in 1883.

STANISLAUS County, National Forest, River, Peak, in Stanislaus, Alpine and Tuolumne Counties.

In 1827 a neophyte Indian chief of the Wallawalla or Cosumnes tribe, named Estanislao after a Polish Saint, ran away from Mission San Jose, of which he was elected town mayor, and became the leader of a band of Indians in the San Joaquin Valley. It is impossible at this time to determine whether the Indian chief was named after Bishop Stanislaus Szczepanowski or Stanislaus Kostka, a Jesuit.

WANDA Lake, in Fresno County.

The lake was named by R.B. Marshall of the U.S. Geological Survey in honor of Mrs. Wanda Muir Hanna, one of the daughters of John and Louie Wanda Muir. John Muir (1838-1914) was a famous naturalist and writer about American wilderness. During his travels he visited Alhambra Valley Ranch near Martinez on the San Joaquin, which belonged to a Polish doctor, John Teophile Strentzel. There he met and later married (April 14, 1880) one of Strentzel's daughters, Louie Wanda. They had several children, including Wanda and Helena. John Muir is buried beside his Polish wife beneath a eucalyptus tree on the Martinez Ranch in a spot he chose himself.

ZABRISKIE Town, Post Office, Railroad Station, Point, in Death Valley, Inyo County.

The town was named after Christian Brevoort Zabriskie who came to Death Valley in 1889 as a representative of the Pacific Coast Borax Company; he later became its executive head. The railroad station was on the Tonopah and Tidewater Railroad of which Zabriskie was secretary-treasurer. Zabriskie Point gives an awe-inspiring view of Death Valley. The Zabriskies belong to a Polish American family of the colonial period. It is descended from Albert Zaborowski who came to New Jersey in 1662.

Zabriskie Point, Death Valley. Photo, Cz. Olechno

ZMUDOWSKI State Park and Beach in Santa Cruz County. Mary Zmudowski in 1950 deeded the land to the State of California with the stipulation the family name was to be used in connection with the park. The park is located on the South Bank of the Pajaro River. The Zmudowski family lived in Watsonville for some time; Martin Zmudowski was a member of a sport team on the Pajaro Hose Company in 1896.

Santa Cruz County. Photo, Martin Dabrowski.

THE POLES IN NORTHERN CALIFORNIA
IN THE 1840's AND 1850's

Witold S. Sworakowski

The history of Poles in California in the 1840's and 1850's and their contribution to the development and growth of this country is quite different from that of any other ethnic group that arrived here during the same period from the states East of the Mississippi. The great bulk of non-Polish immigrants came to California in search of fertile land for agricultural cultivation or, after the discovery of gold in Sutter's mill creek (January 24, 1848), in search of the yellow metal. The former were simple farmers who risked the dangerous trip west, hoping to obtain more and better land. The latter were mostly adventurers from among cities in the East and Middle West, who had nothing or little to lose at home, and expected to attain fast and easy wealth in the "goldland."

The few — perhaps 100 — Poles who came to California in the 1840's and 1850's originated from a different social stratum, and they moved West to find better use for their professional knowledge and skills. Almost all of them had been victims of an abortive national uprising during 1830-1831 in Poland.

A few among these Poles reached California before the American-Mexican War of 1846-1848, when it still was part of Mexico, as participants in the migration of the "wild West." More of them arrived in California during the course of that war, serving as soldiers in American military units that advanced overland across Texas or sailed around Cape Horn. Colonel Jonathan D. Stevenson's regiment, recruited in New York, contained at least six Poles and arrived in San Francisco in the spring of 1847 by boat. After the peace treaty with Mexico had been signed on February 2, 1849, and when the United States acquired "Upper California," still other Poles from the 1834 deportees group arrived in California with American military units, assigned to garrison the new territory. The four companies of

Witold S. Sworakowski, professor emeritus of Stanford University, lives in Stanford.

Dragoons under command of Major Graham also had several Poles, who were traditionally good horsemen. As is known, documentary material on these American army units that moved into California is scarce. The few available lists of officers and soldiers distort Polish names, and not enough research by scholars with a background in the history and language of Poland has been undertaken.

There were also the Poles who arrived in California as part of the gold rush, the Forty-Niners. But only a few of them were adventurous goldseekers. Most came as professionals and staff members of American mining companies, which had moved their operations to California. Others, in 1850 and until the end of the decade, went to California overland or by way of Panama to try their luck in trade and services that did not demand manual labor. By now, the 1834 vintage Poles had grown older and even less willing to undertake gold panning or mining, which demanded physical work.

The following are short profiles of the most outstanding Poles who arrived in California in the 1840's and 1850's, and their contributions to the development and growth to that state's present greatness.

*   *   *

Felix Paul Wierzbicki certainly made the most prominent contribution to the development of California during the early years. As one of the 1834 deportees from Austria, he volunteered in 1846, in New York, for Stevenson's California regiment, and after arrival in San Francisco, received his discharge from the army.

Although a medical doctor, he went to the gold fields shortly after they had been discovered. But he gave up gold panning and made a trip through all gold fields and most of California. This personal study of the land and its conditions resulted in a 68-page pamphlet, *California as It is and as It May Be or a Guide to the Gold Region*, which was published in late 1849 at San Francisco. It described the country, its soil, climate, people, legal procedures for land acquisition, and in some detail, the gold fields and the conditions under which gold was extracted. He warned that the average result of a day's hard physical labor was only one ounce of gold. Richer finds were rare and accidental. In a second edition, Wierzbicki added a chapter on health conditions in the fields and warned against the risks that goldseekers were taking.

The importance of Wierzbicki's publication lies in the fact that it was the first objective and truthful presentation about this land of gold and that it was the first printing in the English language that appeared west of the Rockies and north of Mexico. He gives an interesting description of contemporary towns of California, including San Francisco, Monterey, Stockton and others, mentioning also "the Pueblo de Los Angeles." Dr. Wierzbicki's small book is a remarkable achievement of an exiled Polish intellectual who made California his adopted home.

*   *   *

Wojciech Pulaski, in contemporary sources known as Adalbert Pollasky or Polaskey, became a prominent businessman, at first connected with John A. Sutter's "empire" at Fort Ross and later in Sacramento. He contributed to the development of transportation to and from the gold fields. Two other Polaskeys, Marcus and Louis (obviously sons or relatives of Adalbert) made names for themselves in commerce and railroad development. Marcus founded the town of Polaskey (later renamed Friant) in Fresno county and became a railroad promoter. A spur of the Southern Pacific, running from Fresno through Clovis to Friant, carried the name "Pollaskey Road."

*   *   *

Alexander Zakrzewski was a Polish army engineer, an able cartographer and lithographer, who arrived at San Francisco in 1859 from France. During the same year he drew up an *Official Map of San Francisco, Completed from the field notes of the official survey made by Wm. M. Eddy, Surveyor of the town of San Francisco. Drawn by Alexander Zakrzewski, Ex-Polish Officer, 1849.* This map is held in the county archives at Oregon City, Oregon. It expanded the town limits to the present Larkin and Eighth streets. Zakrzewski later drew several maps of growing San Francisco and other California towns. His are also the many contemporary land maps establishing property rights to old Spanish and Mexican land grants which had to be registered with the new American authorities. He operated a "Topographical Office" at Washington and Montgomery Streets in San Francisco. During the 1860's he was a prominent San Franciscan and co-founder of the Polish Society of San Francisco, which still remains active as Chapter 7 of the Polish National Alliance in the United States.

*   *   *

Casimir Bielawski was an army engineer. He arrived in California in 1853 and for 45 years worked in the United States Land Office in San Francisco, where he reached the position of principal draughtsman

with a salary of $2,000 per year in 1862. With two others, he co-authored in 1865 the *Topographical and Railroad Map of the Central Part of California, and Part of the State of Nevada* which, up to the present, is the basic map for this area. On this occasion, he obviously was able to name the highest mountain in the San Francisco-San Jose area as Copernicus Peak (4,372 ft.) in honor of the famous Polish astronomer. [Today most travel maps of California mark only Mt. Hamilton (4,209 ft.) about two miles southeast of Copernicus Peak]. Fellow cartographers gave recognition to his professional and civic achievements by naming a peak west of Los Gatos Bielawski Mountain. For many years Bielawski served as president of the Polish Society of San Francisco. The great Polish actress, Helena Modjeska, mentions him gratefully in her memoirs as one of the San Francisco Poles who had been helpful in bringing her to the stage in San Francisco.

*   *   *

John Strentzel was another Polish army officer who arrived in this country in 1834. He settled at first in Texas and in 1849, as a doctor of medicine, arrived with a group of immigrants to the San Francisco area. He acquired a ranch in the Alhambra valley near Martinez and became a very successful pioneer horticulturist. He was an enthusiastic naturalist and wanderer through the Sierras. His daughter Ludwika (Louie) Wanda married the famous trailblazer of the Sierras, John Muir. Many years of close association between Dr. Strentzel and Muir were certainly fruitful for both. The historical landmark "Muir House" in Martinez is in fact the house that Strentzel built.

*   *   *

Indeed, by their professional and intellectual qualities as well as hard work, Poles contributed to the growth and present greatness of San Francisco and California as a whole.

FELIX P. WIERZBICKI: ONE OF THE FOUNDERS OF THE FIRST MEDICAL SOCIETY IN CALIFORNIA

Ladislas J. Siekaniec

At the end of September, 1846, as a member of the regiment of Colonel Jonathan D. Stevenson, Dr. Wierzbicki left New York for California, where he arrived the following spring. He had joined this expedition with the idea of becoming a regimental physician. Since there were too many candidates for the commission, he was given the rank of sergeant with the promise of the higher post when a vacancy occurred. Although a vacancy did occur, the commitment to Wierzbicki was not fulfilled; moreover, he was reduced in rank to a private. He appealed to General Kearny of California who acknowledged his grievance as reasonable, and induced Colonel Stevenson to give Wierzbicki an honorable discharge from the United States Army, effective in April, 1847. Later Wierzbicki became an Assistant Surgeon in the United States Army until 1855 when he was discharged.

Wierzbicki did not become seriously infected with the "gold fever," but he traveled up and down California for four months of 1849 and gave medical services in the various camps he visited. Finally he settled in San Francisco to practice medicine, write, take part in politics and invest in real estate.

He aided "in the formation of the first Medical Society in the State," in 1847. The same year he authored the first article on the history of medicine to be published in California. He occupies an impressive position in the mural in Toland Hall, University of California Hospital in San Francisco, depicting the history of medicine in California.

As a hobby, Wierzbicki practiced metallurgy, and when the United States government established a branch mint in San Francisco, he received a position there which he held until his death in 1860.

Ladislas John Siekaniec, O.F.M., is the author of a recently published scholarly work, *The Polish Contribution to Early American Education, 1608-1865*, from which this article is excerpted. He lives in Monroe, La.

CALIFORNIA

AS IT IS, AND AS IT MAY BE,

OR,

A GUIDE TO THE GOLD REGION.

BY F. P. WIERZBICKI, M. D.
SAN FRANCISCO, CALIFORNIA.

FIRST EDITION.

SAN FRANCISCO:
PRINTED BY WASHINGTON BARTLETT.
NO. 8, CLAY-STREET.
1849.

Shortly after Wierzbicki completed his travels up and down California he wrote his famous book, *California, As It Is and As It May Be, or a Guide to the Gold Region.* The first of two editions appeared September 30, 1849, was sixty pages long and priced at five dollars; it sold out immediately. The second edition followed three months later, and had been expanded to seventy-six pages.

Historically, Lyman identified Wierzbicki's book as the first written and published in English, not only in San Francisco but in the State of California. Bancroft considered it the first book ever printed in San Francisco. Abbatt, who in 1927 reprinted Wierzbicki's book in a limited edition of one hundred copies, wrote more conservatively in his preface: "In 1849 he (Wierzbicki) published this book, which soon reached a second and enlarged edition (the one which we reproduce). It was not only one of the first books printed in San Francisco, but one of the first printed in English in this state. In either edition it is exceedingly rare, and until 1919 no copy of it had appeared in the auction room, where it brought $130. Aside from its rarity it is valuable historically as one of the best contemporary accounts of the early days of the Gold Rush."

Allibone holds that it was "one of the first books upon the mines" of California, while the obituary in the *Union* stated several years earlier that Wierzbicki was "author of the first book on the California mines."

The antiquarian value of Wierzbicki's booklet rose from the $130 mentioned in Abbatt's report in 1927 to $660 in 1933. But the book's primary value today is not a monetary one, but its contribution to contemporary history. To the scholars and readers of later generations who have become acquainted with the author only through this book, the words of his epitaph still apply: "Highly esteemed by all who knew him."

HELENA MODJESKA:
THE CALIFORNIA YEARS

Ellen K. Lee

It all began on a cold winter night in Warsaw, in the year 1875. Inside a cheery apartment Helena Modjeska, her husband, Karol Bozenta Chlapowski, and a small group of friends including the young journalist, Henryk Sienkiewicz, began to talk of faraway California. Pamphlets and books, circulated in Europe by the Southern Pacific Railroad and California real estate agents, described it as a beautiful, semi-tropical land where life was idyllic, vast acreages of land could be cheaply purchased, and fortunes were being made by orange growers. Within a few days Chlapowski and his young friends began to talk of forming a California Utopian colony in which their brief hours of labor in the field would be followed by hours devoted to art, literature, and music.

Helena Modjeska also dreamed of going to America, but not to live in a Utopian colony far from civilization. As Modrzejewska, at the age of 35, she was the leading actress at the *Teatr Wielki* in Warsaw, widely admired and honored. But she was also hated by many who were jealous of her fame and the social position she had achieved as the wife of Chlapowski, a nobleman. She longed for a vacation from the stresses and tensions of theatrical life in Poland, and for something more. Many of her best portrayals were in Polish translations of Shakespearean plays. Confident of her own powers, she wished to perform these roles in America and in England also. As she listened to her husband and his friends planning their colony, however, she was amused to realize that they expected *Pani Helena* to be the cook and laundress. While cherishing her own "secret plan"[1] of an American stage debut, she also shared the fantastic dreams of life in sunny California. She recalled these bright hopes:

"Oh, but to cook under the sapphire-blue sky in the land of freedom! What joy! . . . To bleach linen at the brook like the maidens of Homer's *Iliad*! After the day of toil to play the guitar and sing by moonlight, to

Ellen K. Lee is a writer and lecturer in the field of Orange County (California) history. She is the author of numerous articles on Helena Modjeska and other pioneer figures. She has done extensive California maritime research and her *Newport Bay: A Pioneer History*, was published in 1973.

Helena Modjeska. Photograph by Scholl, New York City, 1878. Collection, Lon S. McCoy. Courtesy, Ellen K. Lee.

recite poems, or to listen to the mockingbird! And listening to our songs would be charming Indian maidens, our neighbors, making wreaths of luxuriant wild flowers for us! And in exchange we should give them trinkets for their handsome brown wrists! And oh, we should be so far away from every-day gossip and malice, nearer to God, and better."[2]

Modjeska obtained a leave of absence from the Warsaw theatre and plans for the trip to America were quietly made. Friends understood that it was to be a vacation to see the Centennial Exposition in Philadelphia and to restore Modjeska's health. Almost no one knew of her plans to go on the American stage, and she did not have the permission of the *Teatr Wielki*, to which she was under life contract. One by one the would-be colonists had fallen away and the small party that sailed for America in July, 1876, included only Modjeska with her husband and 15-year-old son, Ralph,[3] artist Julian Paprocki, Jules Sypniewski[4] with his wife and two young children, and a 16-year-old nursemaid named Anusia. Henryk Sienkiewicz was already in America, waiting for them in Anaheim, California, which he and Sypniewski had selected as the location for the new colony. After visiting New York and Philadelphia, they sailed to Panama, crossed the isthmus by train, and boarded a creaky old wooden sidewheel steamer for a long, lazy voyage up the Pacific Coast to San Francisco. Modjeska recalled her first landing in California:

"I remember standing on deck, wrapped up in a blanket, for the cold was quite penetrating, and straining my eyes in the direction of the Golden City. But there was nothing to be seen but the milky mist, and even when the fog became less thick, and at last we entered the bay, we could distinguish only lights piercing the veil of mist, and some nondescript forms that might be rocks, or palaces, vague and mysterious."[5] After a brief stop in San Francisco the Sypniewski family, with Ralph and Anusia, went to Anaheim but Modjeska and her husband, with Paprocki, remained in San Francisco to look into theatrical possibilities.

At the California Theatre, one of the finest in America, they saw America's greatest Shakespearean actor, Edwin Booth (an older brother of John Wilkes Booth who had assassinated President Lincoln a decade earlier) in several Shakespearean productions. Modjeska met John McCullough, an American actor who was also manager of the California Theatre, and decided to return to San Francisco as soon as her husband's colony in Anaheim was under way. Today's reader may wonder why she could not have aspired to a stage debut in Los Angeles. The City of the Angels was but a small, half Mexican community surrounded by orchards, vineyards, and cattle and sheep ranches. Its population had grown to 15,000 during Southern California's land boom of the 1870's, a boom set off partly by those books and pamphlets the Poles had read the previous winter. San Francisco, with a population of about 200,000, was a flourishing city with a number of excellent theatres and a population that loved dramatic entertainment of all kinds. But whatever American city she chose for her debut, Modjeska hoped that if she failed, Warsaw would never know that she had tried at all.[6]

It was late October when Modjeska reached Anaheim. While Chlapowski looked about for a California farm to buy, they and the other colonists crowded into a tiny rented house on a large lot planted with grape vines and fruit trees. They soon discovered that Polish intellectuals were not cut out to be farmers. The best account of their trials and hardships appears in Modjeska's autobiography. While Pani Helena cooked and washed clothes and swept out the dust, Madame Sypniewska took to her bed. The men bought mustangs and joyously rode out to shoot rabbits and quail, but when it came to farming they looked about in vain for the faithful peasants who would have been tilling the fields in Poland. Their American neighbors, however rich, wore old clothes and did their own work. Chlapowski and the others bought overalls and tried to do the same. But the Utopian experiment was a failure.

"Sypniewski," Modjeska recalled, "was the only one with any agricultural knowledge, but he could not apply it well to the new conditions of soil and climate. Besides that, there was no system among our idealists; they worked or not, they discussed a great deal, they sometimes even quarrelled and then made up and hugged each other; in one word, they lived under a nervous tension which could not last long ... Everything seemed to be a sad failure. We had several cows, but there was no one to milk them, and we had to buy milk, butter, and cream from the neighbors. We had chickens, but our fine dogs made meals of the eggs. We had a vineyard, which yielded beautiful muscat grapes, but there was nobody to buy them, and often people would come and fill their wagons with them without more ado; they said that such was the custom of the country ... but the most alarming feature of this bucolic fancy was the rapid disappearance of cash and the absolute absence of even a shadow of income."[7]

Karol Chlapowski, however, who was probably the only one of the colony to fall wholeheartedly in love with California, took possession of a forty-acre farm planted with young orange trees. His deed was recorded on December 19, 1876. By the end of the year the Sypniewski family was probably settled on this ranch. The other colonists were all ready to go elsewhere. The experiment in communal living had lasted for approximately ten weeks. Modjeska was probably the first to leave, going to San Francisco soon after the first of the year to begin learning some of her roles in English. Sienkiewicz went to Los Angeles for a time, and later to the northern part of the state. Leaving Sypniewski in charge of the Anaheim farm, Chlapowski decided to try the healthful, out-of-door life led by the beekeepers and ranchers in the beautiful canyons of the Southern California mountains. About thirty miles from Anaheim, in a wooded glen in Santiago Canyon, he and Paprocki and young Ralph built a beekeeper's shanty near the home of their new friends, Joseph and Maria Pleasants. Here Chlapowski and Paprocki were to live for most of the following year. Years later he and Modjeska would buy the Pleasants' homesite and build their own house there.

The beauties of nature could not, however, obliterate Karol Chlapowski's growing worries. California's promised winter rains failed to come. A severe drought was beginning, the country was already in a financial depression, and his money was nearly exhausted. The colony's hopes were all pinned upon Helena's dramatic success, and that might take months. She was discouraged also, for it had been difficult to find a good English teacher. Word had come from Poland that her life contract with the Warsaw theatre was in jeopardy because of rumors that she was not coming back but planned to act in America. Theatres in San Francisco were closing; actors and actresses were out of work as depression descended upon the city and labor agitation mounted.

Chlapowski took Ralph to San Francisco and rented a small apartment in which Helena and her son could live (she had been staying with Polish friends), and a new English teacher was soon found in the person of 18year-old Johanna Tuholsky. Jo had been brought from Poland by her parents when she was four years old, but spoke English as her native tongue. She refused to accept money for her teaching, but proved to be a most capable instructor as well as a loyal friend. She became Modjeska's constant companion, coaching her patiently in the English words to *Romeo and Juliet, Anthony and Cleopatra,* and *Adrienne Lecouvreur,* all roles she had played time and time again in Poland. She still did not know whether or not she would be able to persuade managers in San Francisco to give her an engagement when word came that she had been fired from her job in Warsaw. By this time her contract with the *Teatr Wielki* had been cancelled. Already she was pawning her silver, jewelry and furs, while in Southern California, the situation was becoming desperate.

Chlapowski's attempts to sell the farm now managed by Sypniewski had been futile. Land prices had plummeted. The ditches bringing water to Anaheim had dried up, no rain had fallen, and many would-be settlers were packing up their belongings, hitching up their covered wagons, and telling Southern California goodbye. Karol's mountain neighbors, the beekeepers, also suffered losses as chaparral failed to bloom and bees died of sheer starvation. Naturalist John Muir, who visited Southern California that year wrote:

"The year 1877 will long be remembered as exceptionally rainless and distressing. Scarcely a flower bloomed on the dry valleys away from the stream-sides, and not a single grain field depending upon rain was reaped. The seed only sprouted, came up a little way, and withered. Horses, cattle, and sheep grew thinner day by day, nibbling at bushes and weeds, along the shallowing edges of streams, many of which were dried up altogether, for the first time since the settlement of the country.

"In the course of a trip I made during the summer of that year . . . the deplorable effects of the drought were everywhere visible — leafless fields, dead and dying cattle, dead bees, and half-dead people with dusty, doleful faces."[8]

Modjeska, in San Francisco, had undergone trials and humiliations in attempting to obtain an audition at the California Theatre, where she was rejected by the interim manager, actor Barton Hill, who did not believe she could act in English, much less Shakespeare, and that she was probably an amateur. Later she wrote to an old Warsaw friend, Jan Jasinski:

"Every week, sometimes every two, Dolek (Ralph) would take something to sell or pawn: now a chain from a small watch, now a silver cup, gewgaws of one sort or another — in a word, that was indeed my time of testing. Of all this my acquaintances knew nothing, nor did they wish to know, and I would have died rather than ask a single one for help. Often the two of us would be hungry at night, and we would joke about it, and then go to bed, consulting with each other as to what it would be we would sell or pawn the next day."[9]

Modjeska later told New York drama critic William Winter about the day when Barton Hill of the California Theatre at last agreed to watch her do one act of *Adrienne Lecouvreur*. "It was no doubt natural and right," wrote Winter, "that, in dealing with a strange applicant for theatrical employment, he should have exercised the functions of his position, but there will always be something ludicrous in the thought of Barton Hill sitting judgment on Helena Modjeska."

"He was very kind — Meester Hill," said the actress; "but he was nervous and fussy, and he patronized me as though I were a leetle child. 'Now,' he said, 'I shall be very critical — ve-ery severe.' I could be patient no longer. 'Be as critical and severe as you like,' I burst out, 'only do, please, *be quiet*, and let us begin!' He was so surprised he could not speak, and I began at once a scene from *Adrienne*. I played it through and then turned to him. He had his handkerchief in his hand and was crying. He came and shook hands with me and tried to seem quite calm."[10] Barton Hill knew he had seen one of the world's great actresses. Upon the return of John McCullough, Modjeska's debut at the California Theatre was scheduled for August 20, 1877. There were still agonizing weeks ahead for the actress and for the colonists in Anaheim as rehearsals began and Modjeska made arrangements for her costumes. The day after her first performance she sent a telegram to her husband in Anaheim. It contained a single word: "Victory." San Francisco at once recognized her genius. *Adrienne Lecouvreur* was followed by the roles of Ophelia and Juliet. It was a sensational beginning of an American career that was to last thirty years.

Helena Modjeska. Woodcut by S. Mrozewski, 1975.

Late in December, 1877, Modjeska began her first tour of eastern American cities. By February she had earned enough money to ease the burden of the colony's Anaheim debts and to send the homesick Sypniewski family home to Poland. They had been living in Anaheim for about a year and a half. Henryk Sienkiewicz also returned to Europe at this time, having spent two years in America. Anusia went to live with a Polish family in San Francisco. Paprocki and Ralph Modjeski remained in America with the Chlapowskis until the following summer. Thus ended the saga of the "Polish colony at Anaheim." But the colony achieved a new legendary fame in the late 1890's when someone remembered that Henryk Sienkiewicz, author of *Quo Vadis?*, had once been a member of a Polish colony at Anaheim. Each retelling of the legend added new exaggerations until it was claimed that 33 artists, writers and musicians had owned thousands of acres of land and had built up a large agricultural enterprise. Modjeska helped to set the record straight again when she described the smallness and simplicity of the venture in her autobiography. Her amusing account has become a classic among pioneer annals of the 1870's but, as she admitted, "We laughed at ourselves to keep others from laughing at us."

After several years of increasing recognition in the United States and England, and in the theatres of her native land, Modjeska returned to California in the summer of 1883 with her husband and son. Ralph Modjeski and Karol Chlapowski (known in America as Mr. Bozenta or "Count" Bozenta), became American citizens. There were visits again in 1885 and in 1886, when Modjeska first acted in Los Angeles with Maurice Barrymore as her leading man, and in 1887 when they at last decided to establish a permanent home in Santiago Canyon and bought the old Pleasants ranch. In 1888 they built the low, rambling white house which Modjeska called "Arden" because the liveoak grove in which it stood reminded her of Shakespeare's Forest of Arden, the setting for *As You Like It*, the play in which she frequently played the part of Rosalind.

In spite of its romantic aura, Arden resembled the wild west more than Shakespeare's placid woodlands. The nearest town was several hours away, by horse or mule-drawn vehicle. The Chlapowskis never had a telephone: lighting was by oil lamps or candles. Mountain lions roamed the hillsides, and rattlesnakes were common. In the summer of 1892, while Modjeska and her family and friends were vacationing at San Juan Capistrano, Chlapowski's ranch manager was murdered by a Mexican employee named Francisco Torres. After Torres had been captured and locked up in the small Santa Ana jail, masked men broke down the door and dragged him off to the main intersection of the town where they hanged him from a telegraph pole. This terrible lynching may have been the reason Arden was offered for sale the following summer. But no buyers appeared, and it continued to be Modjeska's home between theatrical tours.

This was Modjeska Island, Newport Beach, in 1907. Photo, Wojciech Zakrzewski, Mission Viejo.

When Modjeska left California each fall, she could seldom expect to see her home again until the following June, at the end of nine months of strenuous travel in her private railroad car. Chlapowski traveled with her, helping with correspondence, travel arrangements, newspaper interviews, and anything else that would lighten her work load. William Winter regarded him as "one of the kindest, most intellectual, and most drolly eccentric men it has been my fortune to know."[11] Life on the road in the 1880's and 1890's meant eight performances a week, meals eaten on the run, loading and unloading of scenery that sometimes did not fit the stages, cramped and poorly ventilated dressing rooms, and ceaseless travel in smoky, noisy trains. Modjeska, ever a gracious and considerate woman off stage, took her matchless art to the frontier, playing in rude halls in bleak country towns as well as in the fine theatres of New York, Philadelphia, and Chicago. To audiences of those times the wonderful world of the theatre revealed a special splendor which we of the modern era, saturated by motion pictures, television and radio, can scarcely imagine. Those who saw Modjeska never forgot her. Although she never lost her Polish accent, Modjeska was acknowledged in the 1880's and the 1890's to be America's greatest Shakespearean actress. Altogether, during her 30-year American career, she played about 35 roles, 14 of them Shakespearean. It was a remarkable achievement for a Pole who had not learned English until she was thirty-six years old.

To critics who complained that Shakespearean lines should be played only by American or British-born actors, Modjeska cited the universality of his appeal. Commenting on her own accent, she said, "Whenever my pronunciation was found fault with, I could do nothing but accept the criticism in all humility and endeavor to correct the errors of my tongue; yet I persisted without discouragement, and went on studying more and more Shakespearean parts, conscious that their essential value consisted in the psychological development of the characters, and confident that I understood them correctly and might reproduce them according to the author's intention.[12]

As years went by Modjeska's Santiago Canyon home began to have a fame all its own. California neighbors and friends liked to think of the great Polish actress, strolling through her Forest of Arden and reciting her dramatic roles. Maud Durbin, a young actress who later married Otis Skinner, remembered her visit to the Modjeska ranch in 1894. She recalled:

"It was amid the beauty and peace of 'Arden' that I came to know even more than ever the greatness of the woman and the greatness of the artist. In the theatre there had been the rich glamour of the star exalted above her co-players, to whom homage was due and homage was paid by the company and the public. In Arden there was no pomp or pageantry, but the pleasures and annoyances of everyday life. Often we were a dozen at a table, when the temperamental cook, Jesus,[13] who possessed none of the patient virtues his name implied, departed, Madame was equal to the emergency and prepared delectable Polish dishes with the ease and manner of one born to the role of chef. She directed the gardners, she directed the household, she sketched, she read aloud to her small grandson and spent much time in writing and illustrating a fairy tale for him. In the evening we had music and cards, and often dancing, when Madame and Mr. Bozenta entertained their guests with exhibitions of Polish and Russian dances. Tea was always brought in at ten o'clock. Tourists and picnic parties sometimes invaded the grounds and were usually invited into the living room. Her hospitality was frequently imposed upon, or would have been had Madame not always accepted the intruders politely and given them welcome she considered due strangers within her gates."[14]

Modjeska and her husband had many friends in Los Angeles and in the Orange County towns of Anaheim, Tustin, Fullerton, Orange and Santa Ana. She gave generously of her talents and of her brief vacation times to religious and charitable causes. There were readings, dramatic performances, and lawn fetes for the school and orphanage run by the Sisters of St. Catherine in Anaheim, for the Santa Ana Public Library, for St. Joseph's Catholic Church in Santa Ana and St. Boniface Church in Anaheim, as well as for the Sisters of the Good Shepherd and other Catholic institutions in Los Angeles. Modjeska always took an interest in young people, particularly those with artistic talents. Pianist Lester Donahue recalled an occasion when he, as a boy, was taken by the actress, then in her sixties, to call on Paderewski who had come to Los Angeles on tour. Long familiar with railroad switchyards, she led young Donahue down the tracks behind the old railroad station to Paderewski's private car where there was an enthusiastic greeting between the two Poles who had been good friends for years. Paderewski listened to Donahue's playing, encouraged him in his ambitions, and visited his Los Angeles piano teacher. This is only one small example of Modjeska's way of encouraging young talent.

Always a passionate idealist and a great patriot, Modjeska never let anyone forget that she was Polish. She crossed the ocean as often as she could for visits to her native land, to renew her energies and to act in Polish theatres. She and Chlapowski were always generous to Polish causes, in this country as well as abroad. Having had few educational opportunities during her own girlhood, she founded and endowed a school for peasant girls in Zakopane that is still in operation today. Because of her outspoken criticism of the Czarist government during a talk given in Chicago in 1893, Helena Modjeska was exiled from Russian Poland and not allowed to return to Warsaw after 1895. As she approached the end of her life, the burden of this banishment seemed heavier and heavier. Those who knew her during her last years remarked that there was always a sadness about her, as if she were thinking of the martyrdom of her country.

Modjeska's last performance on any stage was in the sleepwalking scene from *Macbeth*, in a benefit for Sicilian earthquake victims given at Los Angeles in February, 1909. Arden had been sold in the autumn of 1906, and after her last theatrical tour, she had rented a house in Tustin for a year before moving to a small cottage on Bay Island in Newport Bay, an island joined to the Newport-Balboa peninsula by a short footbridge. Here she died on April 8, 1909. She was buried in her native Krakow.

Although few people today know much of Modjeska's great stage career, her name continues to be honored in Southern California. She is revered because she experienced the hardships of pioneer days but returned because she loved California, its people, its seashore, and — in particular — its beautiful mountain canyons. The north peak of "Old Saddleback," highest mountain of the Santa Ana range, was named Modjeska Peak in 1909. The 1340 acres of the Modjeska ranch were subdivided years ago, and today many houses and cottages are crowded into the narrow canyon that was once the Forest of Arden. Thousands drive up Modjeska Road each year to visit the bird sanctuary on land beside Santiago Creek that once belonged to the actress and her husband. As Orange County historian Terry Stephenson, who knew her personally, has written: "about the place there will always seem to be the presence of the loved Modieska."[15]

NOTES

1. Helena Modjeska, *Memories and Impressions.* New York: The Macmillian Company, 1910, p. 319.
2. Ibid., P. 250-251.
3. Ralph Modjeski, originally named Rudolf, was Modjeska's son by Gustav Sinnmayer (Modjeski), her first theatrical manager.
4. Sypniewski had met Karol Chlapowski when both were imprisoned in Berlin following their participation in the Insurrection of 1863. Sypniewski and Sienkiewicz left Poland in February, 1876, to select a location for the Polish colony. While Sienkiewicz remained in California, Sypniewski returned to Poland to accompany his wife and children on the return trip.
5. *Memories*, p. 281.
6. Charles deKay, "Modjeska" in *Scribner's Monthly Magazine*, March, 1879, p. 667.
7. *Memories*, pp 304-305.
8. John Muir, *The Mountains of California.* New York: Doubleday & Co., Museum of Natural History. 1961.
9. Marion Moore Coleman, *Fair Rosalind.* Cheshire, Conn., 1969, p. 80.
10. William Winter, *Wallet of Time.* New York: Moffatt & Yard, 1913, pp. 362-363.
11. Ibid., p. 365.
12. *Memories*, pp. 531-532.
13. Jesus Soto was a Mexican-American.
14. Maud Skinner, "Modjeska" in *Theatre Arts Magazine*, June, 1927, pp. 432-433.
15. Terry E. Stephenson, *Shadows of Old Saddleback.* Santa Ana: The Fine Arts Press, 1948, p. 38.

A POST-SCRIPT ON
MODJESKA/PERSONAL LETTER

Dear Father Jacek:

Congratulations on getting your book off to the printer. You must be greatly relieved, and I shall look forward to seeing the book.

Thinking your readers might want to know a little something about the author, I've written a few sentences. I didn't mention my contribution to Sienkiewicz scholarship, the introduction to his Anaheim stories that I wrote for Mrs. Coleman's *Western Septet*. My Modjeska chapters published thus far include an article on the Torres lynching (Torres had murdered the Modjeska ranch manager), a piece on the Rice-Modjeska correspondence, an article on Modjeska's year in Tustin, the talk on her 1897 Santa Ana performance of *Mary Stuart* in San Francisco, and a piece on her autobiography in a recent issue of *Migrant Echo*.

Modjeska Canyon is really a part of Santiago Canyon, and the twin peaks of our Old Saddleback Mountain are properly named Modjeska Peak and Santiago Peak. So it has been very interesting to me that a few years ago my husband and I were able to visit some of the places dear to Modjeska's heart in Poland, and our European tour in May was a bus trip over the old pilgrimage route from Paris to the shrine of Santiago de Compostela in western Spain. Of course, we were just a bunch of pampered tourists and not long-suffering pilgrims, but it was a wonderful trip that really carried us back to the spirit of the Middle Ages. The loveliest churches of all were the little 9th Century ones in remote, out-of-the-way places.

New Modjeska material continues to show up. The Rice family in Tustin recently found three little notes that Modjeska wrote in 1902 and 1903 to Coralinn Rice, her musical friend. Madame Modjeska apparently didn't care for the word *dam*. She and her husband built a dam on one of the Santiago Canyon tributaries to conserve water for their ranch. The Rices apparently took some pictures and sent them to Modjeska. In one of the newly discovered notes she wrote, "Thank you very much for the photographs of our d- -. No, we'll call it Lake Arden — this is much prettier than the other name."

This is amusing because Lon McCoy (son of Modjeska's dentist) once told me that Bozenta's name for the dam was The Development, which he pronounced "devil-opp-ment," with the accent on the "opp." By the way, not all Poles agree with my opinion that Sienkiewicz's

Santa Ana Mountain accounts are partly fictionalized, but that does not downgrade them in any way. I regard them as the finest writing of Orange County's pioneer period.

Best wishes for the progress of the book and for your good health.

Sincerely,
Ellen Lee

South Laguna,
Nov. 1977

RALPH MODJESKI:
FAMOUS BUILDER OF BRIDGES

Tom Szatkowski

The lure of the United States Centennial Exposition of 1876 brought a Polish fifteen-year-old to America. Wanting to see the mechanical wonders of the Centennial Exposition, he agreed to accompany his mother, Helena Modrzejewska, to America. This 15-year old was Ralph Modrzejewski-Modjeski, the future consulting engineer for some of America's most famous bridge projects.

Helena Modrzejewska and her son had left Krakow, Poland, to investigate the possibility of settling in California. Ralph's father, Gustav Sinnmayer Modrzejewski, was manager of a leading theatre in Krakow and had previously toured Poland with his own group of actors. Ralph was born on January 27, 1861. At this time his mother, Helena, was 17. She was preparing for a stage career in Poland. By the time Ralph was 15, his mother had become one of Poland's greatest stage actresses.

After attending the Centennial Exposition in Philadelphia, Helena Modrzejewska-Modjeska and Ralph went to California. It was a difficult trip because the Panama Canal did not exist at this time, and thus an overland journey across Panama was necessary. Ralph became aware of the feasibility and importance of a canal to facilitate travel to the west coast of the United States.

The Modjeski family established their first American residence at Anaheim in Southern California. The family stayed at Anaheim only a short time before they moved to San Francisco. Both mother and son knew very little English. It was in the cosmopolitan atmosphere of San Francisco that they became familiar with America. Modjeska prepared herself for her American theatre debut. Ralph was in the San Francisco school system long enough to learn some English.

At 17, Ralph acted as stage manager for his mother's theatrical company on a tour of the United States. The tour was a financial and artistic success. Later, Ralph accompanied his mother to England where she was to perform. It was at this time that Ralph Modjeski decided to become an engineer. He left his mother in England and

Thomas Szatkowski, Ph.D. in History (University of Southern California), is a free lance writer based in Toluca Lake.

entered Ecole des Ponts et Chaussées in Paris, where he studied four years.

After stage successes in England, Modjeska returned to the United States. During a vacation from school, Ralph visited America to see his mother. On this visit, he had the opportunity to meet his mother's leading men, including Maurice Barrymore, father of Ethel, John and Lionel Barrymore. Ralph could remember holding John Barrymore and Ethel Barrymore on his knee. Contacts with non-theatrical people were also made by the Modjeski family. These contacts grew so extensive that in May, 1905, Modjeska was given a testimonial performance at the New York Metropolitan Opera House. Among those signing a testimonial document presented to Modjeska were Grover Cleveland, Mark Twain and Andrew Carnegie. Some of the success Ralph Modjeski enjoyed as a consulting engineer may have been due to the famous people attracted to Modjeska.

Ralph Modjeski's course of studies in Paris lasted from 1881 to 1885. After graduating with honors, he went to New York. By means of a letter of introduction, he obtained a job in Omaha, Nebraska, rebuilding a railroad bridge. "I got $50 a month for that job," Ralph Modjeski is quoted as saying about the Omaha project. Soon after his work had been completed on the Omaha bridge, Modjeski went into business for himself. His first independent job was to redesign the Rock Island Railway bridge between Rock Island, Illinois and Davenport, Iowa. The Rock Island Company liked him so much that they made him chief engineer in charge of construction for the bridge.

From 1892, Modjeski practiced as a consulting engineer at Chicago. The United States government was among the first to seek his services. In 1903, he was engaged as chief engineer on a fireproof warehouse project for Rock Island Arsenal. Bridges, however, were the primary medium for Modjeski. He worked on so many bridges in so many parts of the United States and Canada that even he could not recall all the sites. This profusion of work was due to the dramatic increase in heavy traffic during the late nineteenth and early twentieth centuries. Countless bridges and roadways, both for automobiles and trains, were needed. The men who controlled these building projects moved in the same social circles as Modjeska.

The Quebec bridge over the St. Lawrence River, completed in 1917, was one of Modjeski's more prominent projects. This bridge had fallen twice before Modjeski, among others, was consulted on the design that was successful. Eighty people were killed in the first fall of the bridge and seventeen in the second fall. The Delaware River bridge at Philadelphia was another of Modjeski's projects. It was completed in 1926.

He claimed as his favorite the Mid-Hudson bridge at Poughkeepsie.

This job was completed in 1929 by the engineering firm which he headed, Modjeski and Masters. The Trans-Bay bridge at San Francisco was the most expensive project Modjeski was assigned. This structure was built by the State of California for the sum of seventy-seven million dollars. It was completed in 1936. Modjeski was chairman of the board of consulting engineers for this project.

Seventy-seven million dollars, during the Depression, was a lot of money to spend on one project. It is a fitting tribute to Modjeski that he was able to attract the attention of the State of California in such unfavorable times. Ralph Modjeski was honored also by smaller communities for his efforts. On completion of the Blue Water bridge connecting Port Huron, Michigan, with Sarnia, Ontario, Modjeski was given a tribute in the form of a biography in the Sarnia *Canadian Observer* of Wednesday, August 10, 1938. His biography was placed prominently on the front page of this newspaper.

Aside from his commercial consulting work, Modjeski treasured among his engineering feats the work of putting in the irrigation system on the ranch of his famous mother. Stanford White, the noted architect, had designed the home for Modjeska's ranch.

Felicie Benda became R. Modjeski's first wife in 1885. He married his second wife, Virginia Mary Giblyn, in 1931. One of Modjeski's sons became an engineer and joined his father's firm.

Sharing his views with others was also an important part of Ralph Modjeski's life. He composed reports to citizens, mayors and city councils detailing his plans for the bridges and roadways these people needed. He wrote many papers and delivered lectures. He lectured at the Massachusetts Institute of Technology in 1924 and in 1929 represented the United States at the World Engineering Congress in Japan. Ralph Modjeski was presented with many awards. The Franklin Institute of the State of Pennsylvania gave him the Howard N. Potts Gold Medal (1914), the Franklin Medal (1922) and the John Fritz Medal (1930). Some of the associations to which Modjeski belonged were: American Institute of Consulting Engineers, American Railway Engineering Association, American Society of Civil Engineers, Art Institute of Chicago and Metropolitan Museum of Art, New York.

A story is told that discouragement set in during Modjeski's engineering studies in France. Seeking solitude away from the rigors of studies in mathematics and mechanics, he turned to music. He had studied piano as a child in Poland, and he had been told that he possessed talent as a musician. A career in music would have seemed to be a more peaceful and appropriate pastime for a man from such a prominent family. However, Ralph Modjeski's interlude with the piano lasted only three months. He returned to his studies and became an engineer. But, in a way, he maintained contact with the musical arts throughout his life. He did this through the bridges he helped to create. Anyone can hear a Modjeski piano concert by looking at or crossing one of these bridges. Modjeski died in 1940, and is buried in Inglewood. The bridges he was associated with are still in use today across the country.

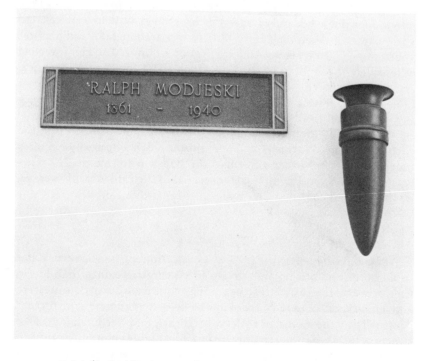

Ralph Modjeski's plaque at Golden West Mausoleum, Inglewood. Photo, Charles Perez.

SIENKIEWICZ IN CALIFORNIA

Gillian Olechno-Huszcza

Henryk Sienkiewicz was born in May of 1846 near Lukow in Poland, and died in November of 1916, at Vevey in Switzerland. He was educated at the University of Warsaw and graduated from the Philological Faculty there in 1870. While he was a student he published various critical articles and book reviews, mainly for *Gazeta Polska*, a newspaper published in Warsaw. His first novel, *Na Marne* (translated variously as In Vain or Run to Waste) appeared in 1872 and his first short story, *Stary Sluga* (An Old Retainer) in 1875. He travelled extensively throughout Europe and Central Africa as well as America. As a gift from the Polish people he received the small estate of Oblegorek near Kielce in 1900 on the occasion of his 30th anniversary as a writer and lived there until he left for Switzerland in 1914. In 1905 he was awarded the Nobel Prize for literature. During the early years of World War I he promoted the cause of Polish independence and organized relief for Polish war victims. His body was removed from Vevey and transferred to the cathedral of Warsaw in 1924.

*　　*　　*

Warsaw in the winter of 1875 was cold, snowing, and dreary. What could be more enticing to a group of romantic idealists than life in California, so far away but so beguiling? This group of artists, writers and musicians, of which Sienkiewicz was a regular member, met habitually at the home of Helena Modjeska and her husband Karol Chlapowski. One such evening, inspired by highly colored accounts in the press of sunshine and gold, food in abundance, wild flowers, Indian braves and maidens all ready to welcome them with open arms, discussion centered around the idea of emigrating. Prosaic details of the frustrations and failures of frontier life were ignored in light of these bewitching dreams of the unknown. However, some discretion did prevail. Sienkiewicz was selected to carry out a reconnoitering expedition. How was this expedition to be financed? Fortunately the problem was solved by his editor, who suggested that Sienkiewicz send back a series of articles on what he found in America during that

Gillian Olechno-Huszcza, Chief of Library Services, LAC/USC Medical Center and the Secretary of the PAHA-Cal. Chapter, lives in Los Angeles.

year of the Centennial of the United States; hence, *Listy z Podrozy do Ameryki* (Letters From a Travel to America).

Enthusiastic endorsement of their idea came from Ignacy Maciejowski, the original heart and soul of the group gathered at the Chlapowski home. He had been the first to leave, frustrated, as were the rest of them, by the Polish Uprising of 1863 and the events of the Franco-Prussian War. He had apparently visited the United States and was very much in favor of California as a place to settle, and his letters to the group written from England were full of exclamations and expressions of delight.

Basing their decision on the fragmentary impressions of others who had gone before, the group decided on Anaheim as the site of their future colony. It was a flourishing community, enjoyed a healthy and sunny climate, and its small population spoke German. Since the would-be colonists all knew German they felt they would have no problem in communication while they learned English. Sienkiewicz, therefore, made his way to Anaheim almost immediately upon his arrival in the United States, stopping only briefly in New York which, with its daily occurences of mayhem in the streets, did not impress him. San Francisco fascinated him and was to draw him back many times. He decided to wait for the Chlapowskis in Anaheim Landing, which at that time was the port of Anaheim. To his dismay he found it to be one of the dreariest wastes he had ever seen in his life, consisting as it did of only six huts and a tavern. He decided, however, to make the best of things and, making friends with the owner, found a place to sleep in the tavern.

While waiting for the rest of the party, Sienkiewicz also visited Los Angeles, where he stayed at a house on Pico Boulevard. With the eager assistance of the local senoritas he made great progress in Spanish and English and was soon able to make himself understood in all essential situations.

Max Nebelung of the tavern became his closest friend, and when they could spare the time they went together into the Santa Ana mountains. The German would sleep outside on the ground but Sienkiewicz preferred to watch the fire and stare into the eyes of the mountain animals. Life in those mountain canyons held an irresistible fascination for him. He was cured of colds, nerves and toothache, and slept like a king. He loved the hunting and even after the Chlapowski group arrived in Anaheim, he did not join them immediately because he could not tear himself away.

If the mountains made Sienkiewicz a man, then the Pacific gave him his true destiny as a writer. At the time of leaving Warsaw he had been in the doldrums but in Anaheim he became transformed. At this time he began his *Szkice Weglem* (Sketches in Charcoal) and, by the time the rest of the company arrived from Warsaw, a number of sketches had been completed. He found a ready and willing audience in Modjeska.

The group was carried away by enthusiasm for the pastoral life but their unrealistic expectations were soon disappointed. Even Sienkiewicz found the digging and the pulling of weeds to be an intolerable chore and began to find excuses not to be around when physical labor was involved. Chlapowski, who had provided the main financing for the group, soon found his capital dwindling while no income was forthcoming. Finally Modjeska decided to recoup the family fortunes by returning to the stage. Early in 1877 she went to San Francisco to study English and prepare for her American stage debut. Sienkiewicz, meanwhile, sailed along the coast to Los Angeles, living for a time in the Mojave Desert, Sebastopol, Hayward, and Mariposa. He later visited San Francisco for Modjeska's opening night on August 20, 1877, at the California Theatre, and attended several more performances, dispatching a long laudatory account of her debut to *Gazeta Polska*, so that her Polish friends could share her triumph.

Sienkiewicz became ill at the end of 1877 after a buffalo hunting trip in Wyoming and was forced to return to San Francisco. By that time Modjeska had left for the East Coast, where she achieved further successes in New York and other cities. While recovering, Sienkiewicz spent his time writing articles on the Chinese and Poles in this country. Minority groups, whether Indians, Chinese, Poles or others, were of great interest to him and he was able to get a good deal of help from a friend, Captain Rudolf Korwin Piotrowski, who had been a commissioner of Immigration for the State of California. Many of the characters in Sienkiewicz's writings are based on personalities he met while in California. In fact this very Captain Piotrowski became Pan Zagloba in The Trilogy (*Ogniem i Mieczem, Potop,* and *Pan Wolodyjowski*), following an incident which took place on the farm in Anaheim involving Anusia, Modjeska's maid. Piotrowski fell into an irrigation ditch while making advances to Anusia and had to be rescued by Sienkiewicz. While Zagloba represents practically the only humor in Sienkiewicz's writings, another story, *A Comedy of Errors*, is amusing in a rather simple and ingenuous way, dealing with a matchmaking problem which arose from a difficulty with the language. This was undoubtedly based on some incident suffered by the Germans of Anaheim while he was there. The story of *Orso*, or *A Circus Hercules*, which was elaborated and extended in *Quo Vadis?* as the story of Ursus and Lygia, was based upon a circus visit to the city of Anaheim. Another character of this period, as Modjeska mentions in her memoirs, is the knight Longin of the family Podbipieta, a man of great height and thinness, whom we meet in *Ogniem i Mieczem,* the first of the great Trilogy. *Memories of Mariposa* was inspired by the Polish political exiles, with their profound homesickness and longing for the sound of their native language, and includes many moving stories. Typical is the account of Putrament, an old prospector whom Sienkiewicz met and addressed in Polish. To his amazement, Putrament answered not in the Polish familiar to Sienkiewicz but in a Polish that had not been spoken since the time of King Stephan Batory. Apparently, in order not to forget the Polish language the old miner read out loud to himself every evening from an old Bible which he called "Wujek." This Bible had been printed some 300 years before in the archaic Polish phraseology.

In fact it was California, and to a somewhat lesser extent his travels elsewhere in America, that made his reputation as a writer. Much of his early writings inclined to a morbid pessimistic tone, indicative of his depression about the future of his country. In America he found none of the inertia of an old and settled civilization. He was inspired by the spirit of optimism and confidence in the future and the surging vitality of the people. Upon his return to Poland he was able to transmit some of this optimism into the hearts and minds of his fellow countrymen through his Trilogy.

That his books are still in print in this country both in Polish and in English translation attests to their continuing popularity. It is fitting that his stay in California should be given the ultimate recognition in the format of a motion picture based on his Nobel Prize winning novel, *Quo Vadis?*

REFERENCES

Coleman, Arthur Prudden and Marion Moore Coleman. *Wanderers Twain; Modjeska and Sienkiewicz; a view from California.* Cheshire, Conn., Cherry Hill Books, 1964.

Encyclopedia Britannica. 1960 ed. S.V. "Sienkiewicz, Henryk." Gardner, Monica M. The *Patriot Novelist of Poland, Henryk Sienkiewicz.* New York, E.P. Dutton, 1926.

Modjeska, Helena. *Memories and Impressions, an Autobiography.* New York, Macmillan, 1910.

Sienkiewicz, Henryk. *Portrait of America: Letters of Henryk Sienkiewicz.* Edited and translated by Charles Morley. New York, Columbia University Press, 1959.

Sienkiewicz, Henryk. *After Bread: A Story of Polish Emigrant Voyage to America.* Translated from the Polish by Vatslaf Hlasko and Thomas H. Bullick. New York, R.F. Fenno, 1897.

Wytrwal, Joseph A. *Poles in American History and Tradition.* Detroit, Endurance Press, 1969.

A picture of a typical Dorek Rusin's award winning sculpture in wood of a bird. Rusin lives in Santa Barbara and exhibits in galleries throughout Santa Barbara County.

PART THREE

VIGNETTES OF POLES IN TWENTIETH CENTURY CALIFORNIA

I'm a third generation American
but am still referred to in the
media and elsewhere as an Irishman.
Who are the Americans?

John F. Kennedy

PADEREWSKI IN PASO ROBLES

Margaret Prasniewski

Ironically, it was that most prosaic of all substances, mud, which first drew Ignace Jan Paderewski to the enchanting California community of Paso Robles. In 1914, the world-famous concert pianist, composer, and statesman was suffering agonies from neuritis, an occupational hazard common to those who work with nerves and hands simultaneously. He was then fifty-four years old. The brutal tour schedules of many, many years were taking their inevitable toll. Concert followed concert in bewildering succession; cities and more cities, hungry audiences demanding etudes, concertos, waltzes; all from one pair of hands, one mind.

Just prior to a concert in Seattle, Paderewski was once again under siege to his old nemesis, neuritis, as he had been for so much of his career. On the advice of a medical friend, he set forth to Paso Robles, famed for its soothing mineral and mud treatments. The gentle terrain was awaiting him, seeming almost to enfold him, its green softness comforting the weary soul as subtly as its mysterious mud soothed the overworked body.

When he arrived in Paso Robles, Paderewski was half a world away from his birthplace of Kurylowka, Poland, yet the scene must have seemed hauntingly familiar. In the first page of his memoirs he describes his birthplace thus:

"It (Kurylowka) was one of the most beautiful places in existence. I cannot tell you about the country, the softness and freshness of the air, the picturesque, undulating landscape . . . the finest orchards I have ever seen. It was a joy to me, a small boy . . ."

Except for the place names, he could well have been describing the tapestry that was early Paso Robles. Its hills rolled in soft green folds, stitched together at random with silver threads of streams, embroidered with clumps of trees, with walnut and almond orchards everywhere. He loved the place on sight, and continued to visit whenever his schedules allowed.

If Paso Robles made a profound impression on Paderewski, he must have made a dynamic impression on the rural community. His arrival

---

Margaret Prasniewski had her short stories published in American magazines, in Great Britain, The Netherlands and in Australia. She lives in Downey.

had the brave flourish of trumpets. Imagine, if you will, Paderewski's first appearance in town. The word spread quickly. The great man was here! In town! A real celebrity, world renowned, who had played for queens and princes and nobility of Europe, was in Paso Robles. Half the inhabitants turned out to greet the arrival of Paderewski in his private railroad coach, "The Colonial," equipped with every modern

Ignacy Paderewski in his orchard, an almond grove, in Paso Robles. Courtesy of Helena Liibke. Picture processed by Martin Dabrowski.

convenience of 1914. It also contained valuable European works of art. They watched him emerge from his coach, the legendary chrysanthemum hair aflame in the golden California sunshine, the unmistakable bearing of artistic temperament at its best. His reputation had, of course, preceded him, but few were quite prepared for the sheer physical magnetism of the man. (The well known British painter, Burne-Jones, had been so impressed at the first sight of Paderewski, that he had immediately dubbed him his "Archangel"). These quiet farmers of Paso Robles nevertheless took this exotic, travelled artist to their hearts, revelling in his achievements, his flair, his difference.

His sojourns at the Paso Robles Hot Springs Hotel were always keenly enjoyed by the townsfolk, who gained first hand experience of Polish hospitality by seeing how warmly Paderewski greeted and treated his guests at the hotel, the opulent dinners over which he presided, and the enormous pleasure he took in pleasing his friends.

He was a great movie fan, and took advantage of his little vacations in Paso Robles to see every movie he could. His favorite movies warranted more than one visit, so he became a well known figure to the other patrons. Like most performers, he was a generous audience indeed. It was not unusual for him to applaud, with enthusiastic cries of "Bravo, Bravo!" any passage which especially moved him. One day the organist thought to compliment the famous man by playing one of Paderewski's waltzes in his honor. The quality of the performance was such that Paderewski, upon hearing his own composition played by the rural organist, rushed from the theatre with his hands clutched firmly over his ears! But the intentions of the organist were the best.

Initially, Paderewski purchased enough land to form a large ranch of over 1,500 acres, calling it "Rancho San Ignacio." Shortly thereafter he purchased another 900 acres for his wife. He farmed almonds and walnuts, the crops of the area, but hardly made a fortune on the venture. (These were the days of the gold boom in California, and he was to remark in later years that he had indeed found a gold mine in California — unfortunately the kind one pours gold into, rather than mining it out.)

Nevertheless, Paso Robles was a continuing pleasure to Paderewski on the occasions when he was able to return. The peaceful reality of life in this rural haven was to rekindle an old dream he had shared with Madame Modjeska on his first visit to her Santa Ana retreat, "Arden" in 1905. The two world famous artists had worked out detailed (if not exactly practical) plans for a free school for artists, where genius could flourish, unhampered by pressures of a world which, they feared, was becoming increasingly materialistic. However, Madame Modjeska died in 1909, and Paderewski shelved the plans for some time.

Many years later he raised the matter once again, this time with his friend Henryk Opienski. But two world wars intervened, and Paderewski's energies became increasingly devoted to the tragic plight of his beloved Poland, to the point where he became as revered a statesman as he was an artist. Thus, the dream of an artists' colony at Paso Robles remained a dream.

Ignacy Paderewski. Wood engraving by Stefan Mrozewski, 1975.

Perhaps for men like Paderewski, many of their most cherished hopes are destined to languish. One lifetime can only last so long; only so much can be accomplished. But the devotion such men inspire in the hearts of their countrymen and their fellow artists throughout the world, are like ripples on a lake, spreading in ever wider circles, into infinity.

Today Paderewski's lands in Paso Robles are in other hands. But almond trees live long. No doubt some of the trees he planted are still being harvested today, just as his music is still being played, and his ideals and love of country are being handed down, generation to generation, by Polish people throughout the world.

HELENA PADEREWSKA:
PASSING THROUGH PASO ROBLES

Helena Liibke/Anne Strakacz Appleton

Helena Paderewska, nee Baroness de Rosen, was born on August 1, 1856. Her father, Baron de Rosen, came from Courland, a small principality on the Baltic; her Greek mother died early and the child was brought up by her Polish paternal grandmother, who lived in Warsaw. At sixteen she was married to Wladyslaw Gorski, a violinist. They had one child, a son, Waclaw. In 1899 the marriage was annuled and Helena Gorska married Ignacy Jan Paderewski.

Much of her time as Paderewski's wife was devoted to charities. Around 1910 she organized a Poultry Raising School. Riond Bosson, the Paderewski property in Switzerland, where Mme. Paderewska raised rare and improved strains of poultry, saw many young girls come over from Poland to study there. With the outbreak of World War I, the school had to close.

In 1915, with Mme. Lazarska's help, Mme. Paderewska established in Paris a small factory of artistic rag dolls which were later sold in America, after Paderewski's concerts. The money was used to help a group of Polish artists who found themselves stranded in Paris without money.

While in America Mme. Paderewska, in touch with the Polish immigration circles, organized women's sewing clubs. Clothing and money were collected and sent to Poland when possible.

Helena Paderewska's great personal achievement was the founding of the Polish White Cross. Poland, as yet unrecognized as an independent state, had no chapter of the International Red Cross. While her husband was forming a volunteer Polish Army in the United States (of non-citizens only), she started a School of Nurses. The graduates went with the Polish Army to France. After the Armistice, the Army and the Nurses were transferred to Poland — still at war with Russia. Named after its commanding general, that was the Haller Army.

As soon as the Paderewskis arrived in Poland (1919), Mme. Paderewska occupied herself with bringing relief to the war-torn and

Helena Liibke was Mme. Paderewska's secretary. Anne Strakacz Appleton's father was I.J. Paderewski's secretary. Both live in California.

famine-depleted population. A chapter of the Polish White Cross was formed under her personal supervision. Numerous canteens were established at army recruiting centers. She was offered a building for a military hospital, which was staffed by her nurses. The hospital itself was equipped with U.S. supplies, which Mme. Paderewska obtained from the American Red Cross in France, where the American Army was liquidating its equipment. Numerous chapters of the Polish White Cross were distributing food and clothing in Poland, generous shipments of which were coming from Polish organizations in America.

Next, Mme. Paderewska established special clubs for paper boys who were poorly clothed and often barefoot. In these clubs the boys were always provided with hot tea or soup or bread, as well as clothing and boots, when available.

Mme. Paderewska also bought a property in Sulejowek, near Warsaw, and founded a home for senior citizens. Most of them were owners of estates in East Poland, who had been driven out by the Bolshevik army and arrived in Warsaw completely destitute. Before leaving Poland in 1920, she transferred the property to the "Association of Assistance to the Intellectuals" in Warsaw. For many years thereafter, she and her husband sent generous financial help to keep the institution going.

In 1921, when Paderewski settled in Paso Robles, California, Mme. Paderewska kept up with charities. The case of Dr. Jakobkiewicz was one example. He arrived in America as a delegate of a Polish committee in Vladivostok in Siberia, asking for help. The needy were more than a thousand Polish children found wandering in the wilderness of the Siberian Tajga. They had to be repatriated or would perish. Mme. Paderewska organized a Bazaar in Paso Robles and got in touch with thousands of her former supporters, who responded with overwhelming generosity. Within a short time the first transport of children was on its way to Poland. Within two years all of the "Siberian children" as they were called, were returned to their country.

The last years of Mme. Paderewska's life were spent in Riond Bosson, where she died after a long illness on January 16, 1934. She was buried in the family tomb at the cemetery in Montmorency near Paris.

A POLISH PRINCE BRINGS POWER
TO SAN FRANCISCO

Don J. Baxter

Of all the major figures in the history of Pacific Gas & Electric, Prince Andre Poniatowski was perhaps the most colorful. A descendant of Polish royalty, he was instrumental in bringing the first hydroelectric power to San Francisco by developments of the Mokelumne River.

Born in Paris in 1864, Prince Andre was reared in luxury among European nobility. Trained as a financier, he brought adventure to a normally staid profession; he was victor in two duels and a big winner in horse racing, both as a bettor and as a gentleman jockey. Bankers sent him to Russia to try to negotiate a loan with the Czar and to South Africa to investigate the gold mines of the Rand. His interests started where those of less venturesome men ended.

Seeking investment opportunities in America, the prince came to San Francisco and formed a syndicate to rework old Mother Lode gold mines, using more modern methods. To get transportation to the mines, he backed railroad builder Thomas S. Bullock in the construction of the Sierra Railway, and to get electric power, his group financed construction of the Blue Lakes Powerhouse on the Mokelumne. Prince Poniatowski saw the vast hydro potential of this river. With his brother-in-law, William H. Crocker, he formed the Standard Electric Co. in 1897 to build Electra Powerhouse. He dreamed of bringing power to San Francisco, 143 miles away — requiring longer transmission at higher voltage than had ever then been attempted.

Larger generators and transformers had to be designed and built. This was done successfully, but the whole project seemed destined to crash when the insulators failed to stand up under the needed 40,000 volts. After agonizing months, a suitable insulator was finally devised. At the same time, workmen balked at working on the reservoirs above the 6,500 foot level. Discovery of big petroleum deposits in California also cut the price the company could get for its electricity. Nevertheless, the project was successfully completed. Electra

Reprinted by permission from *PG & E Progress*, San Francisco, February 1976.

Powerhouse took up the load in 1902 and power flowed through thennovel aluminum conductor (the prince saved $200,000 by using this metal instead of copper) to the mines, to Stockton, Oakland, San Jose and San Francisco.

Prince Andre Poniatowski. Courtesy, *PG & Progress*, San Francisco.

In addition to their railway, mining and power interests, the prince and Crocker built Tanforan race track near the prince's Sky Farm residence in Burlingame. Society folk flocked to see horse racing, previously not considered genteel, as Poniatowski invited friends to the track. Interested in all sports, Prince Andre took boxing lessons, after seeing the Corbett-Fitzsimmons fight in Nevada.

In 1904, having sold his interests, he returned to France with his family, where he continued his active life. In 1954, at the age of 90, Prince Andre Poniatowski died. Up to the end, he lived by his philosophy: "Each hour that we live could be our last, so waste not a single minute of it."

THE WORKS OF JAN DE ROSEN
IN SOUTHERN CALIFORNIA

Gene H. Zygmont

By its very nature, sacral art encompasses more than mere decoration or embellishment of a religious building. Although basically designed for human beings, it transcends this purpose by seeking a higher unity; to express the splendor and glorification of God in artistic achievement. Thus, the artist engaged in sacral art is bringing to his creative work not only his artistic talents, but is, in a sense, acting as an apprentice or assistant to the Creator. He strives to penetrate, illumine, and expand the spirit of the congregation by making spiritual reality immediate and comprehensible.

Because products of artistic endeavor used in the service of the Church must be based on requirements of the rites and ceremonies of the liturgy, an artist must follow prescribed formats and iconographies. For example, the Stations of the Cross must be a narrative representation of Christ's Way to Golgotha. Within this framework, however, the artist has complete freedom of expression and interpretation. Sacral art had its beginnings, as did secular art, in the observation and imitation of nature. Forms and styles evolved and changed with time, so that sacral art of the twentieth century can range from highly realistic to purely abstract, yet still remain true to the theological concepts it represents.

Jan Henryk de Rosen, one of the most successful, contempory sacral artists has, for more than half a century, dedicated his talents to the special needs of the Church. His works are found throughout Europe and the United States. Here, however, we will discuss the sacral art he has produced in Southern California. A multi-talented man, he works in several media — paint, mosaic, and glass. He holds a Ph.D. in literature and taught for many years at Georgetown University in Washington, D.C.

He was born in Warsaw in 1891, and although his father was court painter to the Russian Czars, young de Rosen was not specifically trained to follow in his father's footsteps. Educated in France and Switzerland, he embarked on a literary career after graduation from

Gene H. Zygmont pursues her graduate studies in art history at State University in Long Beach. She lives in Torrance.

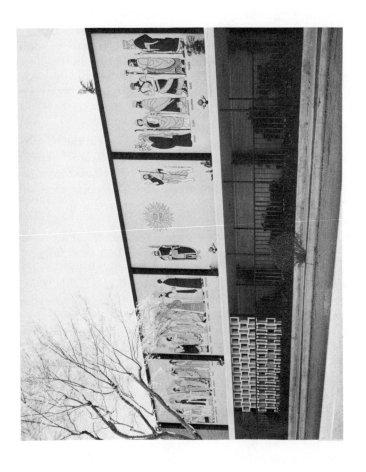

Mosaics by Jan Henryk de Rosen, 1956. St. Catherine Chapel, Anaheim. Architect, J. George Szeptycki and Associates.

the University of Lausanne, but World War I broke out, and he spent the war years serving in the French and Polish armies. After the war he served as military aide to Ignacy Paderewski at Geneva, then spent four years in the Diplomatic Corps of the newly reorganized Polish nation.

In 1925, a painting which he did for the Armenian Cathedral in Lwow proved to be a springboard to a career in sacral arts. This first artistic commission seems also to have set his style, in that he couples a Byzantine palette, richly enhanced with gilt, with classic draughtsmanship. Commissions in Lwow were followed by others outside Poland: the Sobieski Chapel, Kahlenberg, Vienna, Austria, and the Papal Chapel at Castelgandolfo, Italy.

In 1937, the Polish Ambassador, Count Potocki, invited him to the United States to create a mural for the Polish Pavilion at the New York World's Fair, and he has worked in the United States from that time. A highly prolific artist, his works range from a monumental mosaic, *Christ in Majesty*, in the dome of the Immaculate Conception Cathedral in Washington, D.C. to smaller easel paintings in churches throughout the United States.

He has several outstanding works in the Southern California area. For the Chapel at Saint Catherine's Military School in Anaheim, de Rosen created a mural, a mosaic, and a stained glass window on one integrated theme: the philosophical and theological thought throughout the ages, which culminates in the Supreme Knowledge embodied within the Holy Trinity. In the vestibule, a mosaic depicts the development of philosophy throughout the various phases of pre-Christian civilizations: Egyptian, Greek, Judaic, Roman. The Holy Ghost, fount of all knowledge, occupies the central space in this brilliantly executed mosaic. Within the Church, extending the length of a lateral wall, is a mural showing the development of Catholic theology from the time of Christ to Pope Leo XIII. The central figure of Christ is flanked by thinkers, educators, saints, and Doctors of the Church, who helped shape Catholic dogma. Among them are: Saint Catherine, Saint Ursula, St. Thomas Aquinas, St. Augustine, Mikolaj Kopernik, and Dante. A dazzling figure of God the Father, Creator of the Universe, is set in clearstory window between the vestibule and the interior, and acts as unifying factor for the project. The Dominican Sisters, founders and administrators of the school, desired visual interpretation of the importance of education to a better understanding of Catholicism, and this underlying theme was expressed admirably by the artist.

This same kind of spiritual understanding of the purpose of his work is shown in two other projects which he undertook in the area. The

Altar mural in the Church of St. Ambrose, Los Angeles, emphasizes the moment when the Holy Trinity appeared to the Bishop. De Rosen uses rich colors, punctuated by gold and silver, flowing rhythmically from the imposing figure of God the Father at the top of the mural, the crucified figure of Christ, down through the Holy Ghost hovering at His feet, to the kneeling figure of the Bishop Ambrose.

In depicting the Way of the Cross in St. Stephen's Church, Monterey Park, de Rosen employs one large narrative composition which encompasses both lateral walls, rather than the usual fourteen separate panels. From the first Station, showing Christ before Pilate, through the last, in which He is laid in the tomb, the narrative of the Liturgy is underscored by subtle yet definite changes in landscape and atmospheric conditions to denote both the location of the particular Station and the hour at which the event occurred. De Rosen's fine draughtsmanship is evident in unusually well defined anatomy, not only of human figures, but also in the exceptionally well drawn horse, ridden by a Roman centurion, in one of the Stations.

High, highly individual artistic style is apparent in all these works, yet each has followed rigorously the requirements set down by the liturgical need. More importantly, however, he has captured in all of them the essence of what constitutes sacral art, the ability to transcend the visual and to communicate the spiritual.

WIKTOR PODOSKI (1901-1970)

J. George Szeptycki

The year of 1923 when the Polish wood engraver, Wladyslaw Skoczylas, began teaching his first group of students at the Academy of Fine Arts in Warsaw was a very fateful one in the history of Polish art and in the history of international graphic arts as well. Only two years later a dynamic group of young artists started exhibiting amazingly innovative wood engravings in Warsaw galleries, and selling thousands of prints of their works to enthusiastic art lovers. Polish wood engraving became an artistic sensation not only in Poland, but also in the whole of Europe. World museums found it fashionable to include Polish prints in their collections and yearly International Exhibitions of wood engraving became major cultural events on a world-wide scale.

Wiktor Podoski played a doubly prominent role in this movement: first, as a talented wood engraver, and second, as its theoretician and art critic, equipped with a keen, analytical mind. His artistic credo was that, because of the uniqueness of this almost unexplored medium, the wood engravers should not only register visual reality, but rather use it as a point of departure in their search for individual graphic concepts. He emphasized the fact that the luminous white line on the black background was an ideal means for the free interpretation of visual experiences and for experimentation.

It is interesting to note that, at first, the entire group of wood engravers, organized in the Society of Polish Graphic Artists "Ryt," shared a more or less common artistic vision, probably under the influence of their respected teacher. It was only later, as if in following Podoski's advice, that all of them started developing highly diversified styles, based on individual graphic concepts. It should be noted that Stefan Mrozewski, briefly a student of Podoski's, became world famous as a result of his own unique artistic style. Nevertheless, this does not diminish Podoski's position in the field of artistic achievement.

In Podoski's last "California period," extending roughly from 1950 until his death in 1970, and constituting a peak of his artistic activity, he produced a series of dazzlingly rich, nearly abstract forms, textures

J. George Szeptycki, a known architect in Southern California, lives in Los Angeles.

and patterns, constituting a sort of twilight zone between recognizable reality and a brilliant interpretation of this reality in graphic language. His still life compositions, engraved in very small formats, represent the ultimate in artistic discipline, ingenuity and sophistication.

Wood engraving by Wiktor Podoski

In his creative work Podoski never followed momentary emotions or was directed by rash judgment and he remained a penetrating critic of his own work. After the conception of an artistic idea, he lived with it for a long time. He then sketched it loosely in pencil, indicating only the general layout and relative values. The next step was to render it in black ink on white paper with more details and to further develop it on a scratch board, when, for the first time, he could see the approximate effects of a real wood engraving. Finally, when all the details were refined to his complete satisfaction, he transferred the composition to a wood block, and was ready to start cutting.

There is, of course, nothing unusual about this procedure. Many artists follow the same sequence. But in the case of Wiktor Podoski, the process of evolution from the initial notion to the final shape of composition extended for weeks, or more often, for many months. Between each of these steps, Wiktor Podoski spent several hours every day in libraries and bookstores reading and completing his collection of rare books on art, even searching for facsimile reproductions of great works of art. He browsed through the antique stores looking for interesting prints, fabrics, furniture, and oriental rugs, and even organized theatrical productions. He would return to his creative work only when he felt that he had acquired a sufficient perspective to judge it objectively. He was then ready to push it further, but never more than one step at a time. In this slow and deliberate way he always stove for perfection. The results were excellent, and eventually won him a very high professional acclaim and recognition. His work may be found in all most important museums and collections of the world.

Still Nature. Wood engraving by Wiktor Podoski, 1957.

Unfortunately, several of his early blocks and prints were destroyed during the Warsaw Insurrection in 1944. Nevertheless, many of them were saved and are a part of the permanent collection of

Contemporary Graphic Arts Department of the National Museum in Warsaw. After his death, this collection was completed by a deposit of all Podoski's wood blocks of the California period. They are being studied by historians of art, and students of the Fine Art Department of the University of Warsaw.

JAN STYKA AND "THE CRUCIFIXION"

Gene H. Zygmont

A monumental painting, 195 feet long and 45 feet high, created by a Polish artist who had never set foot in California, has been a source of interest and inspiration to over 7,400,000 people from all over the world during the past twenty-five years. The painting is *The Crucifixion*, displayed in the Hall of the Crucifixion at Forest Lawn Memorial Park in Glendale, California. The artist is Jan Styka.

Jan Styka, born in Lwow, Poland in 1858, was contemporary with the Polish painters Jan Matejko, Juljusz Kossak, Jacek Malczewski, Jozef Chelmonski, and Piotr Michalowski. He, like so many of his generation in a partitioned Poland, was fiercely patriotic. During his art student days he vowed to dedicate his genius (of which he personally had no doubt!) to "Art, God, and Poland." Like his compatriot Jan Matejko, Styka leaned to larger-than-life canvasses which emphasized a glorious Polish past. Also like Matejko (who was convinced that his Messianic destiny was to revive the once great Polish State through his historical paintings), Styka believed that his own destiny was to revive the once noble art of religious painting.

A tall handsome man with flashing good looks and tremendous energies, and by all accounts, absolutely irresistible to women, he was as indefatigable after working hours as he was at the easel. It was said that he painted all day, then drank and danced until dawn. Still, his output was prodigious; he once did 15 large canvas paintings in five months. He enjoyed tremendous popularity and won critical acclaim in Vienna, Rome, and Paris while still a relatively young man.

In 1892 he finished a panoramic painting, *Battle of Raclawice*, which depicted Tadeusz Kosciuszko leading peasants armed with scythes and pitchforks to victory over the Russians in the Uprising of 1794. The finished canvas was so huge that a circular building was erected in Lwow to house it. It was there that Ignacy Paderewski saw it and conceived of a painting which would be even more awe-inspiring, because it would have universal appeal. He commissioned Styka to do a painting on the Crucifixion theme. It was to be titled *Golgotha*.

To research the subject and prepare himself for the task, Styka made a pilgrimage to Jerusalem and the Holy Land, where he spent several months sketching. He then traveled to Rome, where Pope Leo XIII blessed his palette and brushes. Meanwhile, a special canvas was being woven in Belgium, and Paderewski was trying to find a building in Warsaw large enough to house it. Unable to do so, he finally obtained a large public building in Lwow for Styka to use as a studio. Here the mammoth canvas, weighted at the bottom, was hung from the ceiling on iron bars, and it was here that Styka worked on his masterpiece, averaging 12 to 14 hours a day.

Golgotha was finished in 1896 and publicly displayed in Lwow. The following year it was moved to Warsaw, to a specially erected building next to the Hotel Bristol, where it drew viewers from all over the world. At the turn of the century, Czar Nicolas II had it placed on exhibit in Moscow; subsequently it was shown in Paris. By this time, word of this stupendous painting had reached America, and it was arranged to have it shown, along with 50 or 60 other Styka paintings, at the St. Louis World's Fair in 1904.

At this point, a suspected art swindle, complicated and compounded by U.S. Customs difficulties, resulted in the other Styka canvasses going to St Louis for exhibit, and *Golgotha* being kept in the Customs House. This proved to be fortuitous, since the St. Louis Exposition building in which the Styka collection was housed burned to the ground, and the work of a lifetime went up in smoke. Eventually, Paderewski arranged to have the painting exhibited in Chicago in 1911.

In 1944 Dr. Hubert Eaton, searching for works to adorn a new burial complex in California, succeeded in locating the painting in a Chicago warehouse. He had heard about the spectacular painting, which had caused such a sensation in Europe a half a century earlier, and was determined to track it down. Even after Eaton had located it, he was involved in a lengthy and complicated legal battle to buy it, but he finally managed to acquire it for Forest Lawn.

Once again the painting presented a housing problem. Styka had apparently never worried about where to hang his colossal canvasses; he let others do that. Faced with this problem, Dr. Eaton solved it in the only possible way: he had a hall built at a cost of more than $1,500,000. It was called the Hall of the Crucifixion, and was a Gothic-inspired building with massive, buttressed walls. On Good Friday of 1951, the work, now retitled *The Crucifixion*, was unveiled in its new location. Since that time it has been viewed on a regular daily basis. Styka, who died in 1925 in Europe, never lived to see his masterpiece in its permanent home.

The Crucifixion is a non-traditional interpretation, and shows the last moment before Christ is nailed to the Cross. He stands atop Golgotha, the Cross lying at His feet, His scarlet robe, crown of thorns, and reed tossed on the ground. He gazes serenely at the darkening, cloudy sky. Behind Him a Roman official is reading the decree of execution. The two thieves, who are scheduled to be crucified along with Him, are in the background. All of the Biblical characters associated with the Crucifixion are portrayed in the vast canvas. The figures, all life-size, and number 1000, are set in a panoramic landscape with a view of Jerusalem in the extreme foreground.

Obviously a painting of such visual and iconographic complexity would be difficult to absorb by most viewers without help. Each of the 2000 seats in the Hall is equipped with a hearing device, allowing viewers to follow the recorded lecture as a light beam moves on the canvas to point out the more important characters depicted.

In the anteroom of the Hall are displayed the palette and brushes which Styka used to paint *The Crucifixion*. There are also three portraits, each with an identifying plaque, and a message. The first, that of Ignacy Paderewski, has a plaque which reads: "He dreamed it." The plaque under the portrait of Jan Styka and painted by his son, Tade, says: "He painted it;" while under the portrait of Dr. Eaton is inscribed: "He preserved it for humanity."

The painting still provokes as much comment as it did when it was painted, over 80 years ago. It has been praised by some art critics, decried by others, and still draws crowds of people who sit in hushed surroundings and gaze at this remarkable painting by an even more remarkable artist, Jan Styka.

AN INTRODUCTION TO STEFAN MROZEWSKI (1894-1975)

Boleslaw Mastai

It was in the early Thirties, and shortly following Mrozewski's swift ascent to fame in Europe, that America first learned of the visionary artist who can be called the Paganini of the burin — for Mrozewski makes use of the engraver's tools to achieve miracles of vibrant suppleness and pulsating luminosity.

Stefan Mrozewski, 1973. California Photo Service, Berkeley.

An exhibition of Polish Art at the Brooklyn Museum on October-November, 1933, presented several of his works, but it was not until 1936 that a complete one-man show was circulated throughout the United States. At the 1939-40 World's Fair, Mrozewski was represented by his famous portraits of Shaw and Wells and the 1934 Polish edition of "Don Quixote" which he had illustrated with twenty-four woodcuts. Since then, numerous exhibitions devoted to Mrozewski's works have been touring the country.

Furnished with representative displays of the artist's work, American art lovers sensed at once that incredible technical skill which aroused so much admiration. "From a technical standpoint," — wrote Adelyn D. Breeskin in *The American Magazine of Art*, April 1936, "the Parsifal illustrations especially are like a sample page of possible tool marks, there is such a rich variety of strokes and dots. In all probability, Mrozewski makes his own tools, for such patterns would certainly not be available in the usual stock in trade." This wizardry however is only a single facet of the artist's genius. For Mrozewski is a poet, a seer of visions, whose native element is fire and light, and his rendering of these is no mere display of pyrotechnics, but a literal translation of his inmost soul.

"The Apocalypse," "La Divina Commedia," "Les Testaments de Francois Villon," "Don Quixote," the works of Marcel Schwob — and lastly, "Firebrand," the life of Dostoevsky, by Henry Troyat — these titles speak for themselves — no mere virtuoso would have dared to approach these works, to illuminate them, in every sense of the word, as Mrozewski has done. It is the profound sincerity, the child-like, unworldly vision of Mrozewski that make him the great artist he is — and it is these qualities above all else that have won for him the enduring affection and admiration which he begins to enjoy in America.

STEFAN MROZEWSKI'S CREATIVITY

Stanley L. Cuba

"Sorcerer of the graving tool" — the phrase captures the essence of Stefan Mrozewski's creativity. The unofficial but appropriate title was given him in the 1930s by Tadeusz Cieslewski, Jr., himself a prominent Polish graphic artist of the interwar period. Mrozewski's wood engravings are the work of a jewelist among jewelers. Their technical subtleties are so exquisite that one finds it difficult to believe that these white-on-black works are indeed wood engravings — each tenuous line carved in relief out of the block. Because of his virtuosity, Mrozewski stands unequalled in his field.

Jerry Lehman, head of an evening school of drawing and painting in Lodz, Poland, initially acquainted Mrozewski with the art and technique of illustration. Formal studies followed, from 1921 to 1925, at the Domestic Arts School in Poznan and the Fine Arts Academies in Cracow and Warsaw. Almost accidentally, it seems, Mrozewski chose to concentrate on wood engraving as a result of his brief studies in the Warsaw Studio of Wladyslaw Skoczylas, founder of the prolific school of modern Polish wood engraving. Skoczylas drew his inspiration from Polish mountaineer (goral) legends and folk talks. Although Mrozewski retained his own artistic style, he did belong to Skoczylas' "Ryt," an association of Polish graphic artists founded in 1926, which included some of interwar Poland's finest wood engravers.

In 1925 Mrozewski joined the expatriate artistic community in Paris. Possessed of a strong will and apparently indefatigable energy, he was determined to make a career for himself as a wood engraver. His Parisian genre scenes brought him to the attention of a Bucharest publishing firm which engaged him, in 1926, to illustrate Dostoevsky's *Les Frères Karamazoff* and Rilke's *Cahiers de Malte Laurids Brigge*. Shortly thereafter he illustrated M. Schwob's *Le Roi au Masque d'Or*, a limited edition of 100 copies published in Paris by Apollo de Lux in 1929. This fine specimen brought him an additional dozen commissions for limited or de Lux editions during the next twenty-one years.

Mrozewski spent 1932 through 1935 in Holland, exhibiting in Amsterdam, Rotterdam, Utrecht (and Brussels, Belgium). In the

Stanley L. Cuba is assistant to the President, The Kosciuszko Foundation, in New York. He hails from Denver, Colorado.

Netherlands he seriously explored and depicted architectonic urban ensembles. From this period, too, dates his "Street Musicians in Bruges," a strikingly beautiful work. A short stay followed in London (1935-1937) during which time he produced a series of excellently engraved portraits of the late King George V, H.G. Wells, G.B. Shaw, Lord Cecil and Sir A.N. Chamberlain.

World War II caught Mrozewski in his native Poland where he belonged to the Polish Underground and used his talents to forge passports for his war-stricken compatriots. After the war he came to California via Western Europe on the strength of a letter he wrote to President Truman, who helped to facilitate his entry into the United States in 1951. On an invitation from the Huntington Hartford Foundation, Mrozewski settled in California where he lived almost uninterruptedly until his death in 1975.

In 1950 Mrozewski's genius received an appropriate American tribute in the form of a one-man show at the Albright-Knox Gallery in Buffalo. The numbered catalog, whose introduction was written by Boleslaw Mastai, was itself a work of art. Printed by Anatol Girs on special, hand-pulled paper, it contained a number of wood engravings by Mrozewski himself. Mr. Mastai called the artist "the Paganini of the burin who makes use of the engraver's tools to achieve miracles . . ."

Also worthy of note are the polychrome frescos which Mrozewski singlehandedly executed in the Polish church in Los Angeles, on West Adams Blvd. They recall similar undertakings by Picasso, Chagall, Matisse and Leger, the artist's contemporaries in Europe. Succeeding years, however, were not always kind to Mrozewski, since his white-on-black works seemed unwelcome in an artistic world increasingly charmed by color and the abstract. His proper recognition by a new generation is only a matter of time.

During a half century of professional artistic activity, Mrozewski produced more than 3,000 wood engravings. Most noteworthy are his illustrations for literary masterpieces by Dante, Cervantes, Villon, Goethe and Rilke. Mrozewski devoted much attention to this aspect of his creativity because he felt deeply that classical literary works were fulfilled and animated when accompanied by artistic illustrations of high calibre. He also possessed a large ouevre consisting of landscapes, portraits of world-renowned figures and genre scenes.

The illustrations for Dante's *Divine Comedy* are undoubtedly Mrozewski's greatest work, not only in terms of size and quality, but also in consideration of the thirty-one years he devoted to their production. From the age of twelve he was enamored of the *Divine Comedy*, the title itself having captured his imagination. Begun in 1938, the 101 illustrations were completed in 1970. In the words of Dr.

Joseph Teplin, they "most surely stand as a monument to perseverence matched by few in the annals of art." To secure a portion of the already-completed blocks from destruction during World War II, Mrozewski hid them in the tomb of Wincenty Kadlubek, the medieval Polish chronicler, and retrieved them on his departure from Poland in the 1940's. Mrozewski's *Divine Comedy* consists of 34 wood engravings for "Hell" and 33 each for "Purgatory" and "Paradise," as well as a masterful portrait of Dante. Each wood engraving measures 10 x 12-1/2 inches, a larger format than is generally used in the medium. Each stands alone and at the same time contributes to the homogeneity of the entire cycle.

His wood engravings reflect not only technical virtuosity and a vivid imagination, but also a remarkable aesthetic sensibility to literature. They contain a wealth of detail that is luxuriant, while at the same time evidencing an inordinate precision. They are delicate, lacy and transparent, yet penetrating, luminous and clear, like etched glass. These characteristics prompted the French art critic, Pierre Mornand, to include Mrozewski among such illustrators as Pierre Bonnard, Raoul Dufy, Andre Derain, Aristide Maillol and Andre Dunoyer de Segonzac when he wrote about wood engraving nearly three decades ago.

Mrozewski was an international representative of the sophisticated interwar school of Polish graphic art. This is somewhat ironic, since he spent the major portion of his career outside the country. His sophistication, notes Clare Leighton, is due to an almost excessive use of the multiple tool which produces "an effect of uniformly silvery grey that is unobtainable by any other means." The attractiveness of Mrozewski's wood engravings has not diminished. They remain both classic and timeless.

STANISLAW SZUKALSKI:
ESOTERIC ARTIST AND THINKER

Gene Harubin Zygmont

Stanislaw Szukalski, with multiple achievements as a sculptor, painter, writer, anthropological researcher, is one of those exceptional individuals who is difficult to categorize. He considers himself primarily a sculptor; however, the bulk of his work was unfortunately destroyed by Nazi bombs in September of 1939 while being exhibited in Warsaw. The works which did survive have been the subject of an ownership dispute between Szukalski and the present Polish government. Thus it is highly unlikely that his sculpture can be viewed or assessed in the foreseeable future. But Szukalski, as a writer, painter, medalist and man of ideas, is very much in evidence and working in California.

To Szukalski, the concept in art is more important than the medium or form. "An artist," he says, "should be a poet, philosopher, a thinker who produces concepts, not just finished sculpture. His art should inspire, infuriate, anger . . ." Szukalski is not concerned about being thought right or wrong. "Art is not math," he explains. "You cannot prove it right or wrong. Art is a manner of perception, therefore anything can be right." He does not believe in using models, believing that working from memory is less hampering in that it permits imagination to be transposed into the finished work. This view has led him to be labeled an "anti-naturalist."

Stanislaw Szukalski has been battling for his individualistic views for more than sixty years. Born in the small town of Warta, Poland, on December 3, 1895, he acquired an interest in sculpture at an early age. The area in which he lived was rich in limestone, soft enough to carve with a small knife. By the time he was eight he was carving birds, mammals, and figures of humans. His father emigrated to the United States, and in 1907 Stas, his mother and sister, joined him in Chicago. There Stas was enrolled in the Art Institute at the age of 12. Two years later he returned to Poland to study at the Krakow Academy of Art, the youngest student ever admitted to the prestigious school. After two and a half years he returned to Chicago, intending to stay for a short visit, but the outbreak of World War I and the death of his father forestalled his return to Europe.

In Chicago, young Szukalski moved in an artistic and cultural milieu which included Clarence Darrow and Ben Hecht. Hecht was to write later of this extraordinary young artist in *Child of the Century*. Young Szukalski began an intensive period of work which lasted until 1923, when he packed up his entire collection and went to Europe. He exhibited in Warsaw in 1923, and drew mixed reviews. While some of his work, particularly his portrait busts, received high praise, other works were denounced as too complex and esoteric. In 1925, at an exhibit in Paris, Szukalski was awarded a Grand Prix, Gold Medal, and other honors.

Mikolaj Kopernik by Stanislaw Szukalski, 1973. Photo processed by Martin Dabrowski.

But subsequent competitions in Poland proved less successful. At an exhibit in Krakow in 1929, Szukalski infuriated both critics and the faculty of the Art Academy with his scathing denunciations of their narrow-minded approach to art. But although denounced by critics, his art was well received by the public. He continued to exhibit in

Poland, as well as in the United States and Paris, visually formulating what he termed "art concepts."

In the fall of 1939, while his exhibit was being shown in Warsaw and Szukalski was working on a monument in Katowice, both cities were subjected to intensive bombing, during the opening days of World War II. Szukalski was buried under rubble in a basement for some 36 hours before he was finally rescued. Only after several months were Szukalski and his American-born wife of five years, Joan, permitted to leave Poland with two small suitcases. His works, or whatever was left of them, remained behind.

In California Szukalski worked for his old friend Ben Hecht in movie studios, and taught drawing to Hollywood notables. His work on complex sculptures which had become his trademark was limited by lack of proper studio facilities, but he did execute several fine pieces, including a miniature panorama of steel factories, commissioned by Bechtel Corporation and now on display in the Gugenheim Museum.

The frustrations of the War and early post-War years turned his attention to other fields. He began work on an autobiography and on an anthropological history of the origin of language, mythology, and evolvement of tribal markings and art motifs. An early-childhood chapter from his autobiography was published in the July 1964 issue of *Atlantic*, under the title "The Mute Singer." His multi-volume anthropological study, copiously illustrated with fine drawings, has been extended to thirty seven volumes, and is not yet complete, he declares. He spends at least eight hours a day researching, drawing and writing.

Although he no longer models large scale sculpture, Szukalski has produced two fine medals in the past four years. One, issued in 1973, commemorated the 500th anniversary of the birth of Mikolaj Kopernik (Copernicus); the other, slated for issue in 1977, is a tribute to the 10,000 Polish officers who were massacred in the Katyn Forest. He has also been kept busy with commissions for portraits, and is represented in collections throughout the United States and England.

A vital, active man, with enough energy for a man half his age, Szukalski is looking ahead to many more fruitful years in which to expound his ideas on art and life. And for Szukalski, the one is the other.

WLADYSLAW GAWLINSKI (1881-1973)

Doris Bernhagen

Born in Obertyn, Poland, November 25, 1881, Wladyslaw Gawlinski's artistic talents were recognized early by the village Catholic priest. This priest encouraged the artist's father to apprentice the lad to a cabinet maker in order to learn the elements of sculpture, since his first efforts had been in the medium of woodcarving. Gawlinski eventually moved to Lwow in search of opportunities for greater knowledge and excellence in his work. During 1919 and 1920 he participated in the defense of the city of Lwow, for which he was awarded several medals of valor. Gawlinski both studied on his own and attended art schools in Poland and in neighboring countries; at the same time, he pursued sculpture professionally as a means of earning his living. This thirst for knowledge and excellence, coupled with his self-discipline and devotion to his work, were dominant characteristics throughout Gawlinski's life.

Though a perfectionist, Gawlinski was also deeply human in his outlook. He was interested in people and loved animals, particularly those graceful and charming cats that have such appeal for artists. His was a positive attitude and an infectious sense of human and he was an interesting conversationalist with a breadth and range of knowledge that enabled him to relate to the interests of almost everyone. He was also a man of deep attachment, both to his native Poland and to the United States, his adopted country.

After World War I, he continued his work as a sculptor in wood, stone, and metal. While working in and managing a statuary studio across from a cemetery in Lwow, Gawlinski also taught drawing and sculpting at the local vocational school, "Szkola Przemyslowa." Because he was a progressive artist and teacher, he emigrated to the United States in 1924 to pursue the latest advances in the commercial art and sculpture; yet he intended to return to Lwow to continue his work there. The economic collapse of 1929, however, forced him to alter his plans, and to remain with his family in Chicago, Illinois. He continued in the art field, teaching and working commercially for the firm of Ted Stein and Sons. Here he specialized in ornamental stone

---

Doris Bernhagen lives in Westwood, Los Angeles.

sculpture which decorated many schools, churches and cemeteries. He had the distinction of being the first gentile sculptor selected to decorate a Jewish temple in Chicago, Illinois.

Gawlinski retired in 1959 and moved to Pasadena, California. Although retired, he continued to be active in the art field, and to extend and enrich his knowledge of his subject. At the time of his death, April 23, 1973, he was still engaged in several projects.

Gawlinski participated in many art exhibitions — at the Chicago Art Institute, the Chicago Polish Arts Club, the Polish University Club of Los Angeles Arts Festivals. After his death, his works were shown at a joint exhibit with Bela Kadar at Wood's Cove Gallery, Laguna Beach, California.

WLADYSLAW (WALTER) ZAWOJSKI: FOUR-DIRECTIONAL MAN

Jacek Przygoda

"An exhibition of approximately 40 highly imaginative airbrush paintings by Wladyslaw (Walter) Zawojski, artist and photographer at the Stanford Linear Accelerator Center (SLAC) is being held during May and June at the Palo Alto Medical Clinic, 300 Homer Ave." wrote *Campus Reporter* (a publication for Stanford University faculty and staff) on May 25, 1977.

"Zawojski's art," the writer continued, "is strongly influenced by his deep interest in science, and represents four directions in his search for self-expression. The first is a group of monochromatic airbrush paintings which he calls 'Art in Science.' Another is a pair of specially processed photographs of subatomic particle 'events' from SLAC's bubble chamber. A third group, 'Forms of Imaginations,' consists of 20 experimental paintings, 'Transcendent Impressions as a Result of the Influence of, and as a Fluid and Continuous Extension of our Animate Nature.' The last is a single experimental painting in acrylic on three pieces of vinyl, creating an illusion of three dimensions.

" 'Paints on a palette?' asked the artist. 'Only the imitation of a rainbow, but the only colors we can use. It is difficult to convey this message, which is almost like trying to play a symphony using only a drum.' "

Who is Zawojski? By way of an answer, an essay entitled "Forms of Imagination" sheds some light:

"Out of the turmoil of war-torn Europe," it states, "came many young people tempered by the fires of ordeal and kept alive by the will to survive. One of these was Walter Zawojski, today an exceptionally gifted man who happens to be the whole 'graphics department' of the Stanford Linear Accelerator Center (SLAC) . . . and one of the most innovative artists working in acrylic lacquers anywhere.

"Born in Przemysl, Poland, Zawojski had his early schooling in Warsaw and Budapest. He studied architecture, stage design and illustration, and by his early twenties was exhibiting at the Vilma Kiralyne Gallery in Budapest. Then in March of 1944 he was arrested by the Gestapo and deported to Germany . . . He managed to escape in 1945 and found his way to safety with the advancing American Fourth Armored Division. Until he could arrange to come to America, he taught drawing and photography at the Amberg Resettlement Center Vocational Training School in Bavaria.

"Once in the United States, Zawojski headed for California, in 1949, to seek identification with science and technology. Among his first positions was with the Graphics Department of Stanford Research Institute, where he had his first U.S. art show in 1957. Since then he has had his work shown in the 1972 'Art in Science' exhibition at the Palace of Fine Arts in San Francisco, at the 1974 AAAS Conference at San Francisco, in San Jose and Monterey."

A third glimpse of W.W. Zawojski is proved by himself. In a "Statement of Project" he wrote, "I believe all the Cosmos is pulsating and vibrating in a perfect rhythm of the unknown — a super-music of which only a minute sample has been extended to our ears. We continuously long for something which we can only dream about

sometimes. Everything pulses in a most glorious beat of music, color and harmony which is only possible to receive as One all together by One who could unify all senses."

Still, the reader is overwhelmed by the outpouring of the ideas about a Great Tomorrow, caught on Today, by this man who brings to mind Pierre Teihard de Chardin's *The Phenomenon of Man*.

The artist has said of himself, "With all modesty, as a Polish emigrant I have to state proudly that my contribution to American 'life' is significant. I have never applied for a job in this country. My activities have been explored on television in Poland, Hungary and Japan. ... I feel it is my ethnic pride that explains my widespread exposure, and I am most happy to read credit lines with a refreshingly Polish name. This is my greatest reward."

THE ART OF KALI-WEYNEROWSKA

James I. Rambo

The story of Kali-Weynerowska really begins in 1939. Just at the time she graduated with highest praise and promise from the Academy of Fine Arts in Warsaw, Poland was invaded. And so, instead of continuing her studies, the young girl became a member of the underground armed forces. Kali was the name under which she was known in the Polish resistance movement. After completing a secret officers' school, as a lieutenant, the former art student became a member of a Diversion and Sabotage Unit, with such assignments as blowing up bridges, tunnels or highways — instead of painting them.

In the tragic Warsaw uprising of 1944 Kali was wounded and decorated for bravery. As a POW she was later taken to a camp in Germany. Once the war ended, she was liberated within the Russian zone and made an adventurous escape into West Germany to turn up under American protection.

Kali managed to reach Belgium in the fall of 1945, where at last she could resume her life as an artist. She started by enrolling in the Royal Academy of Fine Arts in Brussels.

In spite of her marriage to Mr. Henryk Weynerowski, she continued to use her wartime name in signing her paintings. For the following five years she painted in Switzerland, Sweden, Luxembourg, England and France. In 1950 Kali left for Canada where her shows were held in all the major Canadian cities. After she won several prizes and high praise, she was chosen, among others, to represent Canada at the international exhibition of modern art in Sao Paulo, Brazil and in Caracas, Venezuela. In 1953 she moved with her husband to San Francisco.

The word "painter" seems inadequate to describe Kali. The paintings of Kali must be numbered among that rare group which, through the richness of their substance and in the imagination of their execution, appear as art objects as well. In them one discovers delightfully puzzling echoes of other media — of tapestry, mosaic, the "jewelled" porcelain of Sevres and the precious enamels of the Renaissance. In Kali's hands, paint is not a material to be squandered carelessly; it assumes the weight of gold, the lightness of silk, the fragility of glass.

Kali. "Boy with Feather." Panel.

Painters today are apt to be proud creatures who exist in fear of being called craftsmen, believing that craftsmen produce crafts (or "minor" arts), while in some more exalted realm painters produce paintings. The fact remains that painting *is* a craft and one proud enough for the most determined "painter." It is unique only in that it may be used more expressively than most other crafts. What an error to deny the expressiveness inherent in the medium itself! Kali brings prodigies of skill to her art and by aligning herself with the paintercraftsmen of the past, evokes a startling dimension in the present. By calling forth and developing the richness of her medium, she at once extends the richness of her expression.

Perhaps the most arresting single aspect of the inventiveness in Kali's current work lies in the technique she has perfected in rendering of flesh tones. She herself, with a bluntness characteristic of her, refers to this regularized system of precise raised points of pigment, in carefully graduated values of the same tints, as her "gimmick." It is no more a gimmick than are the raised, tooled embellishments of *trecento* Sienese paintings which, with their simplified forms, are areas of brilliantly executed flat pattern. They are an important part of the tradition which Kali is happy to recognize. Through the exact application of these points of paint, Kali is able to produce a seemingly translucent tone that is truly remarkable in its transmutation of texture into light.

It is a satisfaction to trace the development of Kali's art: over the years one finds no campricious change of style — each change being rather the reasoned result of careful and knowing exploration and experimentation. Above all, and in every phase, one senses discipline, but it is a discipline invested with touching humor and suffused with warm humanism; it provides the basis for the success of Kali's striking and evocative canvasses.

EDWARD W. HICKS: PAINTER AND GRANDSON OF A POLISH FORTY-NINER

Jacek Przygoda

Edward W. Hicks, a California landscape painter, was born in 1897 in San Francisco and now lives in Santa Barbara. Hicks' father was Krakus Wichrowsky, but his mother, Jessie Craig, after she married Amos Hicks, changed his name to that of his step-father. His Polish grandfater (Wichrowski, from Krakow) was among the Forty-Niners and, after making some money, went to Missouri near St. Louis, to a German settlement. There he got married and bought a bit of land. The couple commuted between Missouri and California in a covered wagon, because they owned property in both states, including lots in San Francisco.

Edward Hicks attended the University of California at Berkeley, and, after service in the Army during World War I, studied at the Art Students League in New York. He also worked for banks in New York and Brooklyn, as well as on Wall Street. In the capacity of a fledgling investment banker, he was sent to England and lived for two years in London. This provided an opportunity to study the Old Masters in European museums.

After returning to the United States, he continued working for banks, while at night he studied journalism at Columbia University. In December of 1927 he married Alice S. Schenck, his devoted wife for 50 years. In October of 1962 they moved from Fairfield, Connecticut to Santa Barbara. Two years later, Edward W. Hicks became a professional painter.

It has been stated by Edward Selden Spaulding that, "although many artists over the years have capably painted Santa Barbara's landmarks — the Mission, Castle Rock, Rincon Mountain, in particular — Ed Hicks has gone into our costal canyons and found inspiration in the great beauty there for his very fine landscapes. In this work he paints with great distinction the familiar, typical, natural, peaceful California scenes, as remembered and loved by us all — the winding dirt roads of the canyons, the oak-studded hills, the fields of wild flowers."

Seeing his studio, one quickly detects the atmosphere of the artist's nostalgia. Almost each painting speaks its language. A serene meadow, richly carpeted with wild flowers, rolling hills with stubbornly majestic oaks straddling them, scenes without any evidence of curse of urbanization, are the subjects of his most frequently evoked California past. Somehow it seems to reach back to the era of the Gold Rush, to the virginal Golden State, when the "small" was beautiful and men great in their vision of overcoming obstacles.

ANTON GROT: ART DIRECTOR (1886-1974)

Donald Deschner

Born Antoni Franciszek Groszewski, in Kielbasice, Poland, in 1886, Grot attended the Technical College in Koenigsberg (Krolewiec, in Polish), majoring in interior decoration, illustration, and design. In 1909 he came to the United States and was hired by the film producer, Sigmund Lubin, to paint backgrounds and design sets. *The Mouse and the Lion* (1913) was Grot's first film.

In 1922 Grot moved to Los Angeles and made a set of posters advertising Douglas Fairbank's latest film. Fairbanks liked his work and hired Grot to work with William Cameron Menzies on the sets for *The Thief of Baghdad* (1923) and *Dorothy Vernon of Hadden Hall* (1924). When Cecil B. DeMille broke with Famous Players-Lasky and formed his own company, Grot went to work for him and designed three major films, *Road to Yesterday* (1925), *The Volga Boatmen* (1926) and *The King of Kings* (1927). Grot also designed William K. Howard's film, *White Gold*, which employed psychological suggestion through the use of light and sets in the tradition of the Expressionistic German films of the 1920s.

Anton Grot went to work for Warner Brothers as head of the Art Department in 1927. One of the first films on which he worked at this studio was *Show Girl* (1928), directed by Alfred Santell. In 1929 Grot created the settings for three films starring Colleen Moore and directed by William Seiter, *Why Be Good, Smiling Irish Eyes,* and *Footlights and Fools.* During the period when Alexander Korda made films in Hollywood, two of his films had settings by Grot, *Her Private Life* and *Lillies of the Field* (both in 1930).

In a letter dated May 1, 1932, John Barrymore wrote: "You may be a humble artist but you are most certainly a very fine one." Barrymore had recently worked in *Svengali* and its sequel, *The Mad Genius* (both in 1931), with Grot. For these films, Grot made interesting use of tilted floors and ceilings, disproportionate windows and doors, unusual staircases and jagged rooftops, giving the films a nightmarish quality suggesting a distorted mind.

While working on *Doctor X* (1932) Grot said: "The primary purpose of set designing is to establish the mood of the story. In *Doctor X* that

Reprinted by permission from *UCLA Librarian*, Vol. 30, Nos. 7-8. July-August, 1977. Los Angeles, California.

mood is mystery, of course, but we have tried to build menace into the sets. For instance, when we design a set for mystery or melodrama, we know it must be of heavy construction with dark colorings and shadows. When we want to add menace to that, we put in a top-heavy effect over doors and windows, we build in low arches which give the feeling of overhanging danger. We design a set that imitates as closely as possible a bird of prey about to swoop down upon its victim, trying to incorporate in the whole thing a sense of impending calamity, of overwhelming danger." For *Doctor X* a total of 192 sketches and blueprints, many of them completely detailed and all conceived for the eye of the camera, were made by Grot. Other films designed by Grot for Warner Brothers included Busby Berkeley's *Gold Diggers of 1933* and *Gold Diggers of 1935*, and the beautifully designed *Captain Blood* (1935), directed by Michael Curtiz.

Anton Grot. Courtesy, Brooke Whiting, Curator Rare Books, UCLA.

During a radio interview, Grot was asked if his settings were completely realistic. He replied, "On the contrary, I, for one, do not like extremely realistic sets. I am for simplicity and beauty, and you can achieve that only by creating an impression ... *Anthony Adverse* is a period picture. If the sets should happen to be too realistic, it would detract from the action and the beautiful costumes. It had always been my contention that the set must be designed as to blend in with the spirit and the action of the picture."

For the major 1936 production of *A Midsummer Night's Dream*, codirected by Max Reinhardt and William Dieterle, Grot created the fantasy settings. Cedric Gibbons, Chief Art Director at MetroGoldwyn-Mayer, wrote to Grot, "May I compliment you on your work in the *Dream*. It has, I think, more beauty than any picture I have ever seen and I think your work is by far the greatest single contribution to the picture." Other pictures designed by Grot were *The Sea Hawk* (1940), *Dispatch from Reuter's* (1940), and *Sea Wolf* (1941). During this period, Grot invented the "Ripple Machine," which created the appearance of rough seas and waves and was used to great effect first in *The Sea Hawk*.

After World War II, Grot worked in *Mildred Pierce* (1945), for which he made more than 200 drawings of each shot in the film. It was unusual for Grot, or the directors he worked with, to have so complete a story board showing each set-up, angle, and content of the shot. He also worked on *Possessed* (1947), *The Unsuspected* (1947) and *June Bride* (1948).

Anton Grot retired from motion picture work in 1948 and devoted his energies to oil painting. He painted scenes from nature, such as the Carmel coastline and the bird sanctuary at Santa Barbara, portraits, and historical subjects. He died not long after his ninetieth birthday, on March 21, 1974, in Stanton, California.

POLISH ART AND FILM

VOL. I. NO. I   HOLLYWOOD, CALIF. (JULY 1937)   10 CENTS

FREE TRIP TO HOLLYWOOD!

Beginning July 15, 1937, we are offering our readers a contest.

RULES

1. Anyone can take part in this contest, providing the said person is no less than 15 years of age and is a resident of the United States, North America and Canada.

2. Contestants are required to apply by mail for authority to participate in the contest and receive their subscription blanks.

3. The contestant acquiring the greatest number of subscribers during said period, will be presented with a round trip to Hollywood, and all expenses paid for a week's stay. The winner will also have an opportunity to visit the Studios.

4. The contest will be terminated Oct. 15, 1937, the results of the contest will be published in the following issue.

5. Subscriptions may be taken to Oct. 15, inclusively, all receipts and data to be mailed to the Polish Art and Film and bearing the official stamp of the local post office, not later than Oct. 15.

6. In case of a tie, the contest prize will be awarded to both winners.

CLIP THIS COUPON

POLISH ART AND FILM PUBLISHING CO.

1147 N. Hudson Avenue,
HOLLYWOOD, CALIFORNIA
Gentlemen:

I enclose money order for $1.25. Please send me Polish Art and Film Magazine for one year.

Name ....

Address ....

City .... State....................

Hollywood Reports . . . .

Following the completion of her role in "Angel," Marlene Dietrich left for Lake Arrowhead where she will join her daughter, Maria, for several days' vacation . . . Martha Raye and her new husband, Buddy Westmore, are off for a motor trip in the northern part of the state . . . Director Mitchell Leisen who just completed "Easy Living," sailed June 16 on the Normandie for Europe . . . George Raft and Mack Grey are off for Chicago where they will attend the fight . . . Following the completion of his current picture, "Souls at Sea" Director Henry Hathaway and his wife will leave for Honolulu and Jack Benny and Mary Livingston leave the end of the month for several weeks in South America . . . Joan Blondell thinks Baby Norman will be an actor because he makes a scene whenever there's company . . . Louise Fazenda, everybody's favorite, is her own handy man at her ranch, fixing everything from the electric lights to the barn door and has the prettiest roses in the Valley . . . Patric Knowles saved $3 fixing his own car, but paid a mechanic $4.50 to undo the homemade damage . . . Pat O'Brien was all excited when he got China on his radio "as clear as a bell" but wilted when he discovered he had listened to a Fiesta from local Chinatown . . . Tyrone Power's grandmother, Mrs. Adelaide Reaume of Cincinnati, arrived in Hollywood to spend the summer with her grandson . . . Leah Ray thinks there's too much shoptalk so she's going places with Tommy Page, Dallas news reporter . . . Claire Trevor at the Junior League's polo match and barbecue with Billy Bakewell . . . Louise Hovick nightclubbing with famed composer Rudolph Friml . . . Gloria Stuart and Arthur Sheekman, Norman Krasna, Eddie Buzzell and the Groucho Marxes at the new Beverly Hills Tennis Club . . . Michael Whalen and Katherine deMille at the Cocoanut Grove . . . When Charlie Ruggles scheduled swimming party at his redecorated San Fernando home, Jack Haley and Arthur Treacher called all the guests to rent vintage-of-1900 bathing suits for the occasion . . . Haley and Treacher arrived in knee-lengthy, baggy striped swim suits, while the ladies arrived bloomered and stockinged . . . the host had prepared a few gags of his own, with repainted furniture marked "do not sit here," "use combs at your own risks," etc. . . party culminated with a comedy diving act by Haley and Treacher.

JULY. 1937   3

LIFE OF RYSZARD BOLESLAWSKI (1890-1936)

Boguslaw Rostworowski

Six months ago Ryszard Pomian-Szrednicki passed away in his own beautiful shrubbery-and-flower-surrounded mansion on Forester Drive, Palms, California. That was the real name of the genius, creator of many films, famous author, patriot, and great Pole — Ryszard Boleslawski. Through the death of Ryszard Boleslawski, the presentday film world suffered an irreparable loss of one of its leaders, and the Poles lost an ardent promoter of Polish screen art and a film intercessor for Polish culture in the screen world. A few hours after his death, American newspapers brought to the world the stunning and mournful news of his passing in special "extra" editions.

Ryszard Boleslawski was born in 1890, in Debowa Gora, near Plock, Poland. From his parents he inherited the culture of an old and noble family. He lived and developed in an environment created by generous, thoughtful people who dreamed of freedom and beauty in the fertile land of Poland. His name recalls the valorous and meritorious Polish nobility, although family dissonances and the constant struggle of Poland against Czarist oppression took him, after the year 1905, to the distant cities of central Russia. He had a desire to shine and dazzle, and he received a gold medal for his studies at the Czar's gimnazjum. Ryszard Boleslawski, as a young actor, appeared in the famous Moscow Art Theatre. His life brought him into contact with Czarist oppression of the Polish people. He went through the horrors of World War I when he fought in the front line trenches.

After the War he tried to win recognition in his own fatherland, but with no success; he was not understood. He migrated to America, where his appearances were glittering with wit, enlightened with youthful fantasy manifesting itself in a new art, subtle and penetrating, culled from the thousand-year-old Polish culture. This new art was strange to Americans, and for this reason he failed as an actor.

He turned his hand to writing, publishing *Way of a Lancer* and *Lancers Down*. From this time on, fortune began to smile on him. Metro-Goldwyn-Mayer called on him and hired him as a director. He

Adapted from *Polish Art and Film*, Hollywood, July 1937. Courtesy of the Polish Museum of America, Chicago, Illinois.

POLISH ART and FILM

JULY, 1937
PRICE 10¢

☆

• RYSZARD BOLESLAWSKI
(Story on Page 6)

WIN A TRIP TO HOLLYWOOD!

directed such pictures as *Three Musketeers, The Empress, Storm at Daybreak, Les Miserables* and *Strange Woman.* His books were printed in several editions and translated into French, German, Portuguese, Dutch, Danish and Swedish.

Ryszard Boleslawski loved his wife ardently and was truly devoted to his son, John. When he left her, even for a moment, he sent her a messenger with flowers and a tender note. Under her influence and for her he wrote his memoirs and books in which he described the unusual problems in his life and the story of his part in World War I. At the end of his life, Ryszard Boleslawski was happy, famous and wealthy. He passed away on January 17, 1936, and is buried at Inglewood cemetery.

POLISH ART and FILM

| VOL. II. NO. IV | HOLLYWOOD, CALIFORNIA | APRIL, 1938 |

MAIN OFFICES: 1137 NORTH HUDSON AVENUE • TELEPHONE: HOllywood 7603 • HOLLYWOOD, CALIFORNIA
SUBSCRIPTION PRICE: United States - - - - - - - - - - One Year $1.50 • FOREIGN - - - - - - - - - - One Year $2.00

The Publishers Accept No Responsibility for Return of Unsolicited Material

★
BOLESLAW OLECHNOWICZ - - - - - Publisher and Editor
WIKTOR WOJCIECHOWSKI - - - - - - Associate Editor
JOZEFA KUDLICKA - - - - - - - Associate Editor
★

The Polish Art and Film is published monthly by the Polish Art and Film Co., 1137 North Hudson Avenue, Hollywood, California. Entered as Third Class Matter at the Los Angeles Post Office under Section 562, P. L. & R., Permit No. 11169, on February 9, 1938. Copyright, 1937, by Polish Art and Film Co.

The COVER

Jan Kiepura, the Metropolitan's new Polish tenor, has evoked unbounded enthusiasm from large audiences at all his performances during his first season at the Metropolitan.

Critics in New York have attributed it to a naturally-gifted voice, geniality, exuberance, good showmanship. In reviewing "Carmen," Olin Downes of the *New York Times* said, "His presence on the stage gave the whole performance stimulus . . . a gifted singer and also a personable one. Mr. Kiepura not only entertained, but moved his audience."

Concerning the same performance, the following appeared in the *Herald Tribune*: "Jan Kiepura brings to the part of Carmen's soldier lover attributes not often encouraged in operatic tenors, for he is both slender and handsome and an actor of exceptional intelligence and rare perceptive powers. Winningly youthful and naive in the first act, when he falls under the spell of Carmen's seductive allurements, his characterization grew in inten-

sity until it reached a climax of thrilling, tragic impact at the close of the third act."

In Kiepura's debut in "La Boheme" on February 10, Oscar Thompson wrote, "Measured in terms of applause, Mr. Kiepura's success was the most striking of any new singer of the opera season. No opportunity was missed to single him out for special displays of enthusiasm."

Kiepura is married to Marta Eggerth, the Hungarian actress, who has appeared with him in many European films. Now in his early thirties, Kiepura was born at Sosnowiec, Poland, studied law, and then gave it up for an operatic career. He made his debut at the Warsaw Opera in 1925, and appeared the following year at the Vienna Opera in the title role of Gounod's "Faust," following that with a two-year engagement at La Scala in Milan.

For the 1930-31 season he came to this country to sing with Chicago Opera Company, and since that time has devoted himself to the making of motion picture films and performances in the leading European opera houses.

VARIOUS MATTERS

Some reflection on Mother's Day brings us to the realization of the significant part Polish mothers have played and are playing in the development of our artistic heritage. More so than any other nation, Poland owes a great deal to her mothers for the high level of artistic attainment achieved by her sons.

In an oppressed nation which has been in slavery for so many years, artists have continually risen to the fore and presented an artistry typically Polish. Poles have been denied the privilege of speaking or learning their own language. Three nations have tried to absorb them into their own. And despite extreme poverty, coercion, and lack of freedom, her music, her art and her literature have always had and still have a distinct flavor, a distinct nationality. A nation, apparently stifled, has produced artists second to none in the entire world.

What has made this possible? We are not fools enough to believe that ours is a superior race. There is no such thing as racial superiority and knowing this we must wonder

sometimes. Misery certainly does not produce beauty. Then what is it?

The patriotism, sacrifices, hopes and ambitions of Poland's mothers aer the answer; at least in part. All over the world Polish homes contain pianos and violins. Hoping to find some beauty in a sordid world, the Polish mother denies herself everything to make her sons and daughters creators of that beauty which she seeks. She forgets her immediate needs she increases her hardships and lives a life of sacrifice. In your community and mine she toils to make those extra few dollars to buy lessons. She does this for years and years expecting no reward but the satisfaction that she has made something of her children, something which circumstances in a blind world prevented her from being.

The next time we appreciate some Polish works of art let us also appreciate the sacrifices of millions of Polish mothers that are making more of them possible.

—*Wiktor Wojciechowski.*

ZYGMUNT SULISTROWSKI: EXOTIC MOVIE PRODUCER

Kathy S. Hayes

Born in Lwow, Poland, Zygmunt Sulistrowski joined the Polish Home Army during World War II, and was active in the Warsaw Uprising. After the War, Sulistrowski studied at the French Film Academy (IDHEC) in Paris, and then went on to England where he spent two years directing feature-length documentaries.

In 1950 Sulistrowski emigrated to the United States, where he settled in California and established International Film Enterprises, still a thriving company. His specialty is exotic films depicting the culture and religious rites of vanishing cultures in primitive parts of the world.

Sulistrowski's first production, *Naked Amazon*, which he wrote, directed, played and produced, was a winner at the Cannes Film Festival. This film was based on his experiences in the Amazon region of Brazil, where he spent many months living among several tribes, including the still-hostile Gavioes.

This same compulsion for authenticity is the distinguishing mark of all Sulistrowski films. He speaks eight languages, and prides himself on being able to communicate without spoken language when necessary. After totally immersing himself in a culture which interests him, Sulistrowski imports his own professional cast, which he carefully blends with local talent to obtain the greatest possible degree of style and authenticity. According to *Natural History* magazine, some of his work is "an incredible achievement in preserving the graphic expression of vanishing cultures in primitive parts of the world."

Another Sulistrowski film, *Feitico de Amazonas* was chosen Best Film of the Year in Brazil. *Hunza the Himalayan Shangri-La* won a prize at the International Film Festival in Berlin. Other productions include *Happening in Africa, Love in the Pacific, Annie the Virgin of St. Tropez* and *Passion of the Wilderness*.

Sulistrowski describes himself as "always in search of beauty, and mainly of the inner beauty in people, that 'third dimension' . . . which is so often neglected in our fast-moving civilization." While most of his

---

Kathy S. Hayes is a free lance writer based in San Fernando.

Zygmunt Sulistrowski. Photo, *Cinema/TV Today* London, Oct. 16, 1977.

movies center around love, adventure and suspense in remote locations, Sulistrowski takes a firm stand against pornography and violence in films.

This truly cosmopolitan man (Polish-born, French-educated, California-based, and world travelled) has his deepest roots in the Amazon region. He has organized the International Nature Enjoyment Club and International Film Ranch near the Amazon to promote understanding of this unique and fascinating part of the world, and plans to film his next two productions in Brazil: *Macumba God and Devil*, and *The Splendor of the Amazon*.

JAROSLAW ZIELINSKI:
HEAD OF A MUSIC SCHOOL

This Polish pianist, writer and composer was born in Lubicza Krolewska, Poland, on March 31, 1847 and died in Santa Barbara, California, on July 25, 1922. Trained in Poland, J. Zielinski was a pupil of Guziewicz and Wikuli (pianoforte) at Lwow Conservatory. He continued his musical studies under Schulhoff in Vienna and Cerutti (singing) at Milan.

He took an active part in the Polish uprising of 1863-64 against the Czarist Russia, and was badly wounded. Fortunately, he recovered and came to the United States in 1864. Here he joined the Union Army, serving until the end of the Civil War.

After leaving the American Army in 1865, he began to appear as a pianist on the concert platform. He lived successively in New York, Grand Rapids, Michigan, and Detroit. In 1888 he moved to Buffalo, New York, and in 1910 to Los Angeles, California. Here he formed the Zielinski Trio Club and became head of a music school. He wrote several piano-forte pieces and contributed an article, "Poles in Music," to *The Century Library of Music* (Vol. XVIII).

ROMAN MACIEJEWSKI: COMPOSER

Slawa Krance

Roman Maciejewski was born in 1910 in Poznan, Poland. After completing his secondary school education, he studied choral music under the direction of Father W. Gieburowski. Roman graduated from the Warsaw Conservatory of Music, where he studied music composition with Kazimierz Sikorski, and piano with Professor Turczynski.

His first concert was held at the Warsaw Institute of Arts Relations in 1932 and dealt with the newest forms in Polish music, created for the piano and played by both Kazimierz Krance and the composer. In 1934 the government granted Mr. Maciejewski a scholarship for one year's study in Paris, where he worked under the direction of Nadia Boulanger. He also spent some time in England and composed music for the Joos Ballet. The original concert with two pianos was given several times in Paris, London, and Warsaw, always with the participation of the composer and Kazimierz Krance.

During World War II he lived in Scotland, married a member of the Joos Ballet, and composed music for Ingmar Bergman's films. He came to the United States in 1950 and, at the invitation of Artur Rubinstein's children, became involved in the film industry. He has lived in the Los Angeles area for about 25 years, performing as an organist and choir master at the Polish Parish on West Adams Blvd., and at Our Lady of Guadalupe Church in Redondo Beach.

The *Requiem Mass*, his most important composition, was played after World War II at the Festival of Religious Music by the Radio Orchestra of Katowice, and repeated, with the participation of the Roger Wagner Choral, November 1, 1976 at the Music Center in Los Angeles. In addition to writing numerous songs, Roman Maciejewski is credited with such compositions for the piano as mazurkas, lullabies and "Zbojnicki" (a dance of the Tatra mountaineers).

When his friends and admirers learned of his decision to leave California for Europe, they sponsored several farewell receptions in his honor, closing with a gala affair on January 15, 1977.

Slawa Krance lives in Brentwood.

RYSZARD RODZINSKI: MINI- PROFILE

Ryszard Rodzinski, born January 23, 1945 in New York City, is the son of Arthur Rodzinski (the renowned former conductor of the Cleveland Orchestra, Los Angeles Philharmonic and New York Philharmonic) and Halina Rodzinski (born Lilpop-Wieniawski, the grandniece of Henryk Wieniawski).

After attending Oberlin College, Ryszard Rodzinski studied musicology, psychology and the history of art at Columbia University, New York, where he received his master's degree. In 1969 he became artistic assistant to Kurt Herbert Adler at the San Francisco Opera. He is presently the artistic administrator of the Metropolitan Opera in New York City, a position he has held since April, 1975.

STEPHAN PASTERNACKI:
OVER FIFTY YEARS WITH MUSIC

Kathy S. Hayes

Stephan Pasternacki, born in Detroit, Michigan to Polish parents, had a full, interesting and successful career in music which spanned over half a century. He began in New York in 1911 as a song plugger for a music publisher, whose job was to induce performers to give exposure to "their" songs. Without this exposure, in the days before radio and television, the songs would die.

Stephan Pasternacki, Composer/Choir Director.

In 1914 Stephan returned to Detroit to organize a dance band for Frontenac Cafe, where he remained until America entered World War I. While in the Signal Corps in San Antonio, Texas, he produced and wrote songs for several musicals. After the War he returned to Detroit, where he organized a dance band for the Wolverine Hotel, where he advised one of his saxophonists, Carmen Lombardo, to change from C melody to E flat alto sax. This helped set the style for the individual saxophone sound that was later to "identify" the music of Guy Lombardo.

During the 1920's, Pasternacki wrote several songs which made the hit parade, and his orchestra played daily on two radio stations. In 1929, on the advice of a friend, Stephan moved to Hollywood, where the golden era of talking pictures was just beginning. What began as a short stay in Hollywood extended to a life-long career. His first job, as a music advisor, was to familiarize himself with the script, select appropriate and authentic music or songs to be used, and decide how the music was to be recorded. Background music was added to the picture after the final editing was done.

Later, as a music mentor, or song watchman, it was his duty to identify any tune which might have been previously recorded and copyrighted. It necessitated a file of songs in his mind which could be likened to information stored in a computer — a musical accident could cost the studio many thousands of dollars in royalties.

Throughout his life Stephan Pasternacki has retained his interest in his Polish culture and heritage. He has produced a variety of Polish musicals and is still, although retired, a constant participant in various Polish activities, and is a director of the Chopin Choral Group. He is a member of Helena Modrzejewska Art & Culture Club and Polish American Historical Association (PAHA-Calif. Chapter). In June, 1977, Stephan Pasternacki received on the occasion of observance of the twenty-fifth anniversary of California Copyright Conference a special recognition as its founder and first president. He is now its honorary president. Indeed, he has had what very few people acquire — a full, interesting and successful life in one of the greatest arts — Music.

LIBERACE: HIS GLITTERING CANDELABRA

Mindy Kaye

Wladziu Valentino Liberace was born in Wisconsin to a Polish mother and an Italian father. Music was at the heart of the Liberace household. Every member of the family played an instrument. At 4 years of age, Liberace was able to play almost any tune by ear, and at 14 his classical training culminated with a debut as soloist with the Chicago Symphony.

Mindy Kaye is a free lance writer based in Los Angeles.

During the Depression he had to help his family with finances, so he started working the night club circuit under the name of "Walter Busterkeys." All the while he was developing his unique sense of musicianship and showmanship. He began playing the top nightclubs as an intermission pianist and eventually returned to the same night spots as top star with his $150,000 grand piano and the now renowned trademark — a glittering candelabra. Ignace Jan Paderewski, a longtime friend of the family, was the one who advised him to adapt the single name of Liberace.

He was signed as a summer replacement for Dinah Shore on television, which resulted in his winning two Emmy Awards. He was then launched into a diamond-studded orbit that has maintained its velocity to this day. In 1956 he played two Command Performances in London. In 1957 he opened in Las Vegas as the highest paid entertainer in its history; he now has a contract with Caesar's Palace valued at more than $1,000,000.

He has had several television series, and has become known for his flamboyant style and his sartorial splendor. The former depression piano player now spends at least $100,000 a year on his sparkling, brocaded, diamond and jeweled costumes. He commissioned a diamond-studded dune buggy, renovated a mansion in Palm Springs, and co-authored a cookbook, among other activities. He now works 30 weeks a year and remains one of the five highest paid entertainers in show business.

BRONISLAW KAPER: OSCAR WINNER

Mindy Kaye

Bronislaw Kaper was born in Warsaw some time between 1902 and 1908 (the exact date could never be verified). He was graduated from the University of Law and the Frederic Chopin Conservatory of Music, both in Warsaw. He went to Berlin to continue his music studies and there began writing popular songs and music for films, which were then in their infancy. During that period he also conducted a choir of Polish workers, Harmonia, which participated in a competition for choirs sponsored by a Slavic convention in Poznan. In Berlin he also wrote serious concert music, was a member of a piano quartet, and wrote for two great singers of the time, Richard Tauber and Jan Kiepura. While in Berlin he married Elenora (now deceased).

Mr. Kaper next moved to Paris, where he lived for a year and a half. Ludwig B. Mayer, head of Metro-Goldwyn-Mayer, came to Europe seeking talents. He heard "Ninon," a song Mr. Kaper had written, sought him out and signed him to a contract with MGM. Mr. Kaper then came to California and began working for MGM, where he remained for 28 years. He has composed the scores and songs for about 150 movies, including the classic *San Francisco* and the song *Hi-Lilly, Hi-Low,* for which he won an Oscar. His credits include: *The Brothers Karamazov, Lord Jim, Red Badge of Courage, Green Dolphin Street,* and *Gas Light.* He also composed the music for the Broadway musical *Polonaise* with Jan Kiepura and Martha Eggert.

He is a member of the Board of Governors of the Motion Picture Academy; the Board of Directors of the Los Angeles Symphony Orchestra; on the Advisory Board of the Young Musicians Foundation; the Executive Board of the Foreign Language Committee of the Academy of Motion Pictures; and the Executive Board of the Scholarship Committee of the Academy.

Mr. Kaper maintains a close relationship with Polish writers, sports figures, and musicians, especially his closest friend, Artur Rubinstein, and considers himself an unpaid "Polish Ambassador" of the U.S. He was a close friend of Julian Tuwim, the Polish poet, and donated a collection of unpublished letters and verses from Tuwim to the Polish Museum of Literature in Warsaw.

Bronislaw Kaper presently resides in Beverly Hills.

HARRY LOJEWSKI: MGM "EXEC."

Mindy Kaye

Harry (Hieronim V.) Lojewski was born in Detroit, Michigan, of Polish parents, although the family moved to Los Angeles when he was five years old. He started taking piano lessons at the age of ten. Later he attended the University of Arizona but also studied with private teachers, with the aim of becoming a concert pianist.

Following his discharge from the Army in 1946, Mr. Lojewski worked at Metro-Goldwyn-Mayer Studios as a rehearsal pianist; he made his debut as a concert pianist in 1949 at the Wilshire-Ebell (Los Angeles) in an all-Chopin concert. In 1954 he was appointed Music Advisor-Assistant Scorer at MGM, and in 1969 became head of music for television at MGM. In 1972 he was appointed Executive Director of Music for Motion Pictures and Television for MGM, a position he still maintains.

Mr. Lojewski was choir director at Our Lady of Lourdes Church in Northridge for 13 years, during which time he and his choir often appeared on KNXT in the Archdiocesan sponsored program, "Light of Faith." He was invited in 1966 to conduct a choir of 150 voices in his first published English Mass (*Mass in Honor of the Prince of Peace*) at a workshop sponsored by the Archdiocese of Los Angeles and the L.A. Unit of the National Catholic Music Educators Association. He and his choir were appointed official goodwill ambassadors from Los Angeles by Mayor Sam Yorty for the California Bicentennial celebration of the founding of California's first mission, Mission San Diego de Alcala, in San Diego, where they performed his Spanish Mass (Misa de los Mariachis).

Mr. Lojewski is a member of the Academy of Motion Picture Arts and Sciences; American Society of Composers, Authors and Publishers; Composers and Lyricists Guild of America; Broadcast Music, Inc., and the American Federation of Musicians.

He received a Certificate of Recognition in 1972 from the National Academy of Television Arts and Sciences for contributions as music Supervisor for the television program, "Hollywood, the Dream Factory," and again in 1975 for Outstanding Achievement in Music Composition for the television special, "Babe."

Mr. Lojewski is married to Maria-Carmen de Soto, born in Santiago, Cuba and a descendant of Hernando de Soto, discoverer of the Mississippi River and the first Governor of Cuba. They have two children, a son, Victor, who attends a college, and a daughter, Sister Carmen of the Franciscan Sisters of the Immaculate Conception.

HENRY VARS (1902-1977)

Mindy Kaye

Henry Vars, born in Warsaw in 1902, was a graduate of the Warsaw Conservatory of Music. He spent one and one half years in military service, graduating from Officers' School in Wlodzimierz. After leaving the service, he heard American Jazz music of that period, which influenced him very strongly. He started writing songs, and after a brief period of failure, he succeeded as a composer of film music and popular songs.

Unfortunately, World War II interrupted his activities and he was mobilized by the Army. In 1939-40 he was taken prisoner by the Germans, but escaped. Eventually he organized a theatrical group which was so popular that it was invited to tour the Soviet Union, visiting all the major cities.

In 1941, after receiving an invitation from General Anders, the group joined the Polish Army in Russia. They were then transferred to Iran and from there went to Iraq, Palestine, Egypt and on to Italy. They took part many performances for the military as well as civilian populations. In Italy they received first prize in a contest of Allied Forces artistic groups.

In 1947 he was released from the Army and came to the United States. His early years in America were difficult. At the time most of the film production was being done in Europe rather than Hollywood because costs were so much lower there. After several years, he got his first assignment with Columbia Pictures as a composer. The first film he worked on was *The Big Heat*; he then went on to work for several studios — major, minor and independent. He has 39 films to his credit, as well as several song hits recorded by well-known artists including Jimmy Rogers, Doris Day and Bing Crosby. He has composed scores for television shows "Daktari," "Flipper," "Gunsmoke," and others, and has earned the reputation as "the Irving Berlin of Poland." Several hundred of his hits are still being recorded, published and played in Poland.

Among other honors, he was awarded the Cavaliere de Croce Italia, which made him a member of Italian nobility, and an award from President Truman. He was an accomplished caricaturist; among his collection are caricatures of H.S. Truman, Lyndon Johnson, Mao

Henry Vars. Photo, Jack Howard.

TseTung, Jackie Kennedy, Charles de Gaulle, Pandit Nehru, Abdel Gamel Nasser, and many others.

Mr. Vars lived in Beverly Hills with his wife until his death on September 1, 1977. They had two children: one an attorney, the other a housewife, and four grandchildren. One grandchild is a medical student at Stanford University. Mr. Vars' older sister, Josephine Varszawska, was an opera star at La Scala in Milan, Italy. His younger sister, writer and pianist, Franka Frowa, was married to the Italian Consul in Warsaw, and now lives in Milan, Italy.

BOBBY VINTON:
OF "JA CIE KOCHAM ..." FAME

Mindy Kaye

A multi-talented musician as well as singer, Bobby Vinton was born in Canonsburg, Pa., a suburb of Pittsburgh, the son of a locally popular big band leader, Stanley Vinton. At 15 Bobby formed his own band with his friends from high school, playing clubs around the Pittsburgh area. At Duquesne University he studied the oboe and graduated with a degree in Musical Composition. In addition, he became proficient on other instruments in the band, including piano, clarinet, drums, saxophone and trumpet — talents he displays in his nightclub act and on his television show.

His television show, the "Bobby Vinton Show" is the highlight in what has been an illustrious and varied career. As a teenage singing idol of the 60s, he sold over 30 million records and became well established as a popular entertainer, performing in major nightclubs around the country. Some of the songs in his collection of more than a dozen gold records include "Roses Are Red," "Blue on Blue," "Blue Velvet," "Mr. Lonely," "There, I've Said It Again," and many more.

He has appeared on stage in the title role of *The Music Man* and in two major films with John Wayne, *The Train Robbers* and *Big Jake*. In addition to his own series, Bobby has guested on every major talk and variety television show.

His real comeback came when his Number One hit record, "My Melody of Love" was embraced by Polish Americans across the country as their theme song. He wrote the song with Polish and English lyrics. It became the first Polish American hit record, and Bobby became known as the "Polish Prince" and spokesman for millions of ethnics in America — not only Poles, but also Slavs, Italians, Greeks, etc. He explains, "These are the people I'm trying to reach and entertain with my show — the typical working people who come from a hard day's work and want to watch a happy, refreshing, lively show."

JERRY KASPER: MAN OF 'HIGH HOPES'

Jacek Przygoda

Jerome A. Kasper, son of Vincent Kasperowicz and Florence Haworth, was born June 4, 1913 in Philadelphia, Pa. As a ninth-grader he began playing a violin at Polish weddings. Although his first music instructor was his father, Jerry's subsequent instructors included Merle Johnston, foremost saxophone teacher in America; Edmund Wall, first clarinetist with the Franko Goldman band, and Frederick Moritz, principal bassoonist with the Los Angeles Philharmonic. To afford his music lessons, Jerry worked at one time as a hosiery knitter.

Kasper has played and made recordings with Jack Carson, Ginny Sims, Kay Kyser, Jack Smith, Rudy Vallee, as well as Benny Goodman, Tommy Dorsey, Frankie Carle, Horace Heidt, Frank De Vol, and other popular band leaders. He has appeared on TV shows including Groucho Marx, Wladzio Liberace, The King Sisters and The Betty White Show. He was under contract at Paramount Studios and other major movie studios.

Married to Valentine (Violet) E. Lipska-Kuhn in 1936, the couple have three children. Jerry V., Jr., was born in Philadelphia, while Dennis R. and Sandra N. were born in Van Nuys after the family settled in the San Fernando Valley in 1943.

The children have done well. Jerry received his Ph.D. from U.C. Berkeley in 1965, after doing undergraduate studies at California Institute of Technology in Pasadena. He now teaches at UCLA. Dennis received his Ph.D. from California Institute of Technology in 1971, after doing undergraduate studies at Loyola University, and now works for Planning Research Corporation. Sandra became the first woman in California to receive an A.A. degree in Escrow; she is married to Richard Sondomowicz, a Loyola University graduate.

In addition to his first love, music, Jerry Kasper Sr., has been a licensed real estate broker and has held an interest in an escrow company. His favorite field of business endeavor, however, is the stock market.

In music, Kasper can only think of one note at any given moment, which leads him automatically to the next note in the melody. His entire life has personified this truth: his thorough professional education and intelligent dedication to duty at any given time has

Jerry Kasper at the time of working on the "Betty White Show" (KNBC-TV, 1954).

helped him and his family become a well-molded unit of harmony in life, filled with "high hopes." He is in a possession of letter, dated March 19, 1960, that reads:

"Dear Mr. Kasper: This is just a brief note to express my appreciation to you for cooperation in making the record of 'High Hopes.' It has been a great success. Many thanks for your assistance. With every good wish with, I am, Sincerely — John F. Kennedy."

THE SEMONSKI FAMILY: ON THE LAWRENCE WELK SHOW

Mindy Kaye

Joseph Semonski (born in Dunmore, Pennsylvania) and Roberta Semonski (born in Netcong, New Jersey) worked as a musical act: he played accordion and she sang. Their first child, Diane, joined the act and was soon followed by five more daughters: Donna Lee (1958), Moann (1960), Valerie (1962), Audrey (1963) and Michelle (1968). Mr. Semonski originally owned a music store in Dover, New Jersey, and the girls worked in the store, where they had an opportunity to play all the insturments and receive musical training.

Mr. Semonski was Mayor of Great Meadows, New Jersey, and was also the church organist there. When the girls were old enough, they joined the choir and started singing at various town functions. Mr. Semonski retired at 35 to devote himself to his daughters' career, which he launched by taking the family to Disneyworld in Florida. They began performing in Orlando, Florida and received favorable notices in the major newspapers of the area. Lawrence Welk heard of them and auditioned them at a local television studio. Welk not only invited the sisters to come to California but also hired a teacher to teach them to sight-read music. They soon became regulars on the Lawrence Welk Show. They now reside in Van Nuys, California.

Diane, the oldest of the Semonski Sisters, has left the group to strike out on a solo career as songwriter and singer. The other five Semonski Sisters are still performers on the Lawrence Welk Show. In between television appearances, they are joined by their parents in a family act while touring in a motor home.

Mr. Semonski is scheduled to make a recording of Polish polkas and obereks in the near future with Lawrence Welk. Mr. Semonski will do the accordion solos.

The next goal for the Semonski Sisters is to have their own television series.

Semonski Family

GANNA WALSKA:
ALWAYS ROOM AT THE TOP

Jacek Przygoda

Always Room at the Top is the title of a book Ganna Walska wrote and had published in New York in 1943, which spans approximately 25 years of Madame Walska's unusual life. She was born in that part of Poland occupied by Russia, and as a young girl went to St. Petersburg. Enchanted by the Imperial Opera, Ganna took "ten minute" singing lessons. Later in Paris — she reminisces — they lasted "two half-hour periods weekly" with her "illustrious compatriot," Jean de Reszke. Her study of voice continued in New York as well as in Europe, as Mme. Walska kept pursuing her life-dream of becoming an operatic diva.

As a gift from her husband, Harold McCormick (of Harvest International, Chicago), she owned Theatre des Champs Elysées in Paris. "But the sensitivity of my Slavic nature was so great that I was never able to feel happy," Mme. Walska admitted. She also confessed, "while out, dressed up and bejeweled, in a smoky reception hall, sometimes with noisy jazz tearing at my ears, I would smile and look as if I were actually enjoying myself. But this again was only an attempt to overcome my timidity. At the bottom of my heart I was passionately craving the solitude of my room, to cry by myself."

In spite of occasional moods, Mme. Walska's unusually versatile personality illuminated Paris, London, St. Moritz, Salzburg, Rome and various United States cities. Finally, in 1939-40, she came to Santa Barbara to make her home. Here too she devoted her spiritual energy to the pursuit of her "Divine Destiny."

She wrote about America that it was "the only place in the world where a foreigner, within the first generation after immigration, and sometimes even within the space of a few years, becomes a typical citizen, a typical American." And she added, "America — perhaps gives nothing but certainly offers everything. For although we may not be born equal, at least we are born with equal potentiality and so can attain anything."

Mme. Walska did attain an economic independence besides exercising her spiritual freedom and following her artistic inclinations. She was lavishly generous with her money. For example, she was once asked by I. Paderewski's friends "for help to pay his debts on his

California property." Of course she did, without Paderewski ever knowing it. She helped others financially both in Europe and in America.

Ganna Walska remains a unique personality — even if she has been blind for the last two years. She may be blind physically but she still sees herself spiritually as an ardent Polish compatriot.

POLA NEGRI: UNFORGETTABLE QUEEN OF THE SILVER SCREEN

K.Cz./Czeslaw Olechno-Huszcza

Pola Negri, one of the most famous and beautiful film stars of the twenties, came to Hollywood from Poland in 1923 and immediately achieved the recognition of both critics and film fans. For several years she has lived in San Antonio, Texas, where she granted an interview to *Los Angeles Times* reporter Nicholas C. Chriss. *The Sun Times* (Chicago) reprinted this interview in its November 28, 1976 edition. It is a bit of news which will doubtless interest younger readers, who have never seen Pola Negri on the screen. Older readers, on the other hand, will recollect the "golden age" of American film and a fascinating actress of rare beauty and talent.

Barbara Apolonia Chalupiec was born 76 years ago in a part of Poland at that time annexed to Russia. She bagan her career at the age of 13. Chriss writes in his article about the career of Pola Negri in America, yet fails to mention the fact that, when she came to Hollywood, this very young actress was already a famous film star in Europe, a pillar of the German film industry. The first to notice Pola was the famous German director, Ernest Lubitsch, who at the outset of the Hitlerite movement had fled to the United States.

After working a year or so in German films, Pola Negri came to Hollywood. A brunette with green eyes and endowed with outstanding dramatic talent, she was one of the greatest attractions of American films for many years. Her name was linked with many excellent actors, but the greatest sensation was her romance with Rudolph Valentino, whom she intended to marry. The premature death of the actor in 1926 was a great blow to the star. Years later she married a Georgian, Prince Mdivani, but this marriage ended in divorce.

She sparked much admiration with her command of five languages, although she was considered an eccentric. In those days, a woman wearing slacks was unusual; a tiger on a leash was scandalous!

Translated and adapted from an article published on December 3-4, 1976 in a Polish newspaper, in Chicago.

In the interview with Chriss, Pola Negri mentions the Hollywood of fifty years ago. She speaks of her contemporaries, bound by contracts for many years, and of their financial troubles in spite of seemingly huge earnings. At that time, says Pola Negri, high earnings and low taxes enabled artists to provide for the future. The seventy-six year old actress lives in beautiful surroundings and experts have appraised her jewels alone at more than one million dollars.

Pola Negri resigned from her artistic career in 1943, although she has not been inactive. With a small circle of friends, she engaged in charitable work and devotes much time and money to the Universities of St. Mary's and Trinity in San Antonio, Texas. She lives from day to day, returning to the past only when she mentions her films.

Pola does not regret withdrawing from films. "In my days," she says, "they were more romantic; men were romantic and sentimental. In contemporary films we see naked men and women. Can one call that romanticism? Actresses of today place the main emphasis on their love affairs which bring them much publicity. In my days one gained publicity by hard work."

Her name was a household word at the height of her career, and millions of movie goers still remember this sparkling Polish actress with affection.

TED KNIGHT:
RECIPIENT OF EMMY AWARDS

Mindy Kaye

Tadeusz Wladyslaw Konopka was born on December 7, in Terryville, Connecticut, attended Terryville High School, and shortly after graduation entered military service with the First Army Group's Combat Engineers as a radio reconnaissance operator. He was one of the first American troops to enter Berlin during World War II and was awarded five Bronze Battle Stars for Distinguished Service.

After the War, Ted attended the Randall School of Dramatic Arts in Hartford, Connecticut. He worked weekends at Radio Station WCCC until landing a job with WFMY in Greensboro, North Carolina. He next moved to New York and worked with the American Theatre Wing on such classic radio and television programs as "Big Town," "Suspense," and "Lux Video Theatre." After receiving an offer from WJAR he worked in Providence, Rhode Island, where he hosted a children's show, and was master of ceremonies, as well as functioning as a newsman.

In 1957 the Konopka family set out for California. Ted found himself an agent, changed his name and became a prominent supporting actor in Hollywood. His credits include scores of radio and television commercials, and leading roles in legitimate theatre productions at The Player's Ring Theatre, the Omnibus Theatre, the Sombrero Playhouse in Phoenix, Arizona, and the Pasadena Playhouse.

His portrayal of anchorman Ted Baxter on the "Mary Tyler Moore Show" won him the National Academy of Television Arts and Sciences' 1972-73 and 1975-76 Emmy Awards for "Best Supporting Actor in a Comedy." In 1975 the National Father's Day Committee gave him the "Television Father of the Year" Award. In 1976 he received the Polish Ham Award from Warsaw.

In the fall of 1977 Ted will be starring in a Broadway play, "Some of My Best Friends," and in the fall of 1978 he will be appearing in a new television series for CBS.

He lives in Pacific Palisades with his wife Dorothy. They have three children: Ted, Jr., 21, a college student; Elyce, 16, and Eric, 14, both high school students.

KARL LUKAS: VERSATILE ACTOR

Kathy S. Hayes

Karol Lukasiak (Karl Lukas) was born August 21, 1919 in Lowell, Massachusetts. As a child he absorbed the Polish culture and language of his parents; to this day he retains his fluency in Polish (and several other Eastern European dialects) as well as a deep pride in his heritage.

In 1946, after serving four years in the United States Navy as a Demolition Squad Instructor at Texas, A & M, Lukasiak joined the famous Barter Theatre of Virginia, adopted the stage name "Karl Lukas" and toured for awhile with Ernest Borgine. This experience, combined with his rugged looks, won him the role of Lindstrom in the Broadway production of *Mister Roberts*. A six-month run of *Remains to be Seen* followed, and numerous small television roles.

By 1957 Lukas, married two years to Stephanie Kuduk, was a familiar face to millions of television viewers as Private Kadowski on the Phil Silvers Show (Sergeant Bilko). At the same time, Lukas appeared nightly in an off-Broadway production of *Volpone*. At midnight, after "Karl Lukas" was through with his demanding acting schedule, "Karol Lukasiak" began an eight-hour shift in a subway change-booth. At the time, the actor explained his hectic schedule thus: "You see, Lukasiak really wanted a steady job, but Lukas wanted to be an actor. So they compromised — they agreed to cut out sleeping."

Soon afterward, Karl and Stephanie moved to the West Coast and settled in the San Fernando Valley. Lukas' career continuted to flourish: movie credits include *Tall Story, Don't Give Up the Ship, Facts of Life, Under Fire* and *The Thrill of It All.* West Coast Theatre performances include *The Front Page, Of Mice and Men, The Cave Dwellers, People Need People,* and *Always with Love.* Television roles include co-starring and supporting roles in dozens of shows.

Karl Lukas' life belies the myth that actors lead unstable personal lives. He and Stephanie will celebrate their Silver Wedding Anniversary shortly; the couple are devoted to each other and to their two children, Valerie and Mark. The children are happy, outgoing, and active in sports. Mark plays high school basketball, and Valerie is a champion swimmer with over 30 medals, 80 trophies and 250 ribbons collected in nine years of competing. Karl Lukas is active in Knights of

Columbus, winning the "Outstanding Knight of the Month" in 1971. Stephanie, in addition to roles as wife and mother, is a secretary for the City of Los Angeles. They live in Canoga Park.

LORETTA SWIT: THE STAR OF "MASH"

Mindy Kaye

Originally from Passaic, New Jersey, she bagan her theatrical career in New York studying nights at the American Academy of Dramatic Arts while working as a secretary during the day. After two more years of study with Gene Frankel's repertoire theatre, she landed her first job as an understudy to the lead in the national company of *Any Wednesday*. She toured with the company for a year and then continued as understudy with the Broadway Company.

This was followed by roles in the road companies of *The Odd Couple* and *Mame*. When *Mame* closed she came to Los Angeles. Almost immediately, she was cast in a guest-starring role in *Gunsmoke* and has since guested in virtually every major series on television.

She is now beginning her sixth season as a star of the hit series, *MASH*. She has appeared in several television films, and also on a number of variety shows, as well as talk and game shows. Among them are: *Donny and Marie, The Captain and Tennile, Tony Orlando and Dawn,* as well as shows with Sonny Bono, Don Rickles, Merv Griffin, Mike Douglas, *Celebrity Sweepstakes, Password, $10,000 Pyramid, What's My Line? Masquerade Party* and *Match Game*.

In 1974 Ms. Swit was the recipient of the Polish American Congress — Texas Division Heritage Award in San Antonio, given annually to distinguished Americans of Polish origin who have attained prominence and brought honor to their heritage in different areas of activities.

In addition to acting, she enjoys writing and painting. She is adept at portrait work and often dabbles in watercolors and pen and ink drawing. She is also an avid tennis player.

She lives in the West Hollywood Hills with her two Pekingese dogs.

Loreta Swit in her M-A-S-H uniform.

THE "KRAKUSY": POLISH PRIDE AND JOY

Andrzej Nizynski

Following the second World War, a large number of young Polish families settled in Southern California to start a new peaceful life. The cultural center of this Polish community was at the Polish Parish on Adams Blvd. in Los Angeles. As part of the center's theatrical acitivity, four young couples under the direction of Mr. Jankowski organized a dancing group, which in 1956, for the first time in the Los Angeles area, presented Polish Folk Dances in traditional costumes at the International Folk Festival staged at U.C.L.A. For eight years this group represented Polish folk art by performances in Southern California.

In 1964, the Polish community started preparing for the celebration of Christianity of the Polish Nation — "The Millennium." The dance group decided to invite new, younger talent into their ranks and expand group activity. The purpose of the expansion was twofold: not only to grow in number, but also to convey the rich traditions, customs, and beauty of Polish heritage to the younger generation, born in the free world, far away from Poland. Many young high school and college students joined the group and transformed it into a dynamic, colorful dance group where two generations of Poles — parents and youth — joined their talents and energies in one cultural organization. This group, with great pride and dedication, performed well during "The Millennium" ceremonies conducted in the Los Angeles Coliseum in 1966. More than 60,000 Catholics, with His Eminence Cardinal McIntyre, admired the Polish costumes and performance.

A year later, a new chapter unfolded with the arrival in Los Angeles of Marylka Klimek, a famous Polish folk dancer of the Polish state folk ballet "Slask." With great enthusiasm and dynamic personality she helped in the reorganization of the group and introduced new dance arrangements. Within a year, Marylka Klimek became the dance director of the organization, whose members decided to call the ensemble "Krakusy."

Within a year Krakusy expanded their repertoire, staged many shows, and conquered the hearts of the Polish community in Los

Andrzej Nizynski has been involved in the Krakusy's activities. He lives in Los Angeles.

Angeles. They participated in the Annual Folk Festival at U.C.L.A. and Loyola University. For a number of years, Krakusy have proudly demonstrated Polish dances at the International Dance and Art Festival on Catalina Island, where they have performed in front of network television cameras. Krakusy have also received spontaneous applause in the prestigious Los Angeles Music Center for original choreography and beauty of their authentic Polish costumes. Krakusy staged an original Polish spectacular called "The Folklore of Poland" and entertained thousands in the San Gabriel Civic Auditorium and in Beverly Hills.

Marylka Klimek-George, Choreographer, "Krakusy."

The fame of Krakusy has spread to Nothern California. Invitations arrived from San Francisco and Sacramento where Krakusy presented Polish folk dancing, music and songs during the Copernicus celebrations in the Bay area. They repeated the performance at Loyola University, when the 500th anniversary of Copernicus was commemorated with a dedication of the astronomer's memorial sculpture.

Within a couple of years Krakusy have become well-known for the high level of artistic performance, beauty of costumes, and friendly attitude of the members, thus becoming a leading dance group among ethnic cultural organizations. Krakusy blends youth with charm, dance and ballet to portray ancient traditions and folk customs, which are still practiced in the Polish countryside. The authentic Polish-made costumes sparkle with color; elaborate hair styles and traditional music capture the originality of Polish folklore from the mountains to the sea.

Krakusy ensemble is the pride and joy of the Polish community in Southern California, participating in all Polish Parish religious ceremonies, art and folk festivals and historic observances. It is chartered as a cultural youth organization and as an independent section of the Polish Center with the purpose of cultivation and promotion of Polish folk culture in Southern California.

JAN PRASNIEWSKI: FIGURE SKATER

Margaret Kirk

Jan Prasniewski was born in 1955, in England, of Anglo-Polish parents. His father, Jerzy Prasniewski, brought his family to the United States in 1957, and they settled in California immediately.

When Jan was ten years old he developed a keen interest in the art and sport of figure skating. His hobby soon became a lifestyle, with an average of seven hours each day devoted to training sessions. This regimen continued for seven years and brought Jan many honors in competition, including the title of Intermediate Men's Champion, Southwestern United States and Silver Medallist at Pacific Coast Championships (comprising all top skaters west of the Rockies). He also competed successfully in Pair Skating events at the same time.

At seventeen, after graduation from high school, he was approached by the Ice Capades, and toured with their Eastern Company for one year in the United States and Canada. He then accepted an offer to perform in Japan and Hong Kong for one year in a small, exclusive ice show developed by American producers. His third year of professional skating took him on a ten-month tour of major cities in South America, including engagements in Mexico, Venezuela, Columbia, Ecuador and Peru, appearing in a principal role with Ice Follies International.

Margaret Kirk is the author's pen name.

Jan Prasniewski, figure skater, in a dazzling action.

Thus before his twenty-first birthday, he has already travelled a great deal and met many diverse people. He has performed his art in modern stadiums with impeccable facilities — and also in ancient bullrings, with the ice surface laid right over the sand, no roof except the night sky, and audiences of ten thousand persons lining the steeplytiered arenas of the Plaza Del Toros.

JOHN D. F. BLACK: TV WRITER

Mindy Kaye

John Black is a prominent writer of motion pictures and television scripts who has written over 100 television stories for many shows — comedies, dramas and melodramas — including "Shaft," "Man From Atlantis," "The People Doll," and for the "Mr. Novak" series, which had a Polish-American background. He is presently working for NBC on a pilot show with a scientific theme. In addition to producing, he will begin directing in 1977.

Mr. Black was born in Pennsylvania. His grandfather was a glassmaker from Poznan, Poland, but the original family name, Czarniecki, was arbitrarily changed to Black by U.S. immigration authorities because they could not spell it. After attending school in Pennsylvania, he served in the U.S. Army in the Korean conflict. Upon discharge, he relocated in California in order to enter the film and television industry.

Mr. Black and his wife Mary have three sons: Shaun, a graduate of University of California, Davis, is a Doctoral student in Biochemistry at the University of Michigan; Geoffrey is a pre-law student at the University of Southern California; and Christopher will be entering in 1977 Cinema School at the University of Southern California. John D. F. Black currently resides in Los Angeles.

Here is the list of his awards and nominations:

Television:

WITH A HAMMER IN HIS HAND, LORD, LORD/MR. NOVAK/
Writers Guild Award

AN ELEPHANT IS LIKE A TREE/MR. NOVAK/
Braille Award of Merit

DO NOT FOLD, SPINDLE OR MUTILATE
(ABC Movie of the Week)/
Writers Guild Award Nomination

THIEF (ABC Movie of the Week)/
Edgar Allen Poe-Mystery Writers of America Award
&
Emmy Award Nomination

John D.F. Black. Photo, Christine Rose.

FAT HANDS & A DIAMOND RING/INSIGHT/
Catholic Broadcasters of America
Certificate of Merit

ONCE UPON A TIME THERE WAS AIR YOU COULDN'T SEE/
ROOM 222/Emmy Award to ROOM 222 —
Best New Comedy Series

Motion Pictures:
SHAFT/Image Award Nomination

FRANK STANLEY: DIRECTOR OF TECHNICOLOR PHOTOGRAPHY

Mindy Kaye

He was born Franciszek Wladek Boguslavsky in New York City. He attended Stuyvesant High School and Columbia University in New York. His university studies were interrupted when World War II broke out and he joined the U.S. Marines. After returning from the service, he moved to California, where he started working for Technicolor Motion Picture Company in their Lab. He became a cameraman by doing special effects on Cecil B. De Mille's film, *The Ten Commandments* as an assistant cameraman. He was promoted to full cameraman in 1970, and ever since then he has been Director of Photography.

In his capacity of cameraman, Mr. Stanley has worked on locations throughout the world, including Viet Nam, Africa, Norway, Austria, Spain, France, Switzerland, Denmark, etc.

In addition to being Director of Photography, Mr. Stanley is presently President of the International Photographers' Union of the Motion Picture Industry and is active in their apprentice program, whereby ten young people are given the opportunity each year to receive training as cinematographers.

Mr. Stanley's wife, Marian, is a graphic artist, originally from Chicago. They reside in Santa Monica.

CONNIE GALE: DECOUPAGE ARTIST

Jacek Przygoda

The art of paper cutouts or decoupage (in French) or wycinanki (in Polish) has bene known for centuries throughout Europe, including Poland. In Santa Barbara, California, its able representative is Connie Gale. Born in Inowroclaw, Poland, Constance Andrzejewska came for the first time to the City of the Old Mission in 1934. She married Robert Gale, an industrialist, in Cleveland, Ohio, and the couple travelled extensively before settling down to a cattle ranch in Wyoming.

Paper cutout from the Kurpie Region (Poland) by Helena Borowska. Photo, Tadeusz Borowski.

After her husband's death, Constance studied decorative arts at the Maybelle Manning School in Boston. Then she devoted her spare time to the art of decoupage. Her two-story home has become a gallery of her various crafts. Wrote Verne Linderman in the Santa Barbara *News Press*, "decoupage is an old art, thought possibly to have originated in France, in the late 17th century. It involves decorating a box, a chest or screen with pasted cutouts (Connie principally uses lovely old prints). For her montages she plumps up the birds and flowers with papier-mache. Her birds seem to have individuality, as well as beauty and authenticity. The flowers acquire texture. It's an art that takes infinite patience. To her boxes Connie applies 25 to 35 coats of varnish. She usually has at least 10 going at once — and at once means a period of months."

Paper cutout from the Lowicz Region (Poland) by Helena Weyna. Photo, Tadeusz Borowski.

In Poland — explains Constance Gale — cutouts have been made by peasants for centuries. As a folk art it anti-dates paper. Like the Scythians, they used cloth, leather, and also bark of the trees, and sewed them on clothing as ornamentation. Later, when paper became available in the market and at country fairs, young girls bought it eagerly. Starting very young, girls and women developed an unusual proficiency with cutouts. [It can be added here that in the Los Angeles area, Helena Weyna, Helena Borowska, Janina Czyrko, Emilia Romanowska and others are known and admired for their cutouts, paper sculptures, artistic cards and dolls. They too have developed a great dexterity].

Constance Gale has also been interested in pottery and enamel, and is on the Women's Board of the Community Arts Association and has decorated several houses for the Assistance League Christmas House Tour. Connie is also affectionately known at St. Vincent's Day Nursery and the children there were a constant source of joy to her.

SZCZEPAN KAROL ZIMMER:
EDUCATOR, LIBRARIAN, WRITER

Jacek Przygoda

Szczepan K. Zimmer was born in Zborow, Poland, on December 26, 1903. He attended grammar school and gimnazjum in Tarnopol, and later studied at the University of King Jan Casimir in Lwow, where he received his Ph.D. in Philosophy in 1928. He went on to teach at the Trade Gimnazjum and Lyceum in Lwow and Przemysl.

When World War II broke out, Zimmer fought as a Lieutenant in the Polish Army. He was wounded and taken prisoner of war, and remained in German camps until May of 1945. While in the camps, he was active as a lecturer and was elected to serve as president of the Teachers' Association. He supervised and organized all educational activities in the camps.

After the War, in 1945, Zimmer was again elected by the Teachers' Association as President of the Central Committee for Polish Education in West Germany. He was later appointed by the Polish government in London as a delegate of the Ministry of Education. In time occupational authorities acknowledged him as Chief Inspector and Supervisor for Polish Schools in Displaced Persons Camps.

When British authorities relinquished their administrative power to the Germans in 1950, this statement appears in the report of a farewell meeting, dated February 22, 1950: "In recognizing the work of individuals he (Mr. F.O. Finch, Chairman of Displaced Persons Division, C.C.G., Lemgo, B.A.O.R.) made particular mention of Dr. Zimmer whom he had known for three and a half years and who had done such outstandingly good work for Polish education."

In his letter of June 26, 1950, Lieutenant Colonel (retired) H.H. Stackpoole, Displaced Persons Division, C.C.G., Chairman of the Polish Advisory Council, issued the following statement: "Dr. Szczepan Zimmer has been employed as the Senior Polish School Inspector in the British Zone for the past four years. He has also been the Education Member of the Polish Central Advisory Council. During this time he has done really wonderful work in connection with the Organization and Administration of Polish Education in the Zone which he raised to and maintained at a high level."

Not desiring to remain in Germany and not being able to return to his homeland, Zimmer emigrated to the United States in March of 1951. He settled in Chicago, and from 1951 to 1960 worked for Chicago Rawhide Manufacturing Company as a laboratory technician. During this time he married Halina Cieszewska (in 1953) and together they became involved in the activities of the Chicago Polonia.

Szczepan Zimmer.

Zimmer was instrumental in organizing the Political Committee for Polish Affairs for the Polish American Congress, and lectured in the Polish Extension University, Polish Arts Club of Chicago and other societies. In 1957 he and his wife organized a Stanislaw Wyspianski Exhibit to commemorate the 50th anniversary of the poet's death.

Later that year Dr. Zimmer published his first book, *Stanislaw Wyspianski, A Biographical Sketch*; the book was written in Polish and translated into English two years later by his wife.

In 1960 the Zimmers moved to California, and at age 57 Dr. Zimmer enrolled in post graduate courses in Library Science at Immaculate Heart College, and was awarded a Master's Degree in June of 1962. This enabled him to return to books in the capacity of medical research librarian at Los Angeles County General Hospital. Later that same year he organized the Nursing Library for the Nursing School. In 1966 he was appointed Medical Librarian in charge of Unit II Library (Women's Hospital). From 1968 until his retirement in 1973, Dr. Zimmer served as Senior Medical Librarian for all County Medical Libraries of Los Angeles County, University of Southern California Medical Center.

Dr. Zimmer's literary credits include numerous articles written in Polish and English for newspapers and magazines in Chicago, New York, London, Paris and Los Angeles, and covering such subjects as literature, history, education and public affairs.

PUBLICATIONS

1963 — "Jagellonian University Library in Krakow," article in *The Polish Review*, Vol. VIII, No. 1, New York. Followed by a revised and illustrated separate edition.

1968 — *Z Chalupy na Parnas* (From the Hut to Parnasus), a book, study of the poet Jan Kasprowicz. The Poets' and Painters' Press, London, England.

1969 — "Polskie Druki Cyrylickie" ("Polish Cyrillic Prints") an article (in Polish) in the London *Wiadomosci*, No. 1232, November 9, 1969.

1970 — "Pierwszy Polski Drukarz — Kasper Elyan" (The First Polish Printer — Kasper Elyan), article in *The Collective Papers — Polish Congress of Contemporary Science and Culture in Exile*, Vol I, London 9-12, IX, 1970.

1970 — "Krakow First Printing Press," article in *Antemurale*, Vol. XIV. *Institutum Historicum Polonicum Romae*, Rome, London, 1970.

1970 — Translation into Polish, Henry David Thoreau's "Civil Disobedience" with a biographical sketch. Poets' and Painters' *Press Quarterly*, May 1970, London.

1971 — Translation into English, Henry David Thoreau's "Life Without Principle" with an introduction, "The American Storm and Stress Period." Poets' and Painters' *Press Quarterly*, August, 1971.

1972 — Separate Bibliophile edition of the above translation by Poets' and Painters' Press. London, 1972.

STANISLAW KARPINSKI:
AVIATOR/ WRITER

Szczepan Zimmer

General Stanislaw Karpinski, well-known as the last Commander-in-Chief of the Polish Air Force in Great Britain, has an outstanding literary talent in addition to his extensive military achievements. The literary talent was revealed very early in his youth; it is interesting to note that his first poems were devoted to aviation. They were published in 1912 and 1913 in the Warsaw monthly magazine, *The Pilot and Motorist*.

As a pilot during World War I, and throughout his career, he wrote numerous articles devoted to professional aviation problems. In 1924 his article "Tactics of Air Warfare" appeared in the *Bellona* periodical of the Army General Staff. In 1924 Gen. Karpinski published a textbook, *The Building of Airports and Their Conservation*. During the following years, many of his articles appeared in various professional magazines.

Karpinski simultaneously produced literary works. The movie *The Winged Victor*, produced by Aero-film, was based on his screen play. In 1933 his literary gift revealed itself most profoundly in his book *Polish Wings*, dedicated to the youth of Poland. The story was based on Karpinski's adventures and experiences during his early long-distance flights. The book inspired many young readers to show their enthusiasm for flying. The author was deluged by letters from youngsters of all ages. Five years later, in 1938, he published a second book of the same nature, *A Flight Discontinued in Siam*.

With the outbreak of World War II, Lt. Col. Karpinski was working on the Army Air Force Staff. After Poland was overrun by the German and Russian aggressors, he organized the evacuation of the remaining Polish Air Force personnel through Romania to France, and after the surrender of France, on to Great Britain. During the course of W.W. II, as Chief of the Polish Air Force Staff, Commander of Bomber Air Force, Deputy Commander-in-Chief of the Polish Air Force, and finally its Commander-in-Chief, Karpinski gathered enormous material for posterity.

Szczepan Zimmer is well known in America and Europe as a "man of letters." He resides in Los Angeles.

After the war, Karpinski and his wife (also a pilot, whom he met during the war action) settled in California, where he devoted his time to writing. In 1960 *American Anthology* published "The Night in the Desert," a poem in English. From his arrival in the United States, Karpinski worked diligently on his war notes, which were finalized in 1976 and published as *Na Skrzydlach Huraganu* (On the Wings of the Hurricane), a historical novel in Polish. Four volumes were condensed to two huge books (1127 pages), giving a comprehensive picture of the Polish Air Force from the outbreak of W.W. II in 1939 until its end.

No other author could produce as complete a picture of the activities of the Polish Air Force during this period as Gen. Karpinski has. This is indeed a monument honoring all who fought and died believing in a Just Cause. Those who have survived will be grateful to Gen. Stanislaw Karpinski for reminding the world of their heroic battles and sacrifices for the elusive Freedom.

ALICIA POMIAN-POZERSKA: LYRIC POET

Jacek Przygoda

Alicia de Pomian-Pozerska Matulewicz has lived with her mother in San Francisco for 25 years. Born near Wilno, Poland, she grew in the atmosphere of an admiring love for her country and gave her first expression of this devotion in a collection of poems. Unfortunately, they were destroyed during World War II. Her first husband, a Polish Army officer, was murdered in the infamous Katyn forest massacre in April of 1940.

Fleeing with her mother from the Red Army advancing across Poland, she escaped via Czechoslovakia to West Germany where she worked for the American Red Cross. Her supervisor, Elois T. Spencer, helped Alicia, her husband, Jerzy Matulewicz and her mother to emigrate to the United States. Settled in San Francisco, Alicia worked for two decades at the Label Die-Cutting department of Diamond Graphic Arts Division at the Broadway Plant (subsequently acquired by Diamond National Corporation). Retiring as a supervisor and a member of the Lithographers and Photoengravers International Union, she earned an accolade of praises for her honest work.

She also won acclaim as a concert singer, social worker, writer and poet. Her novel *Goodbye Germany* was the first step on the literary road. Two volumes of poetry in Polish, *Najlonowe Skrzydla (The Nylon Wings)* and *Koncert E-moll i Wiersze Inne (Concert in E-Flat and Other Poems)*, were published in Great Britain. She has also written articles for the Polish American press in Chicago and has published her works in the Australian Polish magazine. She currently writes a column in the local Polish Mission Parish Bulletin in San Francisco.

Alicia Pomian-Pozerska's lyric poetry is predominantly characterized by her intense yet subtle feelings. They are of a religious and highly patriotic nature. As an artist she expresses the intimate vibrations of a very sensitive soul; as an observant writer she sees the beauty of the nearby Pacific, the majestic charm of the mountains, the specific qualities of Northern California — all varied and enchanting.

She returns quite frequently in her poems to the Polish landscape, the heroic people there, and their Heavenly Queen, the Blessed Mother, especially venerated at Ostra Brama (the Pointed Gate). Frederic Chopin occupies a unique place in her colorful yet musical poetry.

Her poems are also recognized by the critics for their didactic values. Whether they center upon religious and moral topics or aesthetic and philosophical subjects, the poems are deeply suffused with a genuine humility. The poet suffered enough as a human being not to undervalue the redemptive power of suffering and the treasure of sacrifice.

Alicia Pomian-Pozerska is convinced that, in the poet's creative work, inspiration is first, then the art of sharing it in simple ways with the reader; both are conditioned by an ever-present inner harmony, or at least the attempt to achieve it. This is permeated with a sincere love of God and men, of the world at large and nature.

VICTOR LONDZIN: HUMBLE POET

Jacek Przygoda

Victor Londzin (pen name Leszcza) is a poet who lives with his wife Olga in Los Altos, California; however, his heart and mind are still very much across the ocean in Europe, and, for that matter, in his native Poland.

As a cadet Corporal in the Polish Army, he took part in the 1939 militarily tragic campaign, and was then interned in concentration camps in Dachau and Gusen. After the liberation from the Nazi's terror, Victor launched his literary career. He became a contributor to the Polish newspapers in the West, writing poetry — his first love — essays, reviews of poetry, and prose.

In 1951 Victor emigrated to the United States, where he continued his literary pursuits. He has been a contributor of poetry to major periodicals in the Polish language on this side of the Iron Curtain. Also to his literary credit are translations into the Polish language of the works of modern British, American, German and Czechoslovakian poets. He has published four books, all in Polish: *Time and Insanity*, 1947; *Wooden Horses*, 1967; *A Sketch Book*, 1969 (and *Three Walls*, currently in press).

Londzin has been recognized in the *International Authors and Writers Who's Who*, 1976, and received the Poets and Painters Press Award in London in 1967. His contribution to *Conrad Alive*, a publication in memory of Joseph Conrad's birth centennial, will continue to stand out.

Some of Londzin's critics express the opinion that the form of his poetry is difficult to classify according to accepted standards. They are overlooking the fact, though, that a poet is something more than simply a person with the ability to rhyme a given number of stanzas; a poet is someone able to give humble expression of his inner creative world. And this humility, a very human virtue, personifies Victor Londzin, a poet still searching for form and content.

EWA EMILL: WRITER IN TWO COUNTRIES

Halina Zimmer

Ewa Emill was born in Lwow, Poland. She graduated from Gimnazjum and went on to attend the University of King Jan Casimir, where she supported herself by working in the library. Her first poetry was published in the daily newspapers. She belonged to a group of young poets sponsored by Michal Pawlikowski; their first poetical efforts drew very favorable reviews.

During the Second World War she married a fellow-poet, Jan Mazur, who died shortly after the marriage. Ewa took active part in discussions with poets and writers; seven of her poems appeared in a collection published by the underground press, entitled *The Loyal Flame*. She was also a member of the underground Polish Army.

After the war, Ewa left Lwow for Krakow. She continued her studies at the Jagiellonian University there, and graduated with a Masters' Degree in Philosophy. She worked for a publishing firm, first as a proof reader and later as style editor for *Czytelnik (Reader)*.

In 1953 two of her plays were almost simultaneously performed in subsidized theaters: the drama *W Stwoszowym Domu* (In the Home of Stwosz), directed by Iwo Gall, and a comedy, *Mieszkanie* (Apartment 3), directed by Niewiarowicz. Both plays were performed over 100 times, which is most unusual for contemporary playwrites. The play *In the Home of Stwosz* was also published in book form. The Polish Radio presented several of her radio plays. Somehow, after this wave of success, Ewa Emill found herself unable to continue her literary work in Poland.

Ewa Emill came to California in 1959, at the invitation of her younger sister, Jadwiga Wagner, and her husband. Here she married Adam Skoczowski and chose to make California her permanent home, but it was to be many years before she returned to her literary work.

In 1972 Ewa published her first novel, *Small Lupki Wielkie*; in 1974 a second novel, *Parkowa 8* (Park Avenue 8) appeared, and in 1977 a third novel, *Goscie* (Guests) was published. For the 30th anniversary of the Polish Theatre in London in 1977, Ewa Emill wrote a play, *Hidden Prometheus*, which was honored with an award.

Halina Zimmer, wife of Szczepan, is a translator of the Polish language. They reside in Los Angeles.

The Polish Radio at one time pronounced her a talented playwrite with a deep theatrical intuition and masterful dialogue. Tadeusz Kwiatkowski wrote in December of 1953 in *Dziennik Polski*, "she has true poetical and playwrite's talent." In *Tygodnik Powszechny* #437, Kazimierz Bronczyk wrote: "The author reveals a deep knowledge of contemporary reality, based upon thorough study of source material. She brought out the colorful atmosphere of Krakow during the Renaissance period."

Ewa Emill. Photo, Ted Gurney, Walnut Creek.

Reviewers of Emill's second phase of literary work — outside Poland — are also most favorable in their evaluation. Regarding her book *Small Lupki Wielkie*, Czeslaw Dobek wrote for the London *Tydzien Polski*, "there appears a new remarkable figure, whose work shows unquestionable knowledge of writing." Stefan Legezynski in *Gazeta Niedzielna* No. 1272 appraised her work: "From a literary point of view it is in an unusual class ... the book is professionally written." Tamarra Karren, *Wiadomosci*, No. 1401, wrote, "If this is a debut, then it is a promising debut, and to the emigre literary world another writer of stature is added."

Emill's second book, *Park Avenue 8*, also brought favorable reviews. Jadwiga Rapacka, in *Dziennik Polski*, April 23, 1975 commented, "Ewa Emill is without doubt a talented writer ... the story is interesting, action vivid, with a light dialogue. The only objection found is perhaps too many scenes of atrocity." Janina Surynowa-Wyczolkowska, in *Tydzien Polski* (June 21, 1975) stated: "I am afraid that the book will be read as a thriller ... However, her cynicism is only an exterior cover of its contents beneath, which is a deep feeling for the tragically lost human beings ..."

Ewa Emill's latest book, *Guests*, portrays life among the Polish American ethnic group in Northern California. It also vividly acquaints the reader with the beauty of this State.

EDWARD J. TOLOSKO:
NOVELIST FROM LOMPOC

Jacek Przygoda

Because of his unique perseverance, the first novel of Edward J. Tolosko will be published in 1978 by Farrar, Straus and Giroux. One of seven children, Edward Tolosko was born on June 23, 1922 in San Francisco. After his mother's death in 1928, Ed was brought up in an orphanage in San Rafael, which was a definite factor in his character formation. He worked with the Civilian Conservation Corps on Mount Shasta and subsequently served in the Navy during World War II.

While in Waukegan, Illinois, Ed met and later married Doreen Shauer, a professional singer and Illinois beauty queen. The couple has been blessed with five children; LeeAnn, married to Donald Pharis, Alane Susan, Margaret Jean, Jeanne Louise, married to Stanley Leroy Brinley, and a son, Edward J. Tolosko II. All have exceptionally talented hands and creative minds. Each of them, as their parents hope, will make a mark in this world on their own achievements.

After visiting with the Tolosko's, it was not difficult to follow and admire Ed's life. He is not only a craftsman with his hands, but an original creator in his novels. "Missing family life as a child," confided Mrs. Tolosko, "has made Ed a superior family man, a loving father and husband. His thirst for knowledge began with the great respect he had for his father, Michael, who spoke several languages and was expert at anything he did. This above all was what Ed has emulated.

"Through the child-rearing years, when finances were meager, he had devoted any spare time to devouring encyclopedias. Unable to attend school after the tenth grade, he really had a lot of homework to catch up with. During that period in our life, he started writing poetry for our children. Much humor and tenderness were displayed in these poems. He also looked to their musical education; while telling them stories, they listened to classical symphonic records."

"Novel ideas flowed on paper," continued Doreen. "There were many starts, many different avenues of approach to a major effort at story writing. The long planted germ finally led in 1967 to the beginning of a serious literary work, which has become Ed's first novel, *Sakuran*." The word could mean in Japanese "the path a cherry

blossom petal takes when driven by a troubled wind," or "the paths and destinations of the petal that only God knows of."

As Sue Edelman wrote in the *Lompoc Record* of August 25, 1977, an "electrician, poet, TV repairman, artist, inventor, mechanic, and now fledgling author, Edward J. Tolosko . . . treats (in his novel) another region of the world, another epoch, another culture. His heroes are Samurai — of the prestigious warrior caste of the 13th-century feudal Japan."

When Edward J. Tolosko flew during World War II over Japan, he became interested in that remote part of Asia. Then after the War, while visiting with an Air Force Colonel in Phoenix, Arizona, he saw there a doll representing a Samurai which belonged to the Colonel's Japanese wife. The visitor was fascinated by the doll's fierce expression.

"Tolosko learned," as Sue Edelman wrote, "that Samurai were incredibly skilled in martial arts — of utmost importance to defense in a society as yet unfamiliar with gunpowder. Besides physical perfection, the Samurai were known for their 'giri' . . . total focus drive — great concentration and devotedness to a task."

Tolosko's task from then on was to study the life of Samurai. That he did with the help of his energetic wife. It took almost ten years to arrive at the finished product, but a literary agent in New York found the unsolicited manuscript in substance "perfect as is." After rewriting and some polishing by the author himself, the novel was purchased. That *Sakuran* is only the beginning is the hope of its enthusiastic author, a hope shared by his admiring wife and all five children.

PART
FOUR

POLISH AMERICAN
SOCIETAL LIFE
IN CALIFORNIA

Americans of all ages,
all conditions
and all dispositions
constantly form associations.

Alexis De Tocqueville,
Democracy in America (1835)

immigrant . . . musical chairs

immigrant,
>   *where are you showing?*

>   hoping for gold,
>   trying to break the mold?
>   was it rust you found,
>   empty lust,
>   california or bust?

immigrant,
>   *who are you going?*

>   your children know,
>   they took your trust,
>   sprinkled with old world dust,
>   invaded your dreams,
>   brought your yesterday schemes.

immigrant,
>   *what are you knowing?*

>   alive in two worlds,
>   watching the sands,
>   the countless passing hands,
>   waiting,
>   one more
>   trip home.

                                    E.G. Dabrowska Wissema

AMERICA NEEDS ETHNICITY

Geno Baroni

I met an American Cardinal last year who told me he would be glad when the Bicentennial ended because then, "This ethnic thing will go away."

"It won't go away, Your Eminence," I said, "It won't ever go away."

America needs ethnicity; it needs to understand its own consciousness, its roots, so that it can have a full awareness of what it is as a nation. And yet there are many who, like the Cardinal, wish that ethnicity would go away. The American public is afraid of the word "ethnic." We may recall how upset people were when President Carter used the term "ethnic purity." The press was ready to make this remark into a major campaign issue and many liberals became very upset and worried.

There is a tendency in America, and it is sharpened by the attitudes of many members of the press, to feel that being ethnic is being divisive. There is a tendency to equate ethnicity with being less than a full American — with being aside from, apart from the mainstream of American life. Unfortunately, it is not only the non-ethnics who take this approach. Many ethnics also operate in this fashion.

Many young people do not know who they are. Second and third generation Italians, Poles, Greeks or Lithuanians act as if they were just a little bit ethnic. "We're Americans all the way," they say. And even those who are supposed to be leaders act like this.

It is this type of attitude that must be defeated. America needs the diversity and pluralism that ethnicity brings to it. It needs the uniqueness of our multiple cultural traditions as a counterforce to the tendency toward sameness in American life. There is an overwhelming conformity, a uniformity in America, that can strangle the individual. The background of a rich ethnic tradition can help individuals as well as the nation to combat this movement toward sameness.

A cultural oversoul resides in each of us. This oversoul reflects the backgrounds of our fathers and their fathers before them. It is a sense

Rev. Msgr. Geno Baroni is the assistant secretary of the Department of Housing and Urban Development. He is also Director of the National Center for Urban Ethnic Affairs in Washington, D.C. Reprinted by permission from *Perspectives*, Washington, D.C., Jan-Feb. 1977.

of tradition, of custom, that our forebears brought with them when they came to this new land — to this new America. It must not be lost.

This does not mean that we should be ethnic chauvinists. We should not exalt individual backgrounds at the expense of others. Rather, we should have a participatory ethnicity in which each person is respected for what he is and for his own culture.

There is not yet enough of a sense of pride in our ethnicity. But there are encouraging signs. Barbara Mikulski has been elected to Congress. She is a Polish American who will be more of an American ethnic virtually than any of the ethnic Congressmen now in office. She knows who she is and she knows what her roots are. Both Presidential candidates had ethnic advisors in the election; both had apparently come to the realization that ethnicity was a factor that could not be totally overlooked.

Much work, however, remains to be done. We need to create a society that is a cultural democracy — that has respect for our cultural rights. America must become comfortable when talking about ethnics. No one should become tense because I want to know my own language, my own culture.

Ethnicity should be taught in the schools of America. We should form coalitions among ethnic peoples so that we will have a united front when we go to the educational institutions to ask for courses in our own languages and traditions.

It is important that our young people get involved in civic affairs, in the media, politics, in business. We ought to support and encourage their efforts. We should fight for a third American century that will be a century of cultural justice. We should articulate a new dimension in our society so that a person can be both ethnic and American. We must understand each other and learn to live with our diversity. And America must finally recognize that its greatest strength and unity will be found not by attempting to create a homogeneous society but rather through legitimizing our ethnic and cultural pluralism.

A PROFILE OF THE POLISH AMERICAN COMMUNITY IN NORTHERN CALIFORNIA

Jan Kowalik

The 1970 population census established the number of Polish Americans in California (first generation included) as 115,584.[1] The difference in the American way of interpreting the origin of immigrants challenges the accuracy of these statistics, however. For example, since Poles who arrived from the occupied Poland prior to 1919 were not classified according to their nationality but on the basis of their citizenship, many were registered here as Austrians, Germans or Russians.

Additionally, many persons of Polish origin who have not attained American citizenship were not included in the census. The number of such "aliens" in California was registered at 2,660.[2] Consequently, scholars estimate the number of Poles in California at closer to 125,000.

In order to determine the true size of the Polish American community in Northern California, the 1970 population census and the Standard Metropolitan Statistical Areas (S.M.S.A.) for San Francisco-Oakland and San Jose have been researched.[3] Additional information has been sought from publications concerning the demographic profile of the San Francisco City memberships of various organizations, and from reports of social workers.[4]

Analyzing this data, it has been established that about 25,000 or 22% of all Polish Californians live in Northern California. About 15,000 of them reside in the San Francisco-Oakland-San Jose area, with 4,000 in Sacramento and vicinity. The remaining 6,000 are dispersed within other locations of Northern California.

One of the characteristics of the Poles in San Francisco is their residential stability. The families live in the same house for ten years or longer, and when changing residence, move usually within the same county or state. Those leaving California are in the minority. The steady influx of newcomers, comprising 13% of Polish population (as in other groups coming to California) consists primarily of older individuals seeking better health or desirous of joining relatives. Of

Adapted from "Polonia in Northern California and the History of Its Ethnic Pastorate." *Migrant Echo*, 1976. San Francisco.

those who registered, only 7% were under 24 years, and 68% were over 50 years of age. Therefore the stability could be attributed to the aging society.

According to statistical findings, almost one half of the entire population of San Francisco (371,045 or 44%) comes from some foreign country. Among the ethnic groups, Poles occupy the eighth place; 2,986 of them consider Polish to be their native tongue. One would surmise that Polish is the language generally spoken by the Polish Americans.

A survey shows that of 14,315 Polish Americans in Northern California included in the census, 5,584, or 39%, claimed Polish as their native tongue; 4,555 (32%) listed English, and 2,358 (16%) considered Yiddish to be their native tongue. Other languages mentioned were: German (4.6%), Ukrainian (1.35%), Russian (0.97%), French (0.77%) and Lithuanian (1.29%).

When the Census Bureau distributed its questionnaire with respect to education, it took into account persons over 25 years old exclusively. Of 5,303 Polish Americans (2,961 men and 2,342 women) answering the questionnaire, 42% attended grade school, 31% completed high school, and 26% attended or graduated from college. These statistics, however, do not include the hundreds of Polish immigrants whose European education qualifies them for university positions and for other highly specialized occupations in science and industry.

The greatest percentage of Poles in Northern California is employed either professionally or semi-professionally. Second place is held by skilled craftsmen, followed by merchants, office employees, operators and public service employees. The smallest percentage is comprised of unskilled laborers. The percentage of self-employed Poles, and those in the military, was not tabulated.

The primary religious affiliation of Polish Americans is Roman Catholic. Since the American Hierarchy does not distinguish between the ethnic elements in its annual parochial reports, the exact number of Roman Catholics among Polish Americans is unknown. In addition, Poles also affiliate with Greek and National Catholics, Jews, and numerous denominations of Protestant faiths.

No evidence could be found of the existence of a Polish Catholic church holding regular services in the San Francisco Bay area until after World War II. When Archbishop Joseph Gawlina, to whom the Apostolic See entrusted the care of thousands of Polish immigrants, appealed for a Polish priest, Cardinal Francis Spellman of New York and Archbishop John J. Mitty of San Francisco were the first to respond. As a result of an agreement between the San Francisco

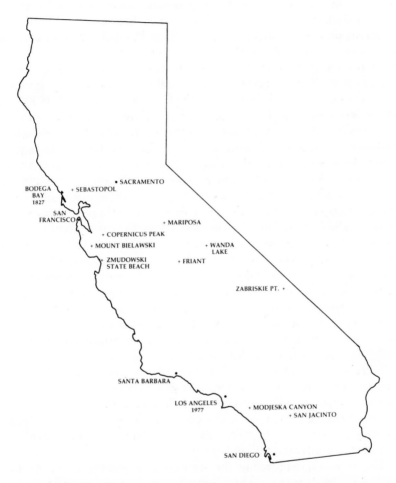

POLISH ECHOES AND STEPS ON THE "SANDS OF TIME" (1827-1977) IN THE THIRTY-FIRST STATE OF THE UNION. Graphic work by Martin Dabrowski, and Catherine Jeschke.

Archdiocese and the Vicar General of the Polish Roman Catholic Mission in Germany, eleven priests were admitted to Northern California and assigned to duties in parishes, hospitals, or chaplains of religious orders. Of this group, Fr. Francis Wajda eventually became the unofficial chaplain of the Polish community.

In his letter to Polish priests sent during the spring of 1955, Archbishop Mitty instructed them to establish three liturgical centers, one of which was to be located at the Church of the Nativity in San Francisco[6] which has served the Slavic population since 1902. With the division of the San Francisco Archdiocese in 1962, the Archbishop reduced the number of centers to two. The activities at the centers were limited to monthly liturgical services and to eucharistic benedictions in Polish. Otherwise, Poles were to continue attending all other services at their respective parish churches. Later, the Archbishop gave verbal permission for a monthly Mass and prayers in Polish to be held at Lone Mountain College in San Francisco.

The duties of the Polish priests who came to Northern California at the end of World War II were only a fragment of their actual activities. The Poles who had come directly from Poland were accustomed to and continued to expect the clergy's active participation in those ethno-cultural traditions which were inseparably linked with religious practices. Thus the newly-arrived priests became moderators of the organization "Veritas" (Frs. Myrda and Woznicki), advisors in religious matters to the Polish American Congress, chaplains at Polish Children's Summer Camps (Frs. Klaia, Maciejewski and Woznicki), Polish Radio Program producers and guest speakers (Frs. Guttman, Degner, Dobkowski, Woznicki, and Przygoda from Los Angeles). Three became financial sponsors and backers of the Polish Documentation Studio (Frs. Przygoda, Stasiak and Woznicki), founded and directed by Jan Kowalik.

By a turn of good fortune, the offer of permanent religious services by the Polish Roman Catholic clergy (Joseph Kania, General Superior of the American-Canadian Province of the Society of Christ), supported by the Polish American Congress, California Northern Division (president, Z. Zakrzewski, Prof. G. Lerski and Prof. W. Sworakowski), Archbishop Joseph T. McGucken of San Francisco, in his decree of February 4, 1976, established the first Polish Mission Parish.[7] Fr. Wojciech Baryski, S.Ch., is in charge of it. St. Adalbert, the Martyr, was selected for its patron saint.

In addition to the individual memberships, the Polish Mission parish enjoyed the participation of 220 families by the end of May, 1976.

It is obvious that during the past twenty five years, the economic and spiritual profile of the Polish American community in Northern

California has undergone a noticeable change.

While continuing in the awareness of their ethnic heritage, the Polish Americans remain loyal to their adopted country, and through the establishment of the Polish American Congress, California Northern Division, Polish Radio programs, Polish Credit Union, Polish Veterans of WWII, Post No. 49, and other organizations, have contributed to the growth of socio-cultural life in Northern California.

REFERENCES

1. U.S. Department of Commerce, *1970 Census of Population.* Subjects Reports, National Origin and Language. Washington, D.C., June 1973.
2. U.S. Department of Justice, Immigration and Naturalization Service. *1974 Annual Report,* App. 6. Washington, D.C.
3. U.S. Department of Commerce, Op. Cit., pp 288, 291, 294 and others.
4. Johanesen, Harry, "A Demographic Profile of the City." *San Francisco Sunday Examiner and Chronicle,* Oct. 29, 1972.
5. Bolek, Francis, *Who's Who in Polish America,* Third Edition. Harbinger House, New York 1943. Damian S. Wandycz, Ed., *Register of Polish American Scholars, Scientists, Writers, and Artists.* The Polish Institute of Arts and Sciences in America, New York, 1969. Jan Kowalik, articles published in *Migrant Echo,* "American Scholars, Scientists and Technicians in California," April 1973; "American Artists and Writers of Polish Origin in California," January & February 1974; "American Motion Picture Artists, Producers, Composers and Conductors of Polish Origin in California," April 1974; "American Writers, Publishers and Journalists of Polish Origin in California," January, February and March, 1975.
6. Archbishop John J. Mitty's letter to Polish priests in the San Francisco Archdiocese, March 10, 1955.
7. Joseph Thomas McGucken, Archbishop of San Francisco. Decree erecting a Polish Catholic Pastoral Mission, February 6, 1976.

POLISH AMERICAN CONGRESS: NORTHERN CALIFORNIA DIVISION

W.J.

The Northern Division organizes national celebrations, lectures, social evenings, and since 1971, an annual bazaar which has become the traditional meeting place of hundreds of Poles from the entire region. Since 1969 the Division, with the aid of affiliated organizations, broadcasts a Polish Cultural Hour program over radio station KQED-FM in San Francisco. This is the only hour-long radio program in Polish in the United States that is not interrupted by advertisements. A Political Committee initiated protests against communist domination and organized support for the Polish people's right to self-determination and full independence.

The Division is active in national conventions of P.A.C. and supports activities of local Captive Nations Committees. It initiated the creation of the Polam Federal Credit Union in 1974 and the Polish Missionary Parish in San Francisco in 1976. In December 1976 the Division had fourteen affiliated Polish organizations and 65 individual and supporting members.

POLISH CLUBS IN THE SAN FRANCISCO BAY AREA

Zdzislaw Zakrzewski

The first Polish organization in California, formed in 1863 and known as the Polish Society in California, still exists as Lodge #7 of the Polish National Alliance, a nation-wide fraternal organization.

In the years following 1863 many other Polish clubs and societies have formed in the San Francisco Bay area. These organizations have a variety of purposes, objectives and programs. They organize and present bazaars, dances, dinners, parties, banquets, festivals, art exhibitions, and many other entertaining and cultural events.

All are affiliated with the Northern California Division of the Polish American Congress, a nation-wide umbrella organization of Americans of Polish descent. The Polish American Congress coordinates and assists each club to represent Polish ethnic culture and interests, and also initiates various projects aimed at enhancing knowledge and recognition of the Polish historical and cultural heritage.

Polish Clubs in the Bay Area include:

In San Francisco, Polish American Catholic University Association (Veritas); Polish American Educational Committee; Polish Literary and Dramatic Circle; Polish National Alliance, Council No. 4; Polish National Alliance, Lodge No. 7; Saint Stanislaus Society; United Polish Societies of San Francisco, and Polish Pastoral Mission for the Archdiocese of San Francisco.

In Oakland there are: Polish American Society of East Bay, and Polish Veterans of World War II, Post 49. The list is rounded out by: POLAM Federal Credit Union in Foster City; Polish American Club of the Peninsula in Palo Alto; Polish American Social Club in Sacramento; Polish Home Army Veteran's Circle in Alameda, and Polish National Alliance, Lodge No. 3159 in Oakland.

Zdzislaw Zakrzewski is a former president of the Pol. Am. Congress, Northern Calif. Div. and runs POLAM Federal Credit Union. He lives in Foster City, Ca.

POLISH CULTURAL HOUR RADIO PROGRAM IN SAN FRANCISCO

W.J.

During the summer of 1969, president Jan Grycz (now deceased) of the Northern California State Division of the Polish American Congress, together with its secretary Adam Pietras, searched for a means to reach a broader spectrum of Polonia in the San Francisco metropolitan area. They decided upon a weekly program in Polish, broadcast over a small local radio station. When the growing audience required a station with more power, the program moved in December 1969, to KQED-FM, an educational station in San Francisco, broadcasting on 88.5 FM. The program (each Sunday from 7:00 to 8:00 p.m.) can now be heard over 50 miles away and the quality of reception has been improved to professional standards.

Broadcast as it is from an educational station, the Polish Cultural Hour carries no commercials. The entire hour, conducted in Polish, is dedicated to cultural matters, music by Polish composers and performers, information on Poland, and announcements of the fourteen organizations affiliated with the Division, among them youth and veterans groups.

The average Polish Hour begins with a short talk on religious matters conducted by the chaplain of the Polish Missionary Parish in San Francisco. In past years, when there was no Polish parish in that city, Rev. Jacek Przygoda from Los Angeles provided taped lectures on religious and philosophical themes. Usually 15 minutes of press reviews is presented, drawn from the American, Polish and emigre press and concentrating on events of interest to the Polish Community. The second half of the Hour usually features current cultural, historic or literary events as well as commemorations of Polish national anniversaries and similar topics.

Since January 1972, Mrs. Helena Sworakowska has been directing the program, preparing the weekly material, narrating it, and searching for local talent to appear on special programs. In a program dedicated to the Warsaw uprising, for example, nine former members of the Home Army took part and discussed personal experiences. During programs dedicated to Generals Anders and Kopanski, more than a dozen former officers and soldiers under their command presented their personal reminiscences about these military leaders. In the past five years, over one hundred local Poles (and many visitors from other parts of the world) were invited to participate in the Cultural Hour of the Polish American Congress in San Francisco.

All of the work on the program — directing, writing, selecting music, performance and technical operations — is based on volunteer participation. Not even transportation or other expenses are refunded. The expenditure for this program is now about $3,000 yearly. This is covered by contributions from affiliated organizations, by donations from listeners and, in part, from the income of an annual bazaar. American friends, non-Poles, contributed in the past five years donations of over $2,500.

In the period 1969-1976, a total of 380 Polish Cultural Hours have been broadcast to the Polish American community in the San Francisco area. A modest estimate of 9,500 hours of volunteer work invested in this program indicates the enormous effort which has made this program possible.

POLAM — FEDERAL CREDIT UNION IN SAN MATEO

Bruno B. Shatyn

POLAM FCU had been founded on Nov. 30, 1973. Its charter provides that POLAM will be a cooperative association organized to promote thrift among its members and to accumulate a fund from their savings to make needed loans to members for useful purposes at reasonable interest rates. Any member of Polish American Congress may be a member of POLAM.

At the Charter Organization Meeting called to order by Mr. Zdzislaw Zakrzewski, the President of the Polish American Congress, Northern California Division, the first Board of Members had been elected as follows: Zdzislaw Zakrzewski, President; Michelle Carmody, Vice-president; Krystyna Chciuk, Secretary; Stanislaw Pieczynski, Treasurer; George Janiszewski, Bruno Shatyn and John Smelski, Members of the Board. Mrs. Zofia Zakrzewski had been elected as Assistant Treasurer.

In the three and a half years of existence, POLAM grew from initially 11 members to an imposing number of 346 with 255 shareholders below $2,000 each. From the initial capital of less than $1,000 to the amount of $870,000 and expecting to pass one million dollars in the calendar year 1977.

POLISH VETERANS OF WORLD WAR II OAKLAND, POST NO. 49

Kazimierz J. Porebski

The principle activity of Polish Veterans Post #49 for the Bicentennial year was obtaining veterans rights for its members. The local committee cooperated with the Central Committee in New York and the Northern California Chapter of the Polish American Congress. Members of the Post sent 120 mailgrams and letters to the United States Senators in Washington, D.C. Similar action by other posts in the country resulted in the passage of HR 71, the Polish Veteran's Bill, in Congress, which was ultimately signed by President Ford. This bill provides some veterans' rights to those Poles who served during either of the World Wars and who have held United States citizenship for at least ten years.

In 1976 the Post was saddened by the death of Rev. Zygmunt Dobkowski, a former army chaplain, and by the passing of Tadeusz Butler. Both were buried with military honors. Many other functions crowded the Post's calendar year, and provided a sense of fraternity for its members.

The author is president of this organization.

POLISH SOCIAL CLUB IN SACRAMENTO

Bohdan Witkowski
(Translated from Polish by Jerzy Prasniewski)

In 1976 the Polish American Social Club of Sacramento, California, conducted twelve general meetings, held on the third Sunday of each month. Average attendance was approximately 100 persons, many of whom assisted in preparing and serving the food which preceded each meeting. The club does not have its own quarters, but a fund for this purpose is growing from year to year and today represents several thousand dollars.

In addition to monthly meetings, four public parties were organized in 1976, each drawing an attendance of about 300 people. In December, members enjoyed a traditional Christmas celebration, with gifts for the children from the ever-popular St. Nicholas. In July a summer picnic was organized to round out the social calendar of the club's year.

The spiritual side of the club's activities has been greatly enhanced by the creation of a Polish sub-parish at St. Anne's Church, in Sacramento. The chaplain is Father Boleslaw Wdowiak (known as Father Bosko) of the order of St. Paul from Bright Mount in Czestochowa, Poland. He also serves as assistant pastor of St. Anne's parish where he celebrates on the third Sunday of every month a Holy Mass in Polish.

A resounding success that can be claimed by the Club and Father Wdowiak has been the creation of a Polish Language School. The school has obtained proper recognition by appropriate educational authorities in the area, and from January 1977 has transferred to regular classes at the Adult School Center. An unusual feature of the classes is that they are attended by members of the community at large, and not only those of Polish descent.

The Club meets at 33rd and 9th Streets, Sacramento.

THE ONGOING WONDER: OUR LADY OF THE BRIGHT MOUNT POLISH PARISH IN LOS ANGELES

Jacek Przygoda

One of the brightest monuments of the Polish American heritage in Southern California is the parish of Our Lady of the Bright Mount in Los Angeles. Especially noteworthy was and is the role of the laity, for without them there would not be a Polish Roman Catholic parish in this part of the country.

As in so many cities and towns across America, lay Polish Catholics settled in this city and its environs, and immediately began seeking a priest of their ancestral heritage. The first was Fr. Jakub Organisciak, who in 1908 celebrated Mass for Poles in the cathedral of St. Vibiana. How large was this original congregation it is difficult to ascertain. It is known, however, that according to the U.S. population census of 1900, there lived in Los Angeles 65 people whose country of birth was Poland (Russian) and 55 from "other" Poland; i.e., 120 Poles (not all Catholics!). As is known, there was no Polish state after the third partition of Poland by Russia, Austria and Prussia (in 1795) until 1918; hence the official U.S. census had difficulty in identifying foreign born Poles.

In the same year, 1908, a committee to collect funds for building a Polish church in Los Angeles was organized. By the end of that year, it was ready for religious services. By 1912, Fr. Konstanty Marciniak took Fr. Organisciak's place and stayed until 1916. Before his departure to Arizona, Fr. Marciniak was instrumental in organizing, in 1913, the Society of St. Joseph of the Polish Roman Catholic Union in America.

Poles also founded several other organizations including the Society of Thaddeus Kosciuszko, a lodge of the Polish National Alliance of America (1904), the "Czytelnia" Society (1905), for the purpose of popularizing the reading of books in Polish, and the Citizens Club (1913). The first Dom Polski (Polish Hall), at the corner of Lima and Vernon Avenue became, from 1908 through 1921, a focal point for Polish cultural undertakings including a school of the Polish language, taught by Olga Bukowska, a close friend of Madame Helena Modjeska. The list of socially active Poles in Los Angeles during the first three decades of this century was headed by the families of Bajerski, Jankiewicz, W.J. Miller, Nowakowski, Rodax, Rydzeski and Walendowski, among others.

Polish religious services, however, had to be discontinued for nine years after the departure of Fr. Marciniak in 1916. Only confessions were available, thanks to Fr. Depta, C.M., stationed at St. Vincent's church. In 1925 Fr. Bronislaw Krzeminski arrived from Poland (diocese of Czestochowa) due to the efforts of Jozefa Kudlicka. Fr. Krzeminski celebrated the first Mass for his faithful on November 1, 1925, in the Polish National Auditorium which was at the corner of 40th Street and South Park Boulevard.

The Poles immediately formed a committee to build another church because the first, the wooden chapel, had been sold. The location was to be at 5134 Towne Avenue and the size commensurate to the increasing numbers of the Polish community. The census of the United States population listed 2,516 Poles in Los Angeles in 1920, and 13,872 in 1930.

On the first Sunday of Advent, November 28, 1926, a happy congregation witnessed the dedication of the new church by Fr. John Condon. "The ceremonies were in charge of Rev. Bronislaw Krzeminski, organizer of the new parish," reported The Tidings (Dec. 3, 1926). "The pews, seating about 300, were filled to capacity. The ground alone . . . cost $7,600. The building [cost] $3,800. The modesty of this figure was made possible through the generous sacrifice of Frank H. Jambor, contractor. On the financial end of it, Mr. F. Bajerski is outstanding. Finances . . . do not worry the new congregation. The balance left on mortgage is $5,000 and this will be wiped out within a few months." The mortgage was indeed paid off, and the deed of the Polish church property was turned over to the Chancery on January 17, 1933. Bishop John Joseph Cantwell acknowledged this fact in a letter of January 25 to Fr. Krzeminski.

The next task before the Polish pastor was the organization of parish life. A flurry of activities followed resulting in setting up the Altar and Holy Rosary Societies (1926); and of the Holy Name of Jesus (1930); St. Cecilia Choir (1926), with Rosalie Galewska, the first organist; Queen Jadwiga (1940); and St. Stanislaus Club (1946). Most importantly, the Polish parish school was opened in 1940, with Franciscan Sisters from Sylvania, Ohio, in charge.

Because the facilities proved to be insufficient to accommodate the growing Polish community, however, a move was in order. A new place was found at 3424 West Adams Boulevard. The first Mass was celebrated there in a temporary chapel on March 3, 1944. The

Interior of the Church of Our Lady of the Bright Mount, Los Angeles. The mosaic picture of our Lady of Czestochowa and the frescoes are the work of Stefan Mrozewski. Photo, Martin Dabrowski.

Archbishop, who authorized the purchase of this new property, agreed on April 27th to the use of the name Our Lady of the Bright Mountnt (Matka Boska Jasnogorska or Czestochowska). Thus, for the third time in the last four decades, Poles had to build a church of their own in Los Angeles. This time it was hoped that it would be permanent. Before that could be undertaken, however, a parish hall became a matter of utmost urgency. It took a little while to get funds, but on May 15, 1950, the hall was blessed and opened for use.

Four years later, on March 1, 1954, Fr. Bronislaw Krzeminski, "who set an example, not only of the tolerance and idealism of Poland, but also of a loyal and active citizen of America," died after twenty-nine years of service to his people. He was buried at Calvary cemetery.

The new administrator of the parish was Fr. Stanislaw Jureko. Born in Poland on August 8, 1899, he became a priest on May 26, 1929, in Fribourg, Switzerland, for service in the Los Angeles diocese. Once in California, Fr. Jureko worked successively in San Diego, Ocean Park, San Pedro, Los Angeles (in the Croatian parish) and in Fillmore, before coming to the Polish parish. Nineteen years of his pastoral work here are highlighted by the construction of the present church, with its furnishings, as well as by the parish participation in the celebration of Poland's Millenium of Christianity.

The Chancery's permission to build the church for Polish Catholics was issued in March of 1955. The building committee was promptly set up. Its president was H. Eric Krol; W. Kobylak, J. Nieder and St. Rymsza, vice presidents; Ch. Babiarz and W. Kosztowniak, secretaries; J. Shubsda, treasurer; L. Niezgodzki, financial secretary; V. Mielcarz, S. Nowakowski and L. Zbylut, auditors. The architect, George J. Szeptycki, gave the first cost estimate at $100,000. Fr. Jureko launched a fervent campaign to raise funds, and in the spring of 1956 construction began. Not only was the enthusiasm of parishioners overwhelming, but their generosity to the church became the pride of the local Polish American community.

The same year, on Sunday, December 9, Bishop Timothy Manning, auxiliary of the archdiocese, solemnly dedicated the new edifice. He said in the memorable homily, "this church is a precious treasure, sort of a shrine, in this archdiocese." In fact, it is the only Polish church in California. Fr. Jureko, assisted by Frs. Thaddeus Shubsda and Boniface Slawik, was the celebrant of the dedication Mass. Fr. John Huchra, S.J., of Chicago, delivered the sermon.

The ceremony was enhanced by the parish choir performing under the direction of Roman Maciejewski, the organist-composer. The beauty of the church interior was highlighted by Stefan Mrozewski's mosaic of Our Lady of Czestochowa and a folkloric fresco painting on the wall behind the main altar, Stations of the Cross made in Italy (a gift of Pola Negri and Margaret West), and stained glass windows. "The Yates and Szeptycki architectural firm deserves special thanks," said Fr. Jureko at the church banquet, held in the parish hall. The function of master of ceremonies for that occasion was assumed by H. Eric Krol. A. Zagorski, Fr. B. Slawik, J. Miller, and the elevated pastor himself, were the speakers. A parish *Pamietnik* (a commemorative book), edited by Jozef Makowiecki, was published later, in 1958.

The observance of Thousand Years of Christianity in Poland by the Los Angeles Polish community became another impressive achievement. Following Fr. Jureko's suggestion, a special Millenium committee was formed on March 21, 1965. Chairmen of its various sections were: O. Klejnot, T. Nowicki, J. Szeptycki, Z. Szumanski, M. Zawadzki, T. Zielinski and S. Zimmer.

The Los Angeles Coliseum throngs witnessed on May 1, 1966, the "Mary's Hour," a very special program. A solemn Mass was offered for the intentions of Poland's Church and Nation to the Blessed Virgin Mary, the Queen of Poland. Another Millenium Mass was celebrated by Cardinal James Francis McIntyre at St. Vibiana cathedral. His Eminence also took part in the Millennium banquet held at the Biltmore Hotel, at which Very Rev. Charles S. Casassa, S.J., then president of Loyola University at Los Angeles, was the main speaker. A historically meaningful, large stained glass window, the work of Ludwik Wiechecki, in the choir loft of Our Lady of the Bright Mount church, is a precious vestige of the Los Angeles Poland's Millennium committee's efforts and of Polish generosity.

In his pastoral work, Fr. Jureko was helped by Fr. Jacek Przygoda and several other Polish priests, both local (A. Saran, B. Slawik) and visitors (V. Jasinski, H. Malak, M. Wojciechowski).

The first resident, Fr. Sylwester Posluszny, was followed in 1966 by Fr. Stefan Kaczmarek, member of the Society of Christ. This society was founded in 1932 by August Cardinal Hlond, Primate of Poland, upon the advice and insistence of Pope Pius XI. Fr. Ignacy Posadzy is considered its co-founder. The initial motherhouse of the Society was located in Potulice, Poland. The main purpose of the Society of Christ is ministry among Polish Catholic immigrants throughout the world. A member of that order, Fr. Zbigniew Olbrys, came to the parish as an assistant to Fr. Jureko on July 1, 1968. Fr. Jozef Furman, S.Ch., also became an assistant, while teaching at St. Bernard's High School, in 1971-72.

On November 29, 1973, after suffering several heart attacks, Fr. Stanislaw Jureko died at St. Vincent Hospital. Bishop Juan A. Arzube presided over the rosary for the deceased pastor and Bishop John J.

Ward was the main celebrant of the funeral Mass the following day. On both days, bereaved parishioners filled the church. In his eulogy, Bishop Ward expressed a deep gratitude to the Polish nation for sending Fr. Jureko, "a great missionary," to the Los Angeles archdiocese. He is buried at Holy Cross Cemetery, "on Polish Hill."

In response to their request, Cardinal Timothy Manning decided to give the administration of the Polish parish in Los Angeles to the Society of Christ. Fr. Zbigniew Olbrys became the new administrator on December 19, 1973.

Fr. Olbrys was ordained priest in 1957 in Poland. Nine years later he was sent to Calgary, Canada, then to Providence, Rhode Island, and finally to Los Angeles. In September of 1974, Fr. Konrad Urbanowski, S.Ch., came to the parish. These two were joined by Bro. Marian Pankanin, S.Ch., the organist and secretary.

Two events stand out so far in Fr. Olbrys' pastorship. For the first time, a Polish Cardinal, Karol Wojtyla of Krakow, Poland, visited the parish and on August 29, 1976, he offered a solemn mass at the Bright Mount to begin the celebration of the golden jubilee of the parish.

This celebration culminated on October 24th when Bishop Wladyslaw Rubin from Rome, the secretary of the Bishops' Synod and the representative of the Primate of Poland, was the main concelebrant of the Thanksgiving Mass. Thus a half century of Polish American Roman Catholic religious experience in an organized form was sealed for posterity.

The title, "Ongoing Wonder" should not now be surprising. Fifty years of the Polish religious presence in Los Angeles and in Southern California have proved to be truly an "ongoing wonder." For in spite of all kinds of obstacles in the past, from within the Polish community itself and various pressures from without, the Polish American Catholic community, richer in experience and guided by Our Lady, looks confidently into its bright future.

SOURCES

1. The R.C. Chancery of Los Angeles Archives. Files on the Polish church.
2. Our Lady of the Bright Mount church files.
3. Kudlicka, Jozefa, "Poles in Los Angeles," *Slavs in California*. Oakland, Ca., 1937.
4. Makowiecki, Jozef, *Pamietnik* (The Commemorative Book). Our Lady of the Bright Mount. Detroit, 1958.
5. *The Tidings*. Los Angeles, Dec. 3, 1926, and several more recent issues.
6. Fr. Z. Olbrys (Personal interviews, 1977).
7. Fr. K. Urbanowski (Personal interview, July 1977).
8. Agnes M. Piehura (Notes from an interview, 1976).

POLISH ELEMENTARY SCHOOL: CHRIST THE KING CHURCH OF LOS ANGELES

Alice Parka

The Polish school in Los Angeles first had its beginning in 1940 at Christ the King Church located at 52nd and Towne Avenue, under the pastorship of the Rev. Bronislaw Krzeminski. It was a fully accredited archdiocesan elementary school, administered and staffed by the Sisters of St. Francis, Congregation of Our Lady of Lourdes, from Sylvania, Ohio. The school had approximately 40 to 50 students attending — comparatively small, because the Polish people resided in various areas throughout the city. The school therefore was comprised of children not only of Polish descent, but also of other ethnic backgrounds. Classes were conducted in the Parish Hall which was divided into two sections. The Polish language was taught for a minimum of three hours a week and consisted of reading, writing, and Polish history.

In 1944, when the new site of the Polish Parish, Our Lady of the Bright Mount, was purchased at 3424 West Adams Boulevard, the school was transferred to this location, and the nuns continued to teach until 1949. Thereafter, the nuns were recalled to Sylvania at the order of their Bishop (since they were a diocesan order) because of the shortage of nuns in their local area.

Since the closing of the elementary school, evening classes in the Polish language are still being conducted once a week at Our Lady of the Bright Mount for adults, and on Saturdays for children from 10:00 a.m. to 2:00 p.m.

Alice Parka is one of the pupils of that school. She lives in Los Angeles.

ST. STANISLAUS CLUB IN LOS ANGELES

Bernice Ault

The St. Stanislaus Club was organized by a small group of young people in September, 1946, under the guidance of the late Father Bronislaus Krzeminski. A name for the club was appropriately chosen in honor of a young Polish saint, Stanislaus Kostka.

The purpose of the club is to provide Catholic activity, social and spiritual, and to assist the Pastor in the upkeep of the Polish parish. Events planned for club members have given the group good Catholic social habits.

The first president, Max Zambel, guided the club through its first year, assisted by Stanley Rymsza, vice-president; Christine Majcher, secretary; and Richard Shubsda, treasurer. The late Max Zambel then chose a most admirable vocation by joining the Order of St. Francis under the name of Brother Stanislaus. Another one of the members, Thaddeus Shubsda, was ordained a priest in April 1950; in a few years he became a Monsignor. February 19, 1977 will be remembered as the day he was consecrated Bishop Thaddeus Shubsda for the Archdiocese of Los Angeles. This was a most memorable event for all people of Polish descent in California.

The working of the Holy Spirit again blessed our Polish Community on April 6, 1977, when member Bill Ustaski was ordained a Deacon by Bishop Shubsda. The ordination was the first such event to take place at Our Lady of the Bright Mount Polish Church. Bill was ordained a priest in June, 1977.

The Shrine of Our Lady, a dream of Father Krzeminski, became a reality when the club aided Father in both moral and financial support. The Parish Church and hall were also constructed through the combined efforts of the group. With the counsel and encouragement of the late Father Stanislaus Jureko, and Father Zbigniew Olbrys, many events have been planned and carried through successfully for the benefit of the parish.

Bernice Ault, member of the Club, lives in Westminster.

POLISH RETIREMENT FOUNDATION IN LOS ANGELES

Alice Parka

When the residence "Szarotka" opened its doors on April 1, 1977, it climaxed the intensive efforts exerted by a compassionate Polish community on behalf of its elderly. For some time, the Polish community had been aware of the need for a retirement home for its senior citizens — ideally, one that would not only provide superior care, but also offer the needed fellowship, and more important, the comfort and friendship of a true Polish-home environment. The initial generosities encouraged others to share their resources and their blessings as expressions of gratitude to the elderly Poles who so generously gave of themselves and their means during their productive years.

In the early part of 1975, the Rev. Zbigniew Olbrys, Pastor of Our Lady of the Bright Mount church, learned of the availability of the property adjacent to the church. Sharing his concern for the elderly, committees were formed to explore the possibility of acquiring the property and converting it to a home for the aged. The Polish community responded with enthusiasm and encouragement.

Thereafter, a Board of Directors was formed consisting of the following officers and members: President, Rev. Zbigniew Olbrys; Vice-President, Mrs. Matthew (Florence) Mika; Secretary, Miss Alice Parka; Assistant Secretary, Roman Zawadzki; Treasurer, Carl Kaymark; Assistant Treasurer, Mrs. Edward (Wanda) Kaminsky; Members, Franciszek Kurnik, Edmund Maciag and Mrs. Aleksander (Maria) Romanski; Legal Advisor, George Kalinski, Attorney-at-Law.

The residence can accommodate 40 persons and is located at 3400 West Adams Boulevard, Los Angeles. It is cared for by Mrs. Tadeusz (Stella) Niemiec, Manager, and administered by Michael Mullen.

THE GUARDIAN ANGEL POLISH NATIONAL CATHOLIC CHURCH IN CALIFORNIA

Robert J. Vrablik

The California Mission of the Polish National Catholic Church was established in Los Angeles in 1959. The charter members, a group of 27 people representing 15 National Catholic families originally from the Midwest and Eastern United States, headed by the late Rev. Clement Sienkiewicz, formed a mission parish.[1] Through the generosity of several Episcopal churches in Southern California, the Polish National Catholics gathered to worship and grew in numbers, increased by members of Eastern parishes settling in California. After the death of Father C. Sienkiewicz in 1964, the Prime Bishop of the Polish National Catholic Church, the Most Reverend Leon Grochowski, enlisted the services of Rev. Edward Kalata for the Los Angeles Mission. Father Kalata, a graduate of the Savonarola Theological Seminary in Scranton, Pennsylvania, was at that time temporarily serving as Rector of the Cathedral Parish in Passaic, New Jersey.

In 1964 the Mission Parish purchased a Spanish style church building at 118 North Commonwealth Avenue in Los Angeles, remodeled it, and built an adjoining hall — all this financed by the parishioners without any outside help. The church has been completely paid for and constitutes the property of the parish, headed by the Parish Priest, assisted by the Parish Council and the Board of Trustees.

Over the eighteen years since the Guardian Angel Parish in Los Angeles was founded, it maintained ties with the rest of the Polish National Catholic Church in the East and has recently sent one of its young men to the Savonarola Theological Seminary to study for the priesthood. The parish is within the jurisdiction of the Central Diocese in Scranton, Pennsylvania, whose present Bishop is the Most Reverend Antoni Rysz.

The parish maintains membership in the Polish National Union (Spojnia), a Ladies' Society of the Adoration of the Holy Sacrament, a Men's Society, and a parish choir whose members also take active part

---

Robert J. Vrablik, member of the church, lives in La Habra.

in performances with other Polish choral groups in Los Angeles. Religion and the Polish language are taught at the church. Polish religious traditions are followed at Christmas and Easter, and a Polish harvest festival and bazaar have become a yearly event. Other social events such as dinners and dances bring together the older and younger generations.

Church services are held weekly in Polish, and every other Sunday of the month in English. Thus ties are kept with the younger generation, which learns about its national and religious heritage.

The success of the Guardian Angel PNCC has inspired other Polish National Catholics in California to form a parish of their own. A Mission Parish in San Diego has been founded, property has been purchased, and the church is being built at 1144 30th Street, San Diego. Father Kalata has been the visiting pastor for the San Diego sister parish since 1974.

REFERENCE

1. Dr. Rev. Stephen Wlodarski, 1974, *The Origin and Growth of the Polish National Catholic Church*. PNCC: Scranton, Pennsylvania.

POLISH AMERICAN CONGRESS: CALIFORNIA-ARIZONA DIVISION

Anthony Saran

The Polish community in Los Angeles, which had since 1939 been organized into the Federation of Polish Societies, received an invitation to join, in 1944, the national convention in Buffalo, New York. By sending one delegate, it participated with 5,000 other representatives in establishing the Polish American Congress during the Memorial Day weekend. Three months later, September 4, 1944, a state-wide meeting was held in Los Angeles to form the California--Arizona Division of P.A.C.; it consisted of Los Angeles, San Diego, Fresno, San Francisco, and Phoenix, Arizona (since 1968 San Francisco has belonged to the Northern California Division). In California, P.A.C. holds monthly meetings, annual election conventions, and sponsors the following annual activities: celebration of the Polish Constitution of May Third, 1791, and Polish Freedom Day, in November.

P.A.C.'s cultural and educational activities were especially intensified during 1960-1966 for the celebration of Poland's Millennium, commemorating one thousand years of Polish Christianity. The Millennium Library was created during this period, which the Congress continues to support. In 1973, the Kopernik Year, P.A.C. issued posters, portraits, seals and bookmarks, as well as installed a plaque to commemorate the 500th anniversary of his birth. The statue, with the plaque, stands in front of the Griffith Park Observatory. The Arizona Chapter sponsored a national and local campaign to change the surname from the Latin Copernicus to the Polish Kopernik.

In more recent years the Congress has assumed an even more politically oriented role to combat derogatory misinformation about Poles and to create a positive image through achievement. When the German Judiciary Committee of Schleswig-Holstein engaged in a massive cover-up of the individual war crimes committed in Poland during World War II, the members of the California-Arizona Division aided in launching a successful campaign to expose effectively the

Rev. Anthony Saran is the associate pastor of Cathedral Chapel, Los Angeles.

atrocities and the Katyn Forest murders.

Through the joint action of P.A.C. and Americans for Freedom of Captive Nations, the United States receives constant reminders to be vigilant in detecting the forces destructive of our freedom.

It is the intent of the P.A.C. to continue functioning effectively in achieving the goal of the local Polonia unification according to the motto: "In Unity, Strength."

Officers for 1977 are: Joseph Koleda, Pres.; Wanda Korba, Mieczyslaw Kowalewski, Genowefa Osinska, Michal Zawadzki, Vice-Presidents; Jean Breese, Financial Secretary; Mary Dziadula, Treasurer; Rev. Anthony Saran, Recording Secretary; Betty Lukasiewicz, Corresponding Secretary. Members of the Board of Directors are: Charles Breese, Izydor Brudzinski, Paul Glab, Josephine Gryn, Veronica Kazmierski, Olgierd Klejnot, Roman Margis, Czeslawa Podlasek, Stanley Szulkiewicz, and Olga Wicker.

"SAMOPOMOC" (THE SELF-AID): THE POLISH FRATERNAL ASSOCIATION IN LOS ANGELES

Izabella Z. Macander

On February 17, 1949 the Polish American Congress, California-Arizona Division, sponsored a special meeting of Polish Americans in Los Angeles. The purpose of this meeting, called by Jerzy Radwan, was to organize a method of providing aid and assistance to Polish immigrants newly arrived from Europe.

To achieve this goal, a new organization was formed and named "Samopomoc" (The Self-Aid), under the direction of its first president, Dr. Tadeusz Nalecz-Mrozowski. The officers and members of Samopomoc labored year after year to increase its ranks and its influence in the Polish American community.

Over the years Samopomoc has inspired the formation of Polish Alma Mater (Polska Macierz Szkolna), a Saturday Polish school for the youth; the Polish Folk Dance Group "Millennium"; the sports club "Polonia," the Polish Theatre "Kruszewska" and the Polish Millennium Library. Although each of these are now autonomous entities, they still occasionally receive financial and moral support from Samopomoc.

As a member of the Polish American Congress, California-Arizona Division, it was represented in the Council of Captive Nations and is also a stockholder in the Polish Hall (Dom Polski).

Samopomoc has participated in American cultural events by organizing exhibitions depicting Polish art and culture, such as the annual Christmas Pageant and Parade held at Disneyland. Outside of the United States, it helps maintain Polish museums and monuments in Switzerland as well as in England. It has also been a great supporter of Polish publications and newspapers by making purchases and donating them to the Polish Library in Los Angeles.

Samopomoc has conducted courses in English for new immigrants, and assisted those seeking employment and adequate housing by making small loans available. Presently the organization's efforts are

---

Izabella Z. Macander, raised and educated in Los Angeles, lives in Bethesda, Maryland.

concentrated on granting scholarships to the youth of the Polish community.

In recent years, a new wave of immigrants, mostly people who again chose freedom and left Poland, has arrived in the Los Angeles area. They are just as much in need of help as were their predecessors. At one of the executive meetings of all Polish organizations in town, this was pointed out and possible programs of action were discussed. Jerzy Kaminski, president of the Polish Credit Union, proposed that P.C.U. establish a special loan account to help new arrivals from Poland. Krystyna Zielkiewicz, current president of Samopomoc, has been a moving force behind this plan. A charter was drafted by Witold Vogt, ratified and signed by officers of participating organizations.

During all these years of existence, Samopomoc has been very much interested in the purchase of a large building or land for use as a center for its expanding activities. Lacking sufficient funds for such a project, Samopomoc enlisted the aid of other Los Angeles Polish organizations and clubs. After years of efforts, River's End Park was purchased, and the Polish Center established. Samopomoc transferred its funds to the Center and became co-owner of the Polish Center Park (Osrodek Polski). A formal merger followed in 1975 to form what is now known as the Polish Center Fraternal Association of California (Osrodek Polski-Samopomoc).

The road travelled by Samopomoc since 1949 has been long and sometimes difficult. But thanks to long-range vision, able and persevering leadership and loyal and generous members, Samopomoc has become one of the socially pivotal forces in the Los Angeles Polish community.

THE POLISH CENTER IN LOS ANGELES

Helena Stelmach

The Polish Center in Los Angeles was founded as a charitable association on February 24, 1967. Initiative to form the Center originated among already exisiting Polish American groups, and included the Polish Fraternal Association-Samopomoc, Polish Combatants in Exile, and the Polish Air Force Association. Its prime mover was the late Tadeusz Zielinski.

As its primary purpose, the Polish Center endeavors to keep Polish traditions alive among Polish American groups in Southern California. In addition, it seeks to make young generations of Polish American descent aware of their cultural roots and the achievements of their predecessors. To fulfill these aims, it was imperative to have a place where members could meet and work effectively. The initial funding for the project came from several Polish fraternal organizations. Later, individual members, who strongly supported the concept of a central meeting place, contributed financially, and with this joint effort, the Polish Center acquired the River's End Recreational Park in Saugus, in June, 1970.

The activities at River's End suffered a serious setback in February 1971, when a major earthquake caused considerable damage to the Recreation Park. Subsequently, with the assistance of the Federal Government, in the form of a loan, and loans from the Polish American Congress Credit Union and from individual members, the damage was repaired and full activities at the park were restored.

In May, 1975, the Polish Fraternal Association of California Samopomoc became affiliated with the Polish Center, and the Association changed its name to Polish Center-Polish Fraternal Association of Los Angeles. With this affiliation, the membership has grown to 350, thus creating a major Polish group in the Los Angeles area. Kazimierz Wnorowski is the president, Roman Babczynski — the administrative secretary, Helena Stelmach — the secretary.

Helena Stelmach is the secretary of the Polish Center. She lives in Canoga Park.

POLISH AMERICAN CONGRESS FEDERAL CREDIT UNION IN LOS ANGELES

Henry Westwalewicz

The Polish American Congress Federal Credit Union was founded as a financial organization in 1970 by Mr. & Mrs. Henry Westwalewicz, Mr. & Mrs. Eugene Mathews, Mr. & Mrs. Jozef Ladowicz, Mr. Zbigniew Marcinkowski, and Mrs. Czeslawa Podlasek. The founders believed there was need for a financial organization geared to serve Polish Americans; thus the PACFCU strives to help Polish Americans to form good thrift habits, learn to control finances effectively, and to extradite themselves, when necessary, from financial difficulties by availing themselves of services provided by an interested financial group.

The PACFCU is one of the twelve most dynamic Credit Unions in the United States, and has won several important Federal awards. In 1976 its assets exceeded $1,000,000.00; and it continues to grow and develop at a remarkable rate.

The organization does not invest in speculative business risks; instead, it specializes in making loans to members. At last count, the rapidly increasing membership list totalled 1237. Benefits and privileges for members include: 6% interest, paid semi-annually, on all funds deposited in savings accounts; all amounts of deposit insured by Federal and Credit Union policies; low interest rate loans with convenient monthly payments; no prepayment penalties, no service or point charges, and free death benefit insurance.

Currently serving as officers are: Rudolph Zatoka, Jerzy Kaminski, Henry Montygierd, and Barbara Martinoff.

POLISH SCOUTING IN CALIFORNIA

Gena Kliszewska

The Scouting movement in Poland began in 1910, and in 1913, at the first International Jamboree in England, Polish scouts were recognized as adhering to the principles laid down by Lord Baden-Powell. From 1920 the Scouting movement grew rapidly in Poland and by 1939 the membership reached 200,000. During World War II Polish scouting contributed much to the struggle against the enemy, both on the battlefield and in the underground resistance movement.

After World War II, the communist regime imposed on Poland did not allow scouting to function according to the principles formulated by Baden-Powell, so the only genuine Polish scouting exists in exile. Although the World Scouting Bureau does not recognize the Polish scouting movement as existing outside the boundaries of Poland, in all the countries inhabited by Polish immigrants Polish scouting is growing successfully and encourages the continuation of the pre-war Polish scouting traditions. It also upholds the culture, history and language of the Polish nation.

Polish scouting in the United States dates back to 1949. The first troops were organized in Chicago where their headquarters remain to this day. In 1976, 2,000 members from all over the world attended the Jamboree of Independent Polish Scouting held in Canada.

There are two Polish scouting centers in California; one in San Francisco, the other in Los Angeles. Coordinator between the two centers is Krystyna Zielkiewicz; assisting her in the San Francisco area is Adam Pietras. The Los Angeles center was organized in 1974. Meetings are held three times a month at the Polish Parish of Our Lady of the Bright Mount, 3424 West Adams Boulevard, Los Angeles.

A group of 50 "Friends of Polish Scouting" is active in the Los Angeles center with Janina Rezler as the chairperson.

The Los Angeles center includes the following troops:

Brownie Troop: "Wawelski Grod," 16 troop members; leaders are Gosia Grzanka and Basia Wojciechowska.

Girl Scout Troop: "Druzyna im. Jagi Falkowskiej," 12 troop members; leader is Wanda Zurawska; assistant leader is Bogna Ladowicz.

Gena Kliszewska lives in Los Angeles.

Young Adult Patrol: "Zastep im. Jagi Falkowskiej," 6 troop members; leader is Wanda Kamieniecka Grycko, assistant leader is Ela Grzanka.

Cubscout Troop: "Woje Krakusa," 15 troop members; leader is Gena Kliszewska, assistant leader is Artur Cybulski.

Boy Scout Troop #26: "Druzyna Nr. 26 im. Tadeusza Kosciuszko," 12 troop members; leader is Franciszek Kurnik, assistant leader is Pawel Dazko.

The Representative for the California Region is Scoutmaster Tadeusz Borowski. The Chaplain for the Los Angeles Region is Rev. Zbigniew Olbrys, Scoutmaster.

The San Francisco center was organized in 1973 and was named in memory of Scoutmaster Tadeusz Butler. Meetings are held three times a month.

The San Francisco center includes the following troops:

Brownie Cubscout Troop: "Wislane Kamyczki," 10 troop members; leader is Walentyna Pietras; assistant, Malgosia Niemiec.

Girl Scout Troop: "Druzyna 'Warta' im. Marii Curie-Sklodowskiej," 16 troop members; leader is Krystyna Chciuk, assistant is Beata Mazur.

Boy Scout Troop: "Druzyna Nr. 10 im. Romualda Traugutta," 12 troop members; leader, Adam Pietras.

The Chaplain for the San Francisco Region is Rev. Wojciech Baryski.

Both centers keep in close contact through overnight campouts, meetings of the leaders and troop members, and through participation in summer camps.

POLISH WOMEN'S ALLIANCE OF AMERICA IN SOUTHERN CALIFORNIA

The Polish Women's Alliance of America, one of the oldest Polish organizations in the country, was founded in Chicago, in 1898, to unite women of Polish descent or conviction in social and civic work; to ensure their welfare and that of their children through beneficial life insurance programs; and to further Polish culture among Polish American youth. For the past 79 years these women have worked tirelessly to achieve these aims by encouraging the formation of affiliate groups throughout the country.

The first such affiliate group of the PWAA in Los Angeles, Group 541, was formed in March, 1928, by Polish women who felt the need for such an organization in Southern California. Since that time, five more groups have been added to the roster. In January, 1948, Council 35 of District 13, which encompassed all groups in the area, was formed and a state president elected. Mrs. Florence Mika is currently serving in that capacity.

The PWAA has raised funds for more worthy causes than can be listed, both here and in Poland. Whenever and wherever help is needed, the women are there to give aid. In addition to major fund raising projects, each group has its own special projects for which it raises funds. These include: American Red Cross, St. Jude Hospital, Orchard Lake Seminary, Polish Retirement Foundation, United Crusade, Our Lady of Bright Mount Catholic Church, Polish Shrine at Doylestown, Pa., Retarded and Blind Children's Hospital in Poland, and countless others. A major fund raiser is the annual Debutante Presentation Ball. Proceeds from this are used for scholarships for members attending universities.

These groups are currently active in Southern California (their respective presidents' names follow):

GROUP 541: *Los Angeles*, Harriett Teachout.

GROUP 752: *Tow. Krolowej Jadwigi*, Maria Buchajeska.

GROUP 784: *Madame Curie Sklodowska* (San Diego) Patricia Fedor.

GROUP 811: *La Jolla*, Wanda Dettling.

GROUP 813: *South Bay*, Helena Klimes.

GROUP 814: *San Fernando Valley*, Camille Howard.

POLISH ARMY VETERANS ASSOCIATION OF AMERICA: P.A.V.A. IN LOS ANGELES

The Polish Army Veteran Association of America — P.A.V.A. (Stowarzyszenie Weteranow Armii Polskiej w Ameryce — S.W.A.P.) was organized in 1921 by veterans of General Haller's "Blue Army," as a benevolent, non-political, non-sectarian and non-profit organization. Its affiliate, Los Angeles Post No. 173, was formed by Lt. F. Truszkiewicz and five veterans in 1937. At that same time, a trio of energetic ladies founded the Ladies Auxiliary.

The purpose of the organization is to assemble former members of the Polish Armed Forces, who have served in either of the two World Wars, and to maintian and propagate the ideals for which they fought. Further, the Association desired to maintain a spirit of brotherhood among its members; to support disabled veterans; to maintain a Veteran's Fund to help former comrades; and to support national unity.

P.A.V.A. observes "Soldiers Day" each August 15th, in remembrance of the victorious Battle of Warsaw of August 1920. In addition, it takes active part in all American and Polish patriotic observances, and has organized special observances for Polish Independence Day and Pulaski Day. Delegates to the Polish American Congress in Los Angeles take active part in its activities.

Lt. F. Truszkiewicz, deceased, served as the first Post Commander. Other Past Commanders were: Z. Swadowski, K. Lazowski, Z. Zielkiewicz, R. Terpilowski. Since 1972, R. Margis has been serving in that capacity. Mrs. G. Osinska is currently presiding over the Ladies Auxiliary.

POLISH VETERANS OF WWII, SOUTHERN CALIFORNIA CHAPTER

The Polish Veterans of World War II Southern California Chapter (SPK), was registered as a non-profit, charitable organization in Southern California in 1963, for these specific and primary purposes:

To provide care for disabled veteran-members unable to work, as well as their widows and orphans; and also, to promote bonds of friendship among members and maintain those ideals for which soldiers of free democratic nations sacrificed their lives, by cooperating with other veteran organizations, both Polish and American.

Cultural and social objectives, which promote friendship and fellowship among members, are an important adjunct to the primary purpose. These include the publication of books, pamphlets and newspapers; the establishment of reading rooms; the organization of literary programs; theatricals; dinner dances and other enter-tainments; in general, promotion of the cultural and social welfare of members. To carry out these corporate purposes, the organization strives to acquire real and personal property by means of purchase or bequest.

B. Fryzendorf presides over the current 90-member corporation. Previous presidents were: M. Kowalewski, W. Tomaszewski, R. Makarewicz, W. Hryniewicki, R. Margis, and A. Romanski.

POLISH AIR FORCE VETERANS ASSOCIATION: PACIFIC COAST WING

Marek J. Mazynski

On December 21, 1951, Dr. Tadeusz Mrozowski organized former Polish airmen residing in the Metropolitan Los Angeles area into the Polish Air Force Association, Los Angeles Squadron. Its parent organization, the Polish Air Force Association, had been founded in 1945 as a universal organization of men and women who could continue the common bond of friendship formed during the war years. Col. W. Zawadzki served as first president of the fledgling group. Other members of the committee were: Dr. T. Mrozowski, vice-president; L. Domanski, secretary; and A. Guluk, treasurer.

The main aims and purposes of the P.A.F.A. are: to aid veterans, widows and orphans and other dependents of former Polish Air Force personnel, both in this country and abroad, by fund-raising social functions; to cooperate with other organizations devoted to the needs and welfare of veterans; and to support those educational and cultural activities which promote the ideals of democracy and freedom of all peoples.

On July 29, 1962, the territory encompassed by the group was extended to include Arizona, Oregon and Washington, and the name was changed to Pacific Coast Wing, Polish Air Force Veterans Association. As such, it was registered in the State of California as a non-profit charitable organization. During the past twenty-five years, it has raised and donated considerable sums to charities. The group is self-sustaining; its headquarters are located at 3424 West Adams, Los Angeles. At present the membership of 120 is headed by M.J. Mazynski.

POLISH RESISTANCE FORCES (HOME ARMY) VETERANS ASSOCIATION IN LOS ANGELES

Kathy S. Hayes

The Los Angeles branch of Home Army (Armia Krajowa) Veterans was established in 1962 after Col. M. Kaminski, with a few friends, wished to install a plaque at the entrance of Polish Parish Church on West Adams Boulevard to commemorate Home Army soldiers who lost their lives in defense of Poland. The response among veterans was so great that a permanent organization seemed necessary. The Los Angeles chapter, formed under Commander Col. M. Kaminski, applied for charter in the world-wide organization of Home Army Veterans.

Members of this organization are veterans of World War II who fought in the underground secret army against the Germans in Poland. This was the largest secret military organization in German-occupied Europe with many sections, including the Partisans (harassed German forts, destroyed bridges and railways), Information and Propaganda (published secret press information on BBC and Polish Radio in London), Intelligence, Training (readiness for D-Day), and Protection of Civilians.

Goals of Home Army Veterans, Los Angeles, include commemorating deceased brothers and sisters at arms, defending the good name of "Armia Krajowa," financial and moral assistance for disabled members and members in hardship situations, as well as social functions. Home Army Veterans is not a political organization; however, it gladly collaborates with other Polish organizations, and remains unswervingly loyal to the United States.

In addition to regular help to disabled veterans in Poland, Germany and France, Home Army Veterans contributes funds to worthy Polish causes: Polish Boy Scouts, Museum in Rapperswil, Sikorski Museum in London, Polish Parish in Los Angeles, Katyn Memorial in London, Restoration of Royal Castle in Warsaw, and many others. A *Quarterly* containing memories of various members has been published for several years, and the publication of books about activities of "Armia Krajowa" has been supported.

Polish Home Army, Christmas Eve, 1943. Stefan Mrozewski.

Col. M. Kaminski served as Commander until 1967 and was succeeded by V. Rokicki, who served until 1972. At that time Col. Kaminski again assumed the post; in 1974 V. Rokicki began a second term, and was assisted during the Bicentennial year by T. Borowski, L. and M. Ciecek, A. Nizynski and E. Terelak.

THE POLISH UNIVERSITY CLUB OF LOS ANGELES

Michele M. Sawa

Founded in November of 1947, by Dr. Thomas M. Potasz, the University Club was instituted in an effort to encourage the interest and advancement of Polish culture. The doctor's dream was to unite college students and graduates of Polish descent.

Today the Club is a well-known organization, featuring programs in literature, science, music and travel. A scholarship fund, instituted by the Club's founder, has been established in order to aid Polish students. The students are able to obtain scholarships by participating in the club's Summer Program for "Polonia's Dzieci" (children of Polonia) which was started in 1975. In the program, college and university men and women act as tutors, field trip guides, and friends to children of the Polish community. Most importantly, the students introduce the children to a study of their Polish heritage.

The program not only culturally and creatively enriches the background of grade school students, but it offers the college students the opportunity to expand their own cultural awareness. This way the children and their teachers not only gain experience and knowledge of their Polish culture, they also learn to work with, understand, and respect each other.

THE POLISH LIBRARY IN LOS ANGELES

Danuta M. Zawadzki

The Polish lending library in Los Angeles was established about 1935, when Polish American community life was centered in Polonia Hall on Avalon Street. One of the very active Polish organizations, the Worker's Self-Aid Fund (Robotnicza Kasa Pomocy), had its office there, and it was to this organization that Mr. Wierzbicki gave his private collection of about 800 books. These books were added to the library belonging to the Polish National Alliance, Group 700 (Czytelnia Polska) and managed by Polonia Hall.

In 1955 Jozef Wlodarczyk, the librarian, left for Arizona and Monika Woroniecka took over the library. Unfortunately, in June 1967 she became ill and Stefan Woroniecki, her husband, became the librarian. In May 1959, he received approval from the Polish American Congress, California-Arizona Division, to organize a special Cultural-Educational Committee which up to 1963 contributed some funds for the purchase of new books.

In 1966 a Library Committee was created. Its members were professional librarians such as Dr. Szczepan Zimmer (MLS), chairman; Danuta Zawadzki (MLS); Zofia Kwiatkowski (MLS); J. Surmacz, Charles Breese and Henry Zebrowski. Dr. Michal Zawadzki became a liaison with the Polish Millennium Committee in Los Angeles. The adopted by-laws of the library followed the American Libraries Association Rules and the Library was registered with the Special Libraries Association under the name "Poland's Millennium Library" in Los Angeles, in December of 1966. This registration gives the library legal status. It can thus accept gifts, bequests, organize lectures, etc. Dr. Michal Zawadzki became its first president and Stefan Woroniecki its first librarian.

During these years Zofia Okon and Jadwiga Szymanska were active in library affairs. In January 1973 Stefan Woroniecki, who was the moving force of the library and to whose dedication and untiring efforts the library owes deep gratitude, passed away. From the roster of original members of the Library Committee, Danuta Zawadzka, several times its president, and Charles Breese, the treasurer, are still officers. Later on Zbigniew Kowalski, the vice-president, Dr.

Danuta M. Zawadzki is a former president of this library. She lives in Los Angeles.

Franciszka Tuszynska, the librarian, and Wanda Jazwinska, the president for 1977, were made officers. Kazimierz Ligus and Marcin Henzel have also been of assistance.

The Millennium Library today is an independent institution. It functions under the sponsorship of the Polish American Congress, California-Arizona Division. Its goal is to acquire, buy, collect and receive books written in the Polish language and those about Poles, Polish Americans and Poland written in other languages. At present there are about five thousand volumes. They include history, literature, biographies, art and geography and novels. There is also a collection of books for young adults, as well as books on music and drama.

POLISH AMERICAN BUSINESS & PROFESSIONAL CLUB IN LOS ANGELES

Jean Breese

The Polish American Business & Professional Club, Inc., of Los Angeles, was organized in 1932 by Frank Jambor, a building contractor, Lech Niemo, an attorney, Thomas Potasz, a doctor, and Roman Rydzeski, a dentist.

Since its inception, this club has been affiliated with the Polish American Congress and has worked in cooperation with other Polish organizations to disseminate information and counsel in business and professional matters. Mrs. D. Sovinski, past president, and Mrs. W. Szatkowski were chairpersons of the Grand Bicentennial Ball for Los Angeles County, held in 1976 at the Hyatt Regency Hotel.

During World War II, the Club was inactive because many of its members were directly involved in the war effort: Lt. Col. Thomas Potasz set up and administered base hospitals for the United States Army; Lech Niemo became acting Polish Consul on the West Coast for the duration of the war; the Honorable Sylwin Strakacz was the Polish Consul on the West Coast after World War II.

Officers for 1977-78 include President Anthony Mantykowski, publisher and representative of the Small Business Administration in Los Angeles; Vice President Joseph Koleda, owner of J.K. Engineering and president of the California Division of the Polish American Congress; Recording Secretary Elizabeth Lukasiewicz, organist and choir conductor; Treasurer Harriet Koleda; Correspondence Secretary Jean M. Breese, A.C.S.W., social service consultant.

The 1977-78 board of directors includes: Carol Blaze, retired accountant and honorary president of the Polish American Congress, California Division; Charles Breese, tool manufacturer and president of the Polish American Citizen's Club; John Kroczko, retired organizer and conductor of a choir which won many awards; Henry Barker, businessman; Roman Terpilowski, businessman; Dorothy Sovinski and Wanda Szatkowski, owners of an interior decorating establishment.

POLISH NATIONAL ALLIANCE
WHITE EAGLE LODGE #3123
SAN FERNANDO

Wanda Korba

The White Eagle Lodge #3123 of the Polish National Alliance was organized in April 1954, by Bertha Czarnecka, a former Commissioner of District 16. PNA is the largest fraternal society composed of Polish Americans, and is dedicated to fostering and propagating Polish heritage, culture and customs.

During the past 23 years Lodge #3123 has been actively involved with civic, cultural and charitable projects.

A yearly event is the traditional Polish Christmas party for youth, which emphasizes the beautiful Polish Christmas customs. Another is the Debutantes Ball, an elegant dinner dance, which raises funds for worthy causes. In 1969 and 1977, Alliance College was the beneficiary of this annual fund raiser. The group has also contributed to the American Red Cross, Boy Scouts of America, Rheumatism Fund, as well as to various scholarship funds. To commemorate America's birthday, the Lodge sponsored a float in the July 4, 1976, San Fernando Bicentennial Parade.

Serving as officers for the current year are: Wanda Korba, President; Zbigniew Podradecki, 1st Vice-President; Gladys Beit-I-Shoo, 2nd Vice-President; Mary Ann Wilk, Financial Secretary; Henry Bodurka, recording secretary; Harrietta Grzegorczyk, treasurer; and Katherine Cichy, Sgt.-at-Arms.

POLISH AMERICAN CITIZENS CLUB IN LOS ANGELES

Jean Breese

The Polish American Citizen's Club was organized in Los Angeles, California in 1913, with these specific goals and objectives:

To foster the principles of American citizenship and promote an active interest in civic affairs among the membership; to provide for the cultural and educational advancement of members and perpetuate Polish culture by encouraging study of Polish traditions; and to cultivate unity, goodwill, and cooperation between members by promoting social events, plays and entertainments.

Charles Breese is currently serving as president; Jean Breese as secretary and Veronica Black as treasurer.

POLISH PHILATELIC AND NUMISMATIC SOCIETY IN LOS ANGELES

Wally Pawlowski

The Polish Philatelic and Numismatic Society was formed on April 14, 1974, through the efforts of Waclaw (Wally) Pawlowski. The purpose of the organization is to bring together individuals interested in collecting stamps, coins, and medals. The Society emphasizes Polish materials, striving thereby also to promote the knowledge of Polish history and culture among its own members, the younger generation and the general public.

To accomplish these goals, the group holds monthly meetings, organizes exhibits and lectures, and prints publications. An outstanding first year achievement was the exhibit of Polish stamps, coins and medals, augmented by Copernicana, Polish P.O.W. stamps, Polish government-in-exile, United Nations and other collections which took place during March, 1975 at the Society's headquarters in Los Angeles, California. It was the first such exhibit of Polish material West of Chicago.

The group is affiliated with the Federated Philatelic Clubs of California, Inc.; the California State Numismatic Association; and the Polish P.O.W. and D.P. Camps Study Group. The Society also corresponds with other Polish philatelic and numismatic groups in the United States and Canada. From an original membership of five: Wally Pawlowski, Jadwiga Pawlowska, M. Pawlikowski, J. Ladowicz and W. Wielkoszewski, the club expanded to 34 members in 1975 and grew to 64 members in 1976. Wladyslaw Wielkoszewski has served as the president of the group since its inception. Other members of the executive board are: M. Komorowski, vice-president; W. Pawlowski, secretary; M. Pawlikowski, treasurer; and Z. Zielkiewicz, director.

THE POLISH COMMUNITY IN SAN DIEGO

Jozef Patyk

The first mention of Polish settlers in the *San Diego Union Newspaper* is March 4, 1902. On that day, Thomas Nalewaja arrived in San Diego from Los Angeles to seek 10,000 acres of land at the eastern edge of the city. According to the newspaper, he and a group of people from Los Angeles, whom he represented, were planning to settle 100 Polish immigrant families on this land. He was already thought to have acquired 100,000 acres of land in Mexico, by the Colorado River, for the same purpose. There is no trace of a realization of this plan but the idea of establishing a compact Polish community continues to survive. Most recently, the development of a place for Polish American retirees in Southern California is often discussed. There is, however, no tendency today to create concentrated Polish communities as was the case at the turn of the century, during the great exodus of immigrants from partitioned Poland.

The coming of Polish settlers to San Diego has not been a mass influx. They have been arriving individually, mostly through Los Angeles and later also through Phoenix, Arizona, and settling throughout the city and county. In most cases, they have migrated from the East or Middle West, or much more often, are descendants of Polish immigrants. Very few of them arrived directly from Poland.

Although the number of San Diegans of Polish origin can be estimated at approximately 6,000, those who take part in Polish organizations or manifest their Polish identity can be counted only in the hundreds. The growing number of inter-ethnic marriages blurs the statistics, and the names themselves are not indicative. However, in spite of the small number who actually preserve their Polish identity, several Polish organizations exist in San Diego.

The oldest organization extant is the Polish National Alliance. On February 4, 1912, 33 persons met in "Castle Hall" to band themselves into an association. Finally, the name "Zywiol Polski na Zachodzie" (The Polish Element in the West) was agreed upon. It became branch Number 1443 of the nationally operating Polish National Alliance, with headquarters in Chicago. The minutes of the first meeting

Jozef Patyk, professor emeritus of Dayton University, Dayton, Ohio, lives in San Diego.

registered 19 members of the association with K.S. Engelman as president, and J. Lebiedzinski, S. Krzywonos, W. Kaczmarek, S. Sniegowski and other officers of this group. At the present time the association counts around 100 members. According to Mrs. Maria Wolan, president of the branch since 1954, blue collar working people join the association while professional persons tend not to apply.

As can be witnessed by the minutes, the members of the association have long been demonstrating their attachment to Polish culture and country of their origin. These sentiments were particularly strong during the two World Wars, when the organization was engaged in collecting help for people in Poland. In conjunction with other organizations, the Polish National Alliance in San Diego has been engaged in several cultural and social programs.

In 1935 a few dozen Polish families moved to San Diego from Buffalo, New York, when an aircraft company in Buffalo established a branch here and transferred its employees. The increase of Polish San Diegans led to the establishment, in 1936, of another Polish association under the name of Polonia Club, later renamed and incorporated as the Polish American Association of San Diego. An important event in the history of this association was the purchase of a house, in 1952, at 1934 Thirtieth Street in San Diego, close to Balboa Park. The house, enlarged in 1967, also became a meeting place for other Polish organizations. Social gatherings, cultural programs, and Polish language classes take place in the house. Though modest by comparison with Polish community houses in the East, it serves the local needs well.

The Polish American Association of San Diego has close to 200 members, mostly of Polish origin. Membership, however, is open to persons of non-Polish origin who are interested in Polish culture, and on one occasion, a member of non-Polish origin was elected as president of the association.

In 1937 the association joined the House of Pacific Relations, a civic organization of San Diego, which coordinates the civic and cultural activities of several ethnic groups. In conjuction with other Polish organizations, the Polish American Association maintains a Polish Cottage in Balboa Park under the sponsorship of the House of Pacific Relations. The Cottage, open every Sunday afternoon, displays Polish art and crafts and Polish food specialities are also served. Thanks to the permanent headquarters in the Polish American Association house, all Polish organizations in San Diego can make joint arrangements to commemorate Polish national anniversaries and other festivities.

As is the case with the Polish National Alliance, so the Polish Women's Alliance is a fraternal organization based on the life insurance system. But it is much more than a fraternal insurance organization, since most of its activities are in the field of cultural and social services. The San Diego branch Number 784 of the organization, with the name Maria Sklodowska-Curie (the Polish scientist and winner of two Nobel prizes) was established in 1946. The most active organizers were Ms. Wanda Dettling and Mrs. Genowefa May, who took over presidency of the association and served for twenty years. She was replaced by her daughter, Mrs. Patricia Fedor, a teacher working for the education center of the San Diego Diocese.

The San Diego branch of the Polish Women's Alliance has over 120 members, forty-five of whom are children. They are very active in performances of Polish dancing and singing, and it is this young group which makes the celebrations lively and colorful. The organization sponsors and supports different activities, and adult members donate their time and money to such institutions as the Childrens Hospital and the Lung Association. The organization also supports Polish cultural groups coming to San Diego to perform.

Of more recent establishment is a Polish Catholic group. As previously noted, the Polish settlers did not establish themselves in any particular section. They are spread throughout the community. The early effort to organize a Catholic parish for the Polish people was unsuccessful. The number of prospective parishioners was small and the territorial principle of the church authorities did not favor a separate Polish parish. In addition, the Catholic hierarchy was involved in attempting to integrate the activities of different ethnic groups.

At this point the Polish National Catholic (non-Roman) Church clergy entered the situation in an effort to organize its church group. Whether this challenge brought a change in the attitude of the Catholic hierarchy to the Polish group is difficult to determine. In 1971 Father Ferdinand Gorka, a Franciscan, was assigned by the Bishop to provide church service for Polish San Diegans. Father Gorka, born and educated in Poland, knows the Polish language well and understands the Polish parishioners' needs and how to organize and cooperate with them.

Early in 1977 the group acquired new status, approved by the Bishop of San Diego. By a majority vote of the faithful gathered in the home of Mr. and Mrs. Leon Kulikowski, it was decided to accept Blessed Maximilian Kolbe (a martyr who volunteered to be executed in a Nazi concentration camp in the place of other inmates), as the group's patron. It is not yet a parish but simply a mission. The Carmelite Monastery Church, 5168 Havley Street, San Diego, accommodates the Polish group. It is a unique church, where services are conducted in several languages for different ethnic groups. Since Polish cultural traditions are intermingled with the Catholic traditions, the parishioners of the Mission are very active in different performances associated with the Polish anniversaries and festivities.

THE POLISH AMERICAN ARTS ASSOCIATION OF SANTA BARBARA

Jolanta Skrzynska

Steeped in the rich history of Spanish land grants, Santa Barbara actively maintains the cultural heritage of the Spanish and Mexican peoples. Quite naturally other nationalities found ways to foster their cultures here too. The existing Finnish, French, German, Swiss and other cultural clubs were recently joined by the Polish American Arts Association.

The PAAA was formed in May of 1976 to give its members the opportunity to come together and work creatively in preserving and promoting Polish culture, heritage and historical traditions that span a thousand years. It also wishes to awaken among young Polish Americans an awareness and pride in Polish cultural achievements and goals. The PAAA is sensitive and attuned to the times by weaving into the fabric of America's culture the best of Polish sources of inspiration and accomplishment.

Within this scope, the PAAA participated in Santa Barbara's Bicentennial Arts Festival held on October 23rd and 24th, 1976. It consisted of a Polish Fine Arts Exhibition in a variety of media at the Brooks Gallery of Art. The PAAA also sponsored a performance of "Krakusy," a folk dance ensemble from Los Angeles. They presented Polish regional dances at the Riviera Theatre.

The Association's lecture series featured a number of notable guest speakers, including Dr. Tymon Terlecki of the University of Illinois, Chicago; Dr. Jerzy Lerski of the University of San Francisco, and George Szeptycki, well-known Los Angeles architect who specializes in churches.

The PAAA has also sponsored during its first year of existence, a Polish language course (now incorporated into the Adult Education Program), a pre-War film series, an exhibition of Polish Art Naive, and other activities in the field of art.

We gratefully acknowledge Janusz Tyszkiewicz-Lacki's leadership as the first president of PAAA. For the 1977-78 season, president Maria Halstead will be assisted by five board members. It can be said that the PAAA is fast becoming a rallying point in the resurgence of artistic creativity among Polish Americans of Santa Barbara.

Jolanta Skrzynska, secretary of the PAAA, lives in Santa Barbara.

THE POLISH PARISH COUNCIL
IN SANTA BARBARA

Catherine Deresiewicz

An oft-repeated saying that "Santa Barbara is the only Mission that was never abandoned" fell on receptive ears in the Polish Roman Catholic parish in Los Angeles. In September of 1976 a busload of people accompanied by Fr. Zbigniew Olbrys from Bright Mount were welcomed at the Old Mission. After the Polish Mass a pot luck dinner was served in Serra Hall.

In December the oplatek (wafer) and live Christmas pageant was announced through eight local parishes. The response from Polish Americans was most encouraging — over 100 were in attendance. Traditional Polish creches were on display as members of the PAAA contributed their artifacts.

Installation of Bishop Thaddeus Shubsda as Vicar General for Santa Barbara County in March of 1977 saw the Polish Parish Council busy and happy.

A book sale followed in June. Proceeds of $120 were realized from the two-day sale of books donated by Catholic Social Service volunteers. Later in the same month, after close of the book sale, a ballet group performance and raffle of fruits and flowers was held.

This first summary chronicle of the Santa Barbara Polish Parish Council ends with a solemn Mass celebrated by Bishop Thaddeus Shubsda on October 28, 1977. A dinner in his honor was served at Serra Hall.

Council's President is Antoni Krzyczkowski; Board Members, Bogdan Deresiewicz and Janusz Tyszkiewicz; Treasurer, Mary Grusinski; and Social Chairman, Catherine Deresiewicz.

Catherine (Kasia) Deresiewicz is the Social Chairman of the Council. She lives in Santa Barbara.

restoration

your time away
the trees sang skyward,
your memories,
lost,
covered
with twenty years
of dust,
the street
marched on
into time
eternal,

back you fly,
to the new home
to the now home
to the last
twenty year home,

back to sunny beaches
reflecting your children's
children's eyes,
reverberating
your tomorrow skies.

                    E.G. Dabrowska Wissema

PART FIVE

DOCUMENTARY
BICENTENNIAL — PEOPLE —
IDEAS — DEEDS

In recent years, what we used to call
immigration history has been transformed
into the study of ethnicity.

Andrew Rolle, *Southern California Quarterly*. Winter 1976.

INTRODUCTORY REMARKS

A Frenchman, Jean Jaures, left this message: "Take from the altars of the past the fire — not the ashes." The realization of his message can be traced throughout Poles' yesteryear as well as present life in California. The latter — and this is precisely in the purview of this documentary section of the book — has been climaxed in Polish Americans' active participation in the United States Bicentennial celebration.

A case in point was the variety of local events organized in 1975 and 1976. Their focal point was the Los Angeles Bicentennial International Hertiage Festival on May 22-23, 1976, on the City Mall. It was preceded by the Polish American Grand Bicentennial Ball. The previous year, a Polish Heritage Weekend was held April 26-27, at Loyola Marymount University.

Each of these three events are extensively documented in this section; other activities within the general framework of the Bicentennial festivities in Los Angeles are outlined in the article, "The Polish American Participation in the Bicentennial in Los Angeles."

To pass the "fire" of history on to forthcoming generations in the United States' third century, three articles present the Polish American Historical Association, California Chapter. The emphasis there is on its Students' Chapter at Loyola Marymount University. Next, an array of 19 personalities are introduced; Bishop Thaddeus A. Shubsda heads this series and an Olympic medalist closes it. In between are featured other achievers of one sort or another. Architect J. George Szeptycki writes in a personal way about his contributions to the church architecture in Southern California. Last, four business firms (one is actually an industrial undertaking) are presented as economic achievers.

All in all, the "slices" of Polish Amnerican life and fascinating people — otherwise Americans like everyone else — featured here provide a first-hand nucleus material for a grass-roots historian in the future. No less revealing are the 130 topics (including people) considered in this book, compiled by 70 contributors and 257 Polish Americans in California (one in Hawaii, one in Arizona and one in Maryland; all connected with California) listed in the *Who's Who* section of the book.

INTERNATIONAL HERITAGE BICENTENNIAL SUBCOMMITTEE SUMMARY OF PROCEEDINGS, May 21, 1974

The first meeting of the International Heritage Bicentennial Team was called to order by Barbara Perry, Executive Director of the City of Los Angeles Bicentennial Committee.

Ms. Perry announced that the theme is UNITY THROUGH DIVERSITY. While it is important for each subcommittee to come up with their own projects, it is necessary to keep the Bicentennial staff advised of their progress.

Points of information and suggestions:

1. Subcommittees will develop brief outline.
2. Since there is no precedent for a Bicentennial there will be changes in guidelines, rules and regulations.
3. It was suggested that each project touch upon the following areas in their projects:
   a) Heritage (Past)
   b) Festival, U.S.A. (Present)
   c) Horizon (Future)
4. City Hall and its facilities will be available (Convention Center, schools, parks, etc.)
5. There are media restrictions — releases for organization bulletins are okay, but any other publicity MUST go through the Public Information Office.
6. Exhibits should be informative as well as practical.
7. It is important to avoid any political overtones.
8. Submit suggestions for additional members of the subcommittee.

After further discussion, it was decided that the next meeting will be held on Tuesday, June 18th at 3:00 p.m. in Room 367 of Los Angeles City Hall.

Please call 485-4421, Ellen Mintz, with your license plate number, color, and make of car so that we may arrange parking.

Those in attendance: Father Jacek Przygoda, John Wesseling, Adolf Dusil, V. Cekanauskas, Rev. Donald Lehti, Rita Weissman, Barbara Rosenstein, Walter Herms, Professor Antony Turhollow, Cheslav Najdziuk, Rev. Lloyd Burke, Maria Fenyas, and Barbara Perry.

Stanislaw L. Lewicki, editor of a special issue of the *Polish Daily News* (Detroit), July 25-26, 1969, commemorating the Three American Astronauts' first landing on the moon.

UNITED STATES BICENTENNIAL

LOS ANGELES CITY CELEBRATIONS

POLISH HERITAGE WEEKEND

Saturday 26 and Sunday 27 of April
1975
Loyola Marymount University
Los Angeles, California

ST. ROBERT'S AUDITORIUM

Saturday
3:30 P.M. Lectures (Sponsored by the Pol. Am. Hist. Ass'n. Cal. Chap.)
"History of the University of Cracow"
Prof. Paul W. Knoll
History Department
University of Southern California

"Henryk Sienkiewicz in California"
Gillian Olechno-Huszcza
Chief Librarian
L.A. County U.S.C. Medical Center

8:00 P.M. Cultural Program

Welcome — Rev. John W. Clark, S.J.
LMU Academic Vice President

Vee Tinnin, Executive Director,
L.A. City Bicentennial Committee

Program M.C. — Ruthanne Simons, LMU
Krakusy M.C. — Theresa Matusiewicz, LMU

KRAKUSY Folk Dance Ensemble

Oberek

"Poles in the United States"
Alicja Brzechwa-White

Kujawiak

Remarks — Karl Lukas (Karol Lukasiak)
Motion Pictures, T.V., Stage Personality

Clog

I N T E R M I S S I O N

Trojak

Tadeusz Luczaj
Vienna International Contest Laureat
Two Songs: Stary Kapral and Polonez
At the Piano: Prof. Mario Silva

"Poles in California"
Barbara Zielinska-Martinoff

Krakowiak

Sunday
8:00 P.M. Polish Guitars Concert
          Zdzislaw Lytkowski, Leader

MAIN LIBRARY

Saturday (afternoon) and Sunday (all day)

Exhibition of Polish Coins and Stamp Collections

MALONE ART GALLERY

Saturday (afternoon) and Sunday (all day)

Polish Art Exhibits
Paintings and Artifacts

MALONE STUDENT CENTER: DEL REY ROOMS

Saturday, 6: P.M.   Polish Dinner

"I feel you can't really be an American
until you accept and celebrate your own
history."

Rev. R. Gaitan, Topeka, Kansas

SACRED HEART CHAPEL

Sunday: 6:30 P.M.

Concelebrated Mass (in Polish)

Homilist (in English)
Rev. Alphonsus Domachowski, S.J.

Hejnal Men's Choir (in Polish)
Waclaw Gazinski, Choirmaster and Organist
Edward Terelak, President

LISTEN to the POLISH RADIO HOUR

KTYM, 1460, Every Sunday at 2:30 P.M.

CONTACT its Program Director:

3424 W. Adams Blvd., Los Angeles, CA. 90018

THE KRAKUSY FOLK DANCE ENSEMBLE ROSTER

Krysia Czarnota
Jody Golowka
Barbara Jankowska
Bozena Kohlman
Laura Martin
Malgosia Niestatek
Basia Nizynska
Ewa Polaczek
Krysia Rokicka
Jeanette Sermak
Carolyn Sermak
Dzidzia Slawinska

Joanna Wnorowska
Marianna Wnorowska
Robert Cichocki
Witek Dudzinski
Marek Gwozdziowski
Tadek Ladowicz
Jacek Nizynski
Nick Pujdak
Mike Pujdak
Robert Pujdak
Tomek Slawinski

Directed by Bozena Kohlman and Marek Gwozdziowski
Choreography: Marylka Klimek-George
Costumes: Irena Kohlman and Zbigniew Szumanski
Decorations: Zbigniew Szumanski
Manager: Andrew Nizynski

THE PROGRAM COMMITTEE

Polish Dinner: Krystyna Zielkiewicz

Exhibits: Arts — Leon S. Kawecki

     Numismatic: W. Pawlowski and W. Wielkoszewski

     Philatelic: Czeslaw Olechno-Huszcza and Zbigniew Zielkiewicz

Ushers: LMU Students

Program Designer: Patricia Olszewski, LMU

Program Hosts: Jerome Kasper, Henrietta Simons,
            Sandi Sondomowicz, and Anthony Turhollow, Jr.

Executive Director: Fr. Jacek Przygoda

PROGRAMS COURTESY of DOMBROWSKI'S FLOWERS
4956 West Century, Inglewood.
Phones: 574-3039 and 678-0604 (from Los Angeles)

THE POLISH AMERICAN PARTICIPATION IN THE U.S. BICENTENNIAL CELEBRATION IN LOS ANGELES

H. Gawlinska, M.W. Wegner and K. Zielkiewicz

Planning for the Bicentennial began in Los Angeles one month after the enactment of US Public Law 93-179 on December 11, 1973, which created the American Revolution Bicentennial Administration "to . . . coordinate, facilitate, and aid in the scheduling of events . . ." in commemoration of the Bicentennial. The City Council confirmed the appointment of Charles S. Casassa, S.J., chancellor of Loyola Marymount University, as chairman of the Los Angeles Bicentennial Committee.

Teams of ethnic and special interest groups sent members to establish the International Heritage Team, which elected Alice Brzechwa-White as its chairperson. Instead of building monuments or producing the customary extravaganza, the commemoration was to be expressed in projects which would promote a better future and improve relationships between the diverse ethnic groups. Through working together, all groups became sufficiently secure to offer input to the much needed "welding" for the creation of the International Heritage Festival.

Since these commemorations sprung from a variety of ethnic groups, the Festival achieved its commemorative motto: "Unity Through Diversity." The event established lasting bonds among the groups, healing many of the previously open social wounds. Of definite value was the Los Angeles Bicentennial Culture Bus — "The Funday Sunday Bus, Line 1776" — which provided inexpensive transportation between art galleries, museums, the zoo, and the time capsule — "Tomorrow's Past" — containing items of popular interest in 1976, which was sealed and installed on the grounds of Griffith Observatory to be opened January 1, 2076.

Just as Poland was the first foreign country to be chosen to host a special U.S. Bicentennial Exhibition, "The World of Franklin and Jefferson," so the local Polish Community was among the first to receive an invitation from Rev. Charles S. Casassa to participate in Los Angeles Bicentennial celebration, through his appointment of Rev. Jacek Przygoda as the chairperson for the Polish American Bicentennial Committee.

In response, Fr. Przygoda and Krystyna Zielkiewicz, vice chairperson, arranged for an informative meeting January 24, 1975, with the Polish Community at the "Kaszubska Hall" of Our Lady of Bright Mount parish. As a result, the Polish American Bicentennial Committee was formed with representatives from the Polish American organizations in Greater Los Angeles. It included: Mark Bielski, Ingeborg M. Klimes, Barbara Martinoff, Clarence Morrissey, Hedy Pawlowski, Joan D. Sovinski, Wanda B. Szatkowski, Dr. Anthony F. Turhollow, Mary W. Wegner, Alice Brzechwa-White, Danuta Zawadzki, Dr. Szczepan Zimmer and Arthur and Gene Zygmont. Through her able leadership, Krystyna Zielkiewicz achieved the cooperation of the entire Polish Community.

Worthwhile projects are costly, and to be successful they require funding. The Polish Fraternal Society "Samopomoc" was the first and major contributor, with Mr. and Mrs. Majewski and Mr. Nalski providing large sums. The highly effective team of Dorothy Sovinski and Wanda Szatkowski skillfully promoted the fund-raising events. Many others aided in a variety of ways and crediting each person individually is impossible, due to limited space. Without the devotion, effort, energy and talent of each participant, neither the Polish pavilion at the International Heritage Festival nor this publication could become a reality.

Each project sponsored by the Polish Bicentennial Committee served a dual purpose: to meet the recommendations of the Los Angeles Bicentennial Committee and to supply the needed funding. The Polish American Bicentennial participation was expressed through the following projects:

The Polish Heritage Weekend of April 26-27, 1975, at Loyola Marymount University, offered lectures on "Contributions of Poles to the Growth of the U.S." by Barbara Martinoff and Alice Brzechwa-White; a talk by TV personality Karol Lukas; an exhibit of the Polish Philatelic and Numismatic Club; a display of Polish dances by the Krakusy Dance Group, and the serving of traditional Polish foods.

The Picnic in June of 1975 at San Antonio Winery, promoted through the efforts of Polish American Business and Professional Club.

Dance and Raffle in September of 1975, at Our Lady of Bright Mount Polish parish brought some additional revenues.

Lecture by H. Toczylowski and A. Kliszewski on "Industrial Poland — Impression from a Visit," sponsored by the Polish Millennium Library, the Polish University Club and Polish American Business and Professional Club, proved to be not only highly informative, but financially rewarding.

The Krakusy Dance Group participated in the Bicentennial International Dance Festival on January 23, 1976 at the Dorothy Chandler Pavillion in Los Angeles. Their lively and colorful dance was an appropriate expression of the Polish American cultural inheritance.

The Polish Arts and Crafts Festival at the Malone Art Gallery of Loyola Marymount University on February 28-29, 1976, paved the way for future art and cultural exhibitions. Thirty-five Polish American artists and artisans participated, displaying their works of watercolors, paintings in oil, ceramics, collages, graphics, photography, sculpture, Christmas ornaments and Easter decorations, etc. A selection from these, for the Los Angeles Bicentennial Ethnic Exhibition, was made by a jury of Mark Bielski, Mieczyslaw Gozdzikowski and Irene Vogt. The Buffet Committee served traditional Polish foods which could please any connoisseur's palate.

The Grand Ball and Banquet, to the music of Eddie Stell's Orchestra, was held April 24, 1976 at the Hyatt Regency Hotel in Los Angeles. This was the main fund-raising project, and featured Eugene Ciejka's and the "Krakusy" Dancers as the main entertainment.

The Polish kiosk-pavilion on the City Mall, created for the International Heritage Festival on May 22-23, 1976, was the final project of the Polish American Bicentennial. The committee, chaired by Krystyna Zielkiewicz, contributed greatly to the achievement of its success. Mark Bielski (helped by his wife, Kasia) was responsible for the skillful coordination, appealing composition and engaging presentation.

The interior of this tent-like, four-sided structure contained the artists' and artisans' works which were selected by the jury at the February 28-29 Polish Arts and Crafts Festival. Large baskets with artistic floral arrangements, donated by Stanley Kersten, adorned the corners of the kiosk.

The pavilion's exterior walls were decorated with Mark Bielski's creation of informative maps, photographs, and plaques offering educational information about Polish culture, history, geography, personalities and their contributions. The artistic composition of the kiosk brought expressions of admiration from other participating nationalities who acknowledged its superior quality. The performance of national folk dances by the "Krakusy" and "Mazury" dance groups also attested to the Polish cultural inheritance.

The establishment of the *Szymanowski Foundation* through the initiative of Miss Anne Cierpik produced three free concerts honoring two Poles, generals of the American Revolutionary War, Tadeusz Kosciuszko and Casimir Pulaski, featuring Karol Szymanowski's works.

The most significant of all the Polish American Bicentennial projects is this book, *Polish Americans in California, 1827-1977, and Who's Who*, sponsored by PAHA, California Chapter. Its editor, Fr. Jacek Przygoda, is responsible for collecting, compiling and editing the literary materials, as well as for a meaningful share of the financial contributions. Krystyna Zielkiewicz has also contributed to fund-raising activities, while Mary Wegner and Jerome Simons have been instrumental in the recording of subscribers and donors to the publishing fund. By opening her home for over a year to the meetings of the sub-committees, Mrs. Wegner has assured continuity in the initial planning of the book.

The realization of this project is in direct response to the Los Angeles Bicentennial Committee's appeal for ethnic groups to record the history of their contributions to America, for the benefit of all Californians. This book has become, in the words of Fr. Przygoda, "our own lasting contribution to the celebration of the United States Bicentennial."

unity through diversity

City of Los Angeles
bicentenial
international heritage
festival

Poland

'May 22,23 1976

POLISH AMERICAN BICENTENNIAL COMMITTEE

Reverend Jacek Przygoda — Chairperson
Mark Bielski
Ingeborg M. Klimes
Barbara Martinoff
Hedy Pawlowski
Joan Dorothy Sovinski
Wanda B. Szatkowski
Dr. Anthony F. Turhollow
Mary M. Wegner
Alicja Brzechwa-White
Danuta Zawadzki
Krystyna Zielkiewicz
Dr. Szczepan Zimmer
Arthur Zygmont
Gene Zygmont

THOSE RESPONSIBLE FOR THE POLISH PAVILION

Chairperson — Reverend Jacek Przygoda
Vice-Chairperson — Krystyna Zielkiewicz
Vice-Chairperson International Heritage Festival — Alicja Brzechwa-White
Liaison L.A. City Hall/Polish Community — Barbara Martinoff
Design & Overall Coordination — Mark Bielski
Historical & Statistical Research — Kasia Bielski
Writing & Editing — George Cybulski
                    Akiko Ono Cybulski
Design Assistants — Jan Bielski
                    Jacek Podhorski
                    Jan Tabencki
Music — Stanislaw K. Cybulski
        Stefan Grubinski
Electrical Installation — Henryk Jankowski
                          Peter Ratajczak
Slides from Poland — Jerzy L. Pujdak
Flower Arrangement — Stanley Kersten

THOSE WHO HELPED RAISE THE FUNDS

POLISH AMERICAN HISTORICAL ASSOCIATION California Chapter
POLISH PARISH — OUR LADY OF THE BRIGHT MOUNT CHURCH, 3424 West
Adams Boulevard, Los Angeles
LOYOLA MARYMOUNT UNIVERSITY
POLISH FRATERNAL ASSOCIATION "SAMOPOMOC"
KLUB SW. STANISLAWA
POLISH RADIO HOUR
CLEM'S POLISH DELICATESSEN, 3002 W. Florence, Los Angeles
COUNTRY CLUB LIQUOR, 300 E. Las Tunas Drive, San Gabriel
HOLLYWOOD WATCH SERVICE, 5453 Hollywood Blvd., Hollywood
JOANNA'S GIFT GALLERY, 473 E. Colorado Blvd., Pasadena

Jadwiga Bukowinska
Helena Brzechwa
Regina Breese
Krystyna Danko
Izabela Frankowska
Zofia Gozdzikowska
Wiktoria Glebocka
Krystyna Gwizdak
M.H. Henzel
Krystyna Kabarowska
Zofia Kabarowska
Teresa Kaminska
Natalia Kaminska
Jerzy Kaminski
Jan Karpinski
Gena Kliszewska
Ingeborg Klimes
Celina Kozak

Alicja Londowicz
Laura Mathews
Wladyslaw Maciejowski
Barbara Martinoff
Marycz
Stanislaw Majewski
Irena Mrozewska
B.I. Mudy
Wladyslaw Nalski
Krystyna Nawroczynska
Tadeusz Nowicki
Henryk Nowowiejski
Stanislawa Niemiec
Pasternacki
J.L. Pawlowski
Alicja Podhorska
Polczynska
Marianna Polaczek

Dorota Prega
Janina Rezler
Leokadia Stasiek
Dorothy Sovinski
Helena Stelmach
Janina Serwacka
Wanda Szatkowski
Slawa Szymak
Franciszka Tuszynska
Irena Vogt
Maria Wegner
Lilia Westwalewicz
Danuta Wojciechowska
Alicja Brzechwa-White
Janina Zdzielnicka
Halina Zimmer
Danuta Zawadzka
Krystyna Zielkiewicz
Jozefa Zrodlo

THE FOLLOWING ARTISTS AND THEIR WORKS ARE REPRESENTED AT THIS EXHIBITION

PAINTINGS

Mrs. Christina S. Eichler
"The Winter"

Mrs. Bozena Grubinski-Salak
"Woman's Face"

Mr. George Kaminski
"Nativity"
"Conversion"
"Duel"

Mrs. Jadwiga Lazowska
"Boat"

Mrs. Barbara Lewicka
"Yacht Club Harbour"
"Polish Old Town"
"Southern California"

Mr. Jacek Podhorski
"Landscape"
"Portrait of a Woman in a Hat"

Miss Edyta Salak
"Old Soldier"
"Old & Young Faces"

Mrs. Helena Tornau
"Testament"
"Plantform Composition"

Mr. William Witkowski
"Sadness"

Mrs. Frances Z. Stampinski
"Sea Shore in France"

Mrs. Miroslawa Harvey
"Poppies"
"Summer Time in Poland"
"After the Rain"
"Merchant from Cashah"

CERAMICS

Mrs. Sophie Janczur
Ornamental Chili Pot
Girl Face Vase
Small Violet Bowl
Small Blue & Yellow Bowl
Plate with Flower Design
King and Two Queens

Miss Edyta Salak
Long Cylinder Vase

Mrs. Henryka Rundzio
Vase — Fish

Mr. James Olczyk
Spanish Lady — Porcelain
Green, Blue, White, Muted Pink — Porcelain

TAPESTRY

Mrs. Yolanta Martusewicz-Shani
"Red Vibration"
"Improvisation"
"Connection in Space"
"Volcanic Eruption"
"Bouquet"
"Sad Glance"
"Double Points"

FOLK ART

Mrs. Helena Borowska
Christmas Mangers (Crèche)
"Villages of Lowicz"
"Bicentennial" w/K. Pulaski, T. Kosciuszko, I. Paderewski

Mrs. Emilia V. Romanowska
"Polish Rooster"

Mrs. Irena Romanowska
All "Pisanki" & 5 egg shell pitchers

Mrs. Helena Weyna
16 Paper Cutouts
1 Felt Cutout

Mrs. Janina Czyrko
All Dolls Dressed in Polish Costumes

PHOTOGRAPHS

Mr. Peter Z. Suszynski
"Cottonwood Greek Canyon Trees, California"
"Big Sur Coast Line, California"
"Pinion Tree — Acent Bristlecone Pine Forest
"Palos Verdes Peninsula 1975"
"Girl Walking in the Park, Denver, Colorado"
"Clown" — Multiple Exposure

Mr. Stanley Wegner
"Winter Scene"
"San Francisco"
"Seashore"
"Condemned"
"Desert Flowers"
"Wave"

THE POLISH AMERICAN BICENTENNIAL GRAND BALL IN LOS ANGELES

Tom Szatkowski

Polish Americans and their friends celebrated the United States Bicentennial with a Grand Ball and Banquet. It was held at the Hyatt Regency Hotel in Los Angeles on April 24, 1976. Months of planning prepared for this premiere: Polish American Bicentennial event in Los Angeles. Chairwomen Joan D. Sovinski and Wanda B. Szatkowski coordinated the efforts of the outstanding planning committee, which had representatives from two community churches and twenty-six Polish American organizations.

The best accommodations were secured for the celebration. The invitations were printed with a red, white and blue cover which divided and opened to reveal the traditional gold eagle of America. To the right of the eagle was an invitation printed in English; to the left of the eagle was an invitation printed in Polish.

A ten-page program including reprints of American historical documents was distributed at the celebration. Among the documents were the Declaration of Independence, the Constitution and Bill of Rights. Persons on the Grand Ball committee, Patrons of the Grand Ball and participating organizations were listed on two pages in the center of the program.

Nine events took place during the celebration night. Among them were the singing of both the United States and Polish national anthems. A U.S. Air Force color guard was present. The Very Reverend Charles S. Casassa addressed the participants and entertainment was provided by Polish folk dancers. Hosts and hostesses saw to the comfort of all guests.

The menu, in the order it was served, consisted of the following: Kartoflanka po polsku (Hot Vichyssoise), Paluszki serowe (Cheese Straws), Salatka po Amerykansku (Chef's Mixed Green Salad), Supreme z pulardy Chasseur z ryzem (Double Breast Chicken Chasseur-Rice Pilaf), Brokuly Polonaise (Broccoli Polonaise), Lody Vacharin z truskawkami Flambé (Ice Cream Log Vacherin with Strawberries Flambé) and Wino Almaden Chablis.

This night in April of 1976 was a time when happy people from Los Angeles, San Francisco, Las Vegas and San Diego gathered to honor America's birthday and prepare for America's future.

Polish American U.S. Bicentennial Celebration in Los Angeles, April 24, 1976. Head table at the Grand Ball and Banquet, Hyatt Regency Hotel. From left: Cyril Holton, Mrs. Stephanie Opid-Holton, Mrs. Charlotte Turhollow, Dr. Anthony Turhollow. Bishop William R. Johnson, George Kalinski, M.C.

LEON S. KAWECKI:
ECHO OF THE U.S. BICENTENNIAL

Kathy S. Hayes

Leon S. Kawecki was born in Poland and studied at the State College of Fine Arts in Poznan, Poland, before continuing his studies in Western Europe and the United States.

Kawecki has exhibited his creative works of art in national and international competitions in Poland, Germany, Mexico and throughout the United States. Since 1959 he has been West Coast Art Director for Mead Packaging Corporation, and since 1971 has been designing illustrated catalog covers for University of California, Irvine.

Kawecki is an artist with a compulsion to elevate the Polish cause. For the Copernican Quincentennial Observation he served as Executive Officer on the Polish American Congress Regional Committee in California-Arizona, and designed numerous bookmarks, stamps, posters, Copernican illustrations, and awards, as well as the bronze-cast plaque for Griffith Observatory. He also designed the multi-color cover for *Mikolaj Kopernik Quincentennial Album*, published in 1973 at LMU in Los Angeles.

For the American Bicentennial, Kawecki designed a commemorative medal, cast in bronze, silver and gold. The obverse shows the Statue of Liberty accompanied by Poland's Statue of King Sigismund III, with the flags of America and Poland traversing the center. The reverse shows a triarch of the Freedom Founders, Kosciuszko, Washington and Pulaski.

Kawecki is a member of the Copernicus California-Arizona Regional Committee, National Society of Art Directors, Art Directors of Los Angeles, Society of Illustrators, American Philatelic Society, California Foreign Coin Club, Polish American Historical Association, Polish University Club of Los Angeles, and is listed in *Who's Who in the West* and in *Men of Achievement*, 1973.

FOR THE RECORD: THE 1973 PAHA — CALIFORNIA CHAPTER MEETING

Helena H. Grams

The second meeting of the PAHA, California Chapter, was held Sunday afternoon, March 4, 1973 in the Rosecrans Faculty Center, Loyola University, Los Angeles, with over 40 people in attendance.

The meeting was called to order and the following agenda was submitted by Rev. Jacek Przygoda and accepted by the Association:

1. Mikolaj Kopernik's Commemorative Festivities in Los Angeles.
   a) Loyola's contribution
   b) Local PAHA's share
   c) Mikolaj Kopernik Album
2. Local Chapter Organization
   a) Executive Board: President, Secretary, Treasurer, Public Relations Officer, Corresponding Secretary, Membership Drive Chairman.
   b) Advisory Council
   c) Headquarters
3. Further Plan of Action
4. Publication of a Local Chapter Bulletin, Editor and Staff
5. PAHA Annual Meeting in San Francisco; our participation in it, e.g., the Host Chapter and eventually members of our Local Arrangements Committee.

I. Introductory remarks on Mikolaj Kopernik, by Father Jacek Przygoda.

"Some of us have recently heard of 'The Theatre of the Absurd' as the newest achievement in the Art of the Theatre. It has been displayed in literature, on the stage, on TV screens.

"Five hundred years ago was born a man who had devoted his life to 'The Theatre of the Absolute,' the Creator of the cosmos. In fact, Mikolaj Kopernik, the man of history and science, had 'stopped the sun and moved the earth.' Better yet, Kopernik has moved people on it. Why? Among other aims, to better know, through astronomy, the symmetry in the Universe and its First Cause.

Helena H. Grams was in 1973-76 the PAHA Chapter recording secretary. She lives in Los Angeles.

"We are gathered here as members and guests of PAHA, California Chapter, to pay tribute to the memory of the famous Polish astronomer. In the ensuing discussion we will consider participation in the Mikolaj Kopernik Celebration on Loyola's campus. This celebration is being planned by an ad hoc faculty committee under Loyola's President, Rev. Donald P. Merrifield, S.J., and will take place from Sunday, April 29 through Thursday May 17, 1973.

"However, prior to the Celebration, Dr. Karol Estreicher will lecture at Loyola University on Wednesday evening, April 18, at 7:30 in Strub Theatre. His topic will be 'Krakow in Mikolaj Kopernik's Time.' No admission charge. Loyola University is expecting a sizable representation of our Los Angeles Polish American community at this event. Please try to attend this promising presentation by Dr. Estreicher so that you may 'spread the word' so to speak.

"The Kopernik Celebration at Loyola will consist of the following: An Academic Convocation on Tuesday, May 1, at 11 a.m. in St. Robert's Hall, at which time will be the unveiling of the Mikolaj Kopernik Bust. There will be a scholarly lecture by Prof. Robert Westman from UCLA, on the evening of Thursday, May 17 at 7:30 in Pereira Hall, Room #31. A week-long display of Copernican paintings, posters, pictures and related materials, organized by Miss Irene Zmurkevych, Cultural Affairs Coordinator, will take place.

"Also, the Polish American Congress was instrumental in planning a Kopernik Commemorative program at the Los Angeles Griffith Observatory for April 19.

"If qualified readers were available, a play honoring Kopernik by Mrs. Helena D. Morrissey could be performed.

"We would also like to invite the Polish Folk Dance Ensemble Krakusy to perform for the Loyola faculty, student body and guests. It will take place on Sunday, April 29, 1973 at 7:30 p.m. in Strub Theatre.

"Fr. Merrifield is very anxious to taste typical Polish delicacies, as are other members of this student body and faculty. So, here's a chance to treat them to Polish American culinary delights.

"All this indicates that the Mikolaj Kopernik Commemoration will become a Polish event at this University. And this is one more reason why Dr. Anthony Turhollow [also a member of the Kopernik Committee] and I would like to ask all of you here present for help. In fact, quite a bit of gracious and efficient help. Suggestions are also welcome."

II. Local Chapter Organization:

According to the Constitution and Standing Rules of PAHA, Article 13, Sections 2, 3 and 4, page 108, the following is reported:

At the time of the first Chapter organizational meeting, held here at

Loyola on Sunday, December 3, 1972, the following were active members of the Association in California and Arizona: Jerzy Lerski, Stefan Pasternacki, Jacek Przygoda, Artur Waldo, Anthony Turhollow and Henryk Westwalewicz.

As of March 15, 1973, the following have joined the Chapter: Tadeusz Bielecki, Anne F. Cierpik, Tadeusz Dudzinski, Eugenia Dziunikowska, Krystyna Eichler, Anna Festen, Stanley Garstka, Hanka Gorska, Helena Grams, Benjamin Grey, Bronislaw Kaper, Gen. Stanislaw Karpinski, Jerome Kasper, Sr., Eugene P. Kulas.

Also becoming Chapter members during the past year are Otto Lauterbach, Wladyslaw Marcinkowski, Zbigniew Marcinkowski, Laura Mathews, Bruno Mudy, Clarence Morrissey, Helen Morrissey, Andrzej Nowakowski, Antoinette Rydzeski, Rev. Antoni Saran, Vlodzimierz Ordon-Sklodowski, Witold S. Sworakowski, Szczepan Zimmer, Edward Szmit, Zygmunt Taube and Helena Tornau.

To complete the list of new members: Franciszka Tuszynska, Richard Uzarewicz, Henryk Wars, Zygmunt Wisznicer, Wilhelm Wolny, Jan Woyski, Daniel J. Zapolski and Rudolph Zatoka.

Grand total as of this date is approximately 44 active members. The membership drive will continue, and we hope to show an even bigger increase during the next year. Membership applications are available through Fr. Przygoda, Loyola University of Los Angeles.

Many people in this socially and culturally maturing community *do* care to record our past achievements and to nurture present and future Polish American cultural and social roles in California. Please do your part to bring all interested persons into our membership ranks.

Executive Board members for 1973 were approved as follows: President, Fr. Jacek Przygoda; Secretary, Prof. Anthony Turhollow; Treasurer, Mr. Jerome Kasper; Public Relations Officer and Chapter Bulletin Editor, Dr. Wlodzimierz Ordon-Sklodowski; Editorial and Corresponding Secretary, Mrs. Helena H. Grams.

Advisory Council members were approved as follows: Anne F. Cierpik, Stanislaus Cybulski, Gen. Stanislaw Karpinski, Eugene P. Kulas, Laura Mathews, Helen Morrissey, Stephan Pasternacki, Zygmunt Taube, Helena Tornau, Artur L. Waldo, Wilhelm Wolny, Daniel J. Zapolski.

Henryk Westwalewicz was elected Membership Drive Chairman and Mr. S. Pasternacki was put in charge of musical programs for the Mikolaj Kopernik Celebrations.

Headquarters for this Chapter will be located at Loyola University of Los Angeles. Its administration is happy to provide PAHA with these facilities as a community service to this Association.

III. Further Plan of Action:

Under this item there was a discussion to further recruitment of new members and discussion of specific endeavors such as the study of Helena Modrzejewska (Modjeska) and Henryk Sienkiewicz's stay in Santa Ana, Felix Wierzbicki's contribution to California history in San Francisco, and other eminent personalities connected with the Polish past in California. As announced at the first local Chapter organizational meeting in December of 1972, a Polish American cultural-historical center in Los Angeles could some day become a reality.

IV. Publication of Quarterly Bulletin:

Dr. Wlodzimierz Ordon-Sklodowski was selected to be Editor of the bulletin; Mrs. Helena H. Grams will serve as editorial secretary.

V. PAHA Annual Meeting in San Francisco:

The California Chapter's role in assisting the National PAHA in preparing plans for the annual meeting at the end of this year in San Francisco is of the utmost importance. As soon as specific plans are submitted by the Chicago Office, appropriate steps to actively participate in the annual meeting will be taken.

Fr. Przygoda had "floated" a loan to help in the publication of *Mikolaj Kopernik Album* by this Chapter. Copies went on sale following this meeting. The *M.K. Album* is the work of Dr. Tadeusz Bielecki.

Eight new PAHA members were enrolled. A wine-tasting hour followed; delicious cookies were donated by Mrs. Vi Kasper. Guests were introduced and warmly welcomed including Mrs. Anne F. Cierpik, Ben Grey, Zygmunt Wisznicer, Rev. Anthony Saran of the Polish American Congress, Mrs. Laura Mathews, Stanislaus K. Cybulski, manager of the Krakusy Polish Folk Dance Ensemble, and many others.

At the close of the meeting, a further appeal was made to attend the forthcoming Mikolaj Kopernik Activities on Loyola Campus.

BULLETIN & NEWSLETTER

P. A. H. A. - California Chapter

SPRING, 1977   LOS ANGELES, CALIFORNIA   Vol. 2   No. I

MEMORABLE PAHA MEETING

Sunday, 19 December, 1976, was another milestone in the life of the PAHA-California Chapter. On that date, our membership held its second semi-annual meeting at the library of the Queen of The Angels Seminary in San Fernando.

A very warm welcome was extended to us by **The Rev. Msgr. J. Reilly**, Rector of the Seminary. In his welcoming words Monsignor expressed his joy in seeing the representatives of the Polish community in this area. He also said that his mind and heart are with those who treasure their past and cultural heritage. He was happy to extend the hospitality to all the PAHA members and their guests.

The purpose of the meeting itself was presented by **Father Jacek Przygoda** in the following motion: "That gathered here Polish Americans in California, actively co-operate in all possible ways in compiling, editing and publishing the book — *Polish Americans in California 1827-1977, and Who's Who.*

The motion was seconded by **Z. Kowalski** and **Z. Zielkiewicz**. A long discussion followed in which participated: **Dr. Stanley Garstka, C. Morrissey, Christiana Dudzinski, Col. M. Haifter, Col. Stan Wyglendowski, Dr. Anthony Turhollow** and others.

Dr. Turhollow presided over the meeting and he and Fr. Przygoda answered all the questions. The vote on the motion followed and *was passed unanimously.*

During the course of the meeting, Fr. Przygoda gave a summary of our role in the Bicentennial celebration in Los Angeles. He thanked all of the committee members for their outstanding contribution of time, energy, effort and talent. He also expressed gratitude for the support received from Polish Americans in our area relative to these historical events.

Following a social hour, a number of persons volunteered to serve on various committees in conjunction with the publication of the book. The following is a *tentative* list of committees and volunteers:

Typing of first draft
Anna Hroscikowski
Maria Tabasz
Ingeborg Klimes
The Simons family

Translations
Father A. Saran
Mr. L. Klimes
Czeslaw Olechno-Huszcza

Publicity
Don Malin (Schools & Colleges)
Jean Breese
Zbigniew Kowalski
Dan Evans
Ed Kaminski
Joseph Koleda (P.A.C.)
Christiana Dudzinski

Research Staff
Doris Bernhagen
Danuta Zawadzki
C. Morrissey

Associate Editors
Al Antczak (Editor, *The Tidings*)
Margaret Prasniewski
Gillian Olechno-Huszcza

Assistant Editors
Jerome Laskowski
Ruthanne S. Eastwood

Managing Editor
Mary Wegner (declined)

Treasurer
Jerome Simons

Fund Raising
Krystyna Zielkiewicz

In conclusion it should be said that the meeting was fruitful and promising in regard to the publication of the planned book, *Polish Americans in California 1827-1977, and Who's Who*, hopefully by the end of 1977. The Executive Board of PAHA is happy to acknowledge the impressive attendance by its members and guests.

IMPORTANT PROGRESS REPORT

We are happy to report to the subscribers (who paid $10.00) and donors (who paid $25.00) that we have collected $5,100.00 towards the publication of our book. The minimum cost estimate we have received so far is $10,000.00. This fact simply means that we have to intensify our campaign for subscribers and donors alike if we want to see the work come to fruition.

As regards to the material for publication to date, we are happy to acknowledge the recently sent article on Polish Americans in Northern California by **Prof. Witold Sworokowski**, Stanford, Calif.

Others who submitted articles are: **Dr. Tom Szatkowski**, Toluca Lake, Calif., who wrote about Ralph Modjeski, the famous bridge builder in America (U.S. and Canada); **Michele M. Sawa**, student of journalism at USC, who prepared an article on Helen E. Bayer; **The Rev. A. Saran**, who gave a history of the Polish American Congress, California Division.

Previously written articles and contributing authors are: **Ellen K. Lee** (South Laguna Beach) who wrote about **Helena Modjeska** in Anaheim; **Gillian Olechno-Huszcza**, on **Sienkiewicz** in California; **Dr. Alfred Wrobel; George Szeptycki; Gene Zygmont; Helena Liibke**, and works by other authors.

We are still expecting more manuscripts, so that our book will represent a well rounded picture of past and presently living Polish Americans in California.

REV. JACEK PRZYGODA — HAIMAN AWARD RECIPIENT

Fr. Jacek Przygoda, Professor Emeritus at Loyola Marymount University, and our Executive Secretary, received the 1976 Haiman Award during the convention of the Polish American Historical Association, held in Washington, D.C., on December 26-28, 1976.

In accepting the Award, Fr. Przygoda commented: "Life grows as it is spent . . . This truism can certainly be ascribed to Mieczyslaw Haiman's published works. They were genuinely researched Polish American history.

"Also his idea, shared with Oskar Halecki after being threshed by Arthur Waldo in the Polish American press, to organize in 1948 the Polish American Historical Association (PAHA), has become a living testimony to Haiman's foresight in the unearthed field, rich in the achievements of Polish personalities as well as Polish communitary life in America.

"Soren Kierkegaard aptly stated: 'that part which cannot become present is not worth remembering.' This dictum is not applying to the Polish American evolving reality, thanks again to Haiman.

"In *Adventures of a Mathematician*, S.M. Ulam made this observation: 'It seems to me that good memory . . . depends to a large extent on the ability to use one's memory properly to find the analogies, past, present and future, which . . . are essential to the development of new ideas.'

"Good historians have this quality. They research and record the past first, then hand over their findings to the present and forthcoming generations, as it was done by M. Haiman. His 'life grew' indeed in the Polish Roman Catholic Union Archives in Chicago. And that fact must be remembered by all of us here, for I cannot agree with presently surfacing attempts of separating the religious experience from the very roots of the Polish American community.

"In closing, I would like you all to know that I am grateful for this Award honoring the name of our memorable historian, Mieczyslaw Haiman. Thank you."

PAHA — CALIFORNIA CHAPTER MEETING AT LMU

Our semi-annual meeting will be held on Saturday, February 26, 1977, at 2:30 PM, in Huesman Hall at Loyola Marymount University

Dr. George J. Lerski, University of San Francisco, will be the speaker.

You and your guests are invited to attend the meeting and enjoy Prof. Lerski's lecture. You will also have an opportunity to meet our youthful PAHA LMU Club members.

SPRING CONCERT IN THE OFFING

Loyola Marymount University Choruses will present a Spring Concert on Sunday, May 15, 1977, in the Sacred Heart Chapel on Campus at 8:00 p.m., accompanied by the Westside Symphony Orchestra and Conducted by **Paul Salamunovich**. Music of interest to Polish Americans and those of Polish descent will be performed, namely the *Stabat Mater* by **Karol Szymanowski**.

POLISH LANGUAGE COURSE AT LMU

The Loyola Marymount University Continuing Education Bulletin for Spring 1977, carried this item of interest:

"America has been enriched by the contribution of Poles and Polish Americans throughout its history, and Poles have made great contributions to the field of science, music, literature and politics. It is therefore surprising that few colleges and universities offer courses in the Polish language. Loyola Marymount is pleased to present this first course in Elementary Polish.

"Students will learn the basics of Polish through oral and written practice. Enrollment is limited to assure small classes which will allow for much individual instruction."

FOR THE RECORD

The following letter of appreciation is worthy of documentation in our PAHA *Bulletin & Newsletter*.

June 9, 1976

Reverend Father J. Przygoda
Loyola Marymount University
7101 West 80th Street
Los Angeles, CA 90045

Dear Reverend Przygoda:

The Los Angeles City Bicentennial Committee wishes to extend its appreciation to you and all those who worked with you for your participation in the International Heritage Festival.

The response from those who attended the festival has been outstanding. It was a memorable event of which Los Angeles can truly be proud.

Again, thank you for your many hours of service which helped to make this first International Heritage Festival such a success.

Sincerely,

The Rev. Charles S. Casassa, S.J.,
Chairman, Los Angeles City Bicentennial
Committee

Layout & Production	Editor	Chapter President
Joe & Bev Timineri	**Jerome S. Laskowski**	**Dr. Anthony F. Turhollow**
	Associate Editor	Executive Secretary
	Gillian Olechno-Huszcza	**Fr. Jacek Przygoda**

THE PAHA STUDENT CHAPTER AT LOYOLA MARYMOUNT UNIVERSITY

Donald P. Malin
Anthony Turhollow, Jr.

In the Spring of 1976 some Polish American students at LMU, and among them Marie T. Hodgson and Donald P. Malin, decided to organize a group of their own.

The first step was to contact Father Jacek Przygoda, Professor and long-time member of the Economics department on the campus. Fr. Przygoda, they found, was already considering the establishment of a student chapter of the Polish American Historical Association. He was well aware of the need to interest Polish American students in their heritage and culture. (Just as surely as the years pass, the young must sooner or later assume the leadership in propagating their culture among themselves, their children and their children's children.)

No sooner had Malin conferred with Fr. Przygoda than he was inundated with applications, pamphlets, and the task of organizing the student chapter of PAHA. In April of 1976, with Don Malin as president, Marie Hodgson as vice president, Mary Tabasz as secretary and Ann Marie Socash as treasurer, the chapter conducted a campaign to establish classes in Polish language and history.

The chapter consulted with Robert Cleymaet, Professor of Modern Languages, and Anthony Turhollow, Professor of History. Fr. Przygoda secured funding for the project, and the administration consented to establish a course on the Polish language, if the chapter could find ten students to take the course. Seventeen students eagerly signed up: Stasia Ahlin, Mary K. Adams, Ed Cilwik, Witold Dudzinski, Eugenia Dziunikowska, Mark Brodka, Marie T. Hodgson, Ann A. Hroscikowski, Marianne K. Murawski, Mary Tabasz, Dr. Anthony Turhollow, Ethel G. Olechno-Huszcza, Anthony Turhollow, Jr., Christine Pilecki, Renate Lichter, Theresa Matusiewicz, Ann Marie Socash and Donald P. Malin.

The students spent the year successfully learning the rudiments of the Polish language along with some cultural background, under the able guidance of Mr. Czeslaw Olechno-Huszcza, Chairman of the Department of Foreign Languages at Morningside High School in Inglewood, and former foreign language examiner (graduate level) at

University of California, Los Angeles. In future years, the Polish language course will be offered every second term, alternating with Russian.

The student chapter organized exhibits at the annual Loyola Marymount University Fair depicting the cultural and culinary aspects of Polish heritage. They also supported concerts of the work of such distinguished Polish composers as Chopin and Szymanowski.

The PAHA Student Chapter at Loyola now lists the following active members: Ann Marie Socash, Randall R. Sobczak, Marianne K. Murawski, Mary Tabasz, Krystyna Pilecki, Theresa Koscki, Ann Hroscikowski, Marie Hodgson, Edward K. Cylwik, Rebecca Simons, Denise Simons, Gregory Simons, Bill Baczek, Renate Lichter, Witold Dudzinski, Mark Brodka, Patricia Olszewski, and Don Malin. In the Fall of 1977, Ann Cugowski, Mary Beth Pokrzywnicki, Jeannette Sermak and John Stanwyck have joined the PAHA Student Chapter at LMU. Don Malin is the president and Mary Tabasz the secretary-treasurer.

BISHOP THADDEUS A. SHUBSDA: PROUD TO BE POLISH

Jacek Przygoda

The first Polish American auxiliary Bishop of the Los Angeles archdiocese was consecrated at St. Vibiana cathedral on February 19, 1977. He is the son of Julian Szubzda and Marianna Jelski, both born in Sitkowo, county of Sokolka, voivodship of Bialystok, Poland. His father came to the United States in 1904, and worked first as a coal miner in Pennsylvania; he then moved to Niagara Falls, New York, and subsequently settled in Buffalo. There he was employed by the Prudential Insurance Company and worked up to the position of the assistant superintendent.

In 1920 he went back to Poland and on the Feast of the Purification of the Blessed Mother, February 2, 1921, was married at St. George parish church in Janow. The couple, after living in Buffalo until 1924, came to Los Angeles. Here the future Bishop, Thaddeus Anthony, was born in 1925. Ted's primary schooling included lessons in the Polish language, taught every Saturday in the Polish Hall on Avalon Avenue by Jozefa Kudlicka. Then, following studies at the junior and major seminary, he was ordained a priest in 1950. Father Ted Shubsda celebrated his first Mass at the Polish church of Our Lady of the Bright Mount in Los Angeles. It is significant to add that the newly ordained priest's father was born on the Feast of the Assumption of the Blessed Virgin Mary, August 15, and his mother on the Feast of the Annunciation, March 25. Father Ted Shubsda's mother was not present at her son's first Mass since she had died in 1943.

In addition to parish work, Father Shubsda has served the Church in many capacities. He has been a Spiritual Director for the Catholic Labor Institute in Los Angeles, was a member of the Matrimonial Tribunal, and worked in the office of the Society for the Propagation of the Faith. Currently he is the pastor of Saint Paul's parish at Bronson Avenue and Washington Boulevard in Los Angeles, and as a Bishop, he is the Episcopal Vicar for Santa Barbara County.

Reminiscing about the past, Bishop Shubsda affectionately underscores his mother's great devotion to the Blessed Sacrament and to Our Lady of Sorrows, and deep respect for priests. His father, who

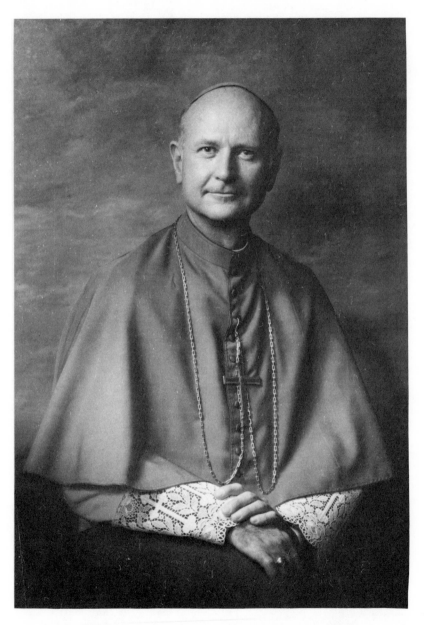

Bishop Thaddeus Anthony Shubsda. Madrid Photography, Glendale.

died two years ago, had a great love for Poland, her history and traditions. He subscribed to Polish American newspapers, and as an octogenarian drove seven miles each way to the Polish church on West Adams Boulevard in Los Angeles. "Oh, yes, he was always proud to be Polish," affirmed his grateful son.

Carl Kaymark, speaking on behalf of all present at the Polish parish hall on the occasion of Bishop Shubsda's pontifical Mass on Sunday, March 27, 1977, stated: "But most of all we are proud that His Excellency is a man of Polish descent and comes from a religiously solid family. Although he lost his mother at an early age, he was truly fortunate in having a noble father. All who knew Mr. Shubsda know what a fine gentleman he was. He always had a big smile and a cheery hello for everyone. He was a man revered in the community and a man who loved his family and his Polish heritage. Many of Bishop Shubsda's exceptional qualities are, no doubt, a direct influence of his father."

When the Bishop's father was 79 years old, he and then Msgr. Shubsda went to Poland. The father took his son to Our Lady of Czestochowa Shrine. It was the first time for each of them to pay homage to Queen of Poland. Now the Bishop's devotion to Our Lady is signified by the picture of Our Lady of Czestochowa on his episcopal mitre.

Bishop Thaddeus Shubsda and his entourage, on the steps of the Polish parish rectory, in Los Angeles, March 27, 1976. Photo Zygmunt Jarosz.

REV. ANTHONY SARAN: INTREPID POLE

Kathy S. Hayes

The road from a log cabin outside Tarnow, Poland, where he was born August 17, 1907, to a Silver Jubilee at Cathedral Chapel, Los Angeles, has been a long and varied one for Father Anthony Saran (Saratowicz). At the age of five, Saratowicz emigrated to America with his mother, a mid-wife who was to bear seven more children after Anthony.

In 1928 Anthony Saran graduated from Harrison Tech high school in Chicago, and entered junior college as a pre-med student, encouraged by his mother. For three years he studied, playing semi-professional baseball to pay expenses. When his money ran out, he wanted to join the Navy, but his mother encouraged him to join a religious order. He spent the next five years studying philosophy at the Resurrection House of Studies in St. Louis, Missouri.

In 1936, Saran went to Poland to study for two years at John Casimir University in Lwow, and then one year at Jagiellon University in Krakow. When Hitler invaded Poland in 1939, he moved· to his grandmother's farm, 50 miles east of Krakow, where he spent the next six years working on the farm, interpreting war news via London Radio (had he been caught, the penalty would have been death) and privately teaching the high school and college students who were forbidden by the Nazis to attend school.

After the Russians drove out the Germans in 1945, Saran began teaching English and History at Adam Mickiewicz High School in Tarnow. In July of 1946 the American Embassy arrived, and Saran registered, and was assigned to sail home in February 1947 on a Liberty Ship.

Back in America, Saran returned to the Resurrection House of Study in St. Louis, graduating in 1951. He then spent two years doing post graduate work in Rome at the Gregorian University. In 1953, at the age of 46, Saran began his first parish work, in Ontario, Canada. He spent two years in Canada, two years at Newman High School in California, five years at the Polish Parish in Chicago, and then four years in Panama City, Florida, where he organized the Polish Millennium Celebration.

In 1966, Father Saran was sent to Healdsburg, California, for two years, and then to St. Anthony's Church in Long Beach to spend three years teaching high school and doing parish work. In 1971 he was given the post of Administrator at Mt. Carmel, Long Beach, and in 1974 moved to Cathedral Chapel, where he celebrated his silver jubilee in 1976.

It has been a long road for the boy born in a log cabin in Poland. Throughout it all he has never lost an abiding love for, and interest in, his Polish heritage. He is an active member of the Polish American Congress, California Division, and has served in the capacity of secretary for many years. He is an active member and past vice president of the Polish American Historical Association. A full life for this man who is 70 years young.

THE CASE OF CONTEMPORARY CHURCH ARCHITECTURE IN CALIFORNIA — A PERSONAL VIEW —

J. George Szeptycki

It was my lifelong dream to be a church architect. During my studies at the Warsaw Polytechnic School of Architecture, my interest in churches expressed itself in the study of church buildings of the past. The very touch of five hundred year old brick seemed to me a romantic experience. At that time, I wrote several articles in art magazines calling attention to historical monuments needing restoration. I also spent a good part of the year of 1938 on a Polish Government Scholarship in Italy, intensely studying the technical aspects of preservation. In 1939, as a young architect, I found myself in Nicholas Copernicus' birthplace, Torun, involved in a preservation program covering the entire Pomeranian District. My professional career was abruptly interrupted by World War II and was to be resumed only after I settled in the United States. I had decided by then to devote the future to my own creative endeavors rather than to restoration of works by others.

St. Ireneus Church, Cypress. J. George Szeptycki, architect.

It took some time after my arrival in California, in 1948, before I was prepared to start a professional practice. The first money I saved permitted me to enter the Graduate School of Architecture of the University of Southern California in 1951. In June of 1952, I was awarded a Master of Architecture Degree, with my design project and thesis devoted entirely to ecclesiastical architecture. California, Florida, Pennsylvania and Illinois state licenses followed.

St. Catherine's Military School Chapel, Anaheim. J. George Szeptycki, architect. Murals and stained glass windows, Jan Henryk De Rosen, 1956.

After a brief time, I found that I, as an Architect of European background, was expected to be an expert in historical styles believed by the majority of my prospective clients to be the only appropriate ones for church structures, while "modern" lines were generally considered unsuitable to express religious spirit. This thinking prevailed among the lay members of the Parish Building Committees and among the clergy. Both groups were obviously forsaking the tradition that the Church was always contemporary in its architecture; Romanesque in the Romanesque times and Gothic in the Gothic times.

It became clear to me that by designing in historical styles I could count on more numerous commissions. I nevertheless decided to reject this temptation for I realized that, aside from new aesthetics, contemporary approaches in architecture encompassed a whole new understanding of a building's relationship to its environment and current state of building technology. Moreover, new exciting forms, planning techniques and ideas were proliferating throughout the world in architectural magazines. Any individual architect could not help but be influenced by others, but by the same token, he was also in a position to affect the development of the entire profession. Because of this, contemporary architecture was in a continuous state of evolution more rapid, profound and inspiring than in any other period in history. Another important factor adding to vitality of contemporary architecture was the activity of the industry, conducting research on a gigantic scale and supplying the market with ever new, more attractive materials, finishes and devices.

The apparent paradox was that in spite of these influences on the architectural profession and on the market, it was much more difficult to be modern in the ecclesiastical than in the commercial field. And there was a reason for it. On one hand, the industrial revolution had created a new class of aggressive industrial and financial entrepreneurs who quickly recognized that the use of sophisticated, mass-produced building components yielded economies in the multi-story commercial structures. They also enjoyed a profusion of available finishing materials, offering the ultimate in luxury and prestigious appearance. On the other hand, the same industrial revolution wiped out the feudal Church patrons whose cultivated artistic taste was responsible for the most daring ideas expressed in the greatest architecture produced in the Western World, that is, Medieval church architecture. In contrast, church buildings of today were founded by a multitude of small lower-middle class donors who felt secure only when they followed the already established patterns.

This situation prevailed when I entered the field of church architecture in 1955 and started working on my first assignment for the Archdiocese of Los Angeles, the Polish Church of Our Lady of the Bright Mount. To my amazement, its simple design was well received, although it represented a sharp deviation from anything the Archdiocese had built before, when Spanish and Mediterranean styles were in exclusive use. Other commissions followed, although almost every project was accompanied by a heated argument for the "Spanish" on one side and persistent counter-argument for the modern on the other. Nevertheless, with time I was able to develop more and more contacts among young pastors and superiors of religious communities who were receptive to the newer ideas.

One of my early projects, which I undertook together with the late Fr. Joseph Myrda of St. Mary's College in Northern California, was a chapel for St. Catherine's Military School in Anaheim, conducted by the Dominican Sisters. Simple basic construction of posts and beams, brick walls and large glazed areas constituted a background for magnificent murals, mosaics and stained glass windows designed by one of the greatest Polish artists working in America, Jan Henryk de Rosen. My interest in selection of a proper structural scheme to harmonize with the artistic concept was valuable, because in the church, unlike commercial buildings, the structural core and connections are totally exposed, and constitute an integral part of its aesthetics.

For another example, the design of the St. Irenaeus Church in Cypress was based on white precast concrete with a massive timber-dominated interior. St. Christopher's Church in West Covina was composed of very large prestressed slabs of concrete sculptured on both sides, precast three-dimensional roof panels, and light post-tensioned concrete framework. The technical and visual qualities of concrete were played to their limits in this structure. The result was a message of logical homogeneity and spatial harmony. The entire area of another church, St. Cyril of Jerusalem in Encino, was covered with self-supporting triangular precast concrete panels, giving a diamond-like effect which was quite striking from inside and out, particularly in combination with the severe mass of sixty-foot high masonry walls.

With time, my architectural concepts became more and more daring. The Church of St. Bede's in La Canada was parabolic in form. The main altar was located at its focal point. A simple wide flat ceiling spanned the entire width, with no intermediate columns, in order to emphasize the spatial integration of the Sanctuary and the Nave. All pews were radially directed toward the altar. Thus, for the first time, I dramatized the space by using two natural illumination patterns in the interior. The Nave had mellow light filtered through the splendid faceted-glass windows, designed by the greatest contemporary artist and craftsman, Gabriel Loire of Chartres, while the Sanctuary was lit by a horizontal narrow window throwing a sharp beam of light on the curved back wall and underscoring the heroic size figure of a Resurrected Christ, executed by one of the most talented artists of the younger generation, Henry de la Vega.

I could continue this list for several pages. It would only stress the point that in every church structure I designed, there were some specific assumptions on which I built my concept as well as some specific problems I had to solve in order to give each structure its unique character. It might be a difficult shape of the lot or a relation to other existing buildings, or zoning requirements. Certain problems, however, repeated themselves in every church structure on the drafting board. The most common and crucial of them was the question of acoustics. Stiffness and hardness of commonly used materials such as concrete, and parallel surfaces of rectangular buildings, had a tendency to produce prolonged echo and poor audibility. In most cases this situation was partly corrected by an electronic sound system and highly directional speakers after the building was completed. But the basic deficiency continued to exist. In the analysis of this all-important problem in church structure, I developed a series of diagrams indicating the position and configuration of walls and ceiling to distribute equally direct and reverberated sound and to eliminate standing waves. It became obvious immediately that, for good acoustics, the basic form of our churches must be modified. For example, the Church of St. Jane Frances de Chantal in North Hollywood took a tent-like shape, with a parabolic roof suspended from a high point above the altar to a low point in the back, thus constituting a sounding board, with non-parallel walls. In St. Norbert's church in Orange, I used a modified set of the same diagrams, which resulted in a flat ceiling and walls set to a specific shape and angles. In both cases the choir loft was located at the same end of the building as the altar. Not only were the acoustics in these two churches perfect, but I also obtained interesting forms, in confirmation of a principle that no good aesthetics can be achieved in architecture if fundamental logic is violated.

The time must be right for new ideas in church architecture, because in the 1950's a National and Interdenominational Guild of Religious Architecture was formed by a group of church architects and artists. I joined the group very early and was an active member until recently. Each year, in different parts of the United States, regional and national conferences and exhibits are organized to demonstrate the best new accomplishments of contemporary church architects and artists. This movement has been reinforced by European architects and artists who, at the same time, produced several significant examples of contemporary church architecture. It is evident that a new era has been born, and contemporary church architecture is now a well-accepted phenomenon.

With my almost 30 completed church buildings and over 300 other structures related to church activities, I became, in my own mind, a church architect, and was known as such. When the Millennium of Poland's Christianity was to be celebrated in 1966, it was sort of natural that I was commissioned by the Pauline Fathers to design the Sanctuary of the Millennium in honor of Our Lady of Czestochowa, in-

Doylestown, Pennsylvania. The task was enormous. The scale of the project was gigantic. Time was short. I worked on this design with a feeling of tremendous responsibility and an understanding that this might be the most important work of my entire life. Now, I think it is.

After reading this article, one may well ask, is it possible for an architect or artist to pass a valid value judgment on his own work? I believe it is. With the passage of time he knows exactly which one of his projects has an artistic impact and which one lacks it. Moreover, looking back at my work, I dare to risk the observation that, during the course of my professional practice as a church architect, I was making continuous progress in grasping the problems involved in church architecture and in quality of design. I am convinced that, besides the Sanctuary of the Millennium, my most recent church structure for St. Mary's Parish in Fullerton, with its entire spatial concept, its relation of the building to its immediate environment, its selection and coordination of sculptures, mosaics, and stained glass windows, its design of all church appointments, and the refinement of details, constitutes a meaningful whole, and is artistically the most mature of my achievements. While working on this building, I was very close to all the artists and craftsmen, and I experienced a great feeling that, together with a team of extremely talented men, I was developing an exciting piece of art.

DR. MIECZYSLAW G. BEKKER: MOON ROVER RESEARCHER

Mieczyslaw G. Bekker was born on May 25, 1905 in Strzyzow, Poland, the son of an accountant. He received his Master's degree in mechanical engineering at the Warsaw Institute of Technology.

From 1931 to 1939 Bekker did research and development work on motorized military vehicles for the Polish Ministry of Defense. Early in 1940 he went to the French Ministry of Armament in Paris to perform similar tasks. During World War II, Dr. Bekker was commissioned as a lieutenant colonel in the Canadian Army and served in the Ministry of Supply and as head of mobility research in the Department of National Defense. He represented the Canadian Army's operations research office at Johns Hopkins University in the U.S., where he evaluated relationships between terrain and vehicles. He retired from the Canadian Army in 1950.

In 1954 Dr. Bekker established the U.S. Army's first Land Locomotion Laboratory at the Detroit Arsenal. He remained at this laboratory to serve as its first director. He also headed the terrain-vehicle laboratory at Steven's Institute of Technology, and has been a lecturer on locomotion mechanics at the University of Michigan.

For the years 1960-1970, Dr. Bekker has directed his major effort to developing wheeled mobility for astronauts to use in their exploration of the lunar surface. He attained his objective in 1971 when the first in a series of mobility systems for lunar rovers, built at AC Electronics, Defense Research Laboratories, Santa Barbara, California, went to the moon; just one year after Dr. Bekker's retirement.

Generally recognized as the father of off-the-road and articulated vehicle concepts for rough terrain of the earth and moon, he is internationally known for his pioneering contributions to the discipline of terrain-vehicle relationships. Military vehicles employing Dr. Bekker's concept are in service in the United States and Canada as well as a number of overseas countries.

As a result of his scientific work, a number of honors have been conferred on Dr. Bekker. Among them are the United States Army's award for meritorious service, the Swedish Royal Military Technical

This article is based on the material published by AC Electronics-Defense Research Laboratories, Santa Barbara, CA., and *SAE Update*, April 1977.

Association's medal for professional achievement, and a certificate of appreciation from the American Ordnance Association for "many, many contributions to vehicle design and ground mobility" which have been widely accepted by the Army, the National Aeronautics and Space Administration, and the civilian industry. In 1977 he was elected as one of the first group of fellows of the Society of Automotive Engineers.

Dr. Mieczyslaw G. Bekker, Moon Rover Researcher, in his studio, Santa Barbara.

In recognition of his contributions to the discipline of off-the-road locomotion, he was awarded the Doctor of Engineering, *honoris causa*, by the Technical University of Munich in November 1962, and by Carleton University, Ottawa, Canada, in 1975.

Dr. Bekker holds a number of U.S., British and Canadian patents and has authored many technical publications and textbooks. A recently completed series of three volumes is hailed by military and civilian authorities as "monumental work" in applying systems analysis methodology to off-the-road locomotive problems. The volumes are entitled *Theory of Land Locomotion: The Mechanics of Vehicle Mobility; Off-the-Road Locomotion: Research and Development in Terramechanics;* and *Introduction to Terrain-Vehicle Systems.*

LECH NIEMO-NIEMOJEWSKI
CHAMPION OF FREEDOM (1888-1973)

Stephan Pasternacki

Lech T. Niemo-Niemojewski was born in St. Paul, Minnesota in 1888. His grandfather took part in the Polish uprising against the Russians in 1863, and was exiled to Siberia. Lech's parents were born in Poland, but brought by their families to America at an early age, to seek the freedom missing in their native country.

After receiving a degree in law from the University of Buffalo, Lech began teaching Polish literature and became interested in the Polish American community activities in Buffalo. He later moved to New York City, where he worked in the field of investments and securities.

In 1930 Lech and his wife Ola Mae, whom he had married in 1923 in Indiana, moved to California. Here in Los Angeles he established a general law practice. After the outbreak of World War II, Niemo organized a group of distinguished citizens under the banner "Friends of Poland." Founding members included Rupert Hughes, Merriam Cooper, Judge Joseph Scott, Adolphe Menjou, Allen Mowbray. First recording secretary of Friends of Poland was Erna Chat-Granicka.

Lech was also instrumental, with the assistance of then-British Consul Eric Cleugh, in the formation of the Committee of United Nations of Southern California.

As a result of his outstanding efforts, Lech Niemo-Niemojewski was made Honorary Polish Consul in Los Angeles by the Polish government in exile (1939-1945). Lectures, speeches and conferences, all in support of true political freedom, took all Niemo's time and energy. Poor health forced him to retire to Vista, California. After a lengthy illness, with his devoted wife at his bedside, Lech T. Niemo-Niemojewski passed away on May 29, 1973.

Throughout his life Niemo remained proud of his Polish background and vividly aware of his ancestors' fight against political, economic and cultural oppression. He fought valiantly for the cultivation of these values among his American compatriots.

Stephan Pasternacki, a known personality in the Hollywood music world, lives in Los Angeles at a place named "Chata Piasta."

JOZEFA KUDLICKA (1870-1962)

Stefan Pasternacki

Never was there anyone more benevolent or charitably inclined than Jozefa Kudlicka — one hundred and forty pounds of heart and goodwill. From her early teens she was filled with a love of her fellow man. As a young girl in Buffalo, New York, she would seek out families in need, then set out to beg for old clothes, discarded furniture, fuel and food to aid them. Once at Christmas time, a black family moved into her neighborhood. They were penniless and little Jozia made special efforts to make their Christmas a happy one. This set a pattern of her life.

As she grew up she joined, organized and activated charitable groups, while she held the post of librarian of the Buffalo Public Library. At the conclusion of World War I, when Herbert Hoover and his Relief Committee came to the aid of Poland in her distress, Jesse, as she was known to her intimates, was one of his chief aides. She was tireless in her efforts to lend a helping hand. Later in life, in 1923, she made her home here in Los Angeles with her daughter Wanda, and husband Jim Marczewski. Here she became one of Poland's best publicity agents.

She had a charming style of speech, always graciously informative. Her talks were very well received, especially by the women's clubs. In 1926 she was instrumental in organizing the Los Angeles Polish church.

When World War II broke out, the Polish government, in arrangement with Mexico, sent several good-sized groups of children to the town of Leon, for interim education and training in the Polish language. It was understood that, at the conclusion of the war, the children were to be returned home as Polish citizens. After months of being buffeted about through India and Asia, the hapless children finally arrived in Los Angeles, on their way to Mexico. They were a bedraggled group of youngsters. Jesse headed the committee to give the poor maltreated children a bit of comfort, by way of food, clothing and candy.

In her later years, having by predisposition a librarian in her make-up, she affiliated herself with the Los Angeles Public Library, and purely through kindly interest, offered her services without pay to substitute for persons who, through illness or some valid reason, could not report to work. This gave her a gratifying sense of doing something for her fellow man.

Jozefa Kudlicka and Sylwin Strakacz. Courtesy, Stephan Pasternacki.

In 1962, at the age of 92, she peacefully went on to join her Maker. Among her final activities was a fervid promotion of the newly-organized Polish American Congress. Up until her last breath, she was a keen observer of current affairs and she can well be remembered as a woman of whom Polish Americans can justly be proud.

THOMAS M. POTASZ (1898-1973)

Michele M. Sawa

Thomas M. Potasz was born December 21, 1898 in New York City, to Polish parents. But when he was quite young, Thomas' family settled in San Francisco. Eventually he became an apprentice with the Union Iron Works, and after four years at the iron works became a skilled journeyman shipfitter. During World War I he tried to enlist in the army. His enlistment was deferred, however, because his ship building skills were needed for the war effort.

The following year, during a flu epidemic, he volunteered as an aide at the San Francisco Community Hospital. His great interest and desire to become a doctor, along with the encouragement of his superiors, led him to enter the medical field.

By attending both day school and night school, he earned the necessary college credits to enroll in the pre-medical program at the University of California at Berkeley for two years. He then entered the Loyola Medical School in Chicago, Illinois. Because of his family's financial problems, he worked his way through medical school by employing the skills he had learned as a shipfitter. He graduated from Loyola in 1927.

After interning at San Diego Community Hospital from 1923 to 1927, the young student passed the state board and received his license as a medical doctor. Dr. Potasz practiced for a year in San Francisco and then did post-graduate work in general surgery at Pennsylvania Medical School from 1928 to 1929. He served a residency in orthopedics at State University and Crippled Childrens Hospital in Oklahoma City, Oklahoma, and then opened his practice as a physician-surgeon in Los Angeles in October, 1931.

During World War II he entered the U.S. Army Medical Corps as a captain, and eventually rose to the rank of a full colonel. At different times during his service, he was commanding officer of the 224 Station Hospital Desert Training; the 149 Medical Battalion Fort Lewis, Washington; and 318th General Hospital, Central Pacific.

After his military discharge, Dr. Potasz entered the field of ophthalmology and took basic courses at various universities

---

Michele M. Sawa is a student at the University of Southern California, Los Angeles. She lives in Downey.

including the University of Southern California. He did his residency at the Chicago Eye, Ear, Throat and Nose Hospital and then went to the Holy Family Hospital in Bihar, India, for exposure to eye cases and operations required by Board of Ophthalmology. He became administrator and instructor in ophthalmology for Chicago's EENT Hospital and because of his background, Dr. Potasz passed the Board and was certified in ophthalmology in 1954. He served on the staff of several hospitals including Daniel Freeman, Viewpark, and Crenshaw.

After his retirement from medicine, he attended Long Beach State College and obtained a Bachelor of Arts degree in art. While working for his Masters degree he became ill, and died August 28, 1973.

Dr. Thomas was always deeply interested in the advancement of Polish culture. As an artist, several of his paintings won first prize awards; as a dedicated individual he helped establish the Polish Business and Professional Club of Los Angeles; he also founded the Polish University Club of Los Angeles for the advancement of Polish culture and to aid Polish students by means of scholarships. The University Club was very close to Dr. Potasz' heart, and he took care to remember it in his will by establishing a monthly income for the club for as long as it should exist.

SYLWIN GEORGE STRAKACZ (1892-1973)

Anne Strakacz Appleton

Sylwin George Strakacz was born in Warsaw on February 17, 1892, the youngest of four children. After graduating from high school he attended the law school of the Imperial University at St. Petersburg, Russia. He returned to Warsaw in 1915 and joined the Ministry of Foreign Affairs. In 1918 he was sent as a special delegate of that office to Sweden, where he was in charge of repatriating Polish workers who had been cut off from their country by the war. When the mission was successfully completed, he started back to Warsaw.

In Copenhagen, in December of 1918, however, he was introduced to Paderewski and his wife, who were about to leave on the British cruiser "Concord" for Danzig. It was a fateful meeting which resulted in a close association lasting twenty-three years. While on that ship, which was taking the Paderewskis to Poland, Strakacz pledged his services to the great man, so that when Paderewski became Prime Minister, Strakacz took the job of his private secretary. In that capacity he served until Paderewski's resignation, at which time, because of loyalty, Strakacz also resigned from the Polish government.

In 1919 Strakacz married Aniela Karszo-Siedlewska; they had one child, a daughter. After a trip to America in 1921 with the Paderewskis, Strakacz returned to Warsaw to become the chief editor of the Polish daily *Rzeczpospolita*, which Paderewski founded in Warsaw in 1923.

In 1928, when Mme. Paderewski's failing health prevented her from accompanying the virtuoso on his concert tours, Strakacz returned to Switzerland to resume his position as a full time secretary to the great man and to be his traveling companion. At the beginning of the second World War, when Paderewski was nominated President of the National Council by the just-formed Polish Government in Exile (with General Wladyslaw Sikorski as Prime Minister), Strakacz became the Government's special envoy and a spokesman for Paderewski, whose health did not allow him to travel to war zones. Strakacz was sent to Marshall Pétain on the delicate mission of evacuating the Polish army

---

Anne Strakacz Appleton lives in Northern California.

organized in France. Most of the units eventually did reach England.

In September of 1940, when Paderewski left Switzerland for the United States, Strakacz and his family accompanied Paderewski and his sister, Antonina Wilkonska. They arrived in New York on November 6, 1940. From that day until Paderewski's death in 1941, Strakacz devoted all his time to aiding the aging statesman in his efforts to bring relief to war devastated Poland. Retaining the title of Minister Plenipotentiary, he resigned as Polish Delegate to the League of Nations in Geneva — a post he held the previous year — and became Paderewski's spokesman to various Polish organizations, as well as to the American press. Among other endeavors he coordinated the arrival of General Sikorski and S. Mikolajczyk on a mission to the United States, and introduced them to the Polish leaders at welcoming rallies. After Paderewski's death, Strakacz was nominated in October 1941 to be Polish General Consul in New York — a post which he held until 1945 when the United States Government officially recognized the Warsaw Communist Regime as Poland's new government. Strakacz then resigned.

In 1947 Strakacz and his wife joined their daughter in Los Angeles, California. There he spent his remaining years as a court interpreter (he was fluent in six languages) as well as an active member of the Republican party, the "Friends of a Free Poland," and "Samopomoc" organizations. Sylwin G. Strakacz died in Los Angeles on May 15, 1973 and is buried at Forest Lawn cemetery in Glendale; he is survived by his daughter and three grandchildren.

HELEN E. BAYER (1894-1971)

Michele M. Sawa

Helen E. Bayer was a prime example of a woman filled with vigor, determination and compassion for those in need. Born Helen Kazmierczyk in Holyoke, Massachusetts, she began her social work in a family effort of aiding Polish immigrants. As children, Helen, her sister Genia, and their brother, the late Monsignor Bernard Kazmierczyk, often gave up their beds to sleep on the floor when the boats arrived from Europe. At the same time, her parents helped all new arrivals from Poland to obtain jobs and to begin settling in this land.

As a young woman, Helen continued in this work by joining the North American Civil League for Immigrants. The League's main objectives were to protect immigrants from exploitation that would hurt their future as American citizens, to teach them about American government and ideals, and, finally, to help them adjust to the new lifestyles they would encounter in the United States.

At the age of 19 Helen married Eugene Schlenk, secretary for the League in Bridgeport, Connecticut. Three years later, as an agent for the League, Mrs. Schlenk performed one of her most noteworthy deeds. She had been sent to Nashua, New Hampshire in the interest of Lithuanian and Polish speaking employees who were striking against the Nashua Manufacturing Company. By gaining the confidence of the strikers, Helen was able to act as intermediary and interpreter between the workers and the cotton mill officials. She persuaded the workers and the mill agents to meet in conference and then appealed to both sides to meet halfway. On April 4, 1916, her efforts resulted in the end of a six-month strike. Once described as "the Joan of Arc of the Nashua strike," Helen was undoubtedly looked upon as a heroine by the 1500 unemployed operatives of the mill.

With the onset of World War I, Eugene Schlenk was called to serve in the armed forces and died overseas. In 1919 Helen married Stanley Bayer and came to California on her honeymoon. She was destined to remain in Los Angeles for the rest of her life, continuing her active participation in humanitarian and social case work.

Helen was in charge of the 1921 Polish entry at the Homeland Art and Craft Exhibit at the Museum of History, Science and Art at Exhibition Park in Los Angeles. The presentation "embodied the patriotism, loves, hopes and ambitions of foreign-born men and women who came to Los Angeles, as well as the fondest regard of Americans for their own country."

Helen went on to become one of the first organizers of Dom Polski in three locations: on Avalon Boulevard, Bonnie Brae, and Third Street. She was a co-founder of the Polish American Citizens Club and a charter member of the Polish University Club. She also served as Commissioner of Polish National Alliance (P.N.A.), and arranged documents for countless Polish displaced persons.

Aside from all of these involvements, Helen devoted herself to educating her two daughters, Helena and Diana. She also ran a real estate, insurance and income tax business, and found time for reading. Able to speak and write fluently in Polish and English, Helen was appointed court interpreter, and so continued to help others.

Helen E. Bayer died in 1971, but her memory lives on within those hearts which were touched and enriched by her undying enthusiasm, compassion and hard work.

HELENA LIIBKE:
SECRETARY TO MME. PADEREWSKA

Jacek Przygoda

Helena Liibke was born on September 8, 1893, to Polish parents in Mainz on the Rhine, Germany, where her father held an engineering position. His specialty — bridges and tunnel construction — first took him, with his family, to Tiflis in the Caucasus, and then to a Siberian camp on the shores of the Lake Baikal, where he worked on the trans-Siberian railroad system.

In 1904 the family, including Helena's two brothers, settled in Warsaw where Helena, after finishing a private high school in 1911, pursued further studies by enrolling in a program of Economic Sciences and Business Administration, from which she graduated in 1914, with honors.

When the first World War broke out she volunteered as a social worker and joined the Warsaw Citizens' Committee. For a year she served in the capacity of a principle of a public high school. In 1916 she joined Z. Szczerbinski's Furniture Firm as bookkeeper and secretary until in 1919, on Paderewski's arrival in Warsaw, her boss recommended her to Mme. Paderewska as a temporary secretary-substitute. That position marked the beginning of her service to the Paderewskis, which lasted as long as they lived.

After Paderewski's resignation as Poland's Prime Minister, in 1920, Helena remained with them and went first to Paris, then Switzerland, and in 1921 to America, where they stayed in Paso Robles, California, for over a year. After 1922, as Paderewski resumed his world-wide tours, Helena attended all the concerts and events honoring the statesman.

In 1929, when Mme. Paderewska became gravely ill and could no longer travel, Helena remained at her side. After Mme. Paderewska's death in 1934, Helena stayed with Mme. Wilkonska, Paderewski's sister, at Riond Bosson, their home in Switzerland.

When, in 1940, Paderewski left for America, Helena remained in Switzerland with her mother, who had arrived from Poland. She became active in establishing letter communication between the Poles in England and their families in Poland. (These letters could not reach Poland if sent directly from England, involved in the war.

Switzerland's neutrality permitted the exchange.) In 1941, when the Paderewski Testimonial Fund, founded by Charlotte Kellog in the United States, opened its branch in Switzerland, Helena became its representative. The Fund helped cover correspondence costs and brought aid to stranded Polish refugees in Switzerland.

When her mother died in 1945, Helena made plans to return to America and eventually settled in Los Angeles, California, in May 1948. She became an American citizen in 1961. Shortly after her arrival in Los Angeles, she took active part in organizing the "Women's International Club," whose president she became in 1953. She also belonged to the "Friends of a Free Poland" and joined "Samopomoc."

TADEUSZ ZIELINSKI:
MAN OF DEEDS (1918-1977)

Jacek Przygoda

Tadeusz Zielinski was born May 12, 1918, in the one-time Polish city of Kijow. In 1926 Tadeusz moved to Czestochowa, Poland, with his family. He went to school in that city but passed his maturity exam in Warsaw, where he enrolled at the University of Warsaw Law School. His interest, however, veered toward journalism and he worked for several years on various newspapers until the outbreak of World War II.

In 1940 Tadeusz escaped Poland in Nazi shackles, and reached France. After the military collapse of France, he joined the Polish Air Force in Great Britain. In 1942, he graduated from an Air Force school in Crawford, and the following year became a pilot in the 304 Squadron of Bombers. Day and night he flew missions over enemy territory. In 1944, he met and married Miroslawa (Mira) Sadowska, a victim of Russian forced labor camps and deportation.

After the War, Tadeusz returned to journalism. From 1947-1949 he was editor and publisher of *The Christian Social Movement*; from 1949-1952 he published London's *The Illustrated Weekly*, and from 1952-1957 worked for *The Last News*, published in Germany.

In February of 1957 Tadeusz, his wife Mira, and their first daughter, Barbara, arrived in Los Angeles where they've made their home for the past 20 years. A second daughter, Eva, was born the following year. Here again, Tadeusz published and edited a bilingual monthly, *Nasze Sprawy* (Our Affairs) for ten years, 1962-1971. In order to make a living, he worked as a surveyor from 1962 until he suffered his first heart attack in 1974.

Tadeusz Zielinski will be best remembered for his intensive social work among and for the Polish community in Los Angeles; not only the publication of *Our Affairs* but his untiring dedication to the Polish Fraternal Association — Samopomoc, and later to the Polish Center — Samopomoc at River's End, in the Saugus area surely stand out. His greatest achievements in California were: a realistic appraisal of the Polish American social and cultural potentials in Southern California, enthusiastic determination in following a chosen path to social progress, and an outstanding "know-how" in dealing with people, especially compatriots.

   Tadeusz Zielinski died at River's End on July 16, 1976, and was buried on July 23rd, 1977, at Holy Cross Cemetery. As Dr. Tadeusz Rowinski said in the eulogy: "He died in his beloved Park like a soldier at his post, which he has chosen himself." His deeds are indeed a legacy and his most eloquent testament for posterity.

THE LATE MICHAL CIESLAK FAMILY: THREE GIRLS AND THEIR MOTHER

Jacek Przygoda

Michal Cieslak met his future wife, Stanislawa Stefania Jaworska while both were serving in the Polish Home Army in the voivodship of Lublin (southeast of Warsaw). They were married in Krasnik in 1943. Michal had returned from Belgium where his immigrant parents lived before World War II, to serve in the Polish Air Force. During the War he was captured and tortured by the Gestapo, and "treated" to two bottles of ammonia, for being a member of the Polish underground. His lungs and stomach were burnt beyond cure.

In 1957 Michal managed to leave Poland for Belgium, and the following year his wife and three small daughters joined him in Charleroi, where he was studying mechanical engineering, a field in which he held a degree from Wawelberg Technical School in Warsaw. After the loss of the Congo colony and the return of the colonists, the Belgian labor market became distinctly unfriendly towards foreigners. Michal tried unsuccessfully to find work in Katanga, Africa.

After rejoining his family in Belgium, the Cieslaks emigrated to the United States in 1962, and settled in Los Angeles. Here Michal found work as an engineer with the Richard Wilk industrial enterprise, where he was employed for six years, until his death in 1969. Michal Cieslak left this life with the deep admiration for R. Wilk, and — along with his family — especially for Mrs. Wilk. She helped the Cieslaks a lot.

All three girls graduated from Catholic high schools and then attended college. Ewa, the oldest, spent one year at the University of Southern California on an architectural scholarship. The following year she transferred to the University of California at Los Angeles. At the same time, she studied in the evening division and earned a Registered Nurse degree. She also painted in watercolors and oils, and spoke three languages fluently.

In December of 1971 Ewa married Nick Nelson. Thanks to a contest she had won in the bank where she was working (and where, incidentally, she received two promotions during her first six months of employment), Ewa and her husband went to Europe for a week. The following year, one Saturday night in August, Ewa was returning from a tennis game when her car was hit by another vehicle at a stop light. Ewa lingered in a coma, never regaining consciousness, for four years; her agony ended in October of 1976.

ACHIEVEMENT

BANK OF AMERICA

AWARD

SCIENCE
AND
MATHEMATICS

WON BY
EVA CIESLAK
1965

Photo, Martin Dabrowski.

Cieslak's second daughter, Anna Marie, studied at U.C.L.A., initially majoring in marine biology, but eventually earning her degree in French. While in France on an annual scholarship, Anna Marie fell in love with a fellow Los Angeleno, George Bukowinski, who was on a similar scholarship. Back home, they were married in June of 1972, and returned to France to study another year. Presently, George teaches French while he works toward his Ph.D. at U.C.L.A., and Anna Marie takes care of their two chidren.

The third daughter, Margaret, is a junior at California State University in Northridge, majoring in psychology. Besides studying she works at two jobs. She is a winner otherwise, also. On August 13, 1976, she earned an unprecedented 985 points on the TV "Cross-Wits" contest. Jack Clark, MC of the show, was flabbergasted, and the audience went wild. Margaret's winnings included a brand new 1977 automobile, a trip to the Caribbean (she wants her mother to go there), and other prizes. All totaled, $5,000 worth.

And their mother? As a career woman, she has been working professionally for the past fourteen years. And her scholarly degree is in endurance. As a wife and mother, she saw her loved ones dying after suffering beyond measure. Whether in Poland, Belgium or the United States, Mrs. Michal Cieslak endured the pain of family separation. Her life so far, in fact, has been permeated with an incessant anxiety and studded with sacrifices.

Small wonder Mrs. Cieslak's living room is adorned with a crucifix, a relic from Poland. Her strength is sustained by the usual courage of a Polish immigrant, and characterized by a special purpose in life: To see her children and grandchildren grow, study and live in a truly free country. Such is the ambition of all immigrant mothers born in Poland.

MARIE ZINGEL:
STUDYING WHILE WORKING

Halina Gawlinska

Marie Toporkiewicz Zingel was born April 9, 1904, in Wilsko, a province of Krakow, Poland. In November 1920, she emigrated to Chicago to join her sister Magdalena and her family, who had left Poland eight years earlier. She began working in a restaurant owned by Magdalena's husband. In the years to come, Marie helped raise his three minor sons who all attained prominence professionally, and for the last ten years of his life, Marie nursed her brother-in-law in his illness.

Within days of her arrival in Chicago, Marie registered for evening classes in English, and two weeks later applied for citizenship, which she attained in 1927.

Chicago's climate proved detrimental to Marie's health. Her physician recommended either a return to Poland, or a move to the drier climate of the West. Marie chose the latter, arriving in Los Angeles in 1929. Here again, Marie undertook a program of working during the day and studying at night, eventually earning her high school diploma.

This was the time of the Great Depression, and Marie could find only part-time work. In 1935, she was employed by a physician to care for his partially paralyzed wife. Her new employer, impressed by her interest in medical books, encouraged Marie to study nursing. Nursing schools at that time, however, required $500 as an admission fee. Marie saved perseveringly, and two years later registered at Mercy College of Nursing in San Diego.

After graduation in 1941, Marie returned to Los Angeles and filed for the State Board Examinations, requesting assignment to care for Poles injured in World War II. She was promised consideration and told to wait. For two years she engaged in general and private duty nursing at St. Vincent's, St. John's in Santa Monica and the Hospital of Good Samaritan, where she provided care for many movie stars, including Howard Hughes.

In August of 1943 Marie was called by the American Red Cross for special assignment at Fort MacArthur Army Hospital in San Pedro. There she was to care for an Army transport of 785 displaced adults and the well-known orphans from Poland en route to Leon, Mexico. She served as a nurse and interpreter, and accompanied them to their destination. (The second transport of 728 adults and orphans brought the unexpected problem of a 7-month-pregnant woman who delivered a premature baby boy at the Army hospital.) In addition to nursing, counseling and escort, Marie arranged with Polish organizations in the United States for warm clothing, blankets, school supplies and other needs of the refugees.

At the conclusion of World War II, Marie returned to private nursing duty in the Los Angeles area. She fell in love and married Michael Zingel in 1945. Together they have visited Poland four times. They are currently living in Santa Monica.

FELICIA KWASIEBORSKA: BORN SOCIAL WORKER

Jacek Przygoda

Born near Krzemieniec, Poland, Felicia, along with two sisters and a brother, came to the United States in 1909 to join their father, Alexander Krutewicz, who had settled in 1905 in St. Louis, Missouri. He had to escape from the Russians; his father, Konstanty, after taking part in the 1863 Insurrection, had died in Siberia.

Felicia's education at the University of St. Louis was interrupted by World War I, when she enrolled in the Polish Gray Samaritans. This group was organized under the auspices of Y.W.C.A. by Mme. Turczynowicz, an American married to a Pole. During World War I the Turczynowiczs and their children moved to Long Island, New York. There the idea of organizing volunteers to do social, charitable and hospital work in Poland, once the War was over, was conceived by Mme. Turczynowicz. In a group of some 30 volunteers, Felicia left for Poland in 1919 and worked there three years for the reconstruction of her native country. The first part of that time she spent in the Kielce voivodship, that second in Brzesc on the Bug River.

Felicia returned in 1922 to St. Louis, where she had previously been instrumental in organizing the International Institute. Promoted to assistant director, she left St. Louis in 1929 to work at the International Institute in Milwaukee, Wisconsin, as a consultant on Immigration and Naturalization, until her retirement in 1958.

Felicia met her future husband, Adam Kwasieborski, in Warsaw in 1920. They were married in 1924 in St. Louis. Adam was a soldier in the General W. Haller Polish Blue Army in France. After the War he served as a liaison officer with the Hoover American Relief for Children, in Poland.

When the Kwasieborskis lived in Milwaukee, Adam worked first for the local Polish American newspapers and then for the Polish National Alliance daily in Chicago.

In 1958 the couple came to Los Angeles. In January of 1976 Adam S. Kwasieborski passed away; Felicia Kwasieborski resumed her social work, this time as a volunteer at the Polish Seniors Foundation on West Adams Boulevard. Her project is the gift shop there.

EDWARD P. DRAKE (KACZOROWSKI): PROLIFIC INVENTOR

Jacek Przygoda

Edward P. Drake was born January 1, 1904 in South Bend, Indiana, son of Joseph Kaczorowski and Veronica Dobski. The family moved to California. Edward returned to South Bend and there married Irena Karpinski. The couple had two sons and a daughter, all born in California, for, in 1925, the Kaczorowskis moved to Los Angeles.

Edward's exceptionally inventive mind was mostly self-taught. His collection of patents, spanning the years between December 11, 1934, and September 4, 1956, lists 32 inventions. Among them: automatic pitting machine, hydraulic control for trail builder, inking device for a printing apparatus, partial product multiplying calculator, binary to decimal converter, and many others.

Drake was a member of The American Society of Mechanical Engineers, American Ordnance Association, National Management Association, State of California Civil and Professional Engineers. He was registered with the National Roster of Scientific and Specialized Personnel, and worked at one time for the City of Los Angeles, and as a Chief Design Engineer, Multiplier Division, for Clary Multiplier Corporation. He was also a member of Knights of Columbus, Council No. 1920, Glendale, and of the Polish Business and Professional Men's Club of Los Angeles.

Edward P. Drake (baptismal certificate issued by St. Hedwidge Church, South Bend, Indiana, January 1, 1904, reads "Erasmus Peter Kaczorowski") died April 29, 1962, in Glendale, California, and is buried at San Fernando Cemetery. He was often heard to say that, "God gave me a good brain, so I can't complain about my poor health."

Irene Drake is a licensed real estate associate saleswoman, and worked professionally for five years. She was instrumental in organizing the Polish Women's Alliance, Group 752. The couple's son, Edward G., works for I.B.M., and son Joseph for Data Processing Division, Western Region. Daughter, Mary Agnes Crowley, a registered nurse, lives in Santa Fe, New Mexico.

EDMUND T. DOMBROWSKI:
"SAY IT WITH FLOWERS"

Kathy S. Hayes

Edmund T. Dombrowski was born in Warsaw, Poland. At age fourteen he emigrated to Los Angeles, California, to join his mother and brothers. Dombrowski mastered the English language, completed high school, and found work as an apprentice machinist. With the care and attention to detail which characterizes Dombrowski's life, he soon became expert in the field of tool and die making. In 1930 he married Violet Muto in Los Angeles, and the couple had two sons.

By the outbreak of World War II, Dombrowski had established his own machine shop in the backyard of his home. With the able assistance of his wife, Violet, and sons, Edmund, Jr., and Stephen, he was able to contribute to the war effort through his skill as a machinist.

The Ed Dombrowski Floral Establishment, Inglewood. Photo, Stephen Dombrowski.

In 1942, the Dombrowski family bought two acres of land, formerly a banana stand. Two glass houses stood on the property, and in their spare time Edmund, Sr., and his sons repaired and restored the structures. By the time both sons were in medical school, Edmund, Sr., and Violet decided to cultivate orchids.

While the elder Dombrowskis began cultivating orchids, son Edmund, Jr., went on to obtain his medical degree. Stephen spent years in medical school before deciding to join his father in the flower business. After four years in the Air Force, Stephen returned home to build a flower shop on the property. "Dombrowski's Flowers" opened on Palm Sunday, 1957.

Twenty years later, Dombrowski's Flowers is a thriving business. The only commercial flower grower within a hundred miles, Edmund, Sr., still does all the orchid cultivating himself, and features thousands of varieties. Dombrowski's Flowers is also still a family business. Stephen manages the flower shop and oversees wholesale sales to other shops, while Stephen's son Tim is learning the art of orchid cultivation from his grandfather.

Edmund Dombrowski is part of the American Dream. This Polish-born Californian, through hard work and strong values, has combined success in business with close ties between himself and his wife, two sons and nine grandchildren.

THE BIRTH OF EASTERN DENTAL MFG. COMPANY

Jacek Przygoda

In 1923, Stanley Victor Pszczolkowski-Preston, a fourteen-year-old Polish youth, went to work for the S.S. White Dental Manufacturing Company in Philadelphia, Pa. He spent the next 24 years mastering the tedious and exacting trade of making dental instruments.

Stanley Pszczolkowski-Preston at work.

In 1947, following the advice of an Armenian friend and co-worker named Khantzian, Stanley migrated to California with his wife and two daughters. In Los Angeles a partnership was formed, and Eastern

Dental Manufacturing Company was born.

By 1960 Mr. Khantzian had passed away, and Stanley carried on the business with the help of three employees, plus his wife who took care of secretarial duties for the growing firm. Business was going very well, with orders coming in from dental supply dealers, dentistry schools and from the U.S. Government.

By 1965 Stanley was desperately searching for skilled help; work was piling up, but trying to find a trained dental instrument maker was like trying to find a needle in a haystack. The work is tedious and exacting, and takes years to master. As a last resort Stanley wrote to a young man he had known in Philadelphia while working for S.S. White Co., to ask if he would be willing to migrate to California.

Charles Nizgorski would be very much interested indeed, and would come out to look the situation over, was the answer. A few months later, with his wife and two young sons, Charles moved to California and joined Eastern Dental Mfg., as a partner.

In 1970, now in his sixties, Stanley sold his interest in the partnership to Charles and retired to live with his wife, Helen Rose, in the mountains of California. Eastern Dental is thriving, run now by Charles with his two sons and nine other employees.

BRONISLAW (BRUNO) MUDY:
HEAD OF EMCO ENGINEERING

Jacek Przygoda

Bruno Mudy was born September 17, 1926, in Poland. While in a forced labor camp in Austria, he was liberated on May 5, 1945, by the United States Army. After a short service with the Polish Guard Company in Germany, he emigrated to Hammond, Indiana, in 1949 under the sponsorship of Mr. and Mrs. Martin Zgoda.

Mudy was drafted by the U.S. Army in September 1950, and after basic training at Camp Polk, Louisiana, served with the 45th Infantry Division. In 1951 he sailed with his unit to Hokkaido Island, Japan. In December of the same year he was shipped to Korea and fought on the central Highlands front until 1952 when he was transferred from active to reserve status.

Back in civilian life, he enrolled in Allied Mechanics Institute in Chicago, and earned a Bachelor's degree in mechanical engineering. While still in school, he worked his way up to manager in charge of production at Cardinal Engineering Company.

Degree in hand, he was hired by Markwart Aircraft Company in January of 1957 and moved to California. The following year he formed a partnership with Al Czerniak to establish Emco Engineering Company in Van Nuys; four years later he became sole owner of the business.

Since then Bruno Mudy has expanded his operations in specialized areas for hydraulic systems in the aircraft and aerospace industries. In 1968 Emco Engineering was incorporated, and in 1973 moved to new and larger facilities in North Hollywood.

Mudy is on the board of directors of National Tool and Die and Precision Machining Association, San Fernando Valley Chapter. He takes an active part in Polish American social and cultural life in the area. He was married in 1963, in Poland, to Maria Teresa Werminska. They have two children, Anthony and Margaret.

WARNO DRUG STORE
AND DEVELOPMENT COMPANY

Jacek Przygoda

Irena and Henryk Warno were born in Poland. Irena was raised and educated in West Germany until 1950 when (with her parents, Wilhelm and Bronislawa Engel) she came to America. She attended St. Rose High School, and graduated from Albany College of Pharmacy in 1959. Henryk was raised and educated in Wroclaw, where he earned degrees in mechanical engineering and physical education. He also won first prize awards in skiing and championship swimming in national contests.

Henryk came to America in 1958 and took further courses in construction. He became an engineer for Skiesclimbers, a division of Western Gear, built power stations and oil refineries for Fuller Company in Southern California, and designed a dust collector. In the meantime, Irena was the sole owner of Corner Drug Store in Seal Beach, which she ran from 1959-1969.

In 1969 Warno Development Company came into existence. The Corner Drug Store (the only Polish American drug store in the Los Angeles area), and Warno Sports (managed by co-owner Richard Engel) are part of Warner Development Company.

The couple has four children. Basia Rosemary Kowalik (a Loyola Marymount University graduate, studies pharmacy in Idaho), Susan is a high school senior, Katherine and John Christopher are also in schools.

Besides belonging to her professional organizations, Irena Warno is one of the vice-presidents of the Polish American Historical Association, California Chapter. Her husband Henryk is on the Board of Directors for that Chapter.

WALTER J. ARCHER (ARCISZEWSKI)

Born in Newark, New Jersey, Walter attended public schools, and went on to become an apprentice to a tool maker. He worked up to the position of manager of the tool shop before he left to establish Vulcan Tool and Manufacturing Company in Maplewood, New Jersey. He owned another business firm, Enterprise Company, in Newark. His specialty was tool engineering; his hobbies were studying architecture and deep sea fishing.

In 1947 he moved to Florida, and in 1950 to Santa Barbara, California, where he went back to work in the construction industry, building homes and apartments. He is married to Janina Szuwalski; the couple have one daughter, Joyce (Mrs. Robert Sebig), and three grandchildren living in Woodside, California.

Walter designed and built their Santa Barbara home in 1954. It is adorned by two Tadeusz (Tade) Styka's highly prized paintings of Walter's wife.

T.T. STANLEY: SEMI-RETIRED DENTIST

T.T. Stanley, the son of a pharmacist, was born and educated in Chicago, Illinois. He opened his first dentistry practice there in 1936. He later moved to Sherman Oaks, but opened his practice in North Hollywood. He is now semi-retired, but continues to keep his license active.

Stanley met his wife, Barbara Lisewski, in Chicago at a Little Theatre where she played as a character actress. They were married in 1937. She is an alumna of the Drama Arts School in Chicago, and a past president of the Polish Arts Drama Club in Chicago. She left the field of drama to become a dental secretary and lab technician for her husband.

Stanley and Barbara live in Santa Barbara, where they play the piano in their leisure time. Barbara collects porcelain, particularly Polish, Italian and Royal Copenhagen, which is her favorite. Both are active devotees of their respective garden clubs, members of the Montecito Country Club, and the Polish American Arts Association in Santa Barbara.

WACLAW (WALLY) PAWLOWSKI: ODYSSEY OF AN IMMIGRANT

Kathy S. Hayes

Waclaw (Wally) Pawlowski was born in Radom, Poland, on September 21, 1923; since 1965 he has lived and worked in Los Angeles County, California. But during those 42 years, Wally traveled over 50,000 miles, was interned in eleven concentration camps, and lived in over a dozen countries.

Pawlowski was attending Technical School in Radom when he was arrested by the Germans on February 18, 1940, at age 17. He spent the next five years in various German concentration camps, until liberated by Canadian forces. He was then 22 years old and weighed 102 pounds. Five months in a hospital doubled his weight and restored his health.

Wally spent the next three years in the U.S. occupied zone, working with motorpools, organizing transports and convoys, and learning the technical aspects of convoys. Nineteen forty eight found Wally organizing the discharge of the Polish Guard Company, before leaving for Australia in February 1949. After 30 days at sea, he landed in Sydney and was to spend eleven years in Australia.

In 1960 Pawlowski began a year long journey to Montreal, Canada, which took him through New Zealand, Fiji Islands, Hawaiian Islands, several other Pacific stopovers, to Vancouver British Columbia, and overland to Montreal. In 1962 he moved to Chicago, where he married Jadwiga Czubek, just arrived from Poland. The couple moved to Los Angeles.

Wally Pawlowski has been active in civic affairs since arriving in California. He promoted the Polish Library in Los Angeles, organized the Philatelic and Numismatic Society, and arranged an exhibit of Polish national and international stamps and coins. He has been awarded the Aeropex '75 for Polish Government in Exile stamps, the Aeropex '77 for Republic of Poland stamps and many others. He has a standing invitation from a Japanese Philatelic Society to exhibit his POW materials in an April 1978 show in Osaka, Japan.

Since his arrival in Los Angeles in 1965, Waclaw Pawlowski has immersed himself in Polish cultural and heritage activities, but he has never lost his dream of returning to a free Poland.

ANDREW CICHY: ONE OF MANY

Kathy S. Hayes

In many ways the life of Andrew Cichy personifies the lives of unknown numbers of Poles who have made California their home because their beloved homeland had become an unpleasant, if not downright dangerous, place to live.

Andrew was born on November 6, 1910, in Wisla, Poland. In 1939, when the Nazis invaded his country, he was working as a railroad man. The Nazis, against Andrew's wishes, mobilized him for a "Bauzug" (construction train) and sent him to the German-Russian front. In 1943 he was drafted, still against his will, into the German army.

After nearly five months of training, he was sent to the battle front in France. He escaped, was recaptured, and escaped again, spending some time dodging the Germans, hiding in fields and ditches, until a U.S. Army truck took him to an assembly point. Soon Andrew was working in the kitchen, a quonset hut, helping feed the 20,000 German P.O.W.'s in camp.

Then a Polish lieutenant gathered a company of 200 men, including Andrew; the company sailed for Italy aboard a U.S. Navy ship, to join the Polish Army, still fighting the Germans in Italy. After the War, Cichy was demobilized along with many of his countrymen, and settled in the southern part of Great Britain.

Andrew worked as a factory worker, to enable him to remain in Great Britain. He later found work in the woolen industry, where he met his future wife, Katherine Slotwinska. She was also born in Poland, and deported by the Nazis to work in Germany. Like her future husband, she went to Great Britain after the Liberation. Andrew and Katherine were married in 1949.

Two years later, with infant John in a basket, the Cichys emigrated to the United States. Work was hard to find for Andrew, and the first three months in this country were very difficult for the young family. Andrew had odd jobs only at first, but eventually found steady employment. In addition to John, four more children were born to the Cichys: Christine (Mrs. M. Langston), Linda, Joe and Andy, Jr.

The story of this family is repeated by thousands of other Polish families, from the early years in Poland, the years of hardship and dislocation during the Nazi and Soviet occupations, the move across the continents to the United States, in this case, to Sepulveda, California.

SEWERYN KULESZA: OLYMPIC MEDALIST

Kathy S. Hayes

Seweryn Kulesza was born in Radom, Poland, on October 23, 1900. His extraordinary talent for equitation showed itself early in life. In 1918 he joined the Polish Cavalry, on its way to the Bolshevik front; he spent 21 years (until the outbreak of World War II) as a cavalry man. Kulesza immediately began training in equitation under a number of renowned instructors. General Adam Kicincki was once heard to remark: "Kulesza is the best rider known to me." By 1929 he was judged ready to enter his first international contest in Nice, France, competing against equitation experts from 12 nations. He won the Cup of Nations, the highest honor, in spite of a broken hand.

Back in Poland, he won the "Puchar Prezydenta" (President's Cup), the most coveted equestrian award in pre-war Poland. The high point of his career was when a team headed by Kulesza won a Silver Medal in the grueling five-day competition at the 1936 World Olympic Games in Berlin. Only a stumble by Kulesza's mount prevented him from taking the Gold Medal.

The outbreak of World War II in 1939 found Kulesza on the front lines of battle against invading Germans. He was captured in battle on September 27, 1939, and interned in Murnau, a German P.O.W. camp; his first wife, Janina, died in Poland, leaving a small daughter, "Myszka."

After being liberated, Kulesza traveled through Italy and reached Great Britain, and then on to Ireland where he spent three years as a colonel in the Irish Army. It was in Ireland he met and married his second wife, Elizabeth; four sons were born of this marriage. His fame as an equestrian led him to be chosen to train the equitation exhibition for the coronation of Queen Elizabeth II in 1952.

In 1957 the Kuleszas left for Belgium, where the Major lived five years working for a private training school in preparing equestrians for the royal court. In 1962 Kulesza left Brussels for Manitoba, Canada, where he spent seven years in Winnipeg. During this period he wrote a riding manual, *Modern Riding*, which was published in New York.

In 1969 Kulesza moved to Houston, Texas, where he stayed eight months as an instructor in a school of riding. The following year he moved to the San Fernando Valley, in California. Now, at the age of 77, Major Seweryn Kulesza still pursues his talent, in Burbank, as an outstanding instructor in equitation. Gen. T. Bor Komorowski wrote in 1966: "Major Kulesza, in my opinion, is one of the best instructors (as a trainer of an international class, ed.), I have ever known."

CONCLUSION

This book was not compiled in a defensive frame of mind, but more accurately, to emphasize the spirit of the paragraph which Joseph Conrad, the great Polish-born English novelist (originally Jozef Teodor Konrad Korzeniowski, 1857-1924) used to dramatically end his novel, *The Nigger of the Narcissus*:

"A gone shipmate," he wrote, "like any other man, is gone forever; and I never met one of them again. But at times the spring-flood of memory sets with force up the dark River of the Nine Bends. Then on the waters of the forlorn stream drifts a ship — a shadowy ship manned by a crew of Shades. They pass and make a sign, in a shadowy hail. Haven't we, together and upon the immortal sea, wrung out a meaning from our sinful lives? Good-bye, brothers! You were a good crowd. As good a crowd as ever fisted with wild cries the beating of canvas of a heavy foresail; or tossing aloft, invisible in the night, gave back yell for yell to a westerly gale."

In reading this book, one cannot help but recall the "good crowd" from the past one-hundred-and-fifty years, including those noted in the text.

No one can disagree with Joseph Conrad's dominant theme, namely the demoralizing influence of isolation, whether physical, social, cultural or spiritual. To forestall that isolation, all must realize that there are no strangers — only the unknown. By reaching out for strangers, people become united as brothers and sisters. This work eliminates, to some small degree, the unknown about Polish Americans in California. It is hoped this book will enable its readers not only to strengthen their bonds of community, but also to enlighten their fellow Americans so that a bond of friendship unites all citizens.

Unusual as it may seem, one of the leading concepts, if not the principal theme of the book, has been the answer to the question, "What is *right* with Polish Americans in California?" Written not in a boastful, clannish manner, but in the spirit of enlightenment, the collection of materials in this monograph recalls with pride the record of one ethnic group in their pursuit of happiness, an integral part of the American Dream. For as long as the American society can allow each ethnic group to retain its cultural heritage, this society will continue as a beacon of hope for the rest of the world, as it was for Polish Americans in California.

In many ways the material presented in the previous parts of this work is a conscious means of correcting the imbalance of California history by bringing into focus this initial study of Poles in California, heretofore a little-known segment in the broad mosaic of diverse peoples who settled and developed this state.

From left: Stanislaw Szukalski, Wiktor Podoski, Alicja Skarbek-Kruszewska and Stefan Mrozewski. Photo, courtesy Irena Mrozewska.

Moreover, in many respects this work aims to do away with the "loss of reality" (a concept coined by Eric Voegelin in his philosophy of consciousness) in the prevailing attitude of the politically and culturally dominant class toward the bulk of the American people.

To some extent this study also reinforces the theses of Maxine Seller, expounded in her recent book:

"the members of an ethnic group share the consciousness of a common historical past;"

"they share common life style and common values;"

"an ethnic community has aspirations for a common future, and these aspirations are focused upon the education of the young."

"Ethnicity is one of the oldest factors in American life; yet it has just begun to be explored;"

"ignorance of ethnicity is self-ignorance — for *all* Americans."[1]

Just as important as the education of the young in dispelling this ignorance of ethnicity, is the need in this "learning society" of the United States to promote the life-long learning of culturally mature Americans.

This book intends not only to promote the above objectives, but also to underscore a special flair among Polish Americans. As was obvious in Part Four (The Polish American Societal Life in California), the myriad of often overlapping societal organizations could be streamlined, inwardly strengthened, and updated within the overall American framework of ethnic integration. This would promote a stronger voice for the Polish Americans in that on-going process of social integration of all Americans.

This diversity is particularly evident in Los Angeles, as noted by Neil C. Sandberg in his *Ethnic Identity and Assimilation: The Polish-American Community, Case Study of Metropolitan Los Angeles*, which "has some forty diverse Polish American organizations, yet the fact that no directory of these groups has been published since 1950 suggests the existence of a community organization gap." "The problem is also manifested in the critical lack of support for Polish Cultural Creativity and for such needs as social and psychological research."[2]

On the other hand, the bicentennial celebration in Los Angeles produced some outstanding and noteworthy evidence of unified creativity on the part of Polish Americans in Southern California. Of some 65 Polish American artists from metropolitan Los Angeles, 35 exhibited their works at an art festival held February 28-29, 1976, in Malone Art Gallery at Loyola Marymount University. A panel of judges headed by Mark Bielski determined the most qualified exhibits from this group to be entered in the city-wide ethnic art exhibition on May 22-23, 1976, on the Los Angeles City Mall.

Education on all levels ranks possibly among the highest achievements of Polish Americans in California. The list of prominent educators continues to expand every year; in addition, financial aid funds, such as the Swantek Trust, directed by Helena Moore, offer assistance to needy Poles who are academically qualified to attend college.

Many organizations continually endeavor to expose their members and the American community at large to the variety and richness of Polish culture. For example, the Chopin choir, under the direction of Stephan Pasternacki, and the Hejnal Choir, directed by Waclaw Gazinski, offer concerts periodically. The "Krakusy," a Polish folk dance ensemble with Marylka Klimek-George as choreographer, and the "Mazur" folk dancers under the direction of Joanna Giedzinska, promote their noteworthy art. Honor is accorded to Anne F. Cierpik for her selfless work for the Szymanowski Foundation. It resulted in the first concert featuring the major works of Szymanowski ever to be performed in America, on October 2, 1977, at Loyola Marymount University. Helena Modrzejewska Art and Culture Club is another active group in this area. To propagate more extensively the Polish American heritage, a state-wide coordinating agency is needed; in fact, it is long overdue.

Gobelins by Yolanta Martusewicz-Shani. Exhibited at the Polish Art Festival, held Feb. 28-29, 1976, at L.M.U., Los Angeles.

On the religious front, Polish American Catholics in California are proud to see their mother parish in Los Angeles growing in prestige and influence. San Francisco now has a Polish Catholic Mission, as does San Diego. Santa Barbara Poles hold periodic religious services, courtesy of the Polish religious ministry in Los Angeles. A new Diocese of Orange also provides occasional services. This growth is a positive reflection of the policy by ecclesiastic authorities in recent years to recognize the religious needs of the bilingual faithful. More important, this policy keeps alive the memory that religious belief was part of the cultural heritage of every immigrant group, including Germans, Italians, Croatians, Poles, and so on.

In the political arena, Polish American representatives will continue to be appointed at all levels of government as they become more involved in taking an active role in public and political affairs. Increased publicity through the communications media — newspapers, magazines, radio and television — will stimulate this interest.

What makes a noticeable impression on the researchers of the Polish American past in California and observers of the present, is the higher proportion of achievers within the Polish American community of California when compared to similar and well-established communities in Illinois, Michigan, New York and so forth.

This work noted that first and foremost were those of Polish descent among the pioneers in the nineteenth century history of this state. Then in the twentieth century, the debt owed by Hollywood to Polish Americans, such as Joseph Tykocinski-Tykociner, inventor of the sound film and other facets of the entertainment world in general, must be singled out. Within the applied and performing arts a researcher must count Polish Americans in the hundreds, including those with Americanized names, as is customary practice in the profession.

A photo of a Polish immigrant family in New Jersey. Picture taken in 1928. The little boy, standing between his parents, is Thaddeus Golas, the future author of *The Lazy Man's Guide to Enlightenment.* He lives in Malibu.

The literary world recognizes Felix P. Wierzbicki, the pioneer-writer in California; Henryk Sienkiewicz, Nobel Prize winner (who worked at one time as a clerk at Jacoby's store on Pico Boulevard in Los Angeles) and several others of a different caliber (like Richard Boleslawski, Frank Riley, Maia Wojciechowska).

HOOVER INSTITUTION
on War, Revolution, and Peace
FOUNDED BY HERBERT HOOVER, 1919

Witold Sworakowski
Collection on Poland

The intellectual field provided especially fruitful ground, including literary figures like the late Waclaw Lednicki, U.C. Berkeley; the late Polish writer, Melchior Wankowicz, at one time of the Huntington Library, San Marino; Edward J. Tolosko, Lompoc; Thaddeus Golas, Malibu; writers like Szczepan Zimmer and Stanislaw Karpinski, Los Angeles; Ewa Emill, Walnut Creek; poets like internationally known Czeslaw Milosz, U.C. Berkeley; Alicja Pomian-Pozerska, San Francisco; Roman Makarewicz, Gardena; Victor Londzin (Leszcza), Los Altos; historiography, Jan Kowalik, San Jose; history, George J. Lerski, San Francisco; Anthony F. Turhollow and Jacek Przygoda, Los Angeles; Bogdan Deresiewicz, Santa Barbara; translator and publisher J. Lubanski, Sutter Creek; Sovietologist Witold Sworakowski, Stanford; political scientists and economists such as George

Lenczowski, U.C. Berkeley; the late Jerzy Karcz, Henryk Minc and Arthur Rachwald, U.C. Santa Barbara; Janusz Zawodny, Claremont Graduate School; Andrzej Brzeski, U.C. Davis; Andrew Korbonski, U.C. Los Angeles; Charles Kowal, a world renowned astronomer at California Institute of Technology, Pasadena; and a host of others along the Pacific Coast. To concretely visualize the extent of Polish presence in today's California, the reader need only peruse the *Who's Who* section of this book.

In closing these summary remarks, it should be clearly stated that anyone at all knowledgeable in the socio-cultural heritage of Polish Americans is aware of these two facts: First, the Poles (along with the "Dutchmen" since their landing in 1608 at Jamestown, Virginia) were the first ones to anticipate "cracks" in the forthcoming American "melting pot" myth.[3] (Symptomatically, 189 years later Helena Modjeska defied the chauvinistic American Protective Association (A.P.A.) in their action against her appearance on the stage in Santa Ana.[4])

Second, "history is for human self-knowledge," as R.C. Collingwood once wrote. And he continued in this vein, "knowing yourself means knowing what it is to be the man *you* are and nobody else is." It follows, to quote again, that "knowing yourself means what you can do; and since nobody knows what he can do until he tries, the only clue to what man can do is what man has *done*. The value of history, then, is what it teaches us what man has done and thus what *man is*." [Italics are Editor's][5]

Jacek Przygoda/Anthony F. Turhollow

REFERENCES

1. Maxine Seller, *To Seek America. A History of Ethnic Life in the United States*, pp. 4, 5, 293. Jerome S. Ozer, Englewood, N.J. 1977.

2. Ibid.

3. Melvin Steinfeld, *Cracks in the Melting Pot. Racism and Discrimination in American History*. Glencoe Press, New York, Beverly Hills. First printing, 1973.

4. Ellen K. Lee, "The Catholic Modjeska," *Polish American Studies*. Chicago, Ill. Vol. XXXI, No. 1, Spring 1974.

5. Jacek Przygoda, "Knowing Yourself, What You Can Do," *Polish American Studies*. Vol. XXX, No. 1, Spring 1973.

INDEX

The names of 500 subscribers and 257 biographees of the WHO's WHO are not repeated in this Index. It encompasses narrative parts only. References "in passing" are not listed.

A

Adams, John, 17, 20
Adams, Mary K., 254
Antczak, Al, 26, 251
Appleton Strakacz, Ann, 70,276
Archer, Walter J., 297
Arendt, Hanna, 227
Arzube, Bishop Juan A., 191
Ault, Bernice, 194

B

Babczynski, Roman, 202
Babiarz, Ch., 190
Bajerski, F., 188
Bancroft, Hubert H., 23, 27
Baranowski, Zygmunt, 23
Barker, Henry, 216
Baroni, Geno, 173
Baryski, Wojciech, 178, 205
Baxter, Don J., 72
Bayer, Helena E., 28, 278-9
Beit-I-Shoo, Gladys, 217
Bekker, Mieczyslaw G., 268-270
Bell, Wanda, 23
Benda, Felicie, 58
Bernhagen, Doris, 93, 251
Bielawski, Casimir, 28, 29, 36, 37
Bielecki, Tadeusz, 248, 249
Bielski, Jan, 240
Bielski, Kasia, 237, 240
Bielski, Mark, 236, 237, 240, 304
Bielski, Martin, 4
Black, John D.F., 149-151
Bielski, Martin, 4
Black, John D.F, 149-151
Black, Veronica, 218
Bodurka, Henry, 217
Bolek, Francis, 23
Boleslawski, Ryszard, 108-110, 307
Bor Komorowski, T., 302
Borowska, Helena, 242
Borowski, Tadeusz, 205, 212
Breese, Charles, 199, 214, 218

Breese, Jean M., 199, 216, 218, 241, 250
Brodka, Mark, 254, 255
Brolaski, Brolaskey, Henry Lyons, 22
Brudzinski, Izydor, 199
Brzechwa, Helena, 241
Brzechwa-White, Alicja, 232, 235, 236, 240
Brzeski, Andrzej, 308
Brzezinski, Zbigniew, 21
Buchajeska, Maria, 206
Bukaty, Franciszek, 18
Bukowinska, Jadwiga, 241
Bukowinski, Anne Marie, 285
Bukowinski, George, 285
Bukowska, Olga, 187
Burke, Lloyd, 229
Butler, Tadeusz, 185, 205

C

Cantwell, Bishop John J., 188
Carmody, Michelle, 184
Carroll, Bishop John, 8
Casassa, Charles S., 191, 235, 243, 253
Cekanauskas, V., 229
Chlapowski Bozenta, Karol, 22, 30, 42-54, 60, 61
Chciuk, Krystyna, 184, 205
Chriss, Nicholas C., 136
Cichocki, Robert, 234
Cichy, Andrew, 300
Cichy, Katherine, 217, 300
Ciecek, L.&M., 212
Cierpik, Anne F., 237, 248, 304
Cieslak, Eva, 285
Cieslak, Margaret, 285
Cieslak, Michal, 284-6
Claiborne, Richard, 18
Clark, John W., 232
Coleman, Marion Moore, 53, 54, 63
Collingwood, R.G., 308
Conrad, Joseph, 302
Cooper, James Fenimore, 9

Cuba, Stanley L., 87
Cugowski, Ann, 255
Cybulski, Akiko Ono, 240
Cybulski, Artur, 205
Cybulski, George, 240
Cybulski, Stanislaw K., 240, 248, 249
Czarnecki, Bertha, 217
Czarnota, Krysia, 234
Czyrko, Janina, 242

D

Dabrowska Wissema, E.G., 172, 226
Dabrowski, Martin, 15, 33, 67, 91, 177, 189
Danielski, Frank, 23
Danielski, Walter, 23
Danko, Krystyna, 241
Dazko, Pawel, 205
Degner, Leon A., 178
Demant, Karol, 23
Deresiewicz, Bogdan, 5, 225, 307
Deresiewicz, Catherine, 225
Deschner, Donald, 104
Dettling, Wanda, 206, 222
Dobkowski, Zygmunt, 178, 185
Domachowski, Alphonsus, 233
Domanski, L., 209
Dombrowski, Edmund T., 291-2
Dombrowski, Edmund Jr., 291
Dombrowski, Stephen, 291
Dombrowski, Violet, 234, 291
Drake, Edward P., 290
Dudzinski, Christiana, 250
Dudzinski, Tadeusz, 248
Dudzinski, Witek, 234, 255
Dusil, Adolf, 229
Dziadula, Mary, 217
Dziunikowska, Eugenia B., 248, 254

E

Eastwood, Ruthanne S., 251
Eichler, Christina S., 241, 248
Engel, Bronislawa & Wilhelm, 296
Engel, Richard, 296
Engelman, K.S., 220
Emill, Ewa, 307

F

Fedor, Patricia, 206, 222
Fenyas, Maria, 229
Festen, Anna, 248
Franklin, Benjamin, 16
Francis, C.W.H., 23
Frankowska, Izabela, 241
Fryzendorf, B., 208
Furman, Jozef, 191

G

Gale, Connie, 153-5
Gallatin, Albert, 10
Garstka, Stanley, 248
Gawlinska, Halina, 235, 287
Gawlinski, Wladyslaw, 93, 94
Gazinski, Waclaw, 233, 304
Giblyn, Virginia Mary, 58
Giedzinska, Joanna, 304
Glab, Paul, 199
Glayre, Piotr Maurycy, 17
Glebocka, Wiktoria, 241
Golas, Thaddeus, 306, 307
Golowka, Jody, 234
Gorka, Ferdinand, 222
Gorska, Hanka, 248
Gozdzikowska, Zofia, 241
Gozdzikowski, Mieczyslaw, 237
Grams, Helena H., 246, 248, 249
Grey, Benjamin, 249
Grochowski, Most Rev. Leon, 196
Grot, Anton, 104-106
Grubinski, Stefan, 240
Grubinski Salak, Bozena, 241
Grusinski, Mary, 225
Grycko, Wanda, 205
Gryn, Josephine, 199
Grzanka, Ela, 205
Grzanka, Gosia, 204
Grzegorczyk, Harrietta, 217
Gwizdak, Krystyna, 241
Gwozdziowski, Marek, 234
Gzowski, Kazimir S., 10

H

Haifter, Mitchel, 250
Haiman, Mieczyslaw, 251, 252
Halecki, Oskar, 252
Halstead, Maria, 224
Harvey, Miroslawa, 241
Hayes, Kathy S., 112, 118, 140, 210, 245, 260, 300, 301
Henzel, Marcin, 215, 241
Hicks, Edward W., 102-103
Hlond, Cardinal August, 191
Hodgson, Marie T., 254, 255
Hollywood, John of, 4
Hordynski, Joseph, 9
Howard, Camille, 206
Howe, Samuel Gridley, 9, 10, 12
Hroscikowski, Ann, 250, 255
Hryniewicki, W., 208
Hunt, Rockwell D., 30

J

Jagiellonian Academy, University, 4
Jambor, Frank, 188, 216
Janczur, Sophie, 241
Janiszewski, George, 184
Jankowska, Barbara, 234
Jankowski, Henryk, 240
Jarosz, Zygmunt, 258
Jaures, Jean, 228
Jazwinska, Wanda, 215
Jefferson, Thomas, 7, 12, 16, 17
Jeschke, Catherine, 177
Johnson, Bishop William R., 244
Jureko, Stanislaw, 190, 191, 192, 19.

K

Kabarowska, Krystyna, 241
Kabarowska, Zofia, 241
Kaczmarek, Stefan, 191
Kaczmarek, W., 220
Kalata, Edward, 196, 197
Kali-Weynerowska, Hanka, 99-101
Kalinowski, Henry, 11
Kalinski, George, 195, 244
Kalussowski, Henry, 10
Kaminska, Natalia, 241, Teresa, 241
Kaminski, George, 201, 203, 241
Kaminski, M., 210, 212
Kaminsky, Wanda, 195
Kaper, Bronislaw, 122, 248
Karcz, Jerzy, 308
Karpinski, Jan, 241
Karpinski, Stanislaw, 248, 307
Kasper, Dennis R., 130
Kasper, Jerome A., 130-132, 234, 24
Kasper, Jerry V., 130
Kasper, Vi, 130, 249
Kawecki, Leon S., 234, 245
Kaye, Mindy, 120, 122, 123, 125, 128,
    138, 142, 149, 152
Kaymark, Carl, 195, 259
Kazmierski, Veronica, 199
Kennedy, John F., 65
Kersten, Stanley, 237, 240
Kirk, Margaret, 146
Kierkegaard, Soren, 252
Klejnot, Olgierd, 191, 199
Klimek-George, Marylka, 234, 304
Klimes, Helena, 206
Klimes, Ingeborg, 236, 240, 241, 25(
Klimes, L., 250
Kliszewska, Gena, 204, 205, 241
Kliszewski, A., 236
Klonowicz, Stefan, 4
Knight, Ted, 138-9
Knoll, Paul, 232

Kobylak, W., 190
Kohlman, Bozena, 234
Kohlman, Irena, 234
Kolbe, Maximilian, 222
Koleda, Harriet, 216
Koleda, Joseph, 199, 216, 250
Kollataj, Hugo, 6, 14, 19
Komorowski, M., 219
Kopernik (Copernicus), Mikolaj, 4, 28, 91,
    92, 145, 198, 245, 246
Korba, Wanda, 199, 217
Korbonski, A., 308
Korwin Piotrowski, Rudolf, 32, 62
Kosciuszko, Tadeusz, 6, 7, 8, 11, 12, 17,
    20, 82, 187, 205, 237, 242, 245
Koscki, Theresa, 255
Koshade, Henrietta D. (Bobby), 23
Kosztowniak, W., 190
Kowal, Charles, 308
Kowalik, Basia, R., 296
Kowalik, Jan, 23, 175, 178, 179, 307
Kowalewski, Mieczyslaw, 199, 208
Kowalski, Zbigniew, 214, 250
Kozak, Celina, 241
Kraitsir, Carl, 10
Krance, Slawa, 116, 117
Kroczko, John, 216
Krol, H. Eric, 190, 191
Krzeminski, Bronislaw, 188, 190, 193, 194
Krzyczkowski, Antoni, 225
Krzywonos, S., 220
Krzyzanowski, Wlodzimierz, 10, 11, 13
Kudlicka, Jozefa, 188, 192, 272-273
Kulas, Eugene P., 248
Kulesza, Seweryn, 301-2
Kulikowski, Leon, 222
Kurnik, Franciszek, 195, 205
Kwasieborska, Felicia, 290
Kwasniewski, Stanislaw, 23
Kwiatkowski, Zofia, 214

L

Ladowicz, Alicja, 241
Ladowicz, Bogna, 204
Ladowicz, Jozef, 203, 219
Ladowicz, Tadek, 234
Laskowski, Jerome S., 251, 253
Lauterbach, Otto, 248
Lazowska, Jadwiga, 241
Lazowski, K., 207
Lebiedzinski, J., 220
Lednicki, Waclaw, 307
Lee, Ellen K., 41, 54, 251, 308
Lehti, Donald, 229
Lenczowski, George, 307

Lerski, George J., 178, 224, 248, 252, 308
Lewanski, Richard C., 28
Lewicka, Barbara, 241
Lewicki, Stanislaw L., 230
Liberace, Wladziu, 120, 121
Lichter, Renate, 254, 255
Ligus, Kazimierz, 215
Liibke, Helena, 67, 70, 251, 280-1
Lojewski, Harry, 123, 124
Londzin, Victor, 307
Lubanski, Josef, 307
Luczaj, Tadeusz, 232
Lukas, Karl, 232
Lukasiewicz, Betty, 199, 216
Luskina, Stefan, 15, 16
Lytkowski, Zdzislaw, 233

M

Macander, Izabella Z., 200
Maciag, Edward, 195
Maciejewski, Roman, 116, 190
Maciejowski, Wladyslaw, 241
Majewski, Mr. & Mrs., 236, 241
Makarewicz, Roman, 208, 307
Makowiecki, Joseph, 191
Malin, Donald P., 250, 254, 255
Manning, Cardinal Timothy, 190, 192
Mantykowski, Anthony, 216
Marciniak, Konstanty, 187, 188
Marcinkowski, Zbigniew, 203, 248
Margis, Roman, 199, 207, 208
Martin, Laura, 234
Martinoff, Barbara, 203
Martusewicz-Shani, Yolanta, 242, 305
Maryanski, Modest, 23
Mastai, Boleslaw, 85
Mathews, Eugene, 203
Mathews, Laura, 203, 241, 248
Matusewicz, Theresa, 232, 254
May, Genowefa, 222
Mazur, Beata, 205
Mazynski, Marek J., 209
Mazzei, Filipio, 17
McCormick, Harold, 134
McCoy, Lon, 43
McCullogh, John, 47
McGucken, Archbishop Thomas J., 178, 179
McIntyre, Cardinal James Francis, 148, 191
Merryfield, Donald P., 247
Mielcarz, V., 190
Mika, Florence, 195
Mikulski, Barbara, 174
Miller, John, 188, 191
Milosz, Czeslaw, 307
Minc, Henryk, 308
Mitty, Archbishop John J., 176, 179

Modjeska, Modrzejewska, Helena, 22, 30, 42-55, 56, 57, 60, 62, 63, 187, 249, 251, 305, 308
Modjeski, Ralph, 44, 46, 47, 56-59
Montygierd, Jerzy, 203
Moore, Helena, 304
Morrissey, Clarence, 236, 248, 251
Morrissey, Helena D., 247, 248
Mrozewska, Irena, 241, 303
Mrozewski, Stefan, 2, 47, 67, 78, 85-89, 189, 211, 303
Mudy, Bruno, 241, 248, 295
Muir, John, 32, 38, 53
Muir Hanna, Wanda, 32, 38
Mullen, Michael, 195
Murawski, Marianne K., 254, 255
Myslicki, Joseph S., 26

N

Najdziuk, Cheslav, 229
Nalecz-Mrozowski, Tadeusz, 200
Nalewaja, Thomas, 220
Nalski, Wladyslaw, 236, 241
Nawroczynska, Krystyna, 241
Negri, Pola, 191
Nieder, Joseph, 190
Niemcewicz, Julian Ursyn, 8, 10, 13, 16
Niemiec, Malgosia, 205
Niemiec, Stella, 195, 241
Niemo-Niemojewski, Lech, 216, 271
Niestatek, Malgosia, 234
Niezgodzki, L., 190
Nizynska, Basia, 234
Nizynski, Andrzej, 144, 212, 234
Nizynski, Jacek, 234
Nowakowski, Andrzej, 248
Nowakowski, Stefan, 190
Nowicki, Tadeusz, 191, 241
Nowowiejski, Henryk, 241

O

Okon, Zofia, 214
Olbrys, Zbigniew, 191, 192, 194, 195, 205, 225
Olczyk, James, 241
Olechno-Huszcza, Czeslaw, 23, 136, 234, 250, 254
Olechno-Huszcza, Gillian, 232, 251, 253, 254
Olewicz, Mrs. M., 23
Opid, Helena, 30
Ordon-Sklodowski, V., 248, 249
Organisciak, Jakub, 187
Osinska, Genowefa, 199, 207

P

Paden, Irene D., 23
Paderewska, Helena, 70-71, 280-1
Paderewski, Ignacy, 12, 52, 66-69, 70, 71, 242, 276
Paine, Thomas, 17, 20
Pankanin, Marian, 192
Paprocki, Julian, 49
Parka, Alice, 195
Pasternacki, Stephan, 118, 119, 241, 248, 271, 272, 304
Patyk, Jozef, 220
Pawlikowski, Marian, 219
Pawlowska, Jadwiga (Hedy), 219, 235, 240
Pawlowski, Wally, 218, 234, 299
Pedzich, Antoni, 15
Perez, Charles, 59
Perry, Barbara, 229
Pieczynski, Stanislaw, 184
Piehura, Agnes, 192
Pietras, Adam, 205
Pietras, Walentyna, 205
Podhorska, Alicja, 241
Podhorski, Jacek, 240, 241
Podlasek, Czeslawa, 199, 203
Podoski, Wiktor, 78-81, 303
Podradecki, Zbigniew, 217
Pokrzywnicki, Mary Beth, 255
Polaczek, Ewa, 234
Polaczek, Marianna, 241
Pollasky, Adalbert, 36
Pollasky, Marcus, 29, 36
Pomian-Pozerska, Alicja, 307
Pongowski, Stanislaus, 22
Poniatowski, Prince Andre, 72, 73
Poniatowski, Count Ladislaus, 23
Poniatowski, King Stanislaw August, 6, 14, 18
Porebski, Kazimierz, 185
Posadzy, Ignacy, 191
Posluszny, Sylwester, 191
Potasz, Thomas, 213, 216, 274-5
Prasniewski, Jan, 146, 147
Prasniewski, Jerzy, 186
Prasniewski, Margaret, 66, 251
Prega, Dorota, 241
Przygoda, Jacek, 22, 95, 102, 130, 134, 153, 156, 161, 164, 168, 178, 182, 187, 191, 229, 234, 236, 238, 240, 246, 253, 282, 284, 289, 290, 293, 295, 296, 307, 308
Pszczolkowski-Preston, Stanley, 293-4
Pudynski, Walter, 26
Pujdak, Jerzy, 240
Pujdak, Mike, 234
Pujdak, Nick, 234

Pulaski (Pollaskey), Albert, 22
Pulaski, Casimir, 7, 13, 237, 242, 245

R

Rachwald, Artur, 308
Radwan, Jerzy, 200
Rambo, James I., 99
Ratajczak, Peter, 240
Reilly, Msgr. John J., 250
Rezler, Janina, 204, 241
Rice, Coralinn, 54
Riley, Frank, 22, 27, 307
Rodzinski, Ryszard, 117
Rogenade, Jacob, 23
Rokicka, Krysia, 234
Rokicki, Vincent, 212
Rolle, Andrew F., 227
Romanowska, Emilia, 154, 242
Romanowska, Irena, 242
Romanski, A., 195, 208
de Rosen, Jan H., 74-77, 263
Rosenstein, Barbara, 229
Rostworowski, Boguslaw, 108
Rubin, Bishop Wladyslaw, 192
Rundzio, Henryka, 241
de Rusillon, Count John, 2
Rusin, Dorek, 64
Rydzeski, Antoinette, 248
Rydzeski, Roman, 216
Rymsza, Stanley, 190, 194
Rysz, Most Rev. Antoni, 196
Rzewuski, Seweryn, 18, 19

S

Salak, Edyta, 241
Salamunovich, Paul, 252
Sandberg, Neil C., 304
Sandburg, Carl, 1
Sapieha, Prince John, 23
Saran, Anthony, 191, 198, 199, 248, 250, 251, 260-261
Sawa, Michele M., 213, 251, 274, 278
Schlichtmann, Margaret E., 23
Sell, Victor, 26
Seller, Maxine, 303, 308
Semonski Family, 132, 133
Sermak, Carolyn, 234
Sermak, Jeanette, 234, 255
Serwacka, Janina, 241
Shaler, William, 27
Sharfman, I. Harold, 22, 27
Shatyn, Bruno, 184

Shubsda, Bishop Thaddeus A., 26, 190, 194, 225, 228, 256-259
Siekaniec, Ladislas J., 38
Sienkiewicz, Clement, 196
Sienkiewicz, Henryk, 22, 30, 42, 44, 46, 54, 60-63, 232, 249, 307
Silva, Mario, 232
Simons, Denise, 255
Simons, Gregory, 255
Simons, Henrietta, 234
Simons, Jerome, 238, 251
Simons, Rebecca, 255
Simons, Ruthanne, 232
Skinner, Maud, 52
Skrzynska, Jolanta, 224
Slawik, Boniface, 190, 191
Slawinska, Dzidzia, 234
Slawinski, Tomek, 234
Smelski, John, 184
Sniegowski, S., 221
Sobolewski, Paul, 10
Socash, Ann Marie, 254, 255
Solinski, Solinskey,
Solinsky, Hugo Charles, 23
Sondomowicz, Richard, Sandra, 130, 234
Sovinski, J. Dorothy, 216, 236, 240, 243
Sovulewski, Gabriel, 23
Stadnicki, Peter, 8
Stampinski, Frances, 241
Stanley, T.T., 298
Stanwyck, John, 255
Staszic, Stanislaw, 6, 16
Steinfeld, Melvin, 308
Stefanowski, Adam, 23
Stefanowski, Mrs. P., 23
Stelmach, Helena, 202, 241
Strakacz, Sylwin, 216, 273, 276-7
Strentzel, John T., 32, 36, 38
Styka, Jan, 30, 82-84
Sulistrowski, Zygmunt, 112-114
Surmacz, J., 214
Surok, Syrec, Francis, 22
Suszynski, Peter, 242
Sutter, John A., 21, 30, 36
Swadowski, Z., 206
Swit, Loretta, 142
Switkowski, Piotr, 16, 17
Sworakowska, Helena, 3, 182
Sworakowski, Witold S., 34, 178, 248, 251, 307
Sypniewski, Jules, 43, 44, 48
Szatkowski, Thomas, 243, 251
Szatkowski, Wanda, 216, 236, 240, 243
Szeptycki, J. George, 75, 78, 190, 191, 224, 228, 251, 262
Szmit, Edward, 248

Szukalski, Stanislaw, 90-92, 303
Szulkiewicz, Stanley, 199
Szymak, Slawa, 241
Szymanska, Jadwiga, 214
Szumanski, Z., 191, 234
Szymanowski, Karol, 237, 252, 255, 305

T

Tabasz, Mary, 250, 254, 255
Tabenicki, Jan, 240
Taube, Zygmunt, 248
Teachout, Harriett, 206
Terelak, Edward, 212, 233
Terlecki, Tymon, 224
Terpilowski, Roman, 207, 216
Timineri, Bev & Joe, 253
Tinnin, Vee, 232
Tochman, Gaspard (Jasper), 10
De Tocqueville, Alexis, 171
Toczylowski, H., 236
Tolosko, Edward J., 307
Tomaszewski, W., 208
Toporkiewicz, Marie, 23
Tornau, Helena, 241, 248
Truskolaski, Joseph, 10
Truszkiewicz, F., 207
Turhollow, Anthony F., 229, 244, 248, 253, 254, 307, 308
Turhollow, Anthony, Jr., 234, 236, 240, 254
Tuszynska, Franciszka, 215, 241, 248
Tykocinski-Tykociner, Joseph, 306
Tyssowski, John, 10
Tyszkiewicz-Lacki, Janusz, 224, 225

U

Ulam, S.M., 252
Urbanowski, Konrad, 192
Ustaski, Bill, 194

V

Vallivode (Waliwoda), Stephen, 22
Vars, Henry, 125-127, 248
Vinton, Bobby, 128, 129
Voegelin, Eric, 303
Vogt, Irena, 237, 241
Vogt, Witold, 201
Vrablik, Robert J., 196

W

Waldo, Artur, 248, 252
Walska, Ganna, 134-5

Wankowicz, Melchior, 307
Washington, George, 7, 8, 12, 15, 17, 19, 245
Ward, Bishop John J., 192
Warno, Henryk, 296
Warno, Irena, 296
Wasick, Regina, 23
Wdowiak, Boleslaw, 186
Wegierski, Kajetan, 8, 17
Wegner, Mary W., 235, 236, 238, 240, 241
Wegner, Stanley, 242
Weissman, Rita, 229
Wesseling, John, 229
West, Margaret, 191
Westwalewicz, Henryk, 203, 248
Weyna, Helena, 242
Wheaton, Henry, 8
Whitney, J.D., 28
Wichrowsky (Wichrowski), Krakus, 102
Wicker, Olga, 199
Wiechecki, Ludwik, 191
Wielkoszewski, Wladyslaw, 219, 234
Wierzbicki, Felix P., 35, 39-41, 249, 307
Wilk, Mary Ann, 217, 284
Wilk, Richard, 284
Wilson, Woodrow, 12
Witkowski, Bohdan, 186
Witkowski, William, 241
Wlodarczyk, Jozef, 214
Wlodarski, Stephen, 196
Wnorowska, Joanna, 234
Wnorowska, Marianna, 234
Wnorowski, Kazimierz, 202
Wojciechowska Basia, 204
Wojciechowska, Danuta, 241
Wojciechowska, Maia, 307
Wojtyla, Cardinal Karol, 192
Wolan, Maria, 221
Woroniecka, Monika, 214
Woroniecki, Stefan, 214
Woznicki, Andrzej, 178
Wrobel, Alfred J., 14, 20, 251
Wyglendowski, Stan, 250
Wyszynski, Eustace, 10
Wytrwal, Joseph, 63

Z

Zabriskie, Christian Brevoort, 32
Zagorski, Antoni, 191
Zakrzewski, Alexander, 36
Zakrzewski, Wojciech, 49
Zakrzewski, Zdzislaw, 178, 181, 184
Zakrzewski, Zofia, 184
Zambel, Max, 194
Zaremba, Bronislaw A., 23

Zaremba, Dionizy, 22, 30
Zatoka, Rudolf, 203, 240, 248
Zawadzka, Danuta, 214, 236, 240, 241, 251
Zawadzki, Michal, 191, 214
Zawadzki, Roman, 195
Zawodny, Janusz, 308
Zawojski, Wladyslaw (Walter), 95-98
Zbylut, L., 190
Zdzielnicka, Janina, 241
Zebrowski, Henry, 214
Zielinska Martinoff, Barbara, 232, 236, 240, 241
Zielinski, Jaroslaw, 115
Zielinski, Tadeusz, 191, 282-3
Zielkiewicz, Krystyna, 201, 204, 234, 235, 236, 237, 238, 240, 241, 251
Zielkiewicz, Zbigniew, 207, 219, 234
Ziengel, Marie, 287-8
Zimmer, Halina, 165, 241
Zimmer, Szczepan K., 156-158, 159, 191, 214, 236, 240, 248, 307
Zmudowski, Martin, 33
Zmurkevych, Irene, 247
Zrodlo, Jozefa, 241
Zurawska, Wanda, 204
Zychlinski, Ludwik, 10, 11
Zygmunt, Arthur, 236, 240
Zygmunt, Gene, 74, 82, 90, 236, 240, 251

PART SIX

POLISH AMERICAN
WHO'S WHO IN CALIFORNIA

History owes its existence to men.

Hanna Arendt
The Human Condition

INTRODUCTION

Estimating the number of Americans of Polish background who reside in California is a very difficult task indeed. The population statistics of the Bureau of Census are not of much help, since they are too preoccupied with the country of origin (as regards the country of emigration), which frequently tells little of the cultural background. For instance, Stanislaw Kopanski, a World War II Polish General, was born in St. Petersburg, raised in Lithuania, educated in Poland, and lived in England. If he had come to California, the Census Bureau would have listed him as "foreign born, United Kingdom." Yet General Kopanski considered himself culturally and ethnically Polish, and in moments of reflection and relaxation would re-read the works of Mickiewicz, Sienkiewicz or Reymont.

So the more pertinent question is, how many Americans in California have a feeling of Polish cultural awareness and care for it? The number is truly unknown. One of the expected benefits of this book is to tell the community at large that quite a number of Polish Americans are alive and well in the Golden State.

This *Who's Who* lists barely a few hundred Polish Americans in California out of potentially thousands. The listing is neither inclusive nor exclusive but presents those men and women known to the editors of *Who's Who*. Unfortunately, there are many who are unknown to them, some who are not aware of the richness of Polish culture and Polish history in California, and still others who may not be aware of the joy and pride that cultural diversity provides. After all, if one is Polish but unaware of one's Polish heritage, even if it were only in part, one is, in the words of the media, "Anglo."

This *Who's Who* represents just a beginning. If one's name does not appear in this edition, it may in the next. The contents of individual entries have been based on submitted materials by the individuals themselves, and it is their sole responsibility. All entries had to be edited to conform to a standard format. As practiced in similar publications, the necessary abbreviations have been adopted and their meaning explained.

Gene H. Zygmont, Editor
Edward M. Kaminski/Arthur L. Zygmont, Assistant Editors

(This was the initial form used in seeking the information for the *Who's Who*.)

POLISH AMERICAN WHO'S WHO IN CALIFORNIA
Biographical Questionnaire

To insure accuracy please write legibly or type. The questionnaire may be filled out in full or *in part* as the respondent wishes. Entries qualified to "WHO'S WHO" will be edited.

FULL NAME _____

                        Last   First   Middle

MAILING ADDRESS _____

                      Number & Street   City   State   Zip Code

RELIGIOUS AFFILIATION (Or None) _____

MARITAL STATUS (check one)   NAME OF SPOUSE IN FULL
Married____Single____

                                          _____

CHILDREN (Name, date & place of birth) _____
_____
_____

BIRTH DATE (Optional)____PLACE OF BIRTH _____

PRESENT CITIZENSHIP: U.S.A. ( )   POLISH ( )   Other _____

COUNTRIES WHERE LIVED (& approximate dates) OR TRAVELED _____
_____

MILITARY SERVICE (countries, military campaigns, dates, rank) _____
_____

P.O.W., CONCENTRATION or FORCED LABOR CAMPS (places, dates) ____
_____
_____

EDUCATION (schools attended, degrees, diplomas) _____
_____
_____

LANGUAGES (spoken, written) _____

EMPLOYMENT or BUSINESS EXPERIENCE (type, where, for how long) _____

_____

MEMBERSHIP IN PROFESSIONAL and/or FRATERNAL ORGANIZATIONS and CLUBS _____

_____

OTHER PERTINENT DATA (Biographical listings, military decorations, awards, honors, prizes, hobbies) _____

_____

DATE____ENCLOSED CHECK for $____SIGNATURE _____

Note: The cancelled check is your receipt.
      If more space is needed for answers, please use the back side of this page or add
      more pages. Do not hesitate to ask questions and spread a *good word* about this
      project. Thank you for your cooperation.

THE *WHO'S WHO*
INFORMATION SEQUENCE

Whenever possible, the *abbreviated* information sequence follows this pattern:

1. Name
2. Residence
3. Present occupation
4. Birthplace/Birthdate
5. Education
6. Marital status/Name of spouse
7. Children
8. Military service
9. Prisoner of War/Concentration Camp and/or Forced Labor Camp Internment
10. Profession/Business experience
11. Membership in Professional/Fraternal/Civic Organizations
12. Published books/papers/articles
13. Honors/Awards/Military/Civilian
14. Other pertinent data
15. Miscellaneous

KEY OF ABBREVIATIONS AND BIOGRAPHICAL CODE

A.A.	Associate in Arts
A.A.U.P.	American Association of University Professors
Acad.	Academy
Acct.	Accountant, Accounting
Act.	Acting
Adj.	Adjutant
Aero.	Aeronautics, Aeronautical
AFB	Air Force Base
Agric.	Agriculture
A.I.A.	American Institute of Architects
A.M.A.	American Medical Association
Amer.	American
Apr.	April

Arch.	Architect, Architecture
Arty.	Artillery
A.S.M.E.	American Society of Mechanical Engineers
Assn.	Association
Assoc.	Associate
Asst.	Assistant
Astro.	Astronomy, Astronomer
Aug.	August
Aust.	Australia
b.	born
B.A.	Bachelor of Arts
Belg.	Belgium
Bldg.	Building
Brig.	Brigadier
B.S.	Bachelor of Science
B.S.A.	Boy Scouts of America
Bus.	Business
c.	Child, Children
Cal.	California
Can.	Canada
Cand.	Candidate
Capt.	Captain
Cath.	Catholic
Cav.	Cavalry
CC	Concentration Camp
c.c.	Country Club
C. of C.	Chamber of Commerce
Chap.	Chaplain
Chem.	Chemistry, Chemical
Chi.	Chicago
Chm.	Chairman, Chairperson
Chpt.	Chapter
C.M.A.	California Medical Association
Cmmdr.	Commander
Co.	Company, County
Col.	Colonel
Coll.	College
Colo.	Colorado
Comm.	Committee, Commercial
Conn.	Connecticut
Cons.	Consultant
Conser.	Conservatory
Contr.	Contributing
Co-op	Cooperative
Cpl.	Corporal
CSU	California State University
CSUDH	California State University, Dominguez Hills
CSULA	California State University, Los Angeles
CSULB	California State University, Long Beach
CSUSF	California State University, San Fernando
CSUSJ	California State University, San Jose

Dec.	December
d.	deceased
Dem.	Democrat, Democratic
Dept.	Department
Des.	Designer
Dev.	Development
Dir.	Director
Dist.	District
div.	Divorced
Div.	Division
Doct.	Doctoral
DP	Displaced Person
DPC	Displaced Persons Camp
East.	Eastern
Econ.	Economist, Economics
Ed.	Editor
Ed.D.	Doctor of Education
Elec.	Electric, Electrical
Eng.	England
Engr.	Engineer
Eur.	Europe, European
Exec.	Executive
Fac.	Faculty
FLC	Forced Labor Camp
Feb.	February
Flt. Off.	Flight Officer
Found.	Foundation
Fr.	France
Frat.	Fraternity
G.B.	Great Britain
Geol.	Geologist, Geology
Gen.	General
Ger.	German, Germany
Gr.	Group
HI	Hawaii
Hon.	Honors, Honorable
Hosp.	Hospital
H.S.	High School
I.E.A.	Institute of Engineers and Architects
Ill.	Illinois
Incl.	Including
Ind.	Industry, Industrial, Indiana
Inf.	Infantry
Ins.	Insurance
Inst.	Institute, Institution
Instr.	Instructor
Intl.	International
It.	Italy
J.A.G.	Judge Advocate General
Jan.	January
Jap.	Japan

J.D.	Juris Doctor
Jour.	Journal
Jr.	Junior
Ju.	June
Jy.	July
K.F.	Kosciuszko Foundation (New York)
LA.	Louisiana
L.A.	Los Angeles
Lab.(s)	Laboratory, Laboratories
Lang.	Language
Lect.	Lecturer
Libr.	Library, Librarian
Lic.	Licensed
Lit.	Literature
L.L.M.	Master of Laws
L.L.D.	Doctor of Laws
Lt.	Lieutenant
Ltd.	Limited
m.	Married
MA	Master
M.A.	Master of Arts
Maj.	Major
Mar.	March
Mass.	Massachusetts
M.B.A.	Master of Business Administration
MD.	Maryland
M.D.	Medical Doctor
Mech.	Mechanical
Med.	Medical, Medicine
Mem.	Member
Met.	Metallurgy, Metallurgical
Mfg.	Manufacture, Manufacturing
Mgmt.	Management
Mgr.	Manager
Mich.	Michigan
Mil.	Military, Military Service
Minn.	Minnesota
M.L.S.	Master of Library Science
M.P.H.	Master of Public Health
Msgr.	Monsignor
Mus.	Music
My.	May
Natl.	National
nee	maiden name
N.J.	New Jersey
N.	North
Nov.	November
Numis.	Numismatic
NY	New York
N.Y.C.	New York City
O.	Ohio

Oct.	October
Off.	Official, Officer(s)
OLBMRCC	Our Lady of the Bright Mount Catholic Church (Polish Parish, Los Angeles)
Org.	Organization, Organized
PA	Polish Army
P.A.A.A.	Polish American Arts Association
P.A.C.	Polish American Congress
P.A.C.F.C.U.	Polish American Congress Federal Credit Union (Los Angeles)
PAF	Polish Air Force
P.A.F.A.	Polish Air Force Association
P.A.H.A.	Polish American Historical Association
Pasa.	Pasadena
P.A.V.A.	Polish American Veterans Association
P.C.	Polish Center
PFAC	Polish Fraternal Association of California (SAMOPOMOC)
Penn.	Pennsylvania
PHA	Polish Home Army, a/k/a Polish Underground Army and Armia Krajowa
P.H.A.V.A.	Polish Home Army Veterans Association
Phar.	Pharmacy, Pharmacist, Pharmaceutical
Ph.D.	Doctor of Philosophy
Phil.	Philosophy
Photo.	Photography
PHS	Polish High School
P.I.A.S.	Polish Institute of Arts and Sciences in America
P.N.A.	Polish National Alliance
Pol.	Poland, Polish, Political
Poly.	Polytechnic
POW	Prisoner of War
P.P.	Past President
P.P.N.S.	Polish Philatelic-Numismatic Society
P.R.C.U.	Polish Roman Catholic Union in America
Pres.	President, Presiding
Princ.	Principal
Prof.	Professor
Prog.	Program
Proj.	Project
Psych.	Psychology
P.T.A.	Parent Teacher's Association
Publ.	Publicity, Publisher
PUC	Polish University College
P.U.C.	Polish University Club
P.W.A.	Polish Women's Alliance
Rad.	Radiologý, Radiologist
RAF	Royal Air Force
R.C.C.	Roman Catholic Church
Rev.	Reverend
Reg.	Registered, Registrar
Regt.	Regiment
Ret.	Retired
Radiol.	Radiology, Radiologist, Radiological

S.B.	Santa Barbara
Sch.	School
Sci.	Science
S.D.	San Diego
Secty.	Secretary
Sect.	Section
Sept.	September
S.F.	San Francisco
Sgt.	Sergeant
S.J.	Society of Jesus, San Jose
S.M.	Santa Monica
S.	South
Soc.	Society, Social
Struct.	Structural
Sup.	Supervisor, Superintendent
Surg.	Surgeon, Surgery, Surgical
Svc.	Service
S.W.G.A.	Screen Writers Guild of America
Tech.	Technical, Technician
Trans.	Transport, Transportation
Treas.	Treasurer
TX	Texas
U.	University
UC	University of California
UCB	University of California, Berkeley
UCD	University of California, Davis
UCI	Univeristy of California, Irvine
UCLA	University of California, Los Angeles
UCSB	University of California, Santa Barbara
UCSC	University of California, Santa Cruz
UCSD	University of California, San Diego
U.K.	United Kingdom
Univ.	University
U.S.	United States
USA	United States Army
U.S.A.	United States of America
USAAF	United States Army Air Force
USAF	United States Air Force
USMC	United States Marine Corps
USN	United States Navy
USSR	Union of Soviet Socialist Republics
Vi.	Vice-
Vet.	Veteran(s)
Virg.	Virginia
V.P.	Vice President
w/	with
W.	West
Wisc.	Wisconsin
Y.M.C.A.	Young Men's Christian Association
Yrs.	Years
&	And

WHO'S WHO

ANTCZAK, ALFONS JOSEPH. San Gabriel. Writer/Editor.b. Detroit, Mich., Aug. 3, 1922. B.S., Loyola U. m. Helen Elizabeth Fitzpatrick. c. Mary, Helen, Margaret, Teresa, Al, Tom, John, Joseph. Mil. Cpl. USAF, 1945. Editorial Staff, *The Tidings*, 30 yrs. Contr. *America, Columbia, Our Sunday Visitor, El Visitante Dominical*. Mem. Cath. Press Council, Newman Club of L.A.

ARCHER, WALTER J. Industrialist. Ret. Santa Barbara. b. Newark, New Jersey. Lived in Florida; since 1950, California. m. Janina Szukalski. d. Joyce (Mrs. Robert Sebig). Hobbies: architecture, collecting paintings.

BALVIN, RICHARD S. Psychologist/Educator. b. N.Y.C. Ph.D., Psych., UCLA — Sch. of Med. Mil. USN, WWII. Philippine Theatre. m., c. D'harimar. Chm., Psych. Dept., CSULA. Mem. Sigma XI; A.A.U.P.; Amer. Psych. Soc.; Psi Chi, Hon. Psych. Assn.; P.U.C.; Pol. Amer. Bus. & Prof. Assn. Co-author several textbooks.

BARC, STANLEY ZDZISLAW. Santa Monica. Retired. b. Buffalo, N.Y., Nov. 26, 1911. Studied: Mich. State U.; U. Chicago; Northwestern U. Mil. Tech. Sgt., USA, 1943-46, Europe, Asia, Pacific. Hosp. Lab. Tech. (HM3), USN, 1948-52, Korea. Floriculturist, tourguide, Chi. Park Dist. 27 yrs. Mem. Quail Gardens Foundation, Self Realization Fellowship, Cetacean Soc.

BARYSKI, REV. WOJCIECH. San Francisco. Clergyman. b. Zaleszczyki, Poland, Apr. 2, 1939. Studied at Seminary of the Soc. of Christ, Poznan, Pol. Came to U.S., 1963.

BEIT-I-SHOO, GLADYS LUCILLE (nee Krasniewicz). North Hollywood. Social worker. b. Brooklyn, N.Y., Feb. 6. B.A., Psych., Alliance Coll., Cambridge Sprs. Penn., 1958. Grad. study, Adelphi U., Garden City, N.Y. m. Dr. Benedict. Social worker, Nassau Co., Minneola, N.Y., 8 yrs.; Red Cross, Van Nuys, Cal., 5 yrs.; Travelers Aid Soc., L.A., 2 yrs. Mem. Nat. Assn. of Soc. Workers; P.N.A. — Gr. 3123; P.P.N.S.

BENDARZEWSKI, JERZY ANDRZEJ. Sherman Oaks. Architect. b. Poland, Dec. 5, 1935. M.A., Arch., Warsaw Poly U. 1961. m. Elizabeth T. c. Joanna, Susanna. Practicing architect: Eng., Fr., Can., U.S.A. Principal w/ Campbell & Bendarzewski, Inc.; C.B.C. Builders, Inc. Lic. Arch., Cal. Mem. Amer. Soc. of Arch. & Engr. Former mem. Toastmasters Intl.

BENDISZ, KAZIMIERZ. San Francisco. Engineer/Instructor. b. Warsaw, Poland, Feb. 11, 1914. Studied: Mil. Coll., Torun, 1933; Poly. Inst., Warsaw, 1937-39; Dipl., Engr., U. Munich, 1947. c. Anna, Zofia. Mil. 1st Lt. PA, 1933-39. POW: Murnau/Bayern, Ger., 1939-45. Ind. Mach. Design., Warsaw. 1963-65; U. Stuttgart, Ger., 1965-68; Engr. Coll. Inst.: S.F.:, 1969-date. Mem. A.S.M.E.

BENNETT, (BIENIASZ) EDWARD. Los Angeles. Retired. b. Rzeszow, Poland, Oct. 13, 1896. M. Phar., Jagiellonian U. Studied: UCLA. m. 1) Stefania Eckhard (div.-dec.) 2) Rose Sturm. c. Tadeusz, Jozef. Mil. Austrian Army, 1916-18; PA, 1939-40. POW: Ger. prison, Epinal, Fr., 1940-41. Jap. CC: Santo Tomas, Los Banos, Philippines, 1942-45. Came to U.S. 1945. Pharmacist, Pol., prior to WWII. Prescription phar., Thrifty Drug Stores, Cal. to retirement.

BERWIN, TED W. Playa del Rey. Electronics Engineer. b. Hamtramck, Mich., Feb. 14, 1928. M.S., Elec. Engr., UCLA. Post. grad. work in progress. m. Caroline Kay. c. Natalie Dawn, Gary Todd, Caryn Suzanne, Christine Ann, Angela Marie. Elec. Engr., Hughes Aircraft Co. Mem. P.A.H.A., Soc. EX. Listed in *Who's Who in the West.*

BIELSKI, MARK. Sunland. Architect. b. Poland. Grad. Arch., S. West Essex Tech. Coll. & Sch. of Art, London. m. Katarzyna. c. Malgorzata, Jan. Mil. PHA, 1943-45; PA, It., 1945-46. Practicing arch.; Eng., 2 yrs., U.S.A. since 1955. Own practice since 1969. Mem. A.I.A.; Natl. Council of Arch. Reg. Boards; West Hills Hunt.

BIENIASZ, JOZEF WLODZIMIERZ. Simi Valley. Civil Engineering. Draftsman. b. Lwow, Poland, Nov. 2, 1922. Grad. PHS, Lubeck, Ger., 1946. Studied Chem. Engr. PUC, London, 1948-52. m. Urszula Grzeskowiak (dec.). c. Anna Grazyna (dec.), Michael Leszek. Mil. PA, 1939; PHA, 1942-45. Lab. Tech., Riker Labs., Northridge, 1954-70; Civil Engr. Draftsman, City of L.A., 1971-date.

BIENIASZ, URSZULA (nee Grzeskowiak). Deceased. b. Poznan, Poland, Apr. 1, 1922. Grad. PHS, Lubeck, Ger., 1946. B.S. Chem., PUC, London. Grad. study, Battersea Poly., London, USC. m. Joseph Wlodzimierz. c. Anna Grazyna (dec.), Michael Leszek. FLC: Lubeck, Ger., 1940-45. Quality Control Chem.: Linoleum Mfg. Co., Staines, Eng., 1953-55; Pabst Brewing Co., L.A., 1955-56; Sr. Research Chem., Purex Corp. Ltd., South Gate, 1956-61. Mem. Amer. Chem. Soc. Two papers on chem. research publ. in *Jour. of Org. Chem.,* 1959 and 1960.

BOBROWSKI, REV. MSGR. KAZIMIERZ JASTRZEBIEC. Huntington Beach. Canon. b. Poznan, Poland, Feb. 22, 1905. Ordained June 16, 1929, Poznan. Pastoral duties: Holy Trinity Parish, Bydgoszcz, Pol. Prof., Heliodor Swiecicki Coll., Miedzychod, Pol. Chap. PA, Rumania. Organized Pol. Sch. for Refugee Children, Bucharest. Chap. Pol. War Refugees, Tel Aviv. Sr. Chap. Far East. Rector, Pol. Cath. Mission, India. Dir., War Relief Svcs., Natl. Cath. Welfare Conference, India. Exec. Dir., Natl. Comm., U.S., Intl. Cath. Child Bureau.

BOGUCKA, JADWIGA KULPINSKA. Philadelphia, Pa. Teacher, Ret. b. Phila. Pa., Oct. 13, 1915. B.S., M.S., Drexel U., 1938, 1946. Special study, Jagiellonian U., 1977. m. Alfred Stanislaw, M.D. c. Piotr. USAF wife, taught school throughout U.S.: Phila. Pa.; Bound Brook H.S., Bound Brook, N.J.; Georgian Court Coll., Lakewood, N.J.; Webster Sch., Fresno, CA., 1943-44; Stege Sch., Richmond, CA., 1947-48. Mem. P.A.H.A.; Pilsudski Institute; K.F.; Polski U. Ludowy, Phila. Pa.; P.K.M. (Polskie Kolko Miedzykolegjalne).

BOROWSKI, TADEUSZ IRENEUSZ. Canoga Park. Design Engineer. b. Warsaw, Poland, Mr. 19, 1916. B.S., Mech. Engr., Warsaw Tech. Coll. m. Helena Szudy. c. Izabela, Tadeusz, Ireneusz. Mil. 2nd Lt., PHA, 1939-44. POW: Altengrabow Hosp., 1944-45. Sr. Design Engr. for space and aircraft ind. Mem. Pol. Amer. Engr. Assn., Chi.; AF Assn.; BSA-Eagle Sounts Assn., U.S.A.; Asst. Chief. Exec., Pol. Scouting Org.

BRODKA, MARK ANDREW. Los Angeles. Student. b. Montebello, Ca., Dec. 8, 1956. Loyola Marymount University; junior, English major, Business minor. Director, Associated Students, LMU. Mem. PAHA, LMU Student Chapter; Krakusy. Travel: Poland, Summer 1973.

BRZESKI, ANDRZEJ. Davis. Professor, Economics. Studied: Catholic U., Lublin, 1946; U. of Lodz, 1947-49; Central Sch. of Planning, Warsaw, 1950-51; UCBerkeley, 1958-61. Mil. PHA, 1944. CC: Borovici, USSR, 1944-46. Prof., Econ., UCDavis, 1963-date. Mem. Amer. Econ. Assn.; Royal Econ. Soc., U.K.; Assn. for Comprehensive Econ.; P.I.A.S.; Mont Pelerin Soc.; J. Pilsudski Institute, N.Y.

BUTLER, TADEUSZ KAZIMIERZ (Deceased). Engineer. b. Warsaw, Poland, My. 10, 1923. Studied: Engr. U., Vienna; PUC, London. m. Halina Teresa Sliwinski. c. Margaret Teresa, Wojciech Edward, Maria Alina, Teresa Barbara. Designer: Companie General de Construcciones, Argentina, 1948-60; Bechtel Corp., S.F., 1960-76. Founder: Pol. Explorer Scouts Org., Argentina; Founder and Pres., Pol. Language Sch., S.F.; Founder: Pol. Scouting Gr., Bay Area; Hon. Mem. Pol. Cath. U. Assn. Veritas; Pol. Second Lancers Regt. Hon. Cross of Valor (for return of regt. banner), Cross of Merit (posthumously) for social work.

CIERPIK, ANNE FELICYA. Los Angeles. Teacher. Ret. b. Chicago, Ill., Apr. 23, 1900. Administrator of Szymanowski Foundation, dedicated to the propagation of the music of Karol Szymanowski (1883-1937) in the United States.

DEGNER, REV. MSGR. LEON A. Walnut Creek. Clergyman. b. Poland. Studied: Priests' Seminary, Pelplin, Chelmno, Poland. CC: Stutthof, Mauthausen, Dachau, Danzig. Pastor, St. Anne's Church, Walnut Creek. Honorary Prelate.

DERESIEWICZ, BOGDAN ANTONI. Santa Barbara. Librarian Emeritus. University of California, Santa Barbara. b. Wrzesnia, Poland, Ju. 9, 1908. M.A., Phil., U. Poznan; M.L.S., Rutgers U. m. Catherine Margaret. Mil. Lt., Inf., PA, 1939. POW: Ger., 1939-45. Prof., secondary schools, Pol., 1930-39. Teacher, DPC, Ger., 1945-50. Univ. libr., several univ., U.S., 1951-75. Libr. Emeritus, UCSB, 1975. Act. Archivist, S.B. Mission Archives, since May 31, 1977. Mem. A.A.U.P.; P.I.A.S.; K.F.; P.A.A.A. Ed., translator of several scholarly works in Latin, Ger., Pol. Contr. to scholarly journals, inc. *Soundings*. His latest work is translation of Hartmann Schedel's *Sarmatia*. *The Early Polish Kingdom*, Plantin Press, Los Angeles, 1976. *Maciej z Miechowa: The Description of Asian and European Sarmatias and What They Contain.* (In Press). Recipient, K.F. Scholarship for research in Pol., 1974-75. Hon. Cross of Valor (four times).

DERESIEWICZ, CATHERINE. Santa Barbara. b. Lebanon, Ill. Jan. 5, 1925. Study: Le Clerc Coll. Belleville, Ill.; Sawyer Bus. Sch.; Santa Ana Coll.; S.B. City Coll. m. Bogdan Antoni. Dental Asst. N.Y.C., Santa Ana, S.F., 15 yrs. Teacher, primary grades. Manuscript typist and photographer for author-husband. Pres. St. Claire Circle of S.B. Mission; Publ. Chm., P.A.A.A.; Soc. Chm., Pol. Parish Council.

DOMANSKI, LUDWIG BOLESLAW. S. Pasadena. Civil Engineer. b. Sielice, Poland, Oct. 22, 1918. Dipl., Civ. Engr., State Tech. Sch., Warsaw; Dipl., Engr. Design, Central Sch. of Arts, London. Study: UCLA, CSULB. Reg. Prof. Civil Engr., State of Cal. m. Inez Grayce. c. Michelle, Patricia, Richard. Mil. PA, 1939; Cadet Off., Eng., 1943; Spec. duty sq. Flt. Off., Italy, 1944; Flt. Lt. Trans. Comm., Eng., 1945. CC: Vorkuta, USSR. POW:

Sagan, Ger., 1944-45. Proj. Engr.: Quinton, Eng., 1958-65; Mgr. Land Dev.: Haver & Assoc., Pasadena, 1965-73; Proj. Engr.: Wheeler & Gray, L.A., 1973-date. Mem. Cal. Soc. of Prof. Engrs.; Soc. of Amer. Mil. Engrs.; Soaring Soc. of Amer.; P.A.F.V.A.; Y.M.C.A. Hon. Cross of Valor, 3 times, Virtuti Militari, Dist. Gold Cross.

DOMBROWSKI, EDMUND THEODORE JR., Redlands. Orthopedic Surgeon. B.A., Pre-Med., M.D., UCLA, 1952, 1956. Residency: Mayo Clinic, 1957-61. m. Eleanor. c. Mark, Linda, Kathy, Edmund T. III, Debbie. Mil. Lt. Cmmdr. USN, 2 yrs. active duty; 8 yrs. reserve duty; Great Lakes Naval Hosp. Mem. Amer. Acad. of Orthopedic Surgeons; Intl. Soc. for Study of Lumbar Spine; Flying Physician, L.I.G.A.; Diplomate, Amer. Board of Orthopedic Surgery. Approx. ten papers presented to Medical Societies nationwide. Several specialized papers on orthopedic surgery problems published in *Journal of Bone and Joint Surgery.* Instrument pilot w/multi engine, comm., & sea plane rating.

DOMBROWSKI, STEPHEN RAYMOND. Los Angeles. Businessman. A.A., El Camino Coll., Torrance, Cal.; USC. m. Nancy Eleanor c. Christopher, Timothy, Stephen II, Todd. Mil. Staff Sgt. USA, Korean Conflict. Self-employed: orchid, plant grower, florist. 20 yrs. Mem. Orchid Soc. of S. Cal.; So. Cal. Floral Assn.; L.A. Airport Rotary Club; P.P., Intl. Rotary Club; Head, Lennox Youth Assn.; Advisor, B.S.A., Troop 263.

DUCHNOWSKI, KAZIMIERZ (Deceased). b. Rajgrod, Poland, Jy. 17, 1891. Studied: Military Sch. of Cav., Tver, Russia. m. 1) Olga (div.) 2) Louise. Off., Russian Army 1913-18; Lt. Col., PA, 1918-39. POW, Murnau, Bavaria, 1939-45. Came to U.S. in 1949, Cal., 1951. Lived in Lancaster, Edwards, Boron, Goleta. Hon.: Virtuti Militari, Cross of Courage (4 times) Gold Cross of Merit. Died May 19, 1973.

DUDZINSKI, TADEUSZ JOZEF. Los Angeles. Structural Engineer. b. Bydgoszcz, Poland, My. 18, 1927. Dipl., Brixton Sch. of Bldg., London. Grad. Study: UCLA. m. Christiane Anna Ida Nerucci. c. Witold, Bogdan, Magali. Mil. PHA, 1940-45; PA, Italy, Eng., 1945-46; Cpl. Pol. Resettlement Corps, 1946-48. Cons., Struct. Engr., Eng., 1953-59; Struct. Engr., Construction firm, Marseilles, Fr., 1953-61; Struct. Engr. Cons., L.A., 1965-date. Mem. Inst. of Pol. Engr. in G.B.; Ca. Soc. of Prof. Engr.; P.C.-P.F.A.C.; P.A.C.; P.C.U.; P.A.H.A. Sustaining mem. B.S.A.; Natl. Audubon Soc.; The Wilderness Society. Reg. Prof. Civil Engr., States of Cal., W. Virg.

EICHLER, CHRISTINA SOPHIE. Los Angeles. Architect. b. Czestochowa, Poland, My. 5, 1921. M.A., Arch. Academie Lebanaise des Beaux Arts — Ecole d'Architecture, Beirut, Lebanon, 1948. m. (div.) c. Joanna Jukowicz. FLC: USSR, 1941. Professional architect since 1948. Mem. O.L.B.M.R.C.C.; P.A.H.A.

ENGEL, TADEUSZ KAZIMIERZ. Long Beach. Mechanical Design Engineer. b. Stryj, Poland, Jan. 14, 1937. Rensselaer Poly. Tech., Troy, N.Y. Mil. USAF, 1957-64. (Pilot-Navigator rank). Mech. Design Engr., Bechtel Corp., Norwalk, Cal.

ENGEL-TYER, VIKTORIA. Long Beach. Teacher. b. Ingelstadt, Germany, Apr. 23, 1947. Grad., CSULB, 1971 w/teaching credential in spec. Early Childhood Educ., pilot proj., providing individualized educational program to meet the needs of every child from kindergarten through third grade. Teaches, Garden Grove Unified Sch. System.

ENGEL, WILHELM. Long Beach. Retired. b. Chrzanow, Poland, Oct. 1903. m. Boleslawa Slominska. c. Irena, Witold, Tadeusz, Wiktoria, Ryszard. Mil. PA, 1919. Mgr. Dairy Co-Op, Stryj, Pol. FLC: Ingelstadt, Bremenhaven. Came to U.S. 1950, moved to Cal., 1962.

FESTEN, ANNE JADWIGA. Los Angeles. Librarian. b. Warsaw, Poland. M.A., Humanities, U. Warsaw; M.L.S., USC. m. Edward. c. Alice. Head Libr., Art Center College of Design, L.A., 1960-date. Mem. P.A.H.A.; Alliance Francaise.

FIELD, STATIA (nee Luckiewicz). Santa Barbara. b. Shenandoah, Penn. R.N., U. Penn., 1929. m. Frank (dec.) c. Frank L.V. Jr. (Ph.D., Harvard U.; Counselor, Bowdoin Coll., Brunswick, Maine). Mem. P.A.A.A. Moved to Santa Barbara, 1976. Hon. First prize award for oil painting, 1953. Paints in oil, watercolor; specializes in dried flower arrangements. Collector, art, artifacts, curios.

FINIE, PHILIP ADAM. Pacific Palisades. Captain, Los Angeles Co. Forestry Dep. Ret. Property Mgmt. & Develop. b. Los Angeles, May 26, 1921, to George A. Finiewicz (from Wilno, Pol.) and Apolonia Rydzicka (from Radzimin, Pol.; they came to U.S., 1909). Studied: Manual Arts H.S., L.A. City College, Cal State and UCLA. m. Anita Mary Sadoch-Kempinska (b. Warsaw; grad. Red Cross School of Nursing; post-grad., Sorbonne, Paris; L.A. City College; Cal State and UCLA.). Two sons: Peter Henry (Loyola U. graduate; post-grad. UCLA, Bus. Adm.; Paul Anthony (Menlo College grad.; attended Loyola U.; Bus. major). Mil. US Army, WWII, South Pacific. Travel, Europe, incl. Poland.

FLORYAN, THADDEUS PHILIP. Los Altos. Colonel, USA, Ret. Consultant. b. Stamford, Conn., May 30, 1916. m. Aline Antoinette Byczkowski. c. Thaddeus P. Jr. B.S., U.S. Military Academy, West Point, 1940; Grad. study: Command and Gen. Staff Coll.; Strategic Intelligence Sch.; Biarritz Army U.; Harvard Bus. Sch.; RAF Control Comm. Sch.; Jagiellonian U.; Warsaw U.; U. of Mexico. Col. USA, 1934-66. Intl. Command of 22,000 U.S., Pol., Brit. forces which combatted Ger. V-1 attacks; Comm.: Redstone Ballistic Missle Gr. Numerous command, high level staff and special assignments. Exec. Lockheed Corp., 1966-70. Consultant-Generalist, 1970-date. Mem. Natl. Defense Preparedness Assn.; World Affairs Council; Assn. of Grad., USMA; PGA Hole-in-one Golf Club; Amer. Inst. of Aero. & Astro. K.F. scholarship, 1938. Hon. Legion of Merit, Bronze Star Medal, Bel. Unit, Croix de Guerre; Korean and European awards. Proposed for next *Who's Who in the West.*

FORTUNKO, CHRISTOPHER MARIAN. Thousand Oaks. Scientist. b. Poland, Dec. 7, 1948. Came to U.S., 1963. B.S., Tufts U., 1970; Ph.D., Stanford U., 1975. Scientist, Science Center, Rockwell Intl., 1975-date. Mem. I.E.E.E., A.S.N.T. Phi Beta Kappa, Ex.

FUZ, GEORGE CONSTANTINE (Deceased). Economist. b. Plock, Poland, Jan. 5, 1925. M.S., Econ., Ph.D., Econ., Netherlands U. of Econ., Rotterdam, 1951, 1952. M.L.S., UCLA. m. Greta Margot. c. Gregory Leon. Mil. PAF, 1944; Br. Allied Control Comm., Intelligence Div., 1945-47. POW: Lubeck, Ger. 1944-45. Bus. Management; Teacher; Librarian; Research Analyst. Corporate Econ., Blue Cross of Cal., 1964-74. Pres. P.A.C. — Cal.-Ariz. Div.; Life Fellow: Royal Econ. Soc.; Mem. Can. Pol. Sci. Assn.; Amer. Libr. Assn.; Amer. Econ. Assn.; Teachers Ins. Assn. of Amer.; UCLA Alumni Assn.; Rotterdam Alumni Assn. Contr. ed.: *Medical Care Review,* U. of Mich. Author: *Morderstwo Sadowe Popelnione w 1939 r. na Obroncach Poczty Polskiej w Wolnym Miescie Gdansku.* (Legal

Murder of the Defenders of the Polish Post Office in the Free City of Gdansk — 1939). Warsaw, 1972. Honorary Degree, Hague Academy of Intl. Law, Peace Palace, the Hague, Holland, for interest and dedication to International Law and Justice.

GALE, CONSTANCE. Artist/Philanthropist. Santa Barbara. b. Inowroclaw, Poland. m. Robert (deceased), industrialist, Cleveland, Ohio. Studied: Maybelle Manning School, Boston. Expert, decorative arts, decoupage. Member, Women's Board, Community Arts Association; PAAA. Helps, St. Vincent's Day Nursery, Assistance League Christmas House Tour.

GARSTKA, STANLEY MARIAN. Riverside. Surgeon. b. Warsaw, Poland, Feb. 22, 1916. Studied: U. Warsaw Med. Sch.; M.D., U. Erlangen Med. Sch., Vienna. m. Martha Alshibaya. Svc.: PHA, 1939-41. CC: Auschwitz, Dachau, Neuengamme, Flossenburg, 1941-45. Sr. Med. Officer, San Bernardino Co.; Private practice in surgery. Mem. P.A.C.; K.F.; P.A.H.A.; Am. Soc. of Abdominal Surgeons. Hon. U.S. Dept. of State Award in recognition of humanitarian surgical services to people of Viet Nam.

GARSTKA, MARTHA. Riverside. M.D., Internal Medicine. b. Kutaisi, Georgia, Transcaucasia (now USSR), Aug. 8, 1915. Study: U. of Berlin, U. of Munich. M.D., U. of Erlangen Med. Sch., Vienna. m. Stanley. Med. Spec., Internal Med.: March AF Base. Also, private practice in Internal Med. Mem. Amer. Board of Internal Med.; P.A.C.; Diplomate of Amer. Board of Internal Med.

GAWLINSKI, WLADYSLAW (Deceased). Sculptor. b. Poland, Nov. 25, 1881. m. Maria. c. Halina. Resided in Los Angeles.

GOLAS, THADDEUS. Malibu. Writer/Editor. b. Patterson, N.J., Ju. 15, 1924. B.A., 1948, Columbia U. Mil. USA, 1942-45. Editor: *Redbook* Magazine, Ballantine Books, Fawcett Publications, Harper & Row. Author: *The Lazy Man's Guide to Enlightenment*, Bantam Books, M. Nancy Monroe Div. (175,000 copies).

GORSKA, HANKA B. Mission Viejo. Architect/Urban Planner. b. Poltawa, Poland. Studied: Liverpool U. — Sch. of Arch., 1944-47; Degree, Eng. Arch., PUC, London, 1949; Post grad. studies: U. Penn., 1968-69; Special conservator study, Warsaw Poly., 1975-76. m. A. Jerzy Gorski. Came to U.S., 1952. 25 yrs. combined experience in architecture, urban & regional planning, historic conservation planning, G.B., U.S.A. Mem. A.I.A.-S. Cal. Chpt.; Amer. Soc. of Planning Officials, Chicago; Natl. Trust for Historic Preservation, D.C.; Soc. of Arch. Hist., Philadelphia; P.A.H.A.; Hon. Pres. (1956-date), P.F.A.C. Author, books on historical preservation in U.S.A. Amer. Assn. of States Award for major accomplishment in field of historic preservation planning, 1971. Smithsonian Inst. Award for study of conservation, restoration of Pol. historic monuments, sites, 1975-76. Currently preparing results of research for publication in both Polish and English.

GORSKI, PIOTR JAN. Los Angeles. Engineer. b. Warsaw, Poland. Studied: Main Sch. of Commerce, Consular Dept., Warsaw; UCLA, Dept., Civ. Engr. Mil. PA, Fr., Bel., U.K., 1939-45. Capt. Br. Army, 1946-48. Served as Consular Agent, Rep. of Pol. Industries for Gold Coast, Nigeria, 1938-39; Lecturer, Staff, Southhampton U., Eng., 1948-52; Asst. Buyer, May Co. L.A., 1952-53; L.A. Co., Dept. of Engr., 1956-75. Mem. P.A.H.A.; K.F.; Cal. Assn. of Prof. Engrs. Hon.: Decorated by Polish, French, English governments.

GOZDZIKOWSKI, MIECZYSLAW. Burbank. Designer/Engineer. b. Poland, My. 10, 1913. Studied: Engr. Mil. Coll., Warsaw. m. Zofia. c. Hanna Siedlecka. Mil. 1st Lt., PA, 1939. POW: Oflag IVA, Arnswalde IID, Grossborn, Lubeka XC, 1939-45. Design Engr., Eng., U.S. Mem. Amer. Soc. of Engr. & Arch.; P.A.H.A.; P.C. — P.F.A.C.; Engrs. & Arch. Inst. Hon. Polish Army Medal.

GRAMS, HELENA HEDWIG. Los Angeles. Legal Secretary. b. Cambridge, Mass., Ju. 5, 1922. Studied: Boston U. m. Employed as legal secretary. Mem. P.A.H.A. (past secty.); Polish Choir, O.L.B.M.R.C.C.

GREY, BENJAMIN. Los Angeles. Attorney-at-Law. b. Plock, Poland, Jy. 7, 1902. L.L.M., U. Warsaw. m. Linda. Mil. Pol. Legion, 1920. Dist. Atty., Lomza, Pol., 1929-32. Private practice, 1932-39. Since 1957, cons. Ger., Pol., compensation matters, L.A. Founder, promoter, charitable, educ. associations.

GRZESIK, JAN ALEXANDER. North Hollywood. Physicist. b. Rybnik, Poland, Aug. 7, 1939. B.A., Phy., UCLA, 1960; M.A., Phy., Harvard, 1961; Ph.D., Nuclear Engr., UCLA, 1977. m. Renata Ewa Wisniewska. c. Renata Lucyna, John Michael. Mem. Tech. Staff, T.R.W., Redondo Beach, 1968-73; 1977-date. Cons.: Phy. Sciences Dept., Rand Corp., S.M., 1973-date; Asst. Research Engr.: Sch. of Engr. & Applied Science, UCLA, 1976-77. Mem. Amer. Phy. Soc.; Phi Beta Kappa. Woodrow Wilson Fellow, 1960-61.

HAIFTER, MITCHEL P.E. San Bernardino. Lt. Col., USAF, Ret. b. Poland, Nov. 12, 1903. Dipl., Cooper Union; M.E., Poly. Inst., N.Y.; Aero. E. Deg., N.Y.U., Sch. of Engr. & Sci.; M.A. Ed., N.Y.U. m. Inez See Myers. c. Mitchel Jr., ALice Marilyn Marks. Mil. Lt. Col., USAF, WWII, Korean Conflict. Prof. Engr., Ret. Teacher, Ret. Lic. Prof. Engr., N.J.; Mem. Prof. Engrs.; Ret. Off. Assn.; Ret. Teachers Assn.; V.F.W.; Masons; Shriners; P.A.H.A.; Pol. Heritage Soc.; Amer. Numismatic Assn.; Cooper Union; PINY; N.Y.U. Engr. & Educ. Res. Off. Assn.; Natl. Assn. for Uniformed Svc. Hon.: Service, Commendation Medals for WWII, Korean Conflict.

HALSTEAD, MARIA TERESA (nee Gadzinowska). Santa Barbara. b. Golina, Poland. m. Clark Paul. Mil. PA, Women's Auxiliary Corps, G.B., Ger., 1943-45. Mem. P.A.A.A. (Pres., 1977). Natl. Soc. of Arts & Letters. Hon. Mem. 308 Pol. Fighter Squad., G.B. Collector, connoisseur, Polish Art, books.

HARTE, ROMAN I. Encino. Film Director/Production Chief. b. Poland, Ju. 22, 1926. Studied: Poly. Sch., Warsaw, 1948-50; Film Acad., Lodz, Pol., 1950-56. Grad. Film Prod. Mgr. & Master of Film Art. m. Daniella. c. Slawomir Joseph Heywood, Monika Hanna. Mil. PHA, 1941-43. FLC: Ger. Production, unit mgr., asst. dir., for state owned Pol. film enterprises. Since 1972, Chief of Prod., Amer. Film Inst. Award winning films inc.: *Generation, Canal, Ashes and Diamonds, Shop on Main Street, Eroica, Sunday Morning, Mother Joan of the Angels, Night Train.* Prod. several experimental films, two winning awards in Brussels, Venice: *Dom,* 1958; *Once Upon a Time,* 1957. Mem. Club A.K., L.A.; Acad. of Motion Picture Arts, Sciences; Soc. of Motion Picture and TV Engrs.

HICKS, EDWARD WILLIS. Santa Barbara. Investm/Banker. Ret. Artist/Painter. b. San Francisco, Cal., Aug. 5, 1897. Studied: Botany, UCBerkeley. m. Alice Schenck. c. Lucy Schenck Van Hylckama, Edward Schenck. Mil. USA, WWI. Supervised defense plant employing 2,000 men during World War II. Moved from Connecticut to Santa Barbara in 1962. Two years later became a professional painter.

HODGSON, MARIE T. Torrance. Student. b. Cal., Feb. 13, 1957. Current study, Loyola Marymount U. Charter Vice-Pres., Student Chpt., P.A.H.A.

JAKIMKO, ADALINE ANN (JACKIE). Bell. Personnel Staffing Specialist: U.S. Civil Svc. Comm. b. N. Amherst, Mass. Hon: City of Bell Award.

JANISZEWSKI, EMIL. Irvine. Engineer. b. Chodorow, Poland, 1928. B.S., Engr. Regent Poly., London. m. Krystyna Renata. c. Andrew, Ewa. Mil. Pol. Cadet Corp., Middle East, Eng. FLC: USSR, 1940-42. Reg. Civil Engr., California. Sup. Struct. Engr., Fluor Engrs., Irvine, 1960-date. Mem. Soc. of Prof. Engrs.; Natl. Soc. of Prof. Engrs.

JAROSZ, ZYGMUNT A. Los Angeles. Architect. b. Poland, 1923. M.A., Arch., U. Wroclaw, Pol. m. Helen. c. Anna B. Mil. PAF. FLC: 1943-44.Reg. Arch., UCLA. Mem. A.I.A.; S. Cal. A.I.A.; UCLA Alumni Assn.

JASIONOWSKI, WALERIAN (Deceased). Alhambra. Engineer. b. Telika, Bessarabia, Feb. 10, 1905. Studied: Poly. U., Warsaw, 1924-26. Grad. Air Force Mil. Coll., Pol., 1928. Mil. Squad. Commdr., PAF, Pol. 1939; Fr., 1940. Wing Commdr., Eng., 1940-44. Merged w/9th Fighter Gr. USAF under Gen. Schramm, 1944. Pol. Staff Coll. Commdr., Weston. Came to U.S. 1953. Engr., L.A. Dept. of Water & Power (Ret. 1970). Hon. Virtuti Militari, Cross of Valor (twice). Died, Ju. 17, 1977.

JUKOWICZ, ESTANISLAO. Los Angeles. Architectural Designer. b. Poland, Aug. 22, 1915. Dipl. Arch., Lebanese U., Beirut. c. Joanne. Mil. PA, USSR, Middle East, 1942-43. FLC: Siberia, USSR, 1940-42. Arch. Asst. Designer: W.E.D. Enterprises, (Walt Disney Productions) 1965-date. Mem. Lorquin Entomological Soc. L.A.

KALINSKI, GEORGE. Marina del Rey. Attorney-at-Law. b. Hamtramck, Mich., Sept. 18, 1935. B.A., magna cum laude Wayne State U.; L.L.M., Harvard U.; J.D., magna cum laude Wayne State U. Mil. Maj. USA, Judge Advocate Gen. Corp. Admitted to practice before the U.S. Supreme Court; U.S. Court of Appeals; (9th Dist. & D.C.); Cal. Supreme Court; Mich. Supreme Court; U.S. Dist. Court: L.A.; Detroit; D.C.; U.S. Tax Court; U.S. Court of Mil. Appeals. Prof., Law: L.A. City Coll.; USA, JAG Sch. Branch Course (U. Virg.). Procurator Advocate, R.C. Archdiocese of L.A., Marital Tribunal. Mem. State Bar, Cal.; State Bar, Mich.; Judge Advocates Alumni Assn.; Judge Advocates Assn. Oliver Br. (Bd. of Dir.); Harvard Club; U. Club, L.A.; P.A.C.; P.U.C.; Pol. Bus. & Prof. Club; L.A. Bar Assn.; Reserve Off. Assn.; Newman Club; S. Cal. Phi Beta Kappa; Wayne State U. Honors Award, Junior, Senior, Gold Keys.

KAMINSKI, EDWARD M. (LARRY) La Mirada. b. Chicago, Ill., Nov. 21, 1913. Pre-med., DePaul U., 1931-35; U. Warsaw, 1937-38. m. Eugenia M. Piechowski. c. Marybeth. Mil. Aviation Cadet: USAF, 1940-41. Mem. Mu Beta Chi (Hon. Sci. Soc.); Alpha Chi; P.A.C.; P.A.H.A.; P.R.C.U. Charter mem., P.P.: Circuit 54, Sports & Soc. Club, P.R.C.U.

KAMINSKI, GEORGE Z. Buena Park. Artist/Businessman. b. Poland, August 8, 1908. Studied: Warsaw U.; Central Sch. of Arts & Crafts, London; St. Martin Sch. of Arts, London. m. Barbara Anderson. Mil. PAF, RAF, 1939-47. FLC: USSR, 1940-41. Owner, Screen Graphics, Anaheim, spec. graphic arts, photoetching, printing. Mem. L.A. Art Assn.; U. Club; P.F.A.C.

KARCZ, JERZY FELIKS (Deceased). Santa Barbara. Professor, Economics. b. Poland, Nov. 8, 1921. B.A., Alliance Coll. Cambridge Sprs., Penn., 1950; M.A., Kent State U., 1952; Ph.D., Columbia U., 1958. m. Irene Matuszak. c. Jan S., Maria W., Jerzy F. Jr., Bartholomew, Joseph A. Mil. Lt. PA, Pol., Fr., 1939-48. POW: Ger., 1940-45. Research: Mid European Studies Center, N.Y., 1953-54; Cons. Rand Corp., S.M., 1954-55; Inst., Soc. Sci., N.Y.C., 1957-59; Asst. Prof., Econ., 1959-64; Assoc. Prof., 1964-68; Prof., Econ., 1968-70: UCSB. Mem. Amer. Econ. Assn.; West. Econ. Assn.; Amer. Assn. for Advancement of Slavic Studies; P.I.A.S.; Assn. for Study Soviet Type Econ.; Comparative Econ. Assn. Hon. Croix de Guerre w/Silver Star, Cross of Valor, Army Medal, War Medal. Listed: *Who's Who in the West*, 1969-70; *International Bibliography*, Fr.; *Royal Blue Book*, Eng.; *American Men of Science* (The Social and Behavioral Sciences). Gen. Ed. *Eastern European Economics*; Ed. *Soviet and European Agriculture*. Dir. Intl. Conference on Soviet Agriculture, 1962. Died Dec. 10, 1970.

KARP, REV. JOSEPH ANTHONY. Anaheim. Clergyman. Diocese of Orange. b. New York City, N.Y., Aug. 1, 1939. Ordained Priest, 1967. B.A., St. Mary's Coll., Orchard Lake, Mich. Span., Loyola Marymount U., L.A.

KARPINSKI, STANISLAW. Los Angeles. Brigadier General. Ret. b. Piotrkow, Poland, Dec. 17, 1891. Dipl., Air Staff Coll., Warsaw, Pol.; L.A. City Coll. m. Stephanie C. Barbara Wojtulanis. Mil. Lt., Russian AF, 1914-18; Capt./Lt. Col., PAF, 1918-39; Dep. Chief, Air Staff, Pol.; Chief, Air Staff, PAF, Fr.; Dep. Comm. in Chief, Bomber Comm., PAF, Eng.; Dep. Comm. in Chief, PAF, Eng.; Dep. Insp. Gen., Resettlement Corps, Eng.; Insp. Gen., Resettlement Corps, Eng., 1939-47. Rank from Lt. Col. to Brig. Gen. Mem. P.A.F.V.A.; P.A.H.A.; Sikorski Inst., London; Pilsudski Inst.; O.L.B.M.R.C.C.; St. Kevin Church, L.A. Hon. Virtuti Militari, Polonia Restituta, Cross of Valor; Golden Cross of Merit; Many Polish, French, English, war and peace medals and decorations. Man of Letters; Author of several books.

KARPINSKI, STEPHANIE C. BARBARA. Los Angeles. Computer Programmer, Ret. b. Warsaw, Poland, Nov. 22, 1912. Studied: Mech. Engr., Warsaw Poly. U.; L.A. City Coll.; Bus. Comp. Prog., L.A. Metropolitan Coll. Mil. Liaison Pilot, PAF, 1939; 2nd Lt., PAF, Fr., 1940; 1st Off., Ferry Pilot, Air Trans. Aux., G.B., 1941-45; Lt. PAF, G.B., 1946. m. Stanislaw N. Elec. Comp. Prog. Librascope Corp., Burbank, 1961; Royal McBee Corp., L.A., 1962; Sr. Clerk, Data Processing: Atlantic Richfield Oil Corp., 1963-74. Mem. P.A.V.A.; P.A.H.A.; Women's Overseas Service League. Hon. Silver Medal of Merit, w/glaives, (twice), Polish Air Force Medal, English War Medal, English Defence Medal.

KASPAREK-OBST, CHRISTOPHER. Monterey. Writer/Translator. b. Edinburgh, Scotland, My. 9, 1945. A.A., Monterey Peninsula Coll.; B.A., UCBerkeley; M.L.S., S.F. State U. m. Malgorzata Tucholska. Polish-English translator of literary and scientific works. Writer. Mem. Alpha Gamma Sigma; Phi Beta Kappa; P.I.A.S.

KASPAREK-OBST, JOSEPH. Monterey. Professor/Writer. b. Branau, Austria, Apr. 20, 1915. Studied: Jan Kazimierz U., Lwow; U. Edinburgh; PUC, London; UCSC. Degrees: L.L.M.; Ph.D., Pol. Science. m. Sylvia Sokolowska-Pozniak. c. Christopher, Hania. Mil. PA, PAF, Pol., USSR, Middle East, U.K., 1939-45. FLC: 1940-41. Assoc. Prof., academic schools in Cal. since 1955. Writer. Mem. P.I.A.S., A.A.U.P., P.A.V.A. Hon. Cross of Valor.

KASPER, JEROME A. Granada Hills. Musician. b. Philadelphia, Penn., Ju. 1913. m. Violet E. Kuhn. c. Jerome V., Dennis R., Sandra Nancy. Musician for past 49 yrs. Played woodwinds with Kay Kyser, Horace Heidt, Tommy Dorsey, Benny Goodman, Clyde Lucas orchestras. Worked, recorded w/Frank de Vol, TV shows. Mem. Locals 802, 47, Amer. Fed. of Mus., Hollywood & New York, P.A.H.A. Past mem. Oxnard Rotary, Elks.

KIBBIE, MARIE PATRICIA. Executive Secretary. Encino. b. Poland. Grad., Cum laude, Holy Family Acad. H.S. m. Daniel C. c. Matthew Michael. FLC: Siberia, USSR, 1940-42. Exec. Secty., American Broadcasting Company.

KILIS, STELLA DIETZ. Norwalk. Realtor. b. Chicago, Ill. Studied: Cerritos Coll., Norwalk; Cal. Sch. of Ins., Pasa. m. Chester Francis. c. Juanita M. Booth, Leonard C. Self-employed as realtor, insurance agent since 1950. Mem. Norwalk-La Mirada Bd. of Realtors; Cal. Assn. of Realtors; Natl. Assn. of Realtors; P.N.A.-Paderewski Lodge 3139; P.A.H.A.; Women of Moose-Norwalk Chpt. 1126; K.F.; Norwalk Women's Club.

KLEJNOT, OLGIERD JAN. Los Angeles. Chemist. b. Tczew, Poland, Mar. 25, 1925. Dipl., Ph.D., Post-doc. study, Ludwig Maximilian U., Inorganic Chem. Inst., Munich, 1952-58. m. Eva Irmina Janczak. c. John Timothy. CC: Ger., 1939-40. Research Spec.: J.P.L., Pasa., 1958-64; Unified Sci. Assoc., Pasa., 1964-65; Cal. Inst. of Tech. (Caltech), Phy. Dept., 1966; Meteorology Research, Inc., Altadena, 1966-70; Air Pollution Cons., 1971-72; Sr. Chem. Truesdail Labs, L.A., 1973-date. Mem. Ger. Alpine Club; Ger. Chem. Soc.; Amer. Chem. Soc.; Sigma Chi. Past Grand Knight & Faithful Navigator, Knights of Columbus; P.P., 1965-68, P.F.A.C.

KLIMEK-GEORGE, MARYLKA TERESA. Los Angeles. Dancer/Director. b. Przedborz, Poland, My. 2, 1934. m. Donald Lee George. c. Dorian, Donna Lee. Toured world-wide as dancer with Polish Folk Dance Group "Slask" 1953-1967.

KLIMES, LUDWIK. Van Nuys. b. Poland. Studied: Academy of Commerce, Krakow. m. Ingeborg M. POW: Ger. Employed, Bendix Pacific.

KLISZEWSKI, MARK ANDREW. San Leandro. Attorney-at-Law. b. Overton, Wales, G.B., Apr. 19, 1949. B.A., U. Santa Clara, S.J., 1970; J.D., UC, Hastings Coll. of Law, 1973. m. Nancy A. c. Kristina, Matthew. Private practice, San Leandro. Mem. Cal. State Bar Assn.; Alameda Co. Bar Assn.; U.S. Court of Appeals, 9th Circuit, U.S. Dist. Court; Lawyers Club, Alameda Co.; S.F. Barristers Club; Cal. Supreme Court.

KODREBSKI, JANUSZ IGNACY. Pacific Grove. Librarian. b. Kasna-dolna, Poland, Dec. 4, 1905. Studied: Officers Artillery Sch., Torun; War Coll., Warsaw, 1936-38; M.L.S., USC. m. Leatrice. Maj., Arty., PA, 1927-45. POW: Oflag IIB, Oflag VIA. Head, Cataloging Dept., Libr., USN Postgraduate Sch., Monterey.

KOGUT, SOPHIA. Long Beach. b. Bobrownik, Poland, 1893. Came to U.S. w/parents, 1901. Lived, Smolen, Pa. w/parents, thirteen brothers, sisters. m. Andrew, at age 15. c. Eight, incl. Frank, Sophia, Steve, Val, Josephine Regrut, Mildred Fujii. Widowed early in life, supported, educated all her children, two of whom are in the professions (dentist, nurse-anesthesiologist), one a businesswoman. Mem. Pol. Natl. Cath. Church, L.A.; P.N.A. Her children, who love and respect her, wish her remembered as a true Polish American pioneer.

KOL, GUSTAV. Newport Beach. Physician. b. Grudziadz, Poland. Studied: Acad. of Med., Gdansk, Pol. m. Barbara Smigielska. c. Matthew. CC: Mathausen, 1944. Private medical practice, Newport Beach.

KOLODNY, NATE. Los Angeles. Insurance Sales. m. Carol Anne. Affiliated w/California Insurance Center, Sherman Oaks.

KONOPKA, ALBIN. Concert Pianist. b. Los Angeles, Cal., Dec., 1950. B.A. Mus. Immaculate Heart Coll. L.A.; M.A. Mus. Juilliard School of Mus. N.Y. Studied w/Mme. Rosina Lhevinne and Beveridge Webster in N.Y., Nadia Boulanger in Paris. Performed with Tulane Symphony Orchestra, Ontario Symphony Orchestra, Broadway musical, *Candide.* Musical director and arranger for Berkshire Theatre Festival, Stockbridge, Mass. Solo recitals in Los Angeles, Santa Fe Springs, Norwalk, Ca.; West Yellowstone, Mon.; Esteli, Nicaragua. Awards include the Young Artist Award and the Sigma Alpha Iota Award.

KOPANIA, MSGR. STEFAN FRANCISZEK. Fremont. Clergyman, Ret. Studied Major Seminary, Wloclawek, Pol. Ordained June 16, 1929. Pastor Lubstowek to 1940. CC: Sachsenhausen, Dachau, 1940-45. Postwar: pastor at DP Camps: Schweinfur, Weiden, Rottweil-Wuert. Chaplain: PA, Eng., Esslingen. Guardian, Pol. orphans, Barcelona. Designated Honorary Prelate by Pope Paul VI in 1976. Currently serves as volunteer chaplain at three convalescent hospitals.

KORBONSKI, ANDRZEJ. Los Angeles. Economist. b. Poznan, Poland, Jan. 2, 1927. B.S., Econ., U. London, 1950; M.A., Econ., Columbia U., 1954; Ph.D., Public Law, Columbia U., 1962. m. Elizabeth G. c. Holly, Ellen. Mil. PA, 1941-45; Pol. Forces in G.B., 1945-48; USA, 1951-53. POW: Lamsdorf, Mulhlberg, Ger., 1944-45. Research Assoc.: Columbia U., 1956-63. UCLA, 1963-date.

KOWALIK, JAN. San Jose. Teacher/Bibliographer. b. Skoczow, Poland, Aug. 28, 1910. Grad. Teacher's Coll., Pol., 1931; Studied Phil., Jagiellonian U., 1935-36; m. Emmy Thea Mock. FLC: Plattenwerk Wrexen, Westphalia, Ger. Elementary, adult sch. teacher, Pol., 1931-39. After WWII engaged in bibliographic research dealing w/Polish subject matter in Intl. sources. Mem. P.A.H.A.; Soc. of Pol. Teachers; Soc. to Defend the West. Border; Union of Pol. Journalists Abroad; Cal. Hist. Soc.; Guttenberg Gesellschaft, Mainz, Ger. Founder: Amer. Pol. Documentation Studio, San Jose. Hon. Gold Cross of Merit. Recipient: Jurzykowski Foundation Grant, 1968, 1971. Godlewska Foundation Award, 1974.

KRANCE, MICHAL. Brentwood. Industrialist. b. Warsaw, Poland. B.A. (equiv.), Gimnazium Realne Wl. Gizyckiego, Warsaw; Technicum, Neu-Stalitz, Ger.; Ecole des Mines, Liege, Belg.; Ecole Super de Fonderie, Paris; Academie des Hautes Etudes Commerciales, Paris. m. Czeslawa Anna. Co-owner, Gen. Mgr., Pres.: L. Kranc & T. Lempicki Met. Works, Warsaw, 1923-39; Founder, Gen. Mgr., Les Decolletages de Commentry, 1938-41; Co-owner, Pres.: Sun Tool & Gauge Corp. N.Y.C.; Co-owner, Century Engr. Corp., Cedar Rapids, Iowa; Sun Machine Corp.; Sun Wire, Glen Cove, N.Y.; Founder: Key Metals Corp., N.Y.C., 1963; Off. of Corp. & Import Div. Mgr.: Harvey Gordon Co., Inc., L.A., 1967-77. Mem. Treas., Pilsudski Institute, N.Y.C.

KROLL, CLEMENS THOMAS. Los Angeles. Printer. b. Milwaukee, Wisc., Jan. 1, 1927. Studied: Notre Dame U. m. Theresa Mae. c. James, Thomas, Daniel. Mil. Sgt. USA —

M.P., Austria, 1945-46. Printer: *Santa Monica Outlook*, Santa Monica Independent Newspapers, 1952-65. Owner: Key Typographers, Culver City, 1965-date. Mem. U.S.C. of C.; United Bus. League; St. Anastasia Men's Club; Holy Name Society.

KROTOSKI, DANUTA MARIA (nee Gwozdziowska). New Orleans, LA. Bacteriologist. b. Preston, England. B.S., UCLA; M.S., Emory U., Atlanta, GA. m. Wojciech Antoni. c. Aleksandra. Teach. Asst., Emory U., 2 yrs. Research Bacteriologist, UCBerkeley, 1 yr. Founder: Pol. Millennium Students Club, L.A.

KROTOSKI, WOJCIECH ANTONI. New Orleans, LA. Physician/Scientist. b. Riga, Latvia, June 20, 1937. B.A., M.D., Ph.D., UCLA. M.P.H., UCBerkeley. m. Danuta Maria Gwozdziowska. c. Aleksandra. Sr. Surgeon (Cdr.) U.S. Public Health Svc., Circumglobal service, 1969-date. Physician, spec., tropical infectious diseases. Scientist, Immunochemistry. Founder: Pol. Millennium Students Club. Mem. Amer. Soc. Tropical Med. & Hygiene Assoc. Mem. Amer. Coll. of Physicians. Published 19 scientific articles.

KRUK, REV. WINCENTY. Oakland. Clergyman, Ret. b. Zawiercie, Pol., Feb. 8, 1908. Study: Jagiellonian U. Pastor of Kielczyslow, Pol. CC: Dachau, 1941-45. Came to U.S., 1951. Served as clergyman in Oakland, S.F., Alameda, San Leandro.

KRZEMUSKI, ADAM K. Beverly Hills. Real Estate Broker. b. Vienna, Austria, Nov. 11, 1915. L.L.M., Johannes Casimiri U., Lwow; L.L.D., Munich U. m. Wincentyna c. Andrzej. CC: Pankrac Prag, Mala Pevnost Terezin, Czech. Law practice, Munich, 1945-50; Foundry Worker, 1950-52; Prod. Control Mgr., 1952-67; Owner, Spring Mfg. Co., 1967-70; Real Estate Broker, 1970-date. Mem. Beverly Hills Realty Board, L.A.C. of C., Cal. Realty Board, Amer. Hist. Soc., H. Modrzejewska Culture & Art Club. P.O.W. Assn., Cal. Bar Assn.

KRZEMUSKI, ANDRZEJ. Beverly Hills. Attorney-at-Law. b. Sep. 19, 1947, Munich, W. Germany. Studied: St. John Vianney H.S., L.A., UCLA., Grad. UCLA Law School, J.D., 1971. Cal. Bar Exam, 1971. Private practice, 6420 Wilshire Blvd., L.A. 90048. Hon. Listings. Speaks: English, Polish, German, Russian.

KRZYCZKOWSKI, ROMAN (Deceased). Santa Barbara. Economist. b. Warsaw, Poland, Mar. 21, 1923. B.S. Elec. Engr., Eng.; M.S., Econ., Ph.D., Econ., London Sch. of Econ., 1952, 1973. m. Maria Krukowska. c. Barbara, Anna. Mil. 2nd Lt./Liaison Off., PA, 1941-42. Engr., Econ. Westinghouse, Baltimore, 1957; Econ. G.E. Tempo, S.B. — European, African Studies Prog., 1959-68; Founder: Pres., Interplan Corp. (Economic Cons.). 1968-75. Died Apr. 22, 1975.

KUGLER, BOLESLAW ANDREW. Encino. Engineer. b. Kielce, Poland, Jan. 1, 1940. B.S., Engr., UCLA; M.S., Mech. Engr., USC. m. Hedy Marie. c. Christine Marie, Andrew Tadeusz. Research, acoustics, vibrations: Measurement Analysis Corp., 4 yrs. Bolt, Beranek & Newman, 8 yrs. Mem. Amer. Soc. of Mech. Engrs.; Acoustical Soc. of Amer. Over 30 published papers on acoustics and noise control.

KULAS, EUGENE P. Tarzana. Marketing Consultant. b. Pittsfield, Mass., Oct. 29, 1921. Grad., Berkshire Coll. of Bus.; Studied: Coll. of Life Underwriters; Spec. studies, Life Insurance, Health Pensions, Profit Sharing, Securities Training. m. Danuta Maria Piotrowska. c. Barbara D., Christopher E. Mil. USA. FLC: Several mos., 1944. Bus. Exp.: Banking, 3½ yrs.; Cost Reduction Spec., Gen. Elec. Co., 10 yrs.; Mutual of Omaha: Sales

Div. Mgr., S.F., 1961-67; Assoc. Dir., Mgmt. Training, 1967-71; Marketing Cons., 1973-date. Mem. Exec. Comm., S.F.C. of C.; Pres., Holy Name Society — St. Thomas More; P.R.C.U.; P.A.H.A.

LAUBE, DANIELA T. San Gabriel. Dentist. b. Poland, Nov. 23, 1946. D.D.S., UCLA, 1968. c. Peter Richard. Private dental practice, 1968-date. Mem. Amer. Dental Assn.; Amer. Women's Dental Assn.; P.A.H.A.; Dental Sorority, MU Chpt.

LAUTERBACH, OTTO E. Los Angeles. Physician/Surgeon. b. Vienna, Austria, Sept. 17, 1915. 6 yrs. study, Jagiellonian U.; D.O., Coll. of Osteopathic Physicians & Surgeons, 1943. M.D., Cal. Coll. of Med., 1962. m. Sandra. c. Halina. Private medical practice, 1942-date. Mem. A.M.A.; C.M.A.; P.A.H.A.; L.A.C.M.A.

LAZAREWICZ, ANDREW RICHARD. Honolulu. Scientist. b. Caracas, Venezuela, Aug. 18, 1950. B.S., Earth & Planetary Sci., Mass. Inst. of Tech., 1972; M.S., Astro., U. Hawaii, 1974; Ph.D. Cand. Geophysics, U. Hawaii. m. Eva Maria Erdman. Planetology Research: Mass. Inst. of Tech.; U. Hawaii; Cal. Tech., Jet Propulsion Lab. Mem. Amer. Assn. for Advancement of Sci., Amer. Geophysical Union, Div. for Planetary Sci., Amer. Astro. Soc., Fed. of Amer. Sci., Theta II, P.A.H.A. Currently, mem. of seismology team, NASA Viking-Mars lander.

LENCZOWSKI, GEORGE. Berkeley. Professor. b. St. Petersburg, Russia, Feb. 2, 1915. L.L.M., U. Warsaw, 1936; Dipl., Civil Law, U. Paris, 1936; J.D., U. Lille, Fr., 1937. m. Bronislawa Szylkiewicz. c. John, Hubert. Mil. Grad. Off., Cadet Sch., Gaza, 1942; Carpathian Brigade: Egypt, Libya, Palestine, Iraq, Tobruk, 1941-42. Pol. Foreign Svc.: Essen, Ger., 1935. Br. Mandate for Palestine, 1938-39; Press Attaché, Pol. Legation, Teheran, Iran, 1942-45; Research Fellow: Sch. of Advanced Intl. Studies, Wash., D.C., 1945-46; Prof., Pol. Sci., Hamilton Coll., Clinton, N.Y., 1946-51; Prof., Pol. Sci., UCBerkeley, 1952-date. Mem. Board of Dir. Middle East Inst., Wash., D.C., 1973-date; Board of Trustees, Coll. Preparatory Sch., Berkeley, 1967-date; Cons. to U.S. industry for Middle East; Chm., Islamic Middle East, Hoover Inst., Stanford, 1974-date. Mem. Amer. Pol. Sci. Assn.; Fellow, Middle East Studies Assn.; P.I.A.S.; P.A.C. — N. Cal. Div. Bohemian Club, S.F.; S.F. Comm. Foreign Relations Faculty Club, UC. Publ. numerous articles on intl. affairs, Middle East politics, economics, in prof. journals. Ed. contr. to several books on Middle East pol., history. Author, *Obligations Contractuelles en Droit International Privé.* Domat-Montchrestien; *Russia and the West in Iran,* Cornell U.P.; *The Middle East in World Affairs* (3 editions), Cornell U.P.; *Oil and State in the Middle East,* Cornell U.P.; *Soviet Advances in the Middle East,* American Enterprise Institute. Listed *Who's Who in America.* Awarded Fellowships from Ford Foundation, 1952-53; Rockefeller Foundation, 1960. Visiting prof. Oxford U., St. Anthony's Coll., 1958. Lect. at universities of Geneva, Tehran, Baghdad; Amer. U., Beirut.

LERSKI, GEORGE JAN. San Francisco. Professor, History. b. Lwow, Poland, Jan. 20, 1917. Studied: Foreign Trade Inst., Lwow; Law, U. Lwow; L.L.M., Pol. Law, Oxford U.; Ph.D. Amer. Hist., Pol. Theory, Georgetown U. m. Belva Jean. c. (five). Mil. PA, Pol., Fr., 1939-40; Educ. Off. PA, Fr., Scotland, 1940-42; Special Envoy (parachuted into enemy occupied Poland, served w/Pol. underground govt.), 1942-44; Pvt. Secty. Prime Minister of Pol., London. Lecturer, Prof., universities in Tokyo, Karachi, Ceylon. Ed. *Polish Daily,* Detroit, Mich. Research Assoc. Hoover Inst. Stanford, 1964-65; Asia Found., S.F., 1965-66. Since 1968, U. San Francisco: Act. Chm., Dept. Pol. Sci., 1968-69; Prof., Hist., Govt., 1969-70; Prof., Hist., 1970-date. Cons. Asia Found., 1966-date; Dept. of Defense: Intl.

Affairs Sec. — Pol. Planning & Natl. Sec. Council, 1970-71. Mem. Amer. Hist. Assn.; Amer. Cath. Hist. Assn.; Phi Alpha Theta; Societe Historique et Litteraire; P.I.A.S.; Pol. Soc. Arts & Sci. Abroad, London; P.A.C. — N. Cal. Div.; P.H.A.V.A.; P.V.A.; P.A.H.A. (Pres. 1974). Numerous articles on hist., pol. sci., intl. relations, pub. in U.S., European, Asian journals. Author, co-author, several books, incl. *A Polish Chapter in Jacksonian America: The United States and the Polish Exiles of 1831.* Madison: U. Wisconsin Press, 1958; *A History of Political Thought: Volume One — Ancient and Medieval.* (Textbook in Jap. translation of Dr. Satoshi Saito) Tokyo: Ricchoscha Publishing Co., 1953; *Origins of Trotskyism in Ceylon: A Documentary History of the Lanke Sama Samaja Party, 1932-1962.* Stanford, 1968. *Jewish-Polish Relations in Modern History 1772-1945,* (planned for publ. 1977). Hon. Cross of Valor, King's Medal for Courage in the Cause of Freedom.

LESKI, LENET (Teofil Wroblewski). Costa Mesa. Industrial Engineer/Designer. b. Skaryszew, Poland, Dec. 5, 1905. Elec. Engr. Deg., Lwow Poly., 1939. m. Virginia Rosini. c. Stephen, Helen. Mil. 1st Lt., PA, Pol., Fr., Scotland, 1938-48. 30 yrs. experience as designer, engr. Power Stations; Commercial, Industrial Plants, incl. gasoline refineries, fertilizer & chem. plants, mines, steel mills. Mem. Sierra Club; Inst. Engrs. & Arch.; P.V. WWII.

LEWICKI, STANISLAW LUDWIK. San Francisco. Writer/Journalist. b. Czerniowce, Jy. 27, 1910. Studied: Pol. Lit., Lang., Jagiellonian U. CC: Ger., WWII. Prior to WWII, journalist, Katowice, Pol. Pub. collection of short stories, *Przez Zycie Na Przelaj.* (Shortcut Through Life), poetry, translations of works of Grillparzer, Geraldy. Short story writer, columnist, poet; contributes regularly to *Wiadomosci,* (The News) London, & the Pol. Literary journal, *Kultura,* Paris.

LIIBKE, HELENA. Los Angeles. Secretary to the late Mrs. Helena Paderewski and family.

LINOWSKI, REV. EUGENE RAYMOND. Van Nuys. Clergyman. b. Cleveland, O., Apr. 25, 1930. B.A., St. Francis Coll., Burlington, Wisc., 1954; Christ the King Theological Seminary, W. Chi., Ill., 1955-59; Slavic Studies, West. Reserve U., Cleveland, O., 1967-70; Hist., John Carroll U., Cleveland, O., 1969; Cand., M.A., Pol. Lit., U. Ottawa, 1970. Served as missionary, Island of Samar, Philippines, as mem. Franciscan Order from Pulaski, Wisc., 1959-63. Presently, Pastor, St. Mary's Byzantine Catholic Church, Van Nuys. Mem. 4th Deg., Knights of Columbus; P.A.H.A.; K.F.; Pol. Amer. Priests Assn., Chi.; Natl. Assn. Cath. Chaplains.

LITYNSKI, ZBIGNIEW JAN. San Rafael. Transportation Specialist. b. Stanislawow, Poland, Ju. 22, 1911. L.L.M., Lwow U.; London Sch. of Foreign Trade & Port Adm., London, 1947-48. m. Zofia. c. Marja. Mil. Capt., PA, Pol., 1939; Fr., 1940; G.B., 1940-47. POW: Hungary, 1939-40. Transportation Spec. London, 1948-50; U.S., 1951-date. Mem. P.V.WWII.; P.A.C.

LOJEWSKI, HARRY VICTOR. Beverly Hills. Musician/Composer. Studied: U. Arizona; L.A. Conservatory. Master Classes: Juilliard Conservatory. m. Maria Carmen. c. Maria Carmen, Victor Girard. Rehearsal pianist, music dir., music advisor, music dir.; Goldwyn-Fox Studios; Head of music, T.V.; Exec. Music Dir. M.G.M., to date. Mem. A.S.C.A.P.; B.M.I. Composer's Guild; Acad. of Motion Pictures.

LONDZIN, VICTOR. Los Altos. Designer. Writer/Poet. Educated in Poland, West Germany. m. Olga. Mil. Cadet Cpl. PA, 1939. CC: Dachau, Gusen. Present occupation, designer. Poets and Painters Press Award, 1967. *The International Authors* and *Writers Who's Who*, Cambridge, England, 1976. Author, three volumes of poetry; essays, articles, book reviews.

LUBANSKI, JOSEF. Sutter Creek. Editor/Publisher. b. Poland. Grad. Forest Engr., U. Poznan. m. (widower). c. Bogdan. Mil. Lt. PA, Pol., Fr., Nor., Eng.; N. Africa, It. Retired, U.S. Forestry Svc. Currently, owner, Correspondence Home Study of Languages. Publishes *Fragments*, selected articles (in translation) from Pol. literary journal, *Kultura*, (publ., Paris). Editor, translator, under pseudonym Charles Joel. Mem. Commando Assn., Eng.; Pol. Commando Vet. Assn., U.S., Eng. Decorated by Polish, French, Norwegian, English governments.

LUCZAJ, TADEUSZ. Los Angeles. Opera, Concert Singer. Studied: Academy of Mus., Warsaw, 1926-30. m. Halszka Karpowicz. c. Andrew. Mil. PHA, Warsaw Insurrection, 1944. Concert appearances: Warsaw Opera, Warsaw Philharmonic, Polish radio. Concert tour: U.S., 1963-64. Won Gold Medal at the Intl. Vocalists Contest, 1933. Hon. Gold Cross of Merit, 1938.

MACANDER, IZABELLA ZOFIA. Bethesda, MD. b. England. B.A., Cult. Anthro., Cert., Latin Amer. Studies, CSULB. Cert. Spanish Language, Saltillo U., Mexico. m. Aleksander. c. Natalia Krystyna. Tech. Writer: Ortho Pharmaceuticals, N.Y.; P.C.L. Health Lab., Colo., Arlen Realty Mgmt. Co., MD., Androlis Research Corp., MD. Taught Pol. language in the Polish School, L.A.

MACKIEWICZ, CZESLAW. Rancho Palos Verdes. Engineer. b. Wilno, Poland, Sept. 3, 1923. Studied: Technische Hochschule, Stuttgart, Ger., 1947-50; B.S., Mech. Engr., U. Bridgeport, Conn. m. Anna Halina. c. Peter C., Christina H., Caroline A. POW: Stalag IXA, 1944-45. Sup., Advanced Design: Hubbell, Inc., 1952-70; Sierra Elec. Div. — Sola Basic Ind. Mem. A.S.M.E., Underwriters Labs., Ind. Advisory Council. Holds six patents in electro-mechanical field.

MAKOWIECKI, JOSEPH LESZEK (Deceased). Glendale. Poet/Author/Editor. b. U.S.A. m. Eugenia. c. Konrad, Isabella. Mil. Gen. Jos. Haller's Army, WWI. Assoc. ed., various publications, Chi., Ill.; Pol. radio news ed., Gary, Ind.; Ed., publication *Jednodniowka*, L.A. Ed. Commemorative book, published after the dedication of the Polish Parish, O.L.B.M. Publ. two volumes of poetry *Poezja Polska* (Polish Poetry). His poem *Na Cichy Brzeg* (Toward the Quiet Shore), dedicated to John F. Kennedy on the occasion of his inauguration (was included in the *Congressional Record*).

MAKOWSKI, JERZY. Torrance. Engineer. b. Poland. M.S., Mech. Engr., Warsaw Tech. U., 1936. m. Anna. c. Maciej, Anna Schumacher, George Jerzy. Mil. PA, G.B., 1940-42. Sr. Asst., Thermodynamics: Warsaw Inst. of Tech., 1938-39. Chief Research Engr. Stratos Div., Fairchild Engine & Airplane Corp., 1944-59; Prog. Mgr.; Sup.; Proj. Engr.: Air Research, 1959-67. Instrumental in design of Amer. SST-ECS. Sr. Scientist: Stratos Div., Fairchild, 1967-73. Lect. Environmental Systems, UC, USC. Eleven articles publ., Pol., U.S., on environmental systems & supersonic travel. Holds three patents.

MALIN, DONALD P. Inglewood. Student. b. Inglewood, Cal., Ju. 11, 1956. Current study, Music, Loyola Marymount U., L.A. Charter Pres. Student Chpt., P.A.H.A., 1976-77.

MALOLEPSZY, MARIAN. Rancho Palos Verdes. Business Executive. b. Lodz, Poland, Jy. 26, 1912. m. Eva F. c. Maria, Kristina, Grazia. Mil. Lt. PA, 1939. POW: Woldenberg, Murnau, Ger. Dist. Mgr. S. Cal. Gas Co., L.A.

MANTYKOWSKI, ANTHONY J. Glendale. Travel Agent. b. Poland. Studied: Vienna U.; Stanford U.; The London Inst. of Applied Research; Bus. U. of Okla. Holds M. Intl. Law, and M.B.A. degrees. m. Jeanine. Mil. PA, Pol., Fr., Belg., Holl., Ger., 1944-45. POW: 1939. FLC: 1940-41. Travel agency owner-manager, 25 yrs. Editor-in-Chief & Publ., *Polonia Review*. Ed., *American Ethnic Voice*, publ. of L.A. Co. Rep. Heritage Council. Pres., Pol. Amer. Rep. Club of S. Cal., 1972-date; Pres. Pol.-Amer. Bus. and Prof. Club, Inc., L.A., 1977; Mem. P.A.C., Kiwanis; Optimist Club; Glendale C. of C.; L.A. Dist. Advisory Council of the U.S. Small Bus. Administration.

MARTINI, FLORIAN K. Santa Barbara. Engineer. b. Warsaw, Poland, Sept. 9, 1915. Mech. Engr., Warsaw Poly. U., 1934-35; M.S., Aero. Engr., PAF Coll., Tech. Grp., Warsaw, 1935-39; Spec. courses, mech., aero., engr. Mil. Capt. PAF, RAF, 1935-48. Sr. Liaison; Proj.; Methods; Design, Engr.: Polaris, Sidewinder, Titan I, II. Currently, partner: S.B. Products Corp., engaged in design, dev. of new products. Mem. Amer. Air Force Assn.; P.A.F.A., — L.A. Wing; Natl. Mgmt. Assn.; Amer. Inst., Aero., Astro. Hon. Virtuti Militari; Cross of Valor (four times); Polish Air Medal (three times); Distinguished Flying Cross; Defence Medal; Air Crew Europe & Clasp; War Medal; Atlantic Star & Clasp; Croix de Combattant. Holds American and British patents.

MATHEWS, (PRZYBYLA) EUGENE A. Long Beach. Engineer. b. Chicago, Ill., Dec. 27, 1920. Studied: Art. Inst., Chi.; Bus. Adm., Wright Coll., Northwestern U.; B.S., Elec. Engr., Brooklyn Poly.; M.B.A., Pepperdine U., 1972. m. Laura J. Kozlofska. c. Veragene Millican, John A. Mil. USAF, 1942-46. Sr. Research Engr.: Rockwell Intl., 1963-67; Sci. Instrumentation Engr.: TRW Systems Gr., Redondo Beach, 1967-69; Celesco Ind., Costa Mesa; Com-Mark, L.B., 1971-date. Mem. Amer. Inst. of Aero., Astro.; Amer. Rocket Soc.; Inst. of Elec. & Elec. Engr.; Inst. Radio Engrs.; Instrument Soc. Amer.; P.N.A.; Amer. Legion; Founding Mem., Dir. P.A.F.C.U.; O.L.B.M.R.C.C.; Amer. Mgmt. Assn.; Wescon — Public Relations Comm. Publ. articles on ballistocardiograph data analysis, spacecraft tape recorder/playback systems, cross cultural research using semantic differential technique. Holds patent in electronic, electromechanical field.

MATHEWS, (PRZYBYLA) LAURA J. (nee Kozlofska). Long Beach. Social Services. b. Bridgeport, Conn., Feb. 14, 1923. A.A., L.B. City Coll. m. Eugene A. c. Veragene Millican, John A. Mil. Pvt. WAC, Ellington Field, Houston, Tex., 1942-43 (served as aircraft elec. maintenance mech). 36 yrs. varied bus. experience. Currently, Sup. L.A. Co. Dept. of Social Services, 1966-date. Active, civic, Pol-Amer. affairs, inc.: teacher, Pol. lang.; Pol. Folk Dance instr.; Pub. Relations, Pub. Dir. for O.L.B.M.R.C.C.; served, Fund Raising Comm., O.L.B.M.R.C.C.; Treas., Comm., Sr. Citizen's Home; numerous others. Contr., articles, poetry, for Pol. newspapers, L.A., N.Y.; co-authored screen play, *The Devil's Partner*. Writer, engr. abstracts, *Astronautics Abstracts*, publ., JPL Labs, Pasa. Mem. S.W.G.A.; Amer. Legion; P.N.A.; P.W.A.; Local 535, Soc. Workers Union, AFL-CIO; Founding Mem., Secty. Bd. of Dir.: P.A.F.C.U.; P.A.H.A. Numerous civic, military awards, incl. USAF Medals (two), Silver Cross (Pol. Govt. in exile).

MATULEWICZ, ALICJA POMIAN-POZERSKA. San Francisco. Writer. b. Wilno, Poland. Studied: Inst. of East. Eur. Educ. Research. m. Jerzy (dec.). Sup. Diamond Intl.

Labels Div., 25 yrs. Contr. writer: *Zgoda*, Chi.; *Nowy Swiat*, N.Y.; *Kresowiak*, Ger.; *Nurt*, Aust.; *Dziennik Polski*, London. Author of novel, *Good Bye Germany*, and two books of poetry. Hon. Gold Cross of Merit, Gold Medal of Merit.

MILLARD, MARY ANN (nee Lisewska)(Deceased). Santa Barbara. Teacher/Pianist. b. Chicago, Ill. M.A., Mus., M.A., Lang., Northwestern U.; Grad., Music Conservatory of Chi. Taught Spanish, Russian languages in L.A. Sch. Syst.; Lang. Dept. Head: Arroyo H.S., over 10 yrs. Classical pianist, tutored aspiring, underpriviledged musicians, gratis. Mem. A.A.U.W.; P.R.C.U. Died July 30, 1975.

MILOSZ, CZESLAW. Berkeley. Professor/Man of Letters/Poet. M. Jur., Slavic Lits., Stefan Batory U., Poland, 1934. Prof., Dept. of Slavic Lang. & Lit., UCBerkeley.

MINC, HENRYK. Santa Barbara. Professor, Mathematics. b. Lodz, Poland, Nov. 12, 1919. Studied: U. Liege, Belg.; Dundee Tech. Coll., Scotland; M.A., Ph.D., U. Edinburgh. m. Catherine Taylor. c. Robert Henry, Ralph Edward, Raymond. Mil. 2nd Lt. PA, Fr., U.K., 1940-48. Asst. Prof. U. Br. Columbia, 1958-60; Assoc. Prof. U. Fla., 1960-63; Prof., Math. UCSB, 1963-date. Mem. Amer. Math. Soc.; Edinburgh Math. Soc.; Israel Math. Union, among others. Published one monograph, nine textbooks, sixty research papers on mathematics. Referee, reviewer for numerous mathematical journals. Listed: *Who's Who in Science, American Men of Science, Who's Who in the West*. Ford Award, Math. Assn. of America, 1966. Lady Davis Fellowship, 1975, 1978.

MIZIOLEK, ANDRZEJ W. Solana Beach. Chemist. b. Hannover, Germany, Feb. 17, 1950. B.S., Chem., Magna cum laude, Wayne State U., 1971; Ph.D., Phys. Chem., UCBerkeley, 1976. Post Doct. Fellow, Chem. Dept., UCIrvine, 1976-date. m. Dr. Karen L. Beemon. Mem. Phi Beta Kappa, Amer. Chem. Society, Psi Lambda Upsilon (Hon. Chem. Frat.), Pol. Boy Scouts, Detroit, Mich. Received Merit Index Award in Chemistry, Michigan Competitive Scholarship.

MOKRZYCKI, GUSTAW ANDRZEJ. Fullerton. Professor, Aeronautics, Ret. M., Mech. Engr., Ph.D., Tech. Inst., Lwow, Pol., 1918, 1925.

MOORE, WANDA HARUBIN. Orange. Deputy City Clerk. b. Hamtramck, Michigan. Studied: Soc., Wayne State U., Det.; Chapman Coll., Orange, Cal.; B.A., Soc., CSU Fullerton, 1973. m. William B. (dec.). c. Michael Craig. Mil. WAC, 1942-46, Pacific Theatre. Varied business experience, legal secty.; congressional secty., (Dr. R.G. Tenerowicz); exec., adm., secty.; financial investigator, Probate Court; social worker. Deputy City Clerk, Orange, 1974-date.

MROZEWSKA, IRENA (nee Blizinska). Walnut Creek. Artist. b. Warsaw, Poland. Studied: Karlowicz Music Sch., Warsaw; Ursulines, Malines, Belg.; Schola Cantorum, Paris; Painting study at Grand Chenier, Paris. m. Stefan. c. Andrzej H. Mil. PHA, 1942-45, ran underground hosp. and logistics, precinct Wloszczowa. After WWII, organized, managed, children's home, Radziwill Palace, Naglowice, 1945-46. Came to U.S. (N.Y.), 1951, moved to L.A., 1952, Walnut Creek, 1963. Taught design, Los Gatos, several seasons. Mem. P.H.A.V.A. Hon. Silver Cross of Merit w/glaives.

MROZEWSKI, STEFAN (Deceased). Walnut Creek. Artist. b. Czestochowa, Poland, 1894. Studied: Sch. of Art, Lodz; Sch. of Decorative Arts, Poznan; Acad. of Arts, Krakow; Acad. of Fine Arts, Warsaw. m. Irena Blizinska. During his lifetime, he illustrated limited editions of Cervantes, Coleridge, Dostoevski, Kossak-Szczucka, Mickiewicz, Schwob, plus major portfolio of 101 engravings of Dante's *Divine Comedy*. Other portfolios: *Polish Millennium of Christianity, Gallery of Polish Saints and Blessed*. Created 160 ex-libris, engraved 40 portraits of famous persons, inc: G.B. Shaw, H.G. Wells, Rudyard Kipling, G.K. Chesterton. Other works inc.: 25 oils, 200 pastels, 20 terracottas, 3,500 engravings. Rep. in Biblioteca Apostolica Vaticana, Rome; private libraries of Royal Families of Holl., Belg., It.; Cal. museums, churches. Died Sept. 8, 1975.

MUDY, BRUNO. North Hollywood. Industrialist. b. Sept. 17, 1926, Poland. Studied: Poland, W. Germany; Allied Mechanics Institute, B.M. Eng., Chicago. Mgr., Cardinal Eng. Co., Chicago. EMCO Eng. Co., Inc., North Hollywood. Mil. W. Ger., USA, Korea. m. Maria T. Werminska. c. Anthony, Margaret. Active, Pol. Am. social, cultural life.

MURAWSKI, MARIANNE KAY. Los Angeles. Student. b. Torrance, Cal., Mar. 9, 1957. Currently working toward Elementary Teaching Credentials, Loyola Marymount U., L.A. Recipient: Cal. State Scholarship, LMU. Listed: *Who's Who Among American High School Students*, 1974-75.

NADOLSKI, LEON. Oakland. Civil Engineer. b. Slawsko Wielkie, Poznan, Poland, Apr. 2, 1917. Studied: Pol. Army Engrs. Acad., Warsaw, 1937-39; Ecole Militaire d'Application du Génie, Versailles, Fr.; Pol. Army Staff Coll., U.K.; Dipl., Engr., PUC, London; Bus. Mgt. Cert., UCBerkeley. m. Jean Mary Bromley Burt. c. Mary Grace, Nina Jean, Leon Mark, Sara Rosalia. Mil. Maj., PA, Pol., 1939; Fr., 1940; U.K., Middle East, It., 1940-45. POW: Hungary (3 mos., 1939). Civil Engr. Kaiser Engr., Oakland; Chief, Civil Struct. Engr. Bechtel Corp. Proj. Mgr., steel complex, Fr., aluminum plant, Tenn. Fellow Amer. Soc. of Civil Engrs.; Mem. Soc. Amer. Mil. Engrs.; Engrs. Club, S.F.; Pol. Amer. Engr. Club, S.F.; V.P., P.A.C. — N. Cal. Chpt. Reg. Civil, Struct. Engr. Cal., Ark., Utah, Ore., Tenn., B.C., Quebec. Listed: *Who's Who in the West*. Hon. Cross of Valor.

NIEDZIELSKI, THEODORE MICHAEL. Phoenix, Arizona. Civic Leader/ Businessman/Musician. b. Bay City, Mich. Studied: Cincinnati Conservatory of Music. m. Gertrude. c. Marge, Dorothy. Exec., menswear retailing, Bay City, Mich., 1938-67. Choral Dir., S.P.E.B.S.Q.S.A., Saginaw, Midland, Bay City, Mich., 1947-49. Choral Dir. Chopin Choral Soc., Bay City, Mich., 1930-65; Halka Ladies Chorus, 1935-42; St. Stanislaus Parish, Bay City, 1926-48. Gen. Conductor: Pol. Singers Alliance of Amer., 1947-49. Mem. Mich. Musical Culture Comm., 1960-65; Pres. P.A.C. — Ariz. Chpt., 1973; Chm. Mikolaj Kopernik 500th Anniv. Comm. Bicentennial Chm., Pol. Amer. Soc. of Phoenix, Ariz., 1975. Pres. Casey Club, Phoenix, Ariz. Hon. Mem. Lutnia Choir, Detroit, Mich., Warsaw, Pol.; Paderewski Choral Soc., Phoenix, Ariz.; Pol. Legion, Amer. Vets. Awarded Honorary Gold Emblem w/Laurel, Alliance of Choral and Instrumental Societies, Warsaw, Poland, 1969. Numerous civic awards in Michigan, Arizona.

NIKLEWICZ, STANLEY. Sacramento. Businessman. b. Poland. Studied at Liceum, Hohenfelds, Ger. m. Emilia C. c. Robert, Elisabeth, Donna, Paul, John. Mil. Staff Sgt., PHA. CC: Mauthausen, Ger. Former owner-operator, retail food stores in Central Cal.; Owner, S&N Co., Sacramento. Contractor, Santa Fe Railroad. Mem. Kiwanis; Pol. Sci. Club, Sacramento; Charter mem. Paderewski Club, S.F. (Pres., 1951-55).

NOWAKOWSKI, ANDREW JAN. Monrovia. Insurance. m. Jadwiga. Mem. P.A.H.A. and professional organizations.

OLBRYS, REV. ZBIGNIEW ARKADIUSZ, S.Ch. Los Angeles. Clergyman. b. Grodno, Poland, Aug. 13, 1932. Ord. Priest, 1957, Soc. of Christ, Poznan, Pol. Came to U.S., 1966. Pastor, Our Lady of the Bright Mount Roman Catholic Church (Polish Parish). Mem. Pol. Retirement Found.; Pol. Scouting Org.

OLECHNO-HUSZCZA, CZESLAW. Los Angeles. Teacher/Businessman. b. Zadworze (Wilenskie), Poland, Aug. 6, 1918. Dipl., Ed., State Teachers Training Coll., Wilno, Pol.; B.A., U. London, Sch. of Slavic, East European Studies, 1950; Dipl., Ed., U. Leeds, Eng., 1951; M.A., Latin, USC, 1958; Can., M.A., Slavic Lang., UCLA. m. Ethel Gillian. c. William Vincent. Mil. PA, Pol., Latvia, USSR, Iran, 1939-41; Pol. Br., Navy: India, S. Africa, G.B., 1942. Lt., RAF, 1942-49. Interned: Ulbroka, Latvia, 1939-40; Yukhnovo, USSR, 1940-41. FLC: Ponoi, Cola Peninsula, USSR, 1941-42. Inst., Pol. Lang.: Pol. Eng. AF Tech. Sch., Halston, Eng., 1946-48; Educ. Off.: RAF, Sealand, Eng., 1948-49; Elect. Engr., Stancil Hoffman Firm, Hollywood, 1952-58; Inst., Foreign Lang.; Dept. Chm.: Morningside H.S., Inglewood, 1958-date. Grad. Lang. Examiner: UCLA (Latin, Pol., Russian), 1963-68. Mem. P.A.H.A.; P.A.F.A.; P.C. — P.F.A.C.; Amer. Translators Assn.; Amer. Fed., Teachers; Modern & Classical Languages Assn.; Amer. Classical League. Hon. Air Force Medal, War Medal. Translator, Polish-English, T. Bielecki, *Warsaw Aflame*, Polamerica Press, 1973; Z. Banasiewicz, *The Warsaw Ghetto*. T. Yoseloff, 1968.

OLECHNO-HUSZCZA, ETHEL GILLIAN. Los Angeles. Medical Librarian. b. Stockport, England, Mar. 1, 1930. B.A., Soc. Studies, Leeds U., Eng., 1951; M.L.S., USC, 1964. m. Czeslaw. c. William Vincent. Libr.: City of Inglewood, 1961-66; Med. Libr., 1966-73; Assoc. Dir., 1973-date: L.A. Co., USC Med. Center. Mem. P.A.H.A.; Med. Libr. Assn.; Med. Libr. Guild of S. Cal.; Amer. Translators Assn.; Ladera Heights Civic Assn.

ORDON, VLADIMIR A. Long Beach. Psychologist/Physiologist. M.Ph., phy., educ., psych.: U. Warsaw, Pol., 1931; Post-grad. study: Clinical sciences, U. Vienna, 1931; Biophysics, U. Berlin, 1935; Ph.D., Communications, Psych., U. Ottawa, 1951. Prior to 1966, a/k/a: Wlodzimierz Sklodowski, Vladimir A. Sklodowski. Psychologist, Physiologist, Biotechnologist, 20 yrs. Currently, Sr. Research Sci., McDonnell Douglas, Huntington Beach. Mem. Amer. Psych. Assn.; Amer. Inst. of Aero. & Astro. (Assoc. Fellow); Aero. Med. Assn. (Assoc. Fellow); Industrial Life Sci. Assn. (Charter Mem.); Ohio Psych. Assn. (Fellow); Human Factors Soc.; Amer. Assn. for Advancement of Sci.; Amer. Cybernetics Soc.; West. Electroencephalography Soc. Author, co-author of approx. 25 technical publications. Listed: *American Men of Science*.

OTFINOWSKI, JOZEF ZBIGNIEW. Menlo Park. Cartographer, Ret. b. Smiela, Ukraine, Jan. 2, 1905. Studied: Mil. Acad., Torun. m. Marcelle. c. Joanna Agnieszka, Danuta Barbara. Mil. Pol.; Fr.; U.K. POW: Soviet, Ger., camps. Cartographer, U.S. Geological Survey, 20 yrs. until retirement.

PADEREWSKI, CLARENCE JOSEPH. San Diego. Architect. b. Cleveland, O., Jy. 23, 1908. B.A., Arch., UCBerkeley, 1932. m. Maxine T. c. Colette J. McCanna, Coleen J. Floyd. Private arch. practice, 1944-48. Partnership: Paderewski, Dean & Mitchell, Arch., 1948-61; Paderewski-Dean & Assoc., 1961-date. Active in civic, professional organizations. Mem. P.P., Fr. Sierra Club; Past mem. Board of Dir. Exec. Comm., Ch., Music Comm.: San Diego Symphony Assn.; Mem. Board of Dir., S.D.C. of C.; S.D. Chpt. Amer. Red Cross; Lions Club Intl.; Calif. State Board, Arch. Examiners; Natl. Council, Arch. Reg. Boards; Chm.: S.D. Copernicus Quincentennial Comm., 1974. Listed: *Who's Who in America*. Coll. Fellows, A.I.A., 1962; S.D. Chpt. A.I.A. Award for design of S.D. Co. U. Hosp.; Hon. Award: S.D. Intl. Airport; Three Outstanding Comm. Leadership Awards, S.D. Central City Assn. Numerous awards for charitable, civic achievements; professional awards for excellence in design.

PATTON, JACK FRANK (Franciszek Piecuch). Palm Springs. Businessman/ Songwriter. b. Amsterdam, N.Y., Oct. 4, 1914. Grad. w/honors, Bernard MacFadden Sch. of Dietetics, Wilmington, Del. Owner, operator, health food stores chain, N.Y., Cal. Financial interest, health food restaurants, L.A. area. Taught nutrition, L.A. High Schools, Coll., 37 yrs. Songwriter, promoter, country western music. Currently, numerous bus. interests, Palm Springs, N.Y. Mem. First Natl. Fitness Council, S. Cal. Nutrition Assn.

PAUKER, EWA TERESA. Topanga. Political Scientist. b. Warsaw, Poland, Feb. 21, 1938. B.A., Pol. Sci., McGill U., Montreal, 1959; M.A., Pol. Sci., UCBerkeley, 1960. m. Guy Jean. c. Anthony J.H. Researcher, Pol. Sci., 1960-70. Approx. twelve papers published.

PAWLOWSKI, EDWARD. Los Angeles. Electronic Technician. b. Warsaw, Poland, Dec. 26, 1916. Studied: Tech. Railway Sch., Warsaw, 1935. m. Irena. PAF, 1937-39; PA: USSR, 1941-42; PAF/RAF, 1942-45; Pol. Resettlement Corp/RAF, 1946-48. POW: USSR, 1939-41. Came to U.S., 1955. Elec. Tech.: Eng., U.S. Mem. P.A.F.A.; P.A.V.A. Hon. Polish Air Force Medal w/bar, France and Germany Star.

PEDZICH, ANTHONY. Garden Grove. Artist/Sculptor. b. Poland, 1910. Studied Law: Stefan Batory U., Wilno. m. Isabel Demby. Mil. PA, 1939; PHA, 1939-44. Took part in Warsaw Uprising, 1944. POW: Stalag 4A, Ger. CC: Dachau.

PETROVICH, ZBIGNIEW. Santa Monica. Physician/Surgeon. b. Warsaw, Poland, Ju. 7, 1938. M.D., Warsaw Med. Acad., 1963. m. Zofia. c. Margaret, Martin. Residencies: Warsaw Gen. Hosp., 1963-64; Warsaw Central Emergency Hosp., 1964; Leeds Reg. Thoracic Surgical Center, Eng., 1964-65; Dept. of Experimental Surg., U. Vienna, 1965-66; Dept. of Surg., Med. Coll., U. Manitoba, 1966 (Teaching Fellow, Surg. Anatomy); St. Boniface Gen. Hosp., Winnipeg, Manitoba, Can., (Radiol.) 1967-68; Vet. Adm. Center, Wadsworth Gen. Hosp., L.A., (Radiol.), 1968-71. Lic. Ariz., Cal., D.C., Texas. Wadsworth Hosp. Center, Radiol. Svc., L.A.: Staff Radiol., 1971-72; Chief, Radiation Therapy Sec., 1972-75; Chief, Radiation Therapy Svc., 1975-date; Cons. Radiation Therapy, 1972; Chief of Center, 1975-date. Adj. Asst. Prof.: UCLA, Sch. of Med., Dept. of Radiol. Sci. Mem. L.A. Radiol. Soc.; Cal. Radiol. Soc.; Amer. Coll., Radiol.; S. Cal. Radiation Therapy Soc.; Cal. Radiation Therapy Assn.; Amer. Soc. of Therapeutic Radiol.; Comm.: UCLA Cancer Center; Vet. Adm. Field Advisory Gr. in Therapeutic Radiol. Papers presented to Cal. Chpt. of Amer. Coll. of Surg.; Amer. Soc. of Therapeutic Radiol.; Radiation Oncology Gr.; Vet. Adm. Radiation Oncology Gr.; USC Co. Comprehensive Cancer Center; Amer. Coll. of Surg.; Radiol. Soc. of N. Amer. Listed: 1978 ed., *Who's Who in the West.*

POLAK, TEODOR. Los Angeles. Physician/Surgeon. b. Poland, Nov. 9, 1928. M.D., Med. Sch., Warsaw. m. Maria. c. Ivona, Eva. Private medical practice, L.A., since 1965. Mem. A.M.A.; C.M.A.; L.A.C.M.A.; Amer. Soc. of Abdominal Surgeons.

PRASNIEWSKI, JAN. Downey. Professional Ice Skater. b. England, Nov. 12, 1955. Trained as skater 10 yrs. World-wide appearances incl., *Las Vegas on Ice,* U.S.A.; *Holiday on*

Ice, Mex.; *Ice Follies International*, world-wide. Mem. U.S. Figure Skating Assn.; Amer. Guild of Variety Artists. Pacific Coast Intermediate Men's Champion, 1970. Gold, silver medalist, numerous skating competitions.

PRASNIEWSKI, JERZY. Downey. Engineer. b. Poland, Jy. 27, 1918. Studied: PAF Officer's Sch., — Tech. Gr., Warsaw; Higher Natl. Cert., England. m. Margaret Mary. c. Jan. Mil. Flt. Lt. —Pilot, PAF (301 Bomber Sq.), Pol., 1939; Fr., Eng., 1940-49. POW: Stalag Luft 3, Sagan, Ger., 1942-45. Engr.: Metropolitan Vickers, Eng.; Cambria Spring Co., L.A. Hon. Cross of Valor.

PRZYGODA, REV. JACEK. San Fernando. Professor, Economics, Ret. b. Poland, Oct. 31, 1910. Studied: Diocesan Seminary, Sandomierz, Pol. Ordained, 1933. M.A., Cath. U. Louvain, Belg., 1947; U. Michigan; Ph.D., Cath. U. Ottawa, Can., 1952. Mil. Underground Army, Belg., 1941-45 (Sr. Chaplain). Teacher, 1933-36; Ed. Diocesan Weekly, Sandomierz, Pol. 1937-38; Pol. Cath. Mission, Belg., Netherlands, Luxembourg, 1938-48; Rector, 1942-48; Instr. Orchard Lake Sch., Mich., 1948-55; Prof., Econ., Loyola Marymount U., 1955-76 (Dept. Chm. 1960-67; 69-70); O.L.Q.A. Seminary, San Fernando, 1976-date. Mem. A.A.U.P.; Amer. Assn. for Soc. Econ.; Cath. Hist. Assn.; P.R.C.U.; Polish Museum; .P.I.A.S.; K.F.; Pi Gamma Mu, Omicron Delta Epsilon, Pi Kappa Thau; P.A.H.A. (Pres. 1972). Contr. Ed. *Sodalis*, Orchard Lake, Mich; Pol. Amer. periodicals, newspapers. Ed. *Glos Polski*, weekly, Brussels, 1945-46. Author, four books, publ. Belg., Rome, 1942-57, also, *Texas Pioneers from Poland*. Waco, Tex., 1971. Ed. *Mikolaj Kopernik Quincentennial*, L.A., 1973. Listed: *Who's Who in the West, Who's Who in American Education, Who's Who in Religion, American Men and Women of Science, Dictionary of International Biography, Community Leaders of America, Men of Achievement*. Hon. Golden Cross of Merit w/glaives; Golden Apple: Teacher of the Year, City of L.A. Scroll, 1976. Haiman Medal, 1976.

PSZCZOLKOWSKI-PRESTON, STANLEY V. Kernville. Manufacturer, Ret. Studied: St. John Cantius Sch., Philadelphia, Penn. m. Helen Rose. c. Cynthia, Marianne. Employed, S.S. White Dental Mfg. Co., Phila., 23 yrs.: Co-owner: 1947-60; Owner, Mgr.: 1960-70; Eastern Dental Instrument Co., L.A. Retired 1970.

PUCHLIK, EDMUND M. Los Angeles. Retired. b. Poland. Studied: Journalism, L.A. City Coll. m. Dacia Haywood. c. Kenneth, Gerald, Edmund. Mil. PAF, G.B., Wing Off., RAF, 304 Sq. & Transport Comm., 1942-49. FLC: Lake Ladoga, USSR, 1940-41. Proofreader, Composing Dept., *L.A. Times*, 1948-76. Mem. P.A.F.A.; Amer. Air Force Assn. — Gen. Doolittle Chpt.; London Club. Hon. Cross of Valor (three times), Star of Europe, Distinguished Gold Cross, Defence Medal, numerous others.

RABEK, JAN WITOLD. Los Angeles. Mechanical, Aeronautical Engineer. b. Poland, Dec. 31, 1912. Studied: Warsaw Poly. U., 1932-38; City & Guild Coll., London U., 1943-45. Grad. Mech. & Aero. Engr. m. Jadwiga. Mil. PAF, 1937-39; Fr., Bomber Pilot, RAF, 305 Pol. Bomb. Squad., 1940-end of war. Intl. experience in aerospace industry as mech. & aero. engr. incl. De Haviland, DuPont, Hughes, R.C.A., Teledyne. Mem. P.A.F.A.; Royal Aero. Soc.; Amer. Helicopter Assn. Hon. Virtuti Militari, Cross of Valor w/two bars (three times), Croix de Guerre, Air Crew Europe Star.

RACHWALD, ARTUR RYSZARD. Montecito. Political Scientist. b. Lublin, Poland, Mar. 19, 1944. L.L.M., U. Marie Curie-Sklodowska, Lublin, Pol., 1967; M.A., Intl. Rel., CSUSF, 1972; Ph.D., Pol. Sci., UCSB, 1975. m. Anna Malgorzata Safader. c. Robert

Ryszard, Inga Barbara. Came to U.S., Apr. 1969. Lecturer, Pol. Sci., UCSB. Mem. Amer. Pol. Sci. Assn.; Council on Foreign Relations; Delta Tau Kappa. Contr., Pol. sci. journals on Polish, Soviet, foreign policy.

RADZIWILL, MACIEJ MIKOLAJ. Monterey. Professor. b. Cannes, France, Feb. 24, 1905. Candidat Ingenieur, Gembloux, Belg., 1924; M.A., Soc. Psych., Harvard, 1949. m. Krystyna. Mil. 2nd Lt. PA, 1939; Capt. Pol. Red Cross, Linz, Austria, 1945-46. POW: Murnau, Ger., 1940-45. Instructor, Pol. Language: Harvard, 1949-50; Lecturer, Slavic Languages, UCBerkeley, 1950-51; Prof., Pol. Dept., Defense Language Instr., 1952-58. Mem. A.A.U.P.; P.V.WWII, Post 49; Harvard Alumni Assn. Hon. Cross of Merit, Cross of Valor.

RETT-WILCZKOWIAK, EUGENIA (nee Dmitrewska). Anaheim. m. Henryk. c. Blanca Alejandra Isabella, Viviana Margarita Griselda. Mil. PHA. POW: Sandbostel, Oberlangen, Niederlangen, Ger. Took part in Warsaw Uprising, 1944. Came to U.S., 1966. Hon. Bronze Cross of Merit w/glaives.

RETT-WILCZKOWIAK, HENRYK. Anaheim. m. Eugenia Dmitrewska. c. Blanca Alejandra Isabella, Viviana Margarita Griselda. Mil. PHA. POW: Sanbostel, Lubeka, 1944-45. Took part in Warsaw Uprising, 1944. Came to U.S., 1966. Hon. Virtuti Militari, Cross of Valor, Order of King George VI (British).

ROWINSKI, TADEUSZ FRANCISZEK. Los Angeles. Dentist. b. Krakow, Poland, Apr. 13, 1905. Grad., Conservatory of Mus., Krakow, 1926; Jur., Jagiellonian U., 1925-27; Dental Sch., Warsaw, 1927-31; Post grad. study: Rostock, Ger., 1931-33; D.D.S., USC Dental Sch., 1970. m. 1) Anna Wanner, 2) Aleksandra Bilewicz (div.). c. Jacek, Kajetan, Justyn. Mil. Arty. Coll., 1924-25; PA, Med. Corps, Pol., 1939; PA, Regt. Dentist, Regt. Bandmaster: 2nd Div., 6th Inf. Regt., Fr., 1939-40: 1st Lt., 16th Armor. Brig., G.B., 1945-48. Interned: Switz., 1940-45. Came to U.S., 1958. Employed as TV repairman, 1960-70. Private practice, dentistry, 1970-date. Mem. L.A. Dental Soc.; Cal. Dental Assn.; Amer. Dental Assn; British Dental Assn.; Pol. Med. Alliance, Chi.; P.F.A.C.; Century Club; Amer. Prof. Prac. Assn. Hon. Croix de Guerre, Polish and British Service Medals.

RUSIN, DOREK. Santa Barbara. Sculptor/Accountant. b. Jaworze-Naleze, Poland, Aug. 1, 1914. Studied: business and commerce, incl. school of accounting, in Pol. m. (div.) c. Anna, Jamie. Mil. Eng. 2nd Lt., Pol. Highlanders, 1939, PA, Fr., 1940; Br. Army, Nigeria, Burma, Normandy, 1941-47. Accountant, London, 7 yrs. Since 1955, self-employed accountant, S.B. Concurrently: sculptor in wood, stone. Numerous one-man shows, exhibits in galleries in S.B., S.B. Museum of Art. Rep. in collections, U.S.A., Can., Aust. Mem. S.B. Art Assn., S.B. Sculpture Guild. Hon. Defence Medal, Polish Star, War Medal.

SAMONEK, EDNA JEAN. Concord. Information Analyst. b. Chicago, Illinois. B.A., Stanford U., 1949. Mil. Maj. USA, 1943-46; 1950-51, European Theatre. Information Analyst, Informatics Inc. to date. Mem. Reserve Off. Assn., Assn. of the USA; P.A.C.

SARAN, REV. ANTHONY. Los Angeles. Clergyman. b. Tarnow, Poland, 1907. Studied: Chicago, John Casimir U., Lwow, Jagiellonian U., Krakow, St. Louis, Missouri. Ordained, 1951. Worked as educator and in parish ministry in several states, incl. Florida and California (Northern and Southern). Active in P.A.C. - Calif. Div. (secretary), PAHA - Calif. Chapter (V.P.).

SAWA, M. STANLEY. Downey. m. Irene Michalina. c. Michele Michalina, Michael Walter. Mem. P.U.C.

SAWA, MICHELE MICHALINA. Downey. Student. b. Lynwood, Cal., Aug. 27, 1957. Current study, USC. Mem. P.W.A.; P.U.C. Hon. Miss Polish California, 1975-76; Polish University Club Scholarship Recipient, 1976; 1975 Debutante, Polish Women's Alliance of America; Honors-at-Entrance, USC, 1975. Listed: *Who's Who Among American High School Students*, 1973-74, 1974-75.

SAWA, MICHAEL WALTER. Downey. Student. b. Lynwood, Cal., Jy. 2, 1959. Current study, UCIrvine. Mem. Phi Delta Theta, Cal Theta Chpt.; P.U.C. Lifetime mem., Natl. Hon. Soc. Hon. John Philip Sousa Award, 1976; Marine Band Award, 1976. Listed: *Who's Who Among American High School Music Students*, 1975-76; *Who's Who Among American High School Students*, 1975-76.

SEREMAK, JAN. Santa Monica. Librarian/Publisher. b. Poland, Mar. 5, 1909. Studied: Poznan U., 1936-39; M. Phil., U. Warsaw; M.L.S., U.S.C. m. Czeslawa. Mil. Lt., PA, 1939. Wide experience as secondary school teacher; Librarian; Publisher, Author, over 100 bibliographies.

SERMAK, JEANNETTE LOUISE. Los Angeles. Student. b. Los Angeles, Feb. 14, 1958. L.M.U., soph., English major. Mem. Phi Sigma Kappa; PAHA, LMU Student Chap.; Krakusy. Travel: Poland, England, France.

SHUBSDA, MOST REV. THADDEUS ANTHONY. Los Angeles. Bishop. b. Los Angeles, Cal., Apr. 2, 1925. Studied: L.A. Coll. (Archdiocesan Minor Seminary); St. John's Major Seminary, Camarillo, Cal. Ordained, 1950. Pastoral duties incl. San Antonio de Padua, St. Vibiana Cathedral. Made Titular See of Trau, West. Yugoslavia. Consecrated auxiliary bishop of L.A., Feb. 19, 1977; appointed Episcopal Vicar for S.B. Co., encompassing 15 parishes and approx. 62,000 Catholics. Currently, pastor of St. Paul's Church, L.A. Mem. Matrimonial Tribunal, Soc. for the Propagation of the Faith.

SIENKIEWICZ-POCZAPOWSKI, STASZEWICZ-SWICKI STEFANIA. Los Angeles. b. Mokra Dabrowa, nr. Pinsk, Poland. Lived, Korzeniow nr. Pinsk, Polesie, Pol. Studied: Ecole Normale Catholique, Fribourg, Switzerland. m. Jan Sienkiewicz. c. Danuta Maria, Roman (dec.). Imprisoned by Russians (1940), Brzesc on Bug River. FLC: N. Kazakhstan, USSR, until 1943. Joined PA, under Br. Command, in Teheran, 1943. WAAF, Eng. to 1947. Came to U.S., 1951. Lived, L.B., N.Y.; Chicago, Ill.; Kingston, Rhode Island; L.A. Mem. P.R.C.U. Hon. War Medal, Defence Medal, Polish Air Force Medal.

SIMONS, JEROME A. Los Angeles. Management Executive. b. Detroit, Mich., Aug. 8, 1922. B.S., Met. Engr., Mich. Tech. U., 1949; M.B.A., Ind. Mgmt., USC, 1964. m. Henrietta G. c. Ruthanne, Denise, Gregory, Rebecca, Thomas, John, Rachel. Mil. USA, European Theatre, 1944-45. Engr. Genl. Motors, Dow Chem., Mich., 1950-60; Rockwell Intl., L.A., 1960-70; Mgmt. Exec.: U.S. Postal Service, 1970-date. Past mem. Assoc. Inst. Met. & Mech. Engrs.; A.F.S.; A.C.S.; V.F.W., among others. Mem. P.A.H.A. Two Purple Heart decorations.

SKOCZOWSKI, ADAM EMIL. Walnut Creek. Chemist. b. Turka, Poland, Oct. 21, 1912: Studied: Ecole des Sciences Politiques, (Sorbonne) Paris; Chem. Tech. Coll., Eng.

m. Maria. Mil. PA, Fr., 1940; G.B., 1945-48. POW: Ger., 1940-45. Served, Pol. Foreign
Off. — Pol. Consulate, Lille, Fr., 4 yrs.; Chevron Research Co. — Standard Oil of Cal., 22
yrs. Mem. Amer. Chem. Soc., Cal. Chpt.; P.V.WWII, S.F.; L'Union des Prisonniers de
Guerre Francais, Paris. Hon. Croix de Combattant.

SKOCZOWSKI, MARIA. Walnut Creek. Writer. Pen name: Ewa Emill. b. Lwow,
Poland. M.A., Phil., Jagiellonian U. m. Adam. Stylistic Ed.: *Czytelnik*, Krakow, 8 yrs. Mil.
PHA, 1939-45. Came to U.S., 1959. Mem. Assn. of Authors (ZAIKS), Pol.; Pol. Literary
Soc., Pol.; P.I.A.S. in America. Author of plays, novels.

SKOWRON (SKOWRONEK), ALEKSANDER. Los Angeles. Physician. b. Warsaw,
Poland, Jan. 6, 1914. Grad., Biol., 1938. Entered med. sch., 1938. Completed med.
studies, internship, 1941. Mil. Off. Med. Corps. Field medical hospitals, Fr., 1940, 1942.
Faculty, Med.: Edinburgh U., 1942-47; Pol. Hospital, Wales, 1947. Practicing physician,
31 yrs. Mem. Amer., Pol., Cal. Med. Assn. Fellow: Royal Soc. of Health, Eng.; Amer.
Thoracic Soc.; Amer. Heart Assn.; Fellow: Amer. & Intl. Coll. of Angiology. Hon. War
Medal, Defence Medal, Croix de Combattant.

SKRZYNSKI, ALEKSANDER JERZY (Deceased). b. Poland, Jan. 10, 1899. Studied:
Krakow Acd. of Art, 1917-18; Krakow Fac., Law & Adm., 1918-23; Oxford U., 1944-45;
Edinburgh Coll. of Art, 1945. Pol. Coll. of Art, London, 1946-47. Camberwell Sch. of
Art, London, 1947-48; Arts Students League, N.Y., 1949. Degree: M., Pol. Law & Pol.
Sci., Oxford U. m. Grazyna Felicia Rychlowska. c. Jolanta, Artur. Mil. PA, 1918-21; Pol.
Insurrection, Silesia, 1921; Capt. PA, Pol., Fr., G.B., 1939-48. Civil Svc., Pol.: Secty.,
Prime Minister, Warsaw, 1923-24; Dept. of Interior, Warsaw, 1925-31; Central Dept.,
Soc. Sec., Warsaw, 1931-34; Insp., Soc. Sec., Lublin, 1934-39. Primarily self-employed as
artist, art inst. after WWII. Art Inst.: Anglo-French Centre, London, 1947-48; Quaker
Educ. Center, Pendle Hill, Penn., 1950; S.B. Hillside House, 1957-58. Exhibited:
Edinburgh, Scotland; London, Carmel, Cal.; One-man shows, Utica, N.Y., Dorchester,
N.Y. Posthumous exhibition, S.B. Museum of Art. Author, two books, published in Pol.
prior to World War II on Polish Parliamentary politics, and numerous articles on the
Polish Social Security system.

SLAWIK, REV. BONIFACE JOHN. Clergyman, Ret. b. Poland, My. 14, 1909. M.A.
Theology, Jagiellonian U., 1938. Ordained, Ju. 26, 1938. Served, Katowice Diocese. Mil.
Chap., WWII: Secty., Pol. Mil. Archbishop, Joseph Gawlina; PA, Middle East, 1942; Maj.
2nd PA Corps, Monte Cassino, 1944. Came to U.S. 1949, moved Cal. 1950. Served, L.A.
Diocese, incl. St. Catherine's Acad., Anaheim; St. Gertrude, Bell Gardens. Pastor
Emeritus, ret. 1973. Hon. Knight of Malta.

SLIWICKI, STANISLAW BOLESLAW. Los Angeles. Architect. m. Barbara
Maliszewska. M.S., Arch., Urban Planning, Tech. U. Krakow, Sch. of Architecture.

SLIWINSKI, MITCHELL STANLEY. Hollywood. Aeronautical Engineer. b. Warsaw,
Poland, Dec. 17, 1907. Dipl., Aero. Engr., Tech. U. Warsaw, 1937-39; Dipl., Eng., PUC,
London. m. Kristina Lobnikar. Tech. Rep., Air Force Dept., Warsaw, 1933-39; M.T.S.,
Hupford Machine Works; Tech. Research Spec., Rocketdyne, N. Amer. Rockwell Corp.,;
M.T.S.: Aerospace Corp. Amer. Inst. of Aero. & Astro. Inc.; Amer. Continental Club;
P.A.C.; P.A.F.A.; P.A.V.A.; P.V.WWII; Pol. Fraternity Assn. Listed: *Who's Who in Aviation*,
1973.

SLIWINSKI, STANISLAW. Concord. Civil Engineer, Ret. b. Wilno, Poland, Aug. 3, 1896. M.S., Civil Engr., Tech. U., Warsaw; Grad. Mil. Engr. Acad., Versailles, Fr., 1932. m. Maria Celina Staniewicz. c. Wanda Jadwiga Kossobudzki, Halina Teresa Butler. Mil. Lt. Col. PA, Corps of Engrs., WWI; Bolshevik War of 1919-20; WWII. POW: German prisons: Grodno, Stralsund, Preusish Holland, Neustadt, Torgau, WWI, 1918. Research Engr., equipment fortifications: Poland. Sup. Field Engr., bridge construction, Highway Dept., Buenos Aires, Argentina. Came to U.S., 1962. Mem. P.A.C.; Pol. Cath. Univ. Assn. Veritas. Hon. Mem. P.V.WWII., Argentina. Founder-mem. Assn. Pol. Vet. WWII, Post 499, S.F. Hon. Chevalier of the Order Polonia Restituta; Cross of Valor; Golden Cross of Merit.

SOVINSKI, JOAN DOROTHY. Toluca Lake. Businesswoman. Studied: Providence Sch. of Nursing. Owner, Regal Drapery Co. Mem. Pol. Amer. Bus. & Prof. Club.

SOVINSKI, JOSEPH MICHAEL. Toluca Lake. Businessman. Studied: UCSD. Owner, Regal Drapery Company.

STACHURA, IRENE A. Kensington. Librarian. M.L.S., UCBerkeley. m. Victor F. c. Renata, Edward. Librarian, Berkeley Public Library. Mem. UC Alumni Assn.; Library Sch. Assn.; P.N.A.; Intl. Inst. of the East Bay.

STANLEY, T.T. Santa Barbara. Dentist. b. Chicago, Ill. Studied Pharmacy, Chicago. m. Barbara Lisewski. Worked, Chicago, North Hollywood. Semi-retired; lives, Santa Barbara. Mem. Montecito Country Club, Garden Club, P.A.A.A.

STANWYCK (STANKIEWICZ), STANLEY. Westminster. Engineer. b. Wilno, Poland, Feb. 20, 1926. B.S., Mech. Engr., Cal. State Poly. U., San Luis Obispo. Grad. study: UCLA, UCIrvine, CSULB. m. Gene Julia. c. Gary, John. Mil. PA, It., 1944-46; Sgt. USMC, 1951-53. Interned, Ger., WWII. Aerospace Engr., McDonnell Douglas, Rockwell Intl., 15 yrs. Mem. P.N.A.; Cal Poly Alumni; ASHRAE.

STONE, ROCHELLE (nee Heller). Los Angeles. Professor/Writer. b. Tilsit, Germany, Dec. 23, 1922. Studied: Liceum Stryj, 1939-40; Handel Conser. of Mus., Munich, 1950; Cand. Med., Ludwig Maximilian U., Munich, 1950; M.A. Slavic Lang., UCLA, 1961; Ph.D. Slavic Lit., Lang., UCLA, 1971. m. Mark. FLC: Kielce Ghetto, 1940-42; Skarzysko, 1943-45. Lect. Asst. Prof.; Slavic Lang., Lit. UCLA, 1960-date. Mem. reviewing staff, lit. quarterly, *World Literature Today.* Contr. numerous articles to lit. journals, U.S., Pol. Author, *Boleslaw Lesmian, The Poet and his Poetry,* University of California Press, 1976. Mem. Assn. of Faculty Women, UCLA; Chm., S. Cal. AATSEEL; Pres. Off., Slavic Sect., Philological Assn. of Pacific Coast. Hon. UCLA nominee, Younger Humanist Summer Stipend, NEH, 1976. Outstanding Teaching Award.

SULISTROWSKI, ZYGMUNT. Hollywood. Movie Producer. b. Lwow, Poland. Studied: French Film Academy, Paris. Worked 2 yrs., London, England. Came to U.S., 1950. Directed, acted in, produced several movies (exotic mostly). His first production, *Naked Amazon,* won at Cannes Film Festival. Plans to film his next two productions in Brazil: *Macumba God and Devil,* and *The Splendor of the Amazon.* Organized, The International Nature Enjoyment Club and International Film Ranch (near Amazon). He describes himself as "always in search of beauty, mainly of the inner beauty in people."

SULKOWSKI, JAN S. San Pedro. Businessman. b. Poland. Studied at Commercial Coll. m. Irena. c. Christine, Barbara, Amelia. Served in Pol., Br., U.S. Merchant Marine. Owner, Liquor Store, Torrance. Mem. C. of C.; Liquor Dealers Assn.

SWORAKOWSKA, HELENA (nee Krzywicka). Stanford. Writer. b. Kaunas, Lithuania. M.A., Hist., Phil., U. Warsaw, 1933. m. Witold Saturnin. c. Michal Tomasz. Director, *Polish Cultural Hour* radio program, S.F., since 1972. Mem. P.A.C. - N. Cal. Div. Hon. Silver Cross of Merit. Author, *Polskie szkolnictwo prywatne w Litwie* (Polish Private Schools in Lithuania), Warsaw, 1935.

SWORAKOWSKI, WITOLD SATURNIN. Stanford. Prof. Emeritus. b. Suczawa, Rumania, Jan. 16, 1903. M., Pol. Sci., Acad. of Pol. Sci., Warsaw, 1933. m. Helena Krzywicka. c. Michal Tomasz. Research Inst. of Nationality Affairs, Warsaw, 1930-33; World League of Poles Abroad, Warsaw, 1933-37; Pol. Foreign Svc.: Riga, Prague, Koven, Curitiba, Chicago (vice-consul), 1937-45; Stanford U., Hoover Inst.: Prof. Emeritus, Curator of East European Collections. Previously, Asst. Dir., Assoc. Dir., Cons. to Dir., 1952-70. Collection on Poland at Hoover Inst. named *Witold Sworakowski Collection on Poland*. Mem. P.A.C. - N. Cal. (Pres. 1977); P.A.H.A. Author, four books, publ. Pol., prior WWII, on education, problems of minorities. Recent publ. incl. *The Hoover Collection on Russia*, Stanford, Cal., 1954; *The Communist International and its Front Organizations*, Stanford, Cal., 1965; *World Communism, A Handbook, 1918-65*, Stanford, Cal., 1973. Hon. Silver Cross of Merit (twice).

SZATKOWSKI, THOMAS JOSEPH. Toluca Lake. Businessman. b. Holyoke, Mass., Jy. 27, 1944. B.A., M.A., Ph.D., USC. Owner, Regal Drapery Co. Mem. P.A.H.A.

SZATKOWSKI, WANDA B. Toluca Lake. Businesswoman. Studied: Northampton Comm. Coll. Owner: Regal Drapery Co. Mem. Pol. Amer. Bus. & Prof. Club.

SZCZEPANSKI, EUGENIUSZ JAN. Rancho Palos Verdes. Consultant. b. Minsk, USSR, Jy. 19, 1919. Studied: Pol. Naval Acad., 1937-39; Deg., Mech. Engr., Gdansk Poly., Pol., 1957; Dipl., Sch. of Econ., Sopot, Pol.; Natl. Tax Training Sch., Monsey, N.Y.; Higher Course in Fed. Taxation, 1966; Bus. Mgmt., UCLA, 1963; Dun & Bradstreet, Inc., Bus. Sch., 1967. m. Stanislawa. c. Zygmunt, Hanna. Mil. Cmmdr.: Pol. Navy, 1939-53. POW: Buchenwald, Braunschweig, Woldenberg, Ger., 1939-45. Mgmt., Naval Logistics: Pol. Navy, 1948-53; V. Dir.: Transport Co., Gdansk, Pol., 1953-59. Bus. Mgmt., Med. Econ., 1963-date. Mem. Pol. Naval Assn., London. Hon. Cross of Valor.

SZCZEPANSKI, STANISLAWA. Rancho Palos Verdes. Pediatrician. b. Korewicze, Poland. M.D., Medical Acad., Gdansk, Pol., 1951. m. Eugeniusz. c. Zygmunt, Hanna. Mil. PHA, Nurse, 1939-44. Poland: Pediatrics Dept., Senior Assist., Med. Acad., Gdansk, 1955-60; Private medical practice, Gdynia, 1951-60. U.S.: Princ. Research Asst.: Radio. Dept., UCLA, 1960-62; Instr., Ped.: USC, Sch. of Med., 1968-73; Instr., Ped.: UCLA Sch. of Med., 1973-date. Private medical practice, Redondo Beach, under name: *Stanislawa Szczepanski Hanka*, 1971-date. Mem. A.M.A.; C.M.A.; L.A.C.M.A.; L.A. Pediatric Soc.; Amer. Med. Soc., Vienna, Austria. Diplomate, Pol. Board of Pediatrics, first, second grade. Hon. Amer. Med. Assn. Recognition Awards.

SZCZEPANSKI, ZYGMUNT JERZY. Hermosa Beach. Management Consultant. b. Gdynia, Poland, Mar. 31, 1948. B.A., Pol. Sci., M.B.A., CSCDH, 1973, 1976. Asst. Dir., Pub. Affairs & Co-ordinator of Sch. Relations: CSCDH, 1973-76; Dir., Sch. & Coll.

Relations, CSCDH, 1976-77. Owner: Zygmunt & Assoc., Publ. Relations, Advertising Mgmt., Cons. Agency, 1976-date. Mem. CSU Conference Planning Comm. & Admissions Council; L.A. Co. Beach Advisory Comm.; Exec. Comm., Amer. Cancer Soc. Listed: *Who's Who Among Student Leaders, Who's Who Among Students in American Universities.*

SZEPTYCKI, J. GEORGE. Los Angeles. Architect. b. Poland, Oct. 6, 1915. B.A., Arch., Poly. Sch. of Arch., Warsaw, 1939; M.A., Arch., U.S.C., 1952; M.A., Econ., U.S.C., 1974. m. Inka. c. Thomas, Christopher. Mil. PHA, 1939-44. Interned, Warsaw Prison "Pawiak," 1942. FLC: Cologne, Thuringen, 1944-45. Lic. Arch. Cal., Fla., Ill., Penn. Planner, Disneyland Masterplan, 1954-55. Master Planner, Designer, Sanctuary of the Millennium of Poland's Christianity, Doylestown, Penn., 1975-date. During past 20 yrs., designed approx. 30 churches, many high schools, elementary schools, institutional buildings. Serves as Art. Dir., Asst. Art Dir., movie studios. Mem. A.I.A.; Guild for Rel. Arch.; Soc. of Motion Pictures & TV Art Dirs. Received City of Los Angeles Certificate of Appreciation for "Outstanding Citizenship and Contribution to the Preparation of the Hollywood Community Plan," 1970, also, Daughters of the American Revolution National Award for "Outstanding Contribution to American Culture," 1971. Author, several magazine articles on art, architecture.

SZMIT, EDWARD WLADYSLAW. Upland. Physician/Cardiologist. b. Poland, Sept. 12, 1931. M.D., Summa cum laude, U. Med. Acad., Lublin, 1955; Cert. Spec., Internal Med., Post Grad. Med. Sch. of Warsaw, 1959; Post Grad. study: Inst. of Cardiology, Warsaw. Med. Internship: St. Louis City Hosp.; Fellowship, Cardiology, Chi. Med. Sch.; Fellowship, Cardiology, White Memorial Med. Center, L.A. m. Halina Apolonia. c. Donna, Andrew. Dept. Supt., Krosno Hosp. (Pol.), teaching internal med.; examiner in cardiac, pulmonary diseases, 1959-62; Research Asst.: Phys., Phar. Dept., Bristol, Eng.; Sr. Reg., St. Bartholomew Hosp. Med. Sch., London, 1965-66; Dir.: Coronary Care Unit, White Med. Center, L.A., 1969-71. Currently, medical practice in cardiology. Mem. A.M.A.; C.M.A.; San Bernardino Med. Soc.; P.A.H.A.

SZPAK, STANISLAW J. San Diego. Chemical Engineer. b. Schenectady, N.Y., Nov. 17, 1920. M.S., Chem. Engr., Tech. U. of Slask, Pol., 1946; Ph.D., Chem. Engr., U. Penn., 1961. m. Bozica. Research Engr.: Gen. Elec. Co., Phila., Penn., 1956-61; Sup.: Stanford Research Inst., S. Cal. Labs., So. Pasadena, 1961-62; Staff Scientist: Lockheed, Palo Alto Research Lab., 1962-68; Research Chem.: Naval Weapons Center, Corona, 1968-70; Mare Is. Naval Shipyard, Vallejo, 1970-72; Naval Electronics Lab. Center, S.D., 1972-date. Numerous publications in *Journal of Electrochemical Society, Journal of Chemistry and Physics.* Patent granted, Apr. 1967.

SZRAJBMAN, SEVERYN SYMCHA. La Habra. Financier. b. Warsaw, Poland, Sept. 17, 1931. Studied: Pol.; Italy; Tokyo; Sofia U.; Oxford, Eng.; UCLA. m. Tuula Marjatta. c. Anne, Roy. Mil. PHA, 1944-46. Survivor, Warsaw Ghetto. Business interests in Cal. Land Development, film production, Intl. Banking. Mem. Optimists Intl.

SZYMANSKI, SLAWOMIR MACIEJ. San Pedro. Tool Designer. b. Krasnystaw, Poland, Aug. 1, 1920. Studied: Natl. Tech. Sch., Warsaw; Warsaw Poly U.; Natl. Maritime Acad., Gdynia; Harbor Coll., L.A. m. Stanislawa Agnieszka. Mil. PHA, 1939-44; Warsaw Uprising. CC: Grossborn, Lubeka. Pres. & Gen. Mgr.: Kasco Machine & Engr., Inc., 1961-date. Mem. Amer. Soc. of Mfg. Engrs. Hon. Cross of Valor.

TABASZ, MARY MARGARET. Los Angeles. Student. Loyola Marymount U., junior. Mem. P.A.H.A., Loyola Belles, Univ. Council; CSF Seal Bearer. Calif. State Scholarship Award winner. Travel: Poland, Czechoslovakia, Austria, France, Germany, Switzerland, Lichtenstein.

TALAGA, JAMES C. Santa Barbara. Businessman/Attorney. b. Oct. 25, 1937. B.A., St. Mary's Coll., Winona, Minn.; L.L.B., J.B., Notre Dame U. m. (div.) c. Allison, Laurie, Jimmy. Mil. Capt., USAF - JAG, 1961-64. Pres. Morzynski-Talaga Coal Co., S.B. Attorney, private practice. Part-time Juvenile Court Judge; Montecito Union Sch. Board, 1970-74, Pres. 1974; Board of Dir. Montecito Protective Assn., 1974-75; Board of Dir., S.B. Co. Bar Assn., 1972; Judge Pro Tem and Small Claims Judge; Pres. S.B. Soc. for Autistic Children, 1976; Vice-Chm. Parents Advisory Gr., Garfield Sch. for the Handicapped, 1977.

TOCZYLOWSKI, HENRYK STANISLAW. Topanga. Engineer, Ret. b. Zakopane, Poland, Dec. 15, 1903. M. Engr., Warsaw Inst. of Tech., 1929. m. Helena Szreder (dec.). c. Ewa Teresa. Mil. PA, Signal Corps: Fr., 1939-40; G.B., 1940-42; Pol. Navy, 1942-46; Lt. Cmmdr., Royal Naval Scientific Svc., 1946-48. Came to U.S. 1970. Engr.: Warsaw, Pol., 1928-39; Royal Naval Signal Est., G.B., 1942-43; G.P.I./B.O.P. Co. Ltd., Can. Mem Inst. of Radio Engr., G.B.; Inst. of Prof. Engr. of Quebec; Inst. of Elec. & Electronic Engrs., U.S.A. Three patents granted.

TOLOSKO, EDWARD J. Lompoc. Novelist. b. June 23, 1922, San Francisco. m. Doreen Shauer. c. Lee Ann, Alane Susan, Margaret Jean, Jean Louis, Edward J. II. Mil. U.S. Navy, WWII. Author, *Sakuran* (to be published, Spring, 1978, by Farrar, Straus & Giroux, New York). Hobbies: music, poetry, painting.

TOPOR, FRANK. Sunnyvale. Engineer, Ret. b. Nowy Targ, Poland, Dec. 22, 1907. Studied: Teachers Coll., Krakow. m. Jadwiga Helena. Mil. 2nd Lt., PA, Pol., 1939; Syria, Egypt, Palestine, 1940-45. Taught school, Pol. 11 yrs. Metal worker, Sweden, 3 yrs. College Instructor, Cal. 5 yrs. Lab Tech. Shockley Transistor Lab.; ITT Semiconductor Lab.; Fairchild Research & Dev. Lab. Palo Alto, 10 yrs. Mem. P.V.WWII. Hon. Africa Star, Defence Medal, War Medal.

TUKAJ-DZIUNIKOWSKA, EUGENIA BARBARA. West Covina. b. Poland, Jan. 15, 1943. Studied: Psych., Loyola Marymount U., L.A.

TURHOLLOW, ANTHONY FRANCIS. Los Angeles. Professor, American History. b. Dec. 1, 1915, N.Y.C. B.S., M.A., Rutgers U.; Ph.D. UCBerkeley. m. Charlotte Elizabeth. c. Charlotte Anne, Anthony, Charles. Mil. USA, Corps of Engrs., 1941-45. Prof., Amer. Hist., Loyola Marymount U., 25 yrs. Hist. cons. USA Corps of Engrs. L.A. Dist. past 10 yrs. Mem. A.A.U.P.; Amer. Hist. Assn.; Org. of Amer. Historians; West. Hist. Assn.; P.A.H.A.; Amer. Cath. Hist. Assn.; Phi Beta Kappa; Phi Alpha Theta; Pi Gamma Mu; Alpha Sigma Nu. Fulbright Lecturer in India. Author, *A History of the Los Angeles District U.S. Army Corps of Engineers 1898-1965.* Los Angeles, 1976.

TYSZKIEWICZ, JANUSZ LACKI. Santa Barbara. Professor/Librarian. b. Poland, Jy. 28, 1900. B.S., Pol. Econ., U. Poznan, 1924. M.L.S., UCBerkeley, 1958. m. Elizabeth Zamoyska. Mil. Capt., PA, 1918-19; 1939-48, Pol., Fr., Ger. Adj. to Gen. Wl. Sikorski, attached to Marshall Montgomery, Pancer & Parachute Corps. Resettlement Off. Language Inst., USA Language Sch., Monterey; Librarian, University Professor. Mem. A.A.U.P.; British Inst. of Mgmt. Hon. Cross of Valor, British War Medal.

VARS, HENRY (Deceased). Los Angeles. Composer. b. Warsaw, Poland, Dec. 29, 1902. Studied composition, composing: Conservatory of Mus., Warsaw. m. Elizabeth. c. Diane, Robert. Mil. PA, 1920, 1939; 2nd Lt. PA, 1941-46. Worked as composer, 47 yrs. Wrote music for 67 Pol. movies, 39 U.S. movies, music for TV series, approx. 100 popular songs. Major works incl., *Symphonie Elegie, Sonatina for Orchestra*, Orchestral Suite: *City Sketches*. Mem. A.S.C.A.P.; A.G.A.C.; A.F.M., Local 47; P.A.H.A. Hon. Cross of Merit w/glaives, Monte Cassino Cross. Died Sept. 1, 1977.

WAGNER, GEORGE JANUSZ. Los Angeles. Engineer/Real Estate Management. b. Wilno, Poland, Jan. 7, 1932. M.S., Struct. Engr., Gdansk Poly. Institute. m. Lenna Maria. c. Barbara, Irene. Formerly professional engr. w/firms in N.Y., L.A., Pasadena. Currently self-employed, real estate management. Licensed prof. engr., State of Cal. Mem. Struct. Engrs. Assn., S. Cal.; Precast Concrete Institute.

WAGNER, LENNA MARIA. Los Angeles. Engineer. M.S., Structural Engr., Gdansk Poly. Institute. m. George Janusz. c. Barbara, Irene. Engineer, private practice, Ismail & Wagner, L.A. Registered professional engr., Poland, State of Cal.

WALLING, LEON CASIMIR. Capistrano Beach. Flight Purser. b. Plains, Penn., Ju. 25, 1920. Studied at Language Schools. m. Margaret Mary Slattery. c. Karen Anne, Lee Burren. Mil. Sgt. USA, 1942-45, Asiatic-Pacific Theatre. Flight Purser, Trans World Airline, 1946-date. Mem. P.A.H.A. Hon. Asiatic-Pacific Ribbon w/5 Bronze Stars.

WEYNEROWSKA, HANKA KALI. San Francisco. Artist (Brush Name — Kali). b. Warsaw, Poland. Studied: Warsaw Academy of Fine Arts; Royal Academy of Fine Arts, Brussels. m. Henryk. Mil. PHA, 1940-45, Warsaw Uprising, 1944. POW: Zeitheim, Ger., 1944-45. Mem. P.A.C.; P.H.A.A. Hon. mem. Artist Equity Assn.

WIERZBIANSKA, ALINA. Oakland. Professor, Philosophy. Dipl., Phil., U. Warsaw. M.L.S., M.A., Fr., UCBerkeley, 1957, 1960. Ph.D., trés honorable, Sorbonne, Paris, 1965. c. Elzbieta Helena Ewa. Lect.: Coll. of the Holy Name, Oakland; U.S.F.; UCBerkeley (Extension). Pres. Pol. Cath. U. Assn., Veritas, 1974-75. Co-edit., *Aesthetics in Twentieth Century Poland*. 1973.

WARNO, HENRYK. Long Beach. Engineer/Businessman. b. Poland. Studied: University of Wroclaw. m. Irena. c. Susan, Katherine, John Christopher. Co-owner, Warno Development Company, Seal Beach. Mem. P.A.H.A. - Cal. Chap. Board of Directors, Prof. organizations.

WARNO, IRENA. Long Beach. Pharmacist. b. Poland. Studied: West Germany; Albany, N.Y., College of Pharmacy. m. Henryk. c. Basia Rosemary, Susan, Katherine, John Christopher. Runs, Corner Drug Store; co-owner, Warno Development Co.; both Seal Beach. Mem. P.A.H.A. - Cal. Chap., v.p. Prof. organizations.

WDOWIAK, JERRY. Pacific Palisades. Manufacturer. b. Poland. Studied: College of Engineering; maj. Dental Technology; Lodz, Poland, grad. 1967. Came to U.S., 1968. m. Krystyna, in Paris, France. c. Bryan, Kareen. Krystyna studied: College of Engineering; maj. Chemistry; Lodz. Came to California, 1970. Jerry's training, Alexander's Porcelain Studio. Jerry Wdowiak Dental Ceramics, Inc., Los Angeles, started in 1971. Mem. National Dental Lab. Assn.

WEGNER, STANLEY. Northridge. Medical Research. b. Poznan, Poland, Apr. 21, 1939. m. Margaret Carolyn Currie. c. Anne Elizabeth, Robert Loren. B.A., Math., CSUN, 1969. Lab. Dir. Cedars-Sinai Med. Center, 1961-72; Research Dir. Century City Cardiovascular Research Found., 1972-76; Pres. Eldeco Medical Prod., Inc., and Comp-U-Med Services Co., 1977-date. Mem. L.A. Co. Heart Assn; Amer. Heart Assn. (Council on Clinical Cardiology). Author, over 30 publications in cardiovascular research.

WESTWALEWICZ, HENRYK. Los Angeles. Engineer. b. Krakow, Poland, Sept. 27, 1913. Studied: La Salle Coll., Chi. m. Lila. Mil. PHA, 1939-45. POW: Lubeck, Ger. After WWII, worked as volunteer social worker for UNRRA. Elec. Designer, Ger., U.S. Founded P.A.C.F.U.C., L.A., served as mgr. 4 yrs. Mem. P.N.A.; P.A.C.; P.P., P.A.H.A., Soc. of Poles in Germany.

WILK, RICHARD BOLESLAW. Santa Barbara. Industrialist. b. Sept. 15, 1916, Siberia, Russia. Studied: Forestry, Eng., Poland; Mechanical Eng., Gr. Britain. Glider pilot, Poland. Automatic pilot specialist, Gr. Br. Instructor, taught in No. 1 RAF School; curriculum director; wrote manuals. m. Mary Frances Hesmer. c. Diana, Jennifer, Michael. Came to California, Jan. 3, 1949. Started, Wilk Quality Electric Instruments, Surgical Instruments Service, Metermaster, Vivonex, Electromatic, and others. Has several patents, mostly in electrical measurements. Co-founder, Precision Measurem's Assn. Mary F. Wilk is V.P. & Treasurer, The Wilk Industries.

WILK, STEFAN PIOTR, D.A.C.R. Studio City. Physician. b. Kamienobrod (Lwow), Poland, 1917. Studied: Lwow Poly., 1937-39; M.D., Dr. Med. Sci., U. Zurich Med. Sch., 1947, 1948. m. Wanda Helen Harasimowicz. c. Diane Lillian. Mil. PA, Fr., 1940. Mil. internee, Switz., 1940-47. Asst. Prof., UCLA Med. Sch., 1954-57; Private practive, radiol., L.A., 1957-date; Dir., Radiol. Queen of Angels Hosp. and Santa Marta Hosp.; Sch., X-Ray Tech., Queen of Angels Hosp.; Drs. Wilk, Aiken & Pirruccello, Inc., L.A. Mem. A.M.A.; C.M.A.; L.A.C.M.A.; R.S.N.A.; A.C.R.; C.R.S.; P.N.A. Author, co-author, numerous scientific medical publications, Switzerland and U.S. Editor, translator, two medical textbooks; one w/world-wide circulation. Winner, Certificate of Merit, Radiol. Soc. of N.A., for scientific exhibit.

WISSEMA, ELZBIETA GRAZYNA DABROWSKI. Rosemead. Artist/Poet. b. London, England, Feb. 7, 1949. Studied: Pasa. City Coll. Contributing poet, *Polish Americans in California, 1827-1977.*

WITT, FRANK R. Reseda. Mechanical Flight Technician. b. Schenectady, N.Y. m. Staycie. c. Robert, Phyllis, Michael. Mech. Flight Tech.: Rockwell Intl., El Segundo, 1952-date.

WITT, STAYCIE. Reseda. Illustrator. b. South Amboy, N.J. m. Frank R. c. Robert, Phyllis, Michael. Illustrator, U.S. Postal Svc., Van Nuys.

WOJCIECHOWSKI, CHRISTOPHER RICHARD. Bel Air. Architect/Builder-Contractor. b. Warsaw, Poland, April 1, 1934. B.A., Arch., U.S.C. m. Elizabeth. c. Jody, Maria, Michael. Architect, Builder-Contractor. Mem. Amer. Arch. Assn. Designed — among others — Hillside Village, Torrance.

WOJCIECHOWSKA-RODMAN, MAIA. Santa Fe, New Mexico. Author/Lecturer. b. Warsaw, Poland, Aug. 8, 1927. Studied: Immaculate Heart Coll., Los Angeles. c. Oriana,

Eleonora. Author, thirteen published books for children and teenagers. One of them, *Till the Break of Day*, had to do with her growing up in Poland; the other was, *Winter Tales from Poland*. Lecturer, public, private schools, universities.

WOJCIECHOWSKI, ZBIGNIEW MIKOLAJ. Burbank. Engineer/Lawyer. b. Warsaw, Poland, Dec. 6, 1925. B.B., Radio-TV Engr., Pacific States U.; J.D., Southwestern U. m. Janet L. c. Mark Z. Mil. Sgt.-Pilot, PAF, G.B., 1945. Engr., Natl. Broadcasting Co., Burbank, 1948-date. Also, law practice. Mem. P.A.F.A.; Cal. State Bar; L.A. Bar Assn.; Burbank Bar Assn.; Cal. Trial Assn.; Amer. Bar Assn.; Judicature Assn.

WOJCIECHOWSKA, ZOFIA Y. Burbank. Retired. b. Warsaw, Poland, Sept. 4, 1894. Studied: Teachers Coll.; Bus. Sch.; Court Clerical Sch. m. Lt. Col. Zygmunt (dec.). c. Zbigniew, Maria, Krysztof. Bus. & prof. experience: Bank off., teacher, court clerk. Ret. Mem. Friends of Pol.; Polish Parish (O.L.B.M.R.C.C.); Pol. Language Sch.; P.W.A. Life mem. P.F.A.C.; Pol. Sch. P.T.A. Hon. City of L.A. Meritorious Service Award, Cross of Merit, Hon. Member Award, PAF.

WOJCIECHOWSKI, ZYGMUNT (Deceased). Lt. Col. PAF, Ret. Los Angeles. b. Warsaw, Poland, Apr. 24, 1896. Grad. Land Engr., Warsaw Poly.; Studied: Pol. Comm. Staff Sch.; Ecole Militaire; Ft. Leavenworth Mil. Comm. Staff Coll. m. Zofia. c. Zbigniew, Maria, Krzysztof. Mil. PA, 1915-29; PAF, 1929-45. Prof. USA Language Sch., Monterey. Mem. P.A.F.A.; Friends of Pol. Decorated by Poland, France, Belgium, incl. Virtuti Militari, Cross of Bravery (three times). Died, Los Angeles, Feb. 28, 1956.

WOYTAK, RICHARD ANDREW. Carmel. Educator. b. Poznan, Poland, Dec. 18, 1940. Studied: Oakland City Coll.; B.A., CSUSF; M.A., Monterey Inst. of Foreign Studies; Ph.D., UCSB. m. Lidia Teresa. c. Adela Alexandra. Mil. E-4, USA. Mem. Amer. Hist. Assn.; Amer. Assn. for the Advancement of Slavic Studies; P.A.H.A.; P.A.C.; P.I.A.S.; Pilsudski Inst. Works published in *East European Quarterly, Slavic Review, Polish Review.*

WOZNIAK, STANLEY M. Torrance. Dentist, Ret. b. Buffalo, N.Y., Mar. 1896. m. Clara G. Jaroch. Mil. USA, Natl. Guard. Private practice. Mem. P.R.C.U.; Amer. Legion.

WOZNICKI, ANDRZEJ MIKOLAJ. San Francisco. Clergyman/Professor. Philosophy. b. Katowice, Poland, Oct. 19, 1931. Studied: Major Seminary, Poznan, 1948-56; B.A., M.A., Cath. U. Lublin, 1956-59; Ph.D., U. Toronto, 1965-67; M.S.L., Pontifical Inst. of Medieval Studies, Toronto, 1963-65. FLC: Ostrow, Tarnow, Pol. 1940-43. Asst. Prof., Phil., 1967-74; Assoc. Prof., Phil., 1974-date, U.S.F.; Act. Chm., Phil. Dept. U.S.F., 1969-70. Mem. Intl. Soc. for Metaphysics, London; Société des Amies de la Théologie et la Philosophie Chrétienne, Rome; Amer. Cath. Phil. Assn., Wash., D.C.; A.A.U.P.; P.I.A.S.A.; P.A.C. - N. Cal. Div., 1968-71; Natl. Comm. on Religious Affairs, PAC, Det., 1969-date. Listed: *International Scholars Directory, Contemporary Writers, Dictionary of International Biography, Men of Achievement, Who's Who in the West.* Award for Polish Cultural Hour, at KQED, BEATA, S.F., 1970. Prof. mountain climbing, part. in expeditions incl. Yukon Centennial Expedition in St. Elias, Can.; Atlas Expedition, N. Africa; Arctic expeditions to Spitzbergen, Greenland, Iceland.

WROBEL, ALFRED JOHN. Professor, History. b. Chester, Penn., 1928. B.A., Humanities, Swarthmore Coll.; M.A., Hist., Columbia U.; Ph.D., Hist., USC. m. Olga Eugenia. c. Pamela K., Peter D., Derek A. Mil. USA, Occupation, Japan, 1946-47.

CSCDH, part time instr., 1967-71; Prof., Hist., El Camino Coll., 1956-date. Mem. Amer. Hist. Assn.; Amer. Fed. of Teachers; F.A.C.C.C. Recipient, Fulbright Research Grant, U. Warsaw, 1963-64.

WYGRZYWALSKI, JERZY (a/k/a George Milton). Hollywood. Businessman. b. Nowy Sacz, Poland. Owner: Quality Light Metric Co., Hollywood, specializing in calibration and measurement equipment.

WYSYNSKY, OTTON V. Montecito. Consulting Petroleum Geologist. B.A.; M.A.; M. Sc.; Ph.D. m. Gertrude. Petroleum geol., engr., in Pol., Rumania, Iraq, Turkey, Peru, Brazil, U.S.A., 1923-50; Petroleum geol.: Cal. State Lands Comm., 1950-70; Cons. petroleum geol., 1970-date. Reg. Geol., Cal. Mem. Amer. Assn. Petroleum Geol.; Amer. Inst. Mining & Met. Engrs.; Assn. Prof. Geol. Scientists.

ZAGOREWICZ, THADDEUS A. San Francisco. Editor/Businessman. b. Poland. Studied: U. Salzburg, Austria; S.F. Police Academy. m. Sophie. c. Christine W., Barbara A. Mil. Lt. PHA, 1939-45; USA, 1945-48; M.Sgt.., USA Intelligence Units, 1951-62. POW, Goerlitz, Ger., 1944-45. Pres. Pol. Welfare Office, Intl. Relief Org., Voecklabruck, Austria; Co-Ed. Pol. monthly *Glos Polski*, Gmunden, Austria. Ed.: *Polak w Kalifornii* (Pol. Californian), S.F., 1951-54; Ed.: *Kronika Zachodnia* (Pol. W. Chronicle), S.F., 1954-55. Ed.: *Polonica Austriackie*, 1945-55 (in manuscript). Pres. self-employed, retail foods. Life Mem. Lions Eye Found., Cal. - Nev., Inc.; 2 V.P.: Lions Intl.; Life Mem. Amer. Rifle Assn.; Rifle & Pistol Assn.; Mem. Non-Comm. Off. Assn., USA; Amer. Legion Post 238, Pacifica; N. Lake Tahoe, C. of C.; Founding Pres.: I. Paderewski Club; Mem. P.A.C. - N. Cal. Chpt. Hon. Silver Cross of Merit.

ZAHORSKI, ADAM T. (Deceased). Aeronautical Scientist. Armour Inst. of Tech., 1924-27; B.S., Aero. Engr., U. Mich., 1928; M.S., Aero. Engr. Cal. Inst. Tech., 1931; Ph.D., Engr. Mech., U. Mich., 1937. Reg. Mech. Engr., Cal.; Consultant, scientist, engr., Lockheed Air Corp.; Northrop Air. Inc.; N. Amer. Aviation, Inc.; Aerophysics Dev. Corp., S.B.; Pres., Chief Engr.: Zahorski Engr., Inc., S.B. Mem. Amer. Assn. f/Advancement of Science; Sigma Xi. Assoc. Fellow: Amer. Inst. Aero., Astro. Listed: *American Men of Science, Who's Who in World Aviation and Astronautica*. Publ. nine papers, field of aero., 1937-62. Several patents, fields of variable gearing, fluid meters, structural sandwich, structural fasteners.

ZAKRZEWSKI, ZDZISLAW. Foster City. Engineer. b. Lwow, Poland, Nov. 11, 1919. Studied: Lwow Poly.; PUC, London. m. Zofia. c. Wojciech, Szczepan, Maciej, Jacek, Agnieszka, Marek. Mil. Pol. Highlanders Brigade, Norway; PAF, G.B. CC: El Deposito de Concentracion Miranda del Ebro, Spain, 1940-43. Engr., Eng., Detroit, Mich.; N.J.; N.Y. Proj. Engr., Bausch & Lomb, Rochester, N.Y.; Staff Engr., Itek Corp., Lexington, Mass.; Proj. Engr., Bay Area Rapid Transit System, S.F.; Mgr. R&D, Finnigan Corp., Sunnyvale; Proj. Engr. Environtech Corp., Belmont. Org. Assn. of Pol. Students Abroad w/20 world-wide chpts. P.P., Pol. Students Assn, G.B., 1944-46; Sarmatia Universal - N.Y. Chpt., 1952-53; Circle of New Polonia, Bayonne, N.J., 1953-56; Pol. Natl. Dem. Party - N.Y. Chpt., 1954-55. Secy. P.V.WWII, Rochester, N.Y., 1958-59; P.P., P.A.C. - N.. Cal. Div., 1973-76; P.N.A. - Gr. 7, S.F., 1968-69. Pres., P.A.C.F.C.U., 1973-date. Co-Dir., Polish Radio Program. Chosen "Man of the Year," Intl. Inst., Oakland.

ZAWADZKI, SIENKIEWICZ-POCZAPOWSKI DANUTA MARIA. Los Angeles. Librarian. b. Warsaw, Poland. Lived Korzeniow, nr. Pinsk, Pol. Studied: Gymnasium, Sisters of St. Family of Nazareth, Warsaw. B.A., U. Rhode Island. M.L.S., Immaculate

Heart Coll., L.A., 1964. m. Michal Ignacy. c. Roman John. Imprisoned by Russians, (1940) in Brzesc on Bug River. FLC: N. Kazakhstan, USSR, 1940-42. Joined Pol. Forces, Buzuluk, USSR, 1942. Mil. Personal Asst., Dept. C-in-C., PAF, under Br. Comm; WAAF, Eng. (Sect. Off., hon. discharged, 1947). Sr. Librarian: HAC, Culver City, 1964-date. Mem. Spec. Libr. Assn.; Amer. Libr. Assn.; P.P., P.F.A.C.; P.P., Pol. Millennium Libr.; P.N.A.; P.R.C.U. Hon. War Medal, Defence Medal, Polish Air Force Medal. Listed: *Who's Who in Library Science.*

ZAWADZKI, MICHAL IGNACY. Los Angeles. Economist. b. Sokolniki, nr. Leczyca, Poland. Son, Halina v. Boetticher, Tadeusz Zawadzki. Lived, Wolka Kozodawska, Co. Grojec, and Lanieta nr. Kutno. Studied: Szkola Mazowiecka, Warsaw; M.S., Coll. of Agric. (S.G.G.W.) & Sch. of Pol. Sci., Warsaw, 1938; B. Litt., U. Oxford, 1959; Ph.D., Agric. Econ., U. Illinois, 1955. m. Danuta Sienkiewicz. c. Roman John. Mil. PAF, 1938-48. Imprisoned by Russians, spent 2 yrs. in jail and FLC, 40 Lagier NKWD, nr. White Sea, USSR. Rejoined PAF, USSR, 1941. Served Iran, Iraq, Palestine. PAF/RAF, G.B., 1942-48, (Flt. Lt., pilot). Research: Econ. of Eastern Europe, U. Chicago, 1955; Agr. Econ., U. Rhode Island, 1955-59. Teacher, econ., U. Rhode Island, Loyola Marymount U., L.A., 1959-61. Part-time instr. econ., CSULB, 1965-67; CSULA, 1968-72. State of Cal. Motor Vehicle Pollution Board, 1961-65; Cal. Dept. of Water Resources, 1965-date. Mem. P.N.A.; P.R.C.U.; P.A.F.A.; P.U.C.; Amer. Farm Econ. Assn.; West. Agric. Econ. Assn.; Pres., Pol. Amer. Dem. Club, S. Cal.; Pres., Chpt. Gdansk, Pol. West. Assn.; V.P., P.A.C. - Cal., Ariz. Div.; P.P., P.F.A.C. Author, co-author, several university publ., articles in prof. journals, bulletin of Cal. Dept. of Water Resources. Hon. War Medal, Defence Medal, Polish Air Force Medal, Golden Cross of Merit. U. Illinios Fellowship, 1953-54. Listed: *Dictionary of International Biography: American Men of Science,* 10 ed.

ZAWADZKI, ROMAN JAN. Los Angeles. Attorney/Engineer. b. London, England. B.S., Gen. Engr., UCLA, 1969; J.D., Southwestern U. Sch. of Law. Civil Engr.: USA, Corps of Engrs., 1969-date; Staff Mem., Comm. Legal Assistance Center, L.A., 1975-76. Mem. Amer. Bar Assn.; State Bar of Cal.; L.A. Co. Bar Assn.; Beverly Hills Bar Assn.; Criminal Courts Bar Assn.; Amer. Soc. Mech. Engrs.; P.A.C.; Intl. Org. of Prof. in Parliamentary Law; Pol. Amer. Dem. Club of S. Cal.; Sgt.-at-Arms, Secy. Toastmaster Intl. Club, 1971-74; V.P., Natl. Fed. of Fed. Employees; Secy. O.L.B.M.R.C.C. Parish Council, 1974-77; Mem. Bd. of Dir., Asst. Secy., Pol. Retirement Foundation, 1975-date. Reg. Civil Engr., Cal. Hon. American Jurisprudence Award, 1975.

ZAWODNY, JANUSZ KAZIMIERZ. Claremont. Professor. b. Warsaw, Poland, Dec. 11, 1921. B.S., Intl. Rel., Iowa, 1950; M.A., 1951; Ph.D., Pol. Sci., 1955. Mil. PHA, 1940-44. Free PA, 1945-48. Resident Grants: Princeton, 1957; Stanford, 1964; Hoover Inst., Stanford, 1965; U. Penn., 1968; Relm Found.; 1966-67; Foreign Pol. Resident Inst., U. Penn., 1967; Amer. Phil. Soc., 1968; Ford Found., Faculty Resident Fellow, 1968-69; Res. Assoc. Center for Intl. Affairs, Harvard, 1968; Sr. Assoc. Mem., St. Anthony's Coll., Oxford, 1968-69. Prof., Pol. Sci., Intl. Relations; Princeton, 1955-58, CSCSF, 1960-61; Washington U., St. Louis, 1963-65. Prof. Claremont Grad. School, Cal., to date. Ed., contr. publications on intl. relations, soc. sci. Author: *Death in the Forest,* story of the Katyn Forest massacre, Notre Dame U. Press, 1962.

ZAWOJSKI, CHRISTOPHER. Los Altos. Swimming Coach. b. Regensburg, Germany, Apr. 16, 1948. A.A., Foothill Coll.; B.A., Psych., Stanford U. Grad. study, CSUSJ. Grad. pilot, Hillview Pilot Training Sch. Mil. USN, USS Enterprise, Viet Nam Combat action, 1968-72; Reserve duty, 1972. Former Flight Simulator Inst., Foothill Coll., Sr. Swim

Coach, Deanza Swim Club; Swim Coach, HI., working w/natl., world ranked Olympic athletes. Mem. Amer. Swimming Coaches Assn.; Aircraft Owners & Pilots Assn. Hon. Navy Commendation Medal for Heroic Achievement, Vietnam Gallantry Cross, Vietnam Service & Campaign Medals, Expeditionary Medal. Other Awards: Red Cross Recognition Certificate, Kalos Kagathos Swimming & Water Polo Forum Citation.

ZAWOJSKI, WALTER (WLADYSLAW). Los Altos. Artist. b. Przemysl, Poland. Grad. Photo. Advanced Sch. of Artistic Photo., Warsaw; Studied: Fine Arts Sch., Budapest; Arch., U. Budapest; M.A., Art, CSUSJ; Post grad. study, Phil. of Esthetics, Theory of Art, to date. m. Maria Perzanowska. c. Christopher, Karen Jackson. Mil. PA, 1939. Internment, Esztergom, Hungary. Mem. of special services for U.S. Occupation Forces, Bavaria. Artist in Visual Comm.: Stanford Research Inst.; Head, Graphic Arts: Stanford Linear Accelerator Center; Illustrator, Cons., S.F. Natural Hist. Museum; Art Inst., practicing artist, own studio. Mem. Advisory Comm., W. Valley Coll.; Artist: Celestial Art. Ed. Publ. Co., Milbrae. Numerous exhibits: Budapest, London, Palo Alto, San Jose, Monterey, S.F. Specializes in unorthodox synthesized, conceptual illustrations, acrylic airbrush, and has received highly favorable critical reviews. Mem. Tech. Illustration Mgmt. Assn.; Palo Alto Art Club; WWII Vet. Assn. Elected Life Member, Phi Kappa Phi, Natl. Hon. Soc., for outstanding scholastic achievement.

ZEBROSKI, EDWIN LEOPOLD. Los Altos. Scientist. b. Chicago, Ill., Apr. 1, 1921. B.S., U. Chicago; Ph.D., UCBerkeley. m. Gisela Karin Rudolph. c. Lars, Zoe, Susan, Peggy, Karen. Formerly, Gen. Electric Co., presently Dir. Systems & Materials, Elec. Power Research Inst., Palo Alto. Fellow: Amer. Nuclear Soc.; Amer. Inst. of Chemists. Mem. Amer. Physical Soc.; A.A.A.S.; Los Altos Hills, C.C. Over 80 publications and patents on energy technology and economics, and nuclear energy. Hon. Charles A. Coffin Award. Listed: *Who's Who in Engineering; American Men of Science.*

ZELAZIK, BOLESLAW. Pasadena. Retired. b. Poland, Nov. 17, 1894. Studied: Teachers Coll., Jedrzejow, Pol. m. (widower). c. Krystyna. Mil. Pol. Legion, 1914-18. POW: Kielce, Checiny, 1917-18. FLC: Passau, Bavaria, 1942-45. Electrician, L.A., 1958-65. Ret. Mem. P.A.V.A.; S.P.K.; P.A.C.; P.R.C.U.; Friends of Pol. Museum, Rapperswil.

ZIELKIEWICZ, KRYSTYNA (nee Zelazik). Pasadena. b. Poland, 1923. Studied: Nazareth, Palestine (now Israel). m. Zbigniew C. c. Izabella. FLC: Archangel, USSR, 1940-41. Nurse (Lt.), PA formed in USSR (after Ger. invasion 1941). Came to U.S., 1956. Pres., P.F.A.C., 1973-75; V.P., P.A.C. - Cal. Div., 1974; Pres., Pol. Scouting Org. in Cal.; Vice-Chm. Pol. Amer. Bicentennial Comm. - L.A., 1975-76; O.L.B.M.R.C.C.; Assumption Blessed Virgin Mary R.C.C., Pasa. Hon. War Medal, 1939-45.

ZIELKIEWICZ, ZBIGNIEW. Pasadena. Surveyor. b. Kutno, Poland, Mar. 11, 1912. Studied: Cadet Corps, Rawicz, Pol.; War College, Pol. m. Krystyna. c. Izabella Macander. Cav. Off., PA. POW: Arnwalde, Grossborn, 1939-45. Mem. P.P.N.S.; P.F.A.C.; Gen. Sikorski Inst.; Cav. Assn., Can. Hon. Cross of Valor, Army Medal.

ZIMMER, SZCZEPAN KAROL. Los Angeles. Librarian/Writer. b. Zborow, Poland, Dec. 26, 1903. M.A., Ph.D., Pol. Lit., Hist., U. Lwow; 1926. M.L.S., Immaculate Heart Coll., L.A., 1962. m. Halina Maria. Mil. Lt., PA, 1939. POW: Ger., 1939-45. Teacher, sch. libr., Tarnopol, Pol., 1925-39; Chief Insp., Sup., Pol. schools, DP Camps, W. Ger. (Br. zone); Lab. Tech., Engr. Dept.: Chi. Rawhide Mfg. Co., Chi.; Research Librarian, Co. Gen. Hosp.; Med. Libr., L.A., 1962-1973. Co-author, three textbooks (in Polish).

Authored literary study on Polish poet, Jan Kasprowicz. Wrote biographical sketch on Stanislaw Wyspianski (Pol. & Eng.). Publ. short hist. of Jagiellonian U. Libr. on 600th anniversary (1964). Translated Henry David Thoreau's *Civil Disobedience* (1970), and *Life Without Principle* (1971), both published by Poets & Painters Press, London, G.B.

ZINGEL, MARIE T. Santa Monica. Nurse. b. Poland, Apr. 9, 1904. R.N., Mercy Coll. Nursing, S.D., 1941. m. Michael. R.N., Red Cross, 1941-43, worked transporting DP's to U.S.; Hosp. exp. incl. St. Vincent's Hosp., L.A.

ZYGMONT, ARTHUR LAURENT (ARTUR). Torrance. Contract Supervisor. b. Detroit, Mich., Oct. 1, 1923. B.S., Econ., U. Detroit, 1949. Grad. study, Wayne State U., Ohio State U. m. Gene (Genia) Harubin. c. Zenon Xavier. Contracting Off., major Aerospace prog., Space & Missile Systems Org., El Segundo. Mem. P.V. Rep. Club; P.A.H.A.; K.F.; Polonus; Cal. Conservative Union.

ZYGMONT, GENE THERESE (nee Harubin). Torrance. b. Hamtramck, Mich., Sept. 15, 1926. B.A., Hist.; B.A., Art Hist.; Grad. study, Art Hist., CSULB, 1975-date. m. Arthur L. c. Zenon Xavier. Contr. ed., *Polish Americans in California, 1827-1977*. V.P., P.A.H.A. Mem. K.F.; Pol. Arts & Culture Found., S.F., Cal. Conservative Union.

ZYGMONT, ZENON XAVIER. Torrance. Student. b. Dayton, O., Sept. 20, 1958. Oceanography major, CSU Humboldt. Traveled: Poland, England, Holland.

SUBSCRIBERS

Abraszewski, Piotr
Antczak, Al
Apostol, Tom & Jane
Archer, Walter J.
Ast, Anthony P.
Ault, Bernice

Babich, Eddie Mr/Mrs
Bala, Walter
Balvin, Richard
Barc, Stanley Z.
Baroni, Rev. Msgr. Geno
Barycki, Rev. Wojciech
Beit-I-Shoo, Gladys
Bekker, M. & J.
Bell, Bezak Flossie
Bell, Lei Lani Ann
Bellen, Jerome & Irene
Bendarzewski, Jerzy A. & Elizabeth T.
Bendisz, K.
Bennett, Edward
Bernhagen, Doris
Bernhardt, William A.
Berwin, Ted W. Mr/Mrs
Biddle, Evelyn H.
Bielecki, Tadeusz & Daniela
Bielski, Mark & Kasia
Bien, Francis I.
Bieniasz, Joseph W.
Bieniasz, Urszula
Bilek, Richard W.
Bilinski, Rev. Donald
Billington, Ray A.
Black, John D.
Black, Veronica
Blatt, Thomas
Bobrowski, Rev. Msgr. Kasimir J.
Bodziak, Bruno F.
Bogucki, Jadwiga K.
Bomba, Raymond
Borowski, Tadeusz I. & Helena M.
Brabec, Witold & Ewa
Breese, Charles C. & Jean M.
Brodka, Mark A.
Bronowicki, K. Mr/Mrs
Brzeski, Andrzej & Nancy
Bukowski, Virginia
Buszek, Andy & Irene
Butler, Halina T.

California State College, Sonoma
Campbell, Ernest & Phyllis
Carr, Stafford & Julia
Cichy, Andrew Mr/Mrs
Cichy, Andy
Cichy, John
Cichy, Linda
Cierpik, Anne
Cieslak, Stanislawa
Clyde, Carl & Veronica
Cokus, Rev. Joseph
Conrad, Henry Mr/Mrs
Cormier-Czaja, Addie
Cuba, Stanley L.
Czyrko, Janine

Dalton, Sandy & Bob
Damasco, Helena
Damiencki, Janina
De Bukowski, Mr/Mrs
Decker, Norman E. & Antoinette
Degner, Rev. Msgr. Leon A.
Deresiewicz, Bogdan
Deresiewicz, Catherine
Dimaria, Vince & Irene
Dobkiewicz, Stefan
Domachowski, Rev. Alphonsus
Domanski, L.B. Mr/Mrs
Dombrowski, Edmund & Violet
Dombrowski, Dr. Edmund Jr.
Dombrowski, Stephen
Domilise, Jerry & Shirley
Dominguez Hills College
Dorman, Josephine
Drake, Irene
Drozanski, Tadeusz & Bozena
Duchnowski, Louise
Dudzinski, Tadeusz & Christiane
Dunlap, Rosemary
Dziadula, Louis & Mary

Eastwood, Jim & Ruthanne
Eichler, Christina S.
Emco Engineering Co.
Engel, Richard
Engel, Tadeusz K.
Engel, William
Engel-Tyer, Viktoria

Faracik, Mieczyslaw & Hela

Finie, Peter H.
Finie, Philip A.
Festen, Anne Mrs.
Field, Statia L.
Floryan, Thaddeus P.
Foamex Co., Inc.
Fortunko, Christopher M.
Foster, Vada
Francki, Janusz & Irene
Frankowska, Zofia
Fuz, George M.

Gale, Constance
Garstka, John A. & Polly
Garstka, Dr. Stanley & Martha
Gasik, Z.J.
Gawlinska, Halina
Gawlinska, Maria
Gawlinski, Wladyslaw
George, Marylka T.
Ginielewicz, Stefan
Golas, Thaddeus
Gorka, Rev. Frederick
Gorska, Hanka Mrs.
Gorski, P.J.
Gorski, Walter Jr.
Gorzenski, William & Sandra
Gozdzikowski, M.
Grams, Helena H.
Grey, Benjamin
Grubola, Edward
Gruchcz-Lesinski, Stanislaw
Grusinski, Anthony & Anne-Marie
Grzesik, John A.
Guardian Angel PNC Church
Gwodz, Robert J.
Gysbers, Bonni S.

Hahn, Dr. George
Haifter, Mitchel
Halstead, Maria
Harte, Roman I.
Hayes, Kathy S.
Hellman, Ludwika
Henzel, M.G. Mr/Mrs
Hicks, Edward M.
Hiszpanski, Jan & Zofia
Hodgson, Marie T.
Holton, Cyril
Holton-Opid, Stephanie

Imbras, Czeslaw

Jakobsen, Wieslaw & Gina
J.K. Engineering
Jakimko, Adeline A.
Janiszewski, Emil
Jankowski, Henry
Janoski, Henry P.
Jarosz, Zygmunt A.
Jasionowski, Walerian
Jeschke, Catherine
Jeschke, Gloria M.
Jeschke, James D.
Jeschke, James P.
Jukowicz, Estanislao

Kabarowska, Zofia
Kadlubowski, Jan A.
Kalinski, George
Kaminski, Edward M.
Kaminski, Z. George
Kaper, Bronislaw
Karcz, Irene
Karp, Rev. Joseph A.
Karpinski, Gen. Stanislaw & Barbara
Kasparek-Obst, Christopher
Kasparek-Obst, Joseph
Kasper, Dennis R. & Jeanne
Kasper, Jerome A. & Valentine E.
Kasper, Jerome V. & Jean
Kasper, Rose
Kawecki, Leon S.
Kaye, Mindy
Kibbie, Daniel & Marie
Kilis, Stella D.
Kleinz, Karl W.
Klejnot, Olgierd J.
Klimes, Ludwik & Ingeborg
Kliszewski, Mark
Knawa, Sr. Anne M.
Knight, Ted
Kocielski, Olek & Lusia
Kodrebski, Janusz I.
Kogut, Sophie
Kol, Dr. Gustav & Barbara
Koleda, Joseph & Harriet
Kolodny, Nate
Konopka, Albin
Kopania, Rev. Msgr. Stefan F.
Korba, Andrew
Korbonski, Andrzej
Korwin-Rhodes, Marta
Kosowicz, Frank
Kowalik, Jan

Kowalski, Zbigniew
Koziol, John E.
Krance, Michael & Slawa
Krawczyk, Edward & Laura
Krekelberg, Rev. Richard G.
Kroczko, John
Kroll, Clement T. & Mae
Krotoski, Dr. Andrzej & Franca
Krotoski, Ludwik N.
Krotoski, Dr.Wojciech & Danuta
Kruk, Rev. Wincenty
Krystaszek, Adam & Vicky
Krzemuski, Adam
Krzemuski, Andrzej
Krzyczkowski, Antoni
Kugler, Boleslaw
Kulas, Eugene P.
Kulesza, Seweryn & Myszka
Kusby, E.D.
Kwasieborska, Felicja

LaDelle, George E.
Langston, M.L. Mr/Mrs
Lankowska, Kasia
Laskowski, Jerome S. & Marian
Lasota, Wladyslaw
Laube, Dr. Daniela T.
Lauterbach, Dr. Otto E.
Lazarewicz, Andrzej & Ewa
Lazowski, Kazimierz
Lee, Ellen K.
Lenczowski, George
Lepak, Chester B.
Lerski, George J.
Leski, Lenet
Lewicki, Robert
Lewicki, Stanley L.
Liibke, H.
Linowski, Rev. Eugene R.
Litynski, Zbigniew
Lockard, Lucile M.
Lojewski, Harry
Londzin, Victor
Loyola Marymount University Library
Lubanski, J.
Luczaj, Andrew & Viola E.
Luczaj, Tadeusz & Halszka
Lukasiak, Karol & Stephanie

Macander, Izabella Z.
Mackiewicz, Czeslaw
Makowiecka-Warwick, Eugenia

Makowski, Jerzy
Malin, Don P.
Mallek, Robert
Malolepszy, M.
Mantykowski, Antoni
Margis, Roman
Martini, Florian
Martinoff, Barbara
Mathews, Eugene
Mathews, Laura J.
Matulewicz, Alicia
McAnany, Tim & Nancy
McGrath, Elsie
Millard, Mary Ann
Milton, George
Minc, Henryk
Miziolek, Andrzej
Modrzejewski, K. & Anna
Moore, Wanda H.
Morrissey, Clarence
Mostwin, Danuta
Mrozewska, Irena
Mudy, Bruno & Maria
Murawski, Marianne K.

Nadolski, Leon
Nalski, Wladyslaw W.
Neterowicz, Jozef
Niedzielski, Theo
Niklewicz, Stanley
Nizynski, Andrew
Novak, Michael
Nowakowski, Andrew J.
Nowowiejski, Henry
Nunis, Doyce B. Jr.

Olbrys, Rev. Zbigniew
Olechno-Huszcza, C. & Ethel G.
Olek, Lillian
Opoczynski, Henryk & Maria
Ordon-Sklodowski, V.A.
Orme, Fenton
Osinska, Genowefa
Otfinowski, Jozef Z.
O'Toole, Ollie & Mildred

Paderewski, Clarence J.
Palusinska, Joasia & Iwonka
Palusinski, Olgierd & Krystyna
Pankanin, Bro. Marian
Parka, Alice
Pasternacki, Stephan
Patton, Jack

Patyk, Josef
Paynter, Jean
Pauker, Ewa
Pawlikowski, Marian
Pawlowski, Edward
Pawlowski, Wally & Hedy
Pedzich, Anthony & Isabel
Petrovich, Dr. Zbigniew
Pharis, Helena E.
Pichly, Doris A.
Podlasek, Czeslawa
Polak, Dr. Teodor
Polam Federal Credit Union
Polczynski, C.
Polish Air Force Veterans Association
Polish American Arts Association
Polish American Business &
Professional Club
Polish American Citizens Club
Polish American Congress — California/
Arizona
Polish American Congress Credit Union,
L.A.
Polish American Democratic Club
Polish Army Veterans Association, L.A.
Polish Arts and Culture Foundation
Polish Center, Los Angeles
Polish Millennium Library
Polish Museum of America
Polish National Alliance, San Fernando
Polish Parish Council, Santa Barbara
Polish Philatelic-Numismatic Association
Polish Resistance Forces, L.A.
Polish University CLub
Polish Veterans of World War II, L.A.
Polish Western Association in America
Polish Women's Alliance, S. California
Prasniewski, Jan
Prasniewski, J. & Margaret
Preston, Stanley & Helen
Priga, Joseph & Olga
Prziborowski, George C.
Przygoda, Rev. Jacek
Puchlik, Edmund
Pugh, Jim & Cecilia

Rabek, Jadwiga & Jan
Rachwald, Arthur & Anna
Radomski, Michal
Radziwill, Maciej M.
Ramolet, Christine
Raycraft, Tom

Regrut, Andrew D.
Reilly, Rev. Msgr. John J.
Renick, M. & Sophie
Rett-Wilczkowiak, Henryk
Riley, Frank & Elfriede
Rokicki, Vincent
Rolle, Andrew F.
Rowinski, Dr. Tadeusz F.
Rusin, Dorek
Rydel, Richard A.
Rylski, Janusz & Dorota
Salagaj, Walter & Marilyn
Samonek, Edna J.
Saran, Rev. Anthony
Savage, Teresa
Sawa, M. Stanley & Irene M.
Sawa, Michelle
Seidl, Zdzislaw
Seminary, Roman Catholic, San Francisco
Seremak, Jan
Sermak, Jeannette L.
Shaw, Robert M. & Danuta
Shubsda, Most Rev. Thaddeus
Siedzik, Wojciech & Christine
Siekiel-Zdzielnicka, Halina
Sienkiewicz, Stefania
Simons, Denise
Simons, Gregory
Simons, Jerome A. & Henrietta
Simons, Rebecca
Skoczowski, Adam & Maria
Skowron, Dr. Alexander
Skrzynska, Jolanta
Slawik, Rev. Boniface
Sliwicki, Stan B.
Sliwinski, Mitchell
Sliwinski, Stanislaw & Maria
Slosarczyk, Czeslaw
Smelski, John
Sondomowicz, Kasimir & Anna
Sondomowicz, Richard & Sandra
Sourk, Anielka D.
Sowinski, Joan D.
Sowinski, Joseph M.
Splawinski, Dolly
Stachura, Irene A.
Stanley, T.T. & Barbara
Stanwyck-Stankiewicz, S.
Stebbins, Charles & Helen
Stebbins, James
Stepaniak, Richard & Heddy

Stone, Rochelle
Styka Gogel, Stanislawa
Sulistrowski, Zygmunt
Sulkowski, S.J.
Sworakowski, Witold & Helena
Szatkowski, Thomas J.
Szatkowski, Wanda B.
Szczepanski, Eugeniusz
Szczepanski, Dr. S. Hanna
Szczepanski, Zygmunt
Szeptycki, George
Szmit, Dr. Edward W.
Szpak, Stanislaw
Szrajbman, S.S.
Szukalski, Stanislaw
Szwede Slavic Books
Szymanski, S.M.

Tabasz, Frank Mrs.
Tabasz, Mary
Talaga, James C.
Terelak, Edward
Toczylowski, H.S.
Tolosko, Edward
Tomaszewski, W.K.
Topor, Frank & J.
Traynor, Stacy
Trzaska, Ed & Eleanor
Tukaj, J. & A.
Tukaj-Dziunikowska, E.B.
Turhollow, Anthony & Charlotte
Tyszkiewicz-Lacki, J. & E.

University of California, San Diego
University of Santa Clara
Urbaniak, Chester
Urbanowski, Rev. Konrad

Van der Marel, Halina
Vars, Henry & Elizabeth
Vernon, Pearl G.
Vinton, Bobby
Vrablik, Robert J.

Wagner, George
Walling, Leon C.
Warno, Henryk & Irena
Wdowiak, Jerry, Dental Ceramics, Inc.
Wdowiak, Jerry & Krystyna
Wegner, Mary W.
Wegner, Stanley
Westwalewicz, Henry
Weynerowska-Kali, Hanka
Whatley, Thomas A. & Maria

White-Brzechwa, Alicia
Wicker, Frank & Olga
Wierzbianska, Alina
Wierzbicka-Kadlubowski, Jozefa
Wilczynski, Mark & Nina
Wilk, Richard B. & Mary
Wilk, Dr. Stefan P. & Wanda
Williams, Mary
Wissema-Dabrowska, E.G.
Witt, F.R. Mr/Mrs
Wojciechowski, Christopher R.
Wojciechowska-Rodnan, Maia
Wojciechowski, Zbigniew M.
Wojciechowska, Zofia J.
Wollonciej, Clara
Wolny, Wilhelm
Woytak, Richard A.
Wozniak, Dr. Stanley & Clara
Woznicki, Rev. Andrzej M.
Wrobel, Alfred J.
Wyglendowski, Stanley J.
Wysynsky, Otton V.
Wyszniewski, Jerzy

Yates, Rose
Yu, Haline

Zagorewicz, Thaddeus A.
Zahorski, Adam
Zakrzewski, Wojciech & Danuta
Zakrzewski, Zdzislaw
Zatoka, Rudolph
Zawadzka, Danuta
Zawadzki, Michael
Zawadzki, Richard
Zawadzki, Roman J.
Zawodny, Janusz K.
Zawojski, Christopher
Zawojski, Walter
Zebroski, E.
Zeitlin, Eugenia F.
Zelazik, Boleslaw
Zielinska, Mira
Zielkiemer, K.
Zielkiewicz, Zbigniew & Krystyna
Ziemann, Rev. G. Patrick
Zimmer, Szczepan & Halina
Zimny, Rev. August
Zingel, Marie
Zygmont, Arthur
Zygmont, Gene
Zygmont, Zenon

ADDITIONAL LIST OF SUBSCRIBERS

Bartak, Andrzej & Anna
Bauler, Rev. Gary P.
Ivers, Bill & Eileen

Krahelski, Mrs. Alexandra
Narbut-Luczynski, George
Sobkowska, Mrs. Cecylia

Topps, Joseph & Dolores

The Polish American Historical Association (PAHA — member of American Historical Association — AHA) seeks to encourage the study of Polish American history, culture, and the European roots of Polish immigrant life in the New World. It also promotes scholarly research and publication in the related fields of sociology, political science, genealogy, and folklore.